Passages from Arabia Deserta

Charles Montague Doughty, explorer, travel-writer and poet, was born in 1843 at Theberton, Suffolk, the son of a clergyman. He failed the medical examination for entry to the navy and instead went to Caius College, Cambridge, where he studied geology but his chief interests were the poetry of Chaucer and Spenser and English philology. After graduating, he wandered about Europe for several years and in November 1876 he embarked upon his historic journey. He spent twenty months in northern Arabia and his penetrating observations on the life, character and people of that land were written up in his famous *Travels in Arabia Deserta* (1888; new edition with an introduction by T. E. Lawrence, 1921). The book's length, over 600,000 words, discouraged a wide readership but in 1908 a first abridgement, *Wanderings in Arabia*, by the distinguished editor, Edward Garnett, brought Doughty long-deserved praise. The book gives a marvellously detailed account of the land through which he travelled, but to Doughty the style of his writing was perhaps even more important than its subject matter. The English language was his constant study and he attempted to rescue it from the decadence into which he considered it had fallen and return it to the tradition of Chaucer and Spenser. His work was studied by T. E. Lawrence and had a profound formative influence on his writing. In 1931 this edition, a second selection from the original massive work, was published and in his introduction Edward Garnett said, 'My object in selecting these passages is that for every old reader to whom *Arabia Deserta* is known, there shall be five new readers, shortly, to whom "Passages" shall be a great experience, exciting not only wonder and admiration, but introducing to them a style consummate in its creative richness.'

Charles Doughty died at his home in Kent in January 1926.

CHARLES M. DOUGHTY

PASSAGES FROM
ARABIA DESERTA

SELECTED BY
EDWARD GARNETT

PENGUIN BOOKS

Penguin Books Ltd, Harmondsworth, Middlesex, England
Penguin Books, 625 Madison Avenue, New York, New York 10022, U.S.A.
Penguin Books Australia Ltd, Ringwood, Victoria, Australia
Penguin Books Canada Ltd, 2801 John Street, Markham, Ontario, Canada L3R 1B4
Penguin Books (N.Z.) Ltd, 182–190 Wairau Road, Auckland 10, New Zealand

First published 1931
Published in Penguin Books 1956
Reprinted 1983

Made and printed in Great Britain by
Richard Clay (The Chaucer Press) Ltd,
Bungay, Suffolk
Set in Monotype Garamond

The Glossary printed at the end of this book
has been prepared by Mr A. C. Fifield
and is based on Mr Doughty's own Glossary
which appears in
Travels in Arabia Deserta

*

A map of North West Arabia and Nejd
appears on pages 8 and 9

PASSAGES FROM
ARABIA DESERTA

The Setting out of the Pilgrim Caravan

A new voice hailed me of an old friend when, first returned
from the Peninsula, I paced again in that long street of Damascus which is called Straight; and suddenly taking me wondering by the hand, 'Tell me (said he), since thou art here again in
the peace and assurance of Ullah, and whilst we walk, as in the
former years, toward the new blossoming orchards, full of the
sweet spring as the garden of God, what moved thee, or how
couldst thou take such journeys into the fanatic Arabia?'

*

It was at the latest hour, when in the same day, and after
troubled days of endeavours, I had supposed it impossible. At
first I had asked of the *Wàly*, Governor of Syria, his licence to
accompany the *Haj* caravan to the distance of *Meddin Sâlih*.
The Wàly then privately questioned the British Consulate, an
office which is of much regard in these countries. The Consul
answered, that his was no charge in any such matter; he had
as much regard of me, would I take such dangerous ways, as of
his old hat. This was a man that, in time past, had proffered to
show me a good turn in my travels, who now told me it was
his duty to take no cognizance of my Arabian journey, lest he
might hear any word of blame, if I miscarried. Thus by the
Turkish officers it was understood that my life, forsaken by
mine own Consulate, would not be required of them in this
adventure. There is a merry saying of Sir Henry Wotton, for
which he nearly lost his credit with his sovereign, 'An am-
bassador is a man who is sent to lie abroad for his country'; to
this might be added, 'A Consul is a man who is sent to play the
Turk abroad, to his own countrymen.'

That untimely Turkishness was the source to me of nearly all the mischiefs of these travels in Arabia. And what wonder, none fearing a reckoning, that I should many times come nigh to be foully murdered! whereas the informal benevolent word, in the beginning, of a Frankish Consulate might have procured me regard of the great Haj officers, and their letters of commendation, in departing from them, to the Emirs of Arabia. Thus rejected by the British Consulate, I dreaded to be turned back altogether if I should visit now certain great personages of Damascus, as the noble Algerian prince *Abd el-Kâder*; for whose only word's sake, which I am well assured he would have given, I had been welcome in all the Haj-road towers occupied by Moorish garrisons, and my life had not been well-nigh lost amongst them later at Medáin Sâlih.

I went only to the Kurdish Pasha of the Haj, Mohammed Saîd, who two years before had known me a traveller in the Lands beyond Jordan, and took me for a well-affected man that did nothing covertly. It was a time of cholera and the Christians had fled from the city, when I visited them formerly in Damascus to prefer the same request, that I might go down with the Pilgrimage to Medáin Sâlih. He had recommended me then to bring a firmân of the Sultan, saying, 'The *hajjâj* (pilgrims) were a mixed multitude, and if aught befel me, the harm might be laid at his door, since I was the subject of a foreign government': but now, he said, 'Well! would I needs go thither? it might be with the *Jurdy*': that is the flying provision-train which since ancient times is sent down from Syria to relieve the returning pilgrimage at Medáin Sâlih; but commonly lying there only three days, the time would not have sufficed me.

I thought the stars were so disposed that I should not go to Arabia; but, said my Moslem friends, 'the Pasha himself could not forbid any taking this journey with the caravan; and though I were a *Nasrâny* what hindered! when I went not down to the *Harameyn* (two sacred cities), but to Medáin Sâlih; how! I an honest person might not go, when there went down every year with the Haj all the desperate cutters of the town; nay the most dangerous ribalds of Damascus were already at

Muzeyrîb, to kill and to spoil upon the skirts of the caravan journeying in the wilderness.' Also they said 'it was but a few years since Christian masons (there are no Moslems of the craft in Damascus) had been sent with the Haj to repair the water-tower or kella and cistern at the same Medáin Sâlih.'

There is every year a new stirring of this goodly Oriental city in the days before the Haj; so many strangers are passing in the bazaars, of outlandish speech and clothing from far provinces. The more part are of Asia Minor, many of them bearing overgreat white turbans that might weigh more than their heads: the most are poor folk of a solemn countenance, which wander in the streets seeking the bakers' stalls, and I saw that many of the Damascenes could answer them in their own language. The town is moved in the departure of the great Pilgrimage of the Religion and again at the home-coming, which is made a public spectacle; almost every Moslem household has some one of their kindred in the caravan. In the markets there is much taking up in haste of wares from the road. The tent-makers are most busy in their street, overlooking and renewing the old canvas of hundreds of tents, of tilts and the curtains for litters; the curriers in their bazaar are selling apace the water-skins and leathern buckets and saddle-bottles, *matara* or *zemzemyeh*; the carpenters' craft are labouring in all haste for the Haj, the most of them mending litter-frames. In the *Perœan* outlying quarter, *el-Medân*, is cheapening and delivery of grain, a provision by the way for the Haj cattle. Already there come by the streets, passing daily forth, the *akkâms* with the swagging litters mounted high upon the tall pilgrim-camels. They are the Haj caravan drivers, and upon the silent great shuffle-footed beasts, they hold insolently their path through the narrow bazaars; commonly ferocious young men, whose mouths are full of horrible cursings: and whoso is not of this stomach, him they think unmeet for the road. The *Mukowwems* or Haj camel-masters have called in their cattle (all are strong males) from the wilderness to the camel-yards in Damascus, where their serving-men are busy stuffing pillows under the pack-saddle frames, and lapping, first over all the camels' chines, thick blanket-felts of Aleppo, that they should not be galled; the gear is not lifted till their return after four months, if they may return alive, from so great a voyage. The mukowwems are sturdy, weathered men of the road, that can hold the mastery over their often mutinous crews; it is written in their hard faces that they are overcomers of the evil by the evil, and able to deal in the long desert way with the perfidy of the elvish Beduins. It is the custom in these caravan countries that all who are to set forth, meet together in some common place without the city. The assembling of the pilgrim multitude is always by the lake of Muzeyrîb in the high steppes beyond Jordan, two journeys from Damascus. Here the hajjies who have taken the field are encamped, and lie a week or ten days in the desert before their long voyage. The Haj Pasha, his affairs dispatched with the government in Damascus, arrives the third day before their departure, to discharge all first payments to the Beduw and to agree with the watee-carriers (which are Beduins), for the military service.

The open ways of Damascus upon that side, lately encumbered with the daily passage of hundreds of litters, and all that, to our eyes, strange and motley train, of the oriental pilgrimage, were again void and silent; the Haj had departed from among us. A little money is caught at as great gain in these lands long vexed by a criminal government: the hope of silver immediately brought me five or six poorer persons, saying all with great By-Gods they would set their seals to a paper to carry me safely to Medáin Sâlih, whether I would ride upon pack-horses, upon mules, asses, dromedaries, barely upon camel-back, or in a litter. I agreed with a Persian, mukowwem to those of his nation which come every year about from the East by Bagdad, Aleppo, Damascus, to 'see the cities'; and there they join themselves with the great Ottoman Haj caravan. This poor rich man was well content, for a few pounds in his hand which helped him to reckon with his corn-chandler to convey me to Medáin Sâlih. It was a last moment, the Pasha was departed two days since, and this man must make after with great journeys. I was presently clothed as a Syrian of simple fortune, and ready with store of caravan biscuit to ride along with him; mingled with the Persians in the Haj journey

I should be the less noted whether by Persians or Arabs. This mukowwem's servants and his gear were already eight days at Muzeyrîb camp.

It was afternoon when a few Arab friends bade me Godspeed, and mounted with my camel bags upon a mule I came riding through Damascus with the Persian, Mohammed Aga, and a small company. As we turned from the long city street, that which in Paul's days was called 'The Straight,' to go up through the Medân to the *Boábat-Ullah* some of the bystanders at the corner, setting upon me their eyes, said to each other, 'Who is this? Eigh!' Another answered him half jestingly, 'It is someone belonging to the *Aiamy*' (Persian). From the Boábat (great gate of) Ullah, so named of the passing forth of the holy pilgrimage thereat, the high desert lies before us those hundreds of leagues to the Harameyn; at first a waste plain of gravel and loam upon limestone, for ten or twelve days, and always rising, to *Maan* in 'the mountain of Edom' near to Petra. Twenty-six marches from Muzeyrîb is el-Medina, the prophet's city (*Medinat en-Néby*, in old time *Yathrib*); at forty marches is Mecca. There were none now in all the road, by which the last hajjies had passed five days before us. The sun setting, we came to the little outlying village *Kesmîh*: by the road was showed me a white cupola, the sleeping station of the commander of the pilgrimage, *Emir el-Haj*, in the evening of his solemn setting forth from Damascus. We came by a beaten way over the wilderness, paved of old at the crossing of winter stream-beds for the safe passage of the Haj camels, which have no foothold in sliding ground; by some other are seen ruinous bridges – as all is now ruinous in the Ottoman Empire. There is a block drift strewed over this wilderness; the like is found, much to our amazement, under all climates of the world.

We had sorry night quarters at Kesmîh, to lie out, with falling weather, in a filthy field, nor very long to repose. At three hours past midnight we were again riding. There were come along with us some few other, late and last poor wanderers, of the Persian's acquaintance and nation; blithely they addressed themselves to this sacred voyage, and as the sun began to

spring and smile with warmth upon the earth, like awakening
birds, they began to warble the sweet bird-like Persian airs.
Marching with most alacrity was a yellow-haired young der-
wîsh, the best minstrel of them all; with the rest of his breath
he laughed and cracked and would hail me cheerfully in the
best Arabic that he could. They comforted themselves by the
way with tobacco, and there was none, said they, better in the
whole world than this sweet leaf of their own country. There
arose the high train of Hermon aloft before us, hoar-headed
with the first snows and as it were a white cloud hanging in the
element, but the autumn in the plain was yet light and warm.
At twenty miles we passed before *Salâmen* an old ruined place
with towers and inhabited ruins, such as those seen in the
Hauran: five miles further another ruined site. Some of my
companions were imaginative of the stranger, because I inquired the names. We alighted first at afternoon by a cistern
of foul water *Keteyby*, where a guard was set of two ruffian
troopers, and when coming there very thirsty I refused to
drink, 'Oho! who is here?' cries one of them with an ill countenance, 'it is I guess some Nasrâny; auh, is this one, I say,
who should go with the Haj?' Nine miles from thence we
passed before a village, *Meskîn*: faring by the way, we overtook a costard-monger driving his ass with swagging chests of
the half-rotted autumn grapes, to sell his cheap wares to the
poor pilgrims for dear money at Muzeyrîb: whilst I bought of
his cool bunches, this fellow, full of gibes of the road, had descried me and 'Art thou going,' cried he, 'to Mecca? Ha! he is
not one to go with the Haj! and you that come along with him,
what is this for an hajjy?' At foot pace we came to the camp
at Muzeyrîb after eight o'clock, by dark night; the forced
march was sixteen hours. We had yet to do, shouting for the
Aga's people, by their names, to find our tents, but not much,
for after the hundreds of years of the pilgrimage all the Haj
service is well ordered. The mukowwems know their own
places, and these voices were presently answered by some of
his servants who led us to their lodging. The morrow was one
of preparation, the day after we should depart. The Aga counselled me not to go abroad from our lodging. The gun would

be fired two days earlier this year for the pilgrims' departure, because the season was lateward. We had ten marches through the northern highlands, and the first rains might fall upon us ere we descended to Arabia: in this soil mixed with loam the loaded camels slide, in rainy weather, and cannot safely pass. There was a great stillness in all their camp; these were the last hours of repose. As it was night there came the waits, of young camp-followers with links; who saluting every pavilion were last at the Persians' lodgings, their place, as they are strangers and schismatics, doubtless for the avoiding of strifes, is appointed in the rear of all the great caravan with the refrain *bes-salaamy bes-salaamy, Ullah yetowwel ummr-hu, hy el-ády, hy el-ády Mohammed Aga!* 'go in peace, good speed, heigho the largess! We keep this custom, the Lord give long life to him'; and the Persian, who durst not break the usage, found his penny with a sorry countenance.

The new dawn appearing we removed not yet. The day risen the tents were dismantled, the camels led in ready to their companies, and halted beside their loads. We waited to hear the cannon shot which should open that year's pilgrimage. It was near ten o'clock when we heard the signal gun fired, and then, without any disorder, litters were suddenly heaved and braced upon their bearing beasts, their charges laid upon the kneeling camels, and the thousands of riders, all born in the caravan countries, mounted in silence. As all is up the drivers are left standing upon their feet, or sit to rest out the latest moments on their heels: they with other camp and tent servants must ride those three hundred leagues upon their bare soles, although they faint; and are to measure the ground again upward with their weary feet from the holy places. At the second gun, fired a few moments after, the Pasha's litter advances and after him goes the head of the caravan column: over fifteen or twenty minutes we, who have places in the rear, must halt, that is until the long train is unfolded before us; then we strike our camels and the great pilgrimage is moving. There go commonly three or four camels abreast and seldom five; the length of the slow-footed multitude of men and cattle is near two miles, and the width some hundred yards in the

7

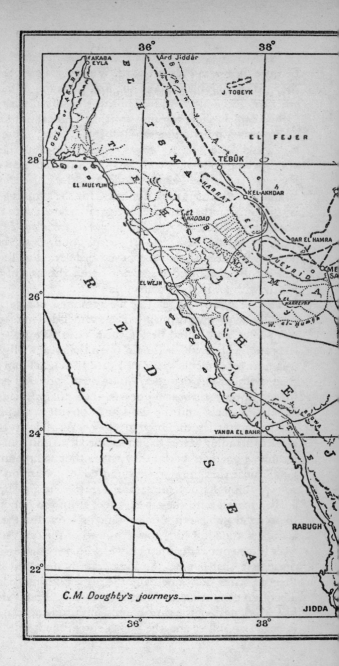

C. M. Doughty's journeys ___ _ _ _

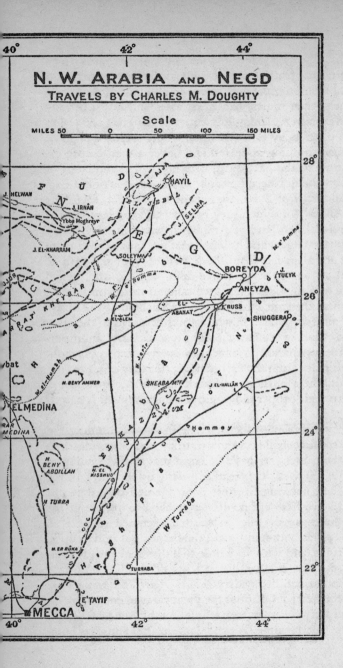

N. W. ARABIA AND NEGD
TRAVELS BY CHARLES M. DOUGHTY

Scale

MILES 50   0   50   100   150 MILES

40°   42°   44°

28°

J. HELWAN

F   Ü   D

N   J. IRNÁN

Ybba Moghreyr

J. EL-KHARRÁM

SOLEYMA

E

G

J. AJJA

HAYÍL

EL JEBEL

J. SELMA

W. e Rumma

D

BOREYDA

ANEYZA

J. TUEYK

26°

JUDD

RUMMA

RARRAT' KREYBAR

J. EL-ALEM

EL-ABANAT

E'RUSS

SHUGGERA

N

bat   H

W. El HUMM

N. BENY AMMER

W. Jerir

SHEABA MTS

J. EL-HALLÁN

ELMEDÍNA

RAR MEDÍNA

EL HEJAZ

A'ÚM

Hemmey

24°

H. BENY ABDILLAH

H. EL KISSMUD

PISN

H TURRA

W Turraba

H. ER RÚKA

H

22°

TURRABA

E'TAYIF

■MECCA

40°   42°   44°

open plains. The hajjàj were this year by their account (which may be above the truth) 6,000 persons; of these more than half are serving men on foot; and 10,000 of all kinds of cattle, the most camels, then mules, hackneys, asses and a few dromedaries of Arabians returning in security of the great convoy to their own districts. We march in an empty waste, a plain of gravel, where nothing appeared and never a road before us. Hermon, now to the backward, with his mighty shoulders of snows closes the northern horizon: to the nomads of the East a noble landmark of Syria, they name it *Towîl éth-Thalj* 'the height of snow' (of which they have small experience in the rainless sun-stricken land of Arabia). It was a Sunday, when this pilgrimage began, and holiday weather, the summer azure light was not all faded from the Syrian heaven; the 13th of November 1876; and after twelve miles way, (a little, which seemed long in the beginning,) we came to the second desert station, where the tents which we had left behind us at Muzeyrîb, stood already pitched in white ranks before us in the open wilderness. Thus every day the light tent-servants' train outwent our heavy march, in which, as every company has obtained their place from the first remove, this they observe continually until their journey's end. Arriving we ride apart, every company to their proper lodgings: this encampment is named *Ramta*.

It is their caravan prudence, that in the beginning of a long way, the first shall be a short journey; the beasts feel their burdens, the passengers have fallen in that to their riding in the field. Of a few sticks (gathered hastily by the way), of the desert bushes, cooking fires are soon kindled before all the tents; and since here are no stones at hand to set under the pots as Beduins use, the pilgrim hearth is a scraped out hole, so that their vessels may stand, with the brands put under, upon the two brinks, and with very little fuel they make ready their poor messes. The small military tents of the Haj escort of troopers and armed dromedary riders, *Ageyl* (the most *Nejd* men), are pitched round about the great caravan encampment, at sixty and sixty paces: in each tent fellowship the watches are kept till the day dawning. A paper lantern after sunset is hung before every one to burn all night, where a sentinel stands with his musket, and they suffer none to pass their lines unchallenged. Great is all townsmen's dread of the Beduw, as if they were the demons of this wild waste earth, ever ready to assail the Haj passengers; and there is no Beduwy durst chop logic in the dark with these often ferocious shooters, that might answer him with lead and who are heard from time to time, firing backward into the desert all night; and at every instant crying down the line *kerakô kerakô* (sentinel!) the next and the next men thereto answering with *haderûn* (ready). I saw not that any officer went the rounds. So busy is the first watch, whilst the camp is waking. These crickets begin to lose their voices about midnight, when for aught I could see the most of their lights were out; and it likely the unpaid men spare their allowance: these poor soldiers sell their candles privily in the Haj market.

In the first evening hour there is some merrymake of drum-beating and soft fluting, and Arcadian sweetness of the Persians singing in the tents about us; in others they chant together some piece of their devotion. In all the pilgrims' lodgings are paper lanterns with candles burning; but the camp is weary and all is soon at rest. The hajjies lie down in their clothes the few night hours till the morrow gun-fire; then to rise suddenly for the march, and not knowing how early they may hear it, but this is as the rest, after the Pasha's good pleasure and the weather.

At half past five o'clock was the warning shot for the second journey. The night sky was dark and showery when we removed, and cressets of iron cages set upon poles were borne to light the way, upon serving men's shoulders, in all the companies. The dawn discovered the same barren upland before us, of shallow gravel and clay ground upon limestone.

Punishment of a Caravan Thief

I was startled, where I reposed in my little travelling tent, by wailing cries and a rumour from the Persians' pavilion: in such a mukowwem's great canvas lodging might well assemble an hundred persons. In the midst is a square settle, which is carried in pieces, whereupon three personages may be seated cross-legged; and housed within is all his gear and two camel litters. There entering, I was witness of a sorrowful execution. I took by the elbow one of this throng of grave faces, to know what was going forward. He whispered, 'An *haràmy*' (thief). The accused was put to the torture – but if the wretch were innocent, for his health broken what god or human afterthought might make him amends! – Terrible in this silence sounded the handstrokes and his mortal groans. I asked again 'Why is he beaten so?' *Answer*. 'Until he will confess where it is hidden, the cursed one!' – 'And if they beat on thus he will be dead!' *Answer*. 'Except he confess, they will leave no life in him.' As I went through them, I heard that already four stout fellows had wearied their arms over him, and the fifth was now in the beginning of his strength. With an earnest countenance, he heaved in his two hands a tough plant and fetched down every stroke upon him with all his might. This malefactor was laid prone, men held down his legs, some kneeled upon his two shoulders and kneaded him, without pity. The writhing worm and no man, after the first cries drawn from him, now in a long anguish groaned hideously; I thought, within a while he must be beaten in pieces and is already a broken man for his life after. It was perilous for me to tempt so many strangers' eyes, but as humanity required, I called to them, 'Sirs I am an hakîm; this man may not bear more, hold or he may die under your handling!' – words which, besides their looking upon the speaker, were not regarded. Soon after I saw the grovelling wretch lifted from the earth, he had confessed his fault; some then bearing up under his arms and all men cursing him, he walked as he could and was led forth. (Of that lying down to be beaten before the judge's face we read in Moses.) This was an Arab caravan servant of Bagdad and greyheaded: bursting a lock he had stolen the purse with £40 of his Persian master, a foolish young man, and hid it beside their tent in the earth.

This power of execution is with the chiefs of the pilgrim companies, and they repress the most dangerous spirits in the caravan: many among the Haj servants are lurkers from justice and from the military conscription. '*Khalîl Effendi*' (said the Persian when he found me alone) 'what is the meddling with the man's punishment? wouldest thou to Medáin Sâlih, or no? This may be told to-morrow in the ears of the Pasha; then they will know you, and you will be turned back. Come no more forth in the public view.' But as an European I trod every day upon the *mesquin* oriental prudence; in camp he would have me remain in my little tent separately. It is perilous in the Haj to lodge alone at night, and I hired one of the drivers to cook my supper and set up the tent when we alighted and at night to sleep by me.

Mount Seir: Beduin Horsemen

Here the 19–20 November our tents were stiffened by the night's frost. Mount Seir or J. Sherra before us (*sherra* is interpreted high), is high and cold, and the Arab's summer clothing is as nakedness in the winter season. The land is open, not a rock or tree or any good bush to bear off the icy wind; it is reported, as a thing of a late memory, that wayfaring companies and their cattle have starved, coming this way over in the winter months. In the night they perished together, and the men were found lying by the cold ash-pits of their burned-out watch-fires. Not far from this wady, in front, begins that flint beach, which lies strewn over great part of the mountain of Esau; a stony nakedness blackened by the weather: it is a head of gravel, whose earth was wasted by the winds and secular rains. This land-face of pebbles shines vapouring in the clear sun, and they are polished as the stones and even the mountains in Sinai by the *ajàj* or dust-bearing blasts. The widespread and often three-fathom deep bed of gravel, is the highest platform of land in all that province; the worn flint-stones are of the washed chalk rock lying beneath, in which are massy (tabular) silicious veins; we see such gravel to be laid out in shallow streaming water, but since this is the highest ground, from whence that wash of water? The land-height is

4,000 feet above the sea! The Arabs name all this region *Ard Suwwan*, the Flint-Ground; the same which is in the old Geographers *Arabia Petraea*. But, a marvell this gravel is not ancient, as the antiquity of man; I have found in it such wrought flint instruments as we have from some river and lake gravels and loams of Europe. Journeying from this wady, we passed six or seven ancient mile-stones by the wayside, without inscriptions. At twelve miles' end we crossed the head of a deep and dry torrent (or *seyl*) named by the Haj *Durf ed-Drawish* 'butter-skins of the poor Derwishes,' whose course is not west to the Dead Seaward, but eastward in the desert; so they say 'all this land "seyls" (or shelves, so that the shower-waters flow) towards the *Tchôl Bagdad*.' In the hollow banks, when last I came by, I had found a night's lodging. Further in our march we see the soil under our feet strangely bestrewed with lava, whose edge is marked upon the gravel-land as it were a drift which is come from the westward, where we see certain black vulvanic bergs. Here, and where we journeyed still for fifty more miles, Esau's land is a great barrenness of gravel stones. We are in the marches of the *Howeytát*, not a small Beduin nation, whose borders are the two seas. They are liker nomad fellahîn than Beduins; many among them use husbandry, all are tent-dwellers. – I should not wonder were they found to be Nabateans. *Ibn Jeysey* is sheykh of the Howeytát *Daràwessha*, of the mountain of Edom; in his circuit is Petra. Early in the afternoon we passed by a broken turret; so small a sign of human hands is comfortable to the eyes in this desolate country. From hence three hours eastward upon the desert side, are the ruins of some considerable place, *Borma* or *Burma*.

Before sunset we came to encamp a little short of the *Kellat Anezy*, where is but a cistern for rain water, kept by two lubbers, sons of old Damascene tower-guards and of Shobek mothers; but commonly they live at home in their village. My pilgrimage companions would hardly believe me that I had drunk after rain the year before of this birket, they had never found water there. Some miles from thence, westward, are ruins of a place which the Arabs name *Jardanîa*, I went aside to

see it at my former passing:* and that there is shadow and
shelter, it is often a lurking place of land-loping Beduw, so
that of the armed company with whom I rode, there was
one only who would follow me for a reward. I found a four-
square town wall nearly thirty feet high and dry building in
courses, of the wild lava blocks. There are corner towers and
two mid-bastions upon a side, the whole area is not great: I
saw within but high heaps of the fallen down lava house-
building, a round arch in the midst and a small birket. What
mean these lofty walls; is not the site too small for a city?
neither is the soil very fit hereabout for husbandry; less town
than fortress, it might be a *praesidium*, in these parts, upon the
trade road. Thereby stands a black vulcanic mountain which
is a landmark seen from Maan. Here passing, in my former
journeys, we saw Arab horsemen which approached us; we
being too many for them, they came but to beg insolently a
handful of tobacco. In their camps such would be kind hosts;
but had we fallen into their hands in the desert we should have
found them fiends, they would have stripped us, and perchance in a savage wantonness have cut some of our throats.
These were three long-haired Beduins that bid us *salaam*
(peace); and a fourth shock-haired cyclops of the desert, whom
the fleetness of their mares had outstripped, trotted in after
them, uncouthly seated upon the rawbone narrow withers of
his dromedary, without saddle, without bridle, and only as an
herdsman driving her with his voice and the camel-stick. His
fellows rode with naked legs and unshod upon their beautiful
mares' bare backs, the halter in one hand, and the long bal-
anced lance, wavering upon the shoulder, in the other. We
should think them sprawling riders; for a boast or warlike
exercise, in the presence of our armed company, they let us
view how fairly they could ride a career and turn; striking
back heels and seated low, with pressed thighs, they parted at
a hand-gallop, made a tourney or two easily upon the plain;
and now wheeling wide, they betook themselves down in the
desert, every man bearing and handling his spear as at point to

* In the summer of 1875 Doughty had journeyed through Edom to
Petra. — E.G.

strike a foeman; so fetching a compass and we marching, they a little out of breath came gallantly again. Under the most ragged of these riders was a very perfect young and startling chestnut mare, – so shapely there are only few among them. Never combed by her rude master, but all shining beautiful and gentle of herself, she seemed a darling life upon that savage soil not worthy of her gracious pasterns: the strutting tail flowed down even to the ground, and the mane (*orfa*) was shed by the loving nurture of her mother Nature.

The settled folk in Arabian country are always envious haters of the nomads that encompass them, in their oases islands, with the danger of the desert. These with whom I journeyed, were the captain of the Haj road at Maan and his score of soldiery, the most being armed peasantry of the place, which came driving a government herd of goats, (the unwilling contribution of the few unsubmitted Idumean villages) to sell them at *Nablûs* (Sichem). Shots were fired by some of them in the rear in contempt of the Beduw, whose mares, at every gunfire, shrank and sprang under them, so that the men with their loose seats were near falling over the horses' heads. 'Nay Sirs!' they cried back, 'nay Sirs, why fray ye our mares?' The Beduw thus looking over their shoulders, the peasantry shot the more, hoping to see them miscarry; he of the beautiful filly sat already upon his horse's neck, the others were almost dislodged. So the officer called to them, 'Hold lads!' and 'have done lads!' and they 'Our guns went off, wellah, as it were of themselves.' And little cared they, as half desperate men, that had not seen a cross of their pay in sixteen months, to obey the words of their scurvy commander. They marched with a pyrrhic dancing and beating the tambour: it is a leaping counter and tripping high in measure, whilst they chant in wild manner with wavings of the body and fighting aloft in the air with the drawn sword. Those Beduins roughly demanded concerning me 'And who is he?' It was answered 'A Nasrâny,' – by which name, of evil omen, the nomads could only understand a calamity in their land: and they arrogantly again in their throats 'Like to this one see ye bring no more hither!' As I heard their word, I shouted 'Arrest, lay hands on them!'

They thought it time to be gone, and without leave-taking
they turned from us and were quickly ridden under the horizon.

The Akaba: The Dying Derwish

We approached at noon the edge of the high limestone platform of J. Sherra, *Masharîf es-Shem* of the old Mohammedan
bookmen, 'The brow of Syria or the North.' And below begins Arabia proper, *Béled el-Aarab*: – but these are distinctions
not known to the Beduish inhabitants.

The Haj road descending lies in an hollow ground, as it were
the head of a coomb, of sharp shelves of plate-flint and limestone. We are about to go down into the sandstones, – whereof are the most sands of Arabia. A ruinous kella and cistern
are here upon our left hand. The caravan column being come
to the head of the strait passage, we are delayed in the rear
thirty minutes. The caravaners call such a place *Akaba*, 'A
going up'; this is named the Syrian or northern, *es-Shemîya*.
I found here the altitude 4,135 feet. Upon a rock which first
straitens our descending way was seated, under a white para-
sol, the Pasha himself and his great officers were with him:
for here on the 24th of November we met again the blissful
sunshine and the summer not yet ended in Arabia. The caravan
lines are very loose, and long drawn out in the steep, which is
somewhat encumbered with rocks above. As the camels may
hardly pass two and two together the Pasha sees here at leisure
the muster of the hajjàj slowly passing; the pilgrims have
alighted from the cradle litters and their beasts' backs and all
fare on foot. My unlucky new camel, which had been purchased from the Beduins at Maan and not broken to this
marching, tied, burst her leading-string at the Pasha's feet,
which made a little confusion and I must run to bring all in
order again. But I was confident, although he had seen me in
Arabic clothing at Damascus, that he should not now know
me. The Akaba is long and, past the Pasha's seat, of little difficulty. The Beduins name this going-down *Batn el-Ghrôl* 'belly
(hollow ground) of the Ogre' or else 'strangling place,' *fen
yughrulûn ezzillamy*; a sink of desolation amongst these rusty

ruins of sandstone droughty mountains, full of eternal silence and where we see not anything that bears life. The Akaba is not very deep, in the end I found, where the pilgrims remounted, that we were come down hardly 250 feet. The length of the caravan was here nearly an hour and there was no mishap. Camels at a descent, with so unwieldy fore-limbs, are wooden riding; the lumpish brutes, unless it be the more fresh and willing, let themselves plumb down, with stiff joints, to every lower step. These inhospitable horrid sandstones resemble the wasting sandstone mountains about *Sherm* in Sinai.

Below we are upon a sand bottom, at either hand is a wall of sand-rock, the long open passage between them descends as a valley before us. Upon the left hand, the crags above are crusted with a blackish shale-stone, which is also fallen down to the foot, where the black shingles lie in heaps shining in the sun and burnished by the desert driving sand. This is the edge of a small lavafield or *harra*: I had seen also erupted basalt rock in the descent of the Akaba. After three miles the way issues from the strait mountains and we march upon a large plain *Debîbat es-Shem*, *Ard Jiddàr*, of sand; heavy it is to handle and oozing through the fingers. Few miles from the road upon our right hand are cloud-like strange wasted ranges of the desolate Hisma.

I saw one fallen in the sand, half sitting half lying upon his hands. This was a religious mendicant, some miserable derwish in his clouted beggar's cloak, who groaned in extremity, holding forth his hands like eagles' claws to man's pity. Last in the long train, we went also marching by him. His beggar's scrip, full of broken morsels fallen from his neck, was poured out before him. The wretch lamented to the slow moving lines of the Mecca-bound pilgrimage: the many had passed on, and doubtless as they saw his dying, hoped inwardly the like evil ending might not be their own. Some charitable serving men, Damascenes, in our company stepped aside to him; *ana mèyet*, sobbed the derwish, I am a dying man. One then of our crew, he was also my servant, a valiant outlaw, no holy-tongue man but of human deeds, with a manly heartening word, couched by an empty camel, and with a spring of his stalwart arms,

lifted and set him fairly upon the pack saddle. The dying derwish gave a weak cry much like a child, and hastily they raised
the camel under him and gathered his bag of scattered victuals
and reached it to him, who sat all feeble murmuring thankfulness, and trembling yet for fear. There is no ambulance service
with the barbarous pilgrim army; and all charity is cold, in
the great and terrible wilderness, of that wayworn suffering
multitude.

After this there died some daily in the caravan: the deceased's goods are sealed, his wayfellows in the night station
wash and shroud the body and lay in a shallow grave digged
with their hands, and will set him up some wild headstone by
the desert road side. They call any pilgrims so dying in the
path of their religion, *shahûd*, martyrs. But the lonely indigent
man, and without succour, who falls in the empty wilderness,
he is desolate indeed. When the great convoy is passed from
him, and he is forsaken of all mankind, if any Beduw find him
fainting, it is but likely they will strip him, seeing he is not yet
dead. The dead corses unburied are devoured by hyenas which
follow the ill odour of the caravan. There is little mercy in
those Ageyl which ride after; none upon the road, will do a
gentle deed 'but for silver.' – If we have lived well, we would
fain die in peace; we ask it, a reward of God, in the kind
presence of our friends! – There are fainting ones left behind
in every year's pilgrimage; men of an old fibre and ill-com-
plexion, their hope was in Ullah, but they living by the long
way only of unwilling men's alms, cannot achieve this extreme
journey to Mecca. The fallen man, advanced in years, had
never perhaps eaten his fill, in the Haj, and above 200 miles
were passed under his soles since Muzeyrîb. How great is
that yearly suffering and sacrifice of human flesh, and all lost
labour, for a vain opinion, a little salt of science would dissolve
all their religion!

Arabian Perils: the Semites

And now come down to Arabia, we are passed from known
landmarks. Two chiefly are the perils in Arabia, famine and

the dreadful-faced harpy of their religion, a third is the rash weapon of every Ishmaelite robber. The traveller must be himself, in men's eyes, a man worthy to live under the bent of God's heaven, and were it without a religion: he is such who has a clean human heart and long-suffering under his bare shirt; it is enough, and though the way be full of harms, he may travel to the ends of the world. Here is a dead land, whence, if he die not, he shall bring home nothing but a perpetual weariness in his bones. The Semites are like to a man sitting in a cloaca to the eyes, and whose brows touch heaven. Of the great antique humanity of the Semitic desert, there is a moment in every adventure, wherein a man may find to make his peace with them, so he know the Arabs. The sour Waháby fanaticism has in these days cruddled the hearts of the nomads, but every Beduin tent is sanctuary in the land of Ishmael (so there be not in it some cursed Jael). If the outlandish person come along to strange nomad booths, let him approach boldly, and they will receive him. It is much if they heard of thee any good report; and all the Arabs are at the beginning appeased with fair words. The oases villages are more dangerous; Beduin colonies at first, they have corrupted the ancient tradition of the desert; their souls are canker-weed beds of fanaticism. – As for me who write, I pray that nothing be looked for in this book but the seeing of an hungry man and the telling of a most weary man; for the rest the sun made me an Arab, but never warped me to Orientalism. Highland Arabia is not all sand; it is dry earth, nearly without sprinkling of the rains. All the soft is sandy; besides there is rocky moorland and much harsh gravel, where the desolate soil is blown naked by the secular winds. The belts of deep sand country and borders about the mountain sandstones, which are called *Nefúds*, are perhaps of kin with those named, in England, 'greensands.' Commonly the Arabian desert is an extreme desolation where the herb is not apparent for the sufficiency of any creature. In a parcel of desert earth great as an house floor, you shall find not many blades and hardly some one of the desert bushes, of which the two-third parts are no cattle-meat but quite waste and naught.

Tales of the Cholera Years

Before the sunset we came to our white tents pitched beside the ruinous kella, without door and commonly abandoned, Dàr el-Hamra 'the red house'. Ruddy is the earth and the rocks whereof this water-castle is built. High and terrible it showed in the twilight in this desolation of the world. We are here at nearly 4,200 feet. After marching above one hundred miles in forty-three hours we were come to the water, – water-dregs teeming with worms. The hot summer nights are here fresh after the sunset, they are cold in spring and autumn, and that is a danger for the health of the journeying pilgrimage, especially in their returning jaded from tropical Mecca. Eswad told me a dolorous tale of a cholera year, now the third or fourth past, in the ascending Haj: he thought there died in the marches and in the night stations, an hundred (that is very many) every day. 'The deceased and dying were trussed with cords upon the lurching camels' backs until we reached, said he, this place; and all was fear, no man not musing he might be one of the next to die, and never come home to his house; the day had been showery, the rain fell all that night incessantly. The signal gun was fired very early before dawn and the Haj removed in haste, abandoning on the wet ground of the dark desert, he thought, 150 bodies of dead and dying. At length those which survived of the pilgrimage, being come upon the wholesome Peraean highlands, were detained to purge their quarantine at ez-Zerka eight days.' He thought it was hardly the half of them which lived to enter again, by the Boábat Ullah, to the pleasant streets of Damascus. Many are their strange Haj tales of cholera years, and this among them. 'There was a poor man who dying by the way, his friends, digging piously with their hands, laid him in a shallow grave; and hastily they heaped the sand over their dead and departed with the marching caravan. Bye and bye in this dry warmth, the deceased revived; he rose from his shallow burial, and come to himself he saw an empty world and the Haj gone from him. The sick staggered forth upon their footprints in the wilderness, and relieved from kella to kella, and from nomads to nomads, he came footing over those hundreds of waste miles to Damascus and arrived at his own house; where he was but scurvily received by his nighest kin, who all out of charity disputed that it was not himself, since some of them but lately laid him in the grave, stark dead, in Arabia. They had mourned for him as dead; now he was returned out of all season, and they had already divided his substance.'

Medáin Sâlih: The Kella Garrison

In a warm and hazy air, we came marching over the loamy sand plain, in two hours, to Medáin Sâlih, a second merkez on the road, and at the midst of their long journey; where the caravan arriving was saluted with many rounds from the field-pieces and we alighted at our encampment of white tents, pitched a little before the kella.

The Ajamy would have me write him immediately a full release and acquittance. I thought it were better to lodge, if I might, at the kella; the *kellâjy*, surveyor of this and next towers, had once made me a promise in Damascus, that if I should ever arrive here he would receive me. The Beduins I heard to be come in from three days' distance and that to-morrow they would return to their wandering menzils. I asked the Persian to transport my baggage, but because his covenant was out he denied me, although my debtor for medicines which he had upon the road freely, as much as he would. These gracious Orientals are always graceless shortcomers at the last, and therefore may they never thrive! Meanwhile the way-worn people had bought themselves meat in the camp market of the Beduin fleshers, and fresh joints of mutton were hanging soon before all the Haj tents. The weary Damascenes, inhabitants of a river city, fell to diligently washing their sullied garments. Those who played the cooks in the fellowships, had gathered sticks and made their little fire pits; and all was full of business.

Here pilgrims stand much upon their guard, for in this they think, the most thievish station upon the road to Medina,

which 'thieves' are the poor Beduins. A tale is told every year
after their cooks' wit, how 'the last time, by Ullah, one did
but look round to take more sticks and when he turned again
the cauldron was lost. This cook stepped upon his feet and
through the press he ran, and laid hand upon a bare-foot
Beduwy the first he met; and he was he, the cursed one, who
stole back with the burning pot covered under his beggarly
garment.' Friendly persons bade me also have a care, I might
lose a thing in a moment and that should be without remedy.
There came in some of the poor nomads among us; the citizen
hajjies cried upon them 'Avaunt!' some with staves thrust
them, some flung them headlong forth by the shoulders as
wild creatures; certain Persians, for fear of their stealing, had
armed themselves with stones. – Yet afterward I knew all
these poor people as friendly neighbours, and without any
offence. There were come in some of their women, offering to
sell us bunches of mewed ostrich feathers, which they had
taken up in the desert. The ribald akkâms proffered them again
half-handfuls of broken biscuit; yet are these fretted short
plumes worth above their weight in silver, at Damascus.
Eswad, who was a merry fellow, offended at this bargaining
with a dishonest gesture; 'Fie on thee, ah lad for shame!' exclaimed the poor young woman: – the nomads much despise
the brutish behaviour of the towns-people. I went through
the encampment and came under the kella, where sweetmeat-
sellers, with stone counterpoises, were selling pennyworths of
dates upon their spread mantles; which wares are commonly
carried in the desert journeys upon asses. I spoke to one to
lend me his beast for money that I might fetch in my baggage.
'My son, (answered the old man, who took me for one of the
Moorish garrison,) I have therewith to do, I cannot lend him.'
I returned to the Ajamy; he would now lend me a mule, and
when I had written him his quittance, the cloudy villain
changed to fair weather; I saw him now a fountain of smiles
and pleasant words, as if he fed only with the bees among
honey flowers, and bidding el-Eswad drive the load he
brought me forward with the dunghill oriental grace and false
courtesy. As I was going 'Khalîl Aga (said the best of the

akkâms) forgive us!' they would have me not remember their sometimes rude and wild behaviour in the way. We found that kellâjy standing before the gate of his kella, (thereover I saw a well engraved Arabic inscription); busy he was receiving the garrison victual and caravan stores. He welcomed me shortly and bade me enter, until he should be out of hand. Loiterers of the garrison would hardly let me pass, saying that no strangers might come in there.

But what marvellous indifference of the weary hajjies! I saw none of them set forth to view the monuments, though as much renowned in their religion as Sodom and Gomorrah, and whereof such strange fables are told in the koran. Pity Mohammed had not seen Petra! he might have drawn another long-bow shot in Wady Mûsa: yet hardly from their camp is any of these wonders of the faith plainly visible. The palmers, who are besides greatly adread of the Aarab, durst not adventure forth, unless there go a score of them together. Departing always by night-time, the pilgrims see not the Cities of Sâlih, but the ascending Haj see them. Eswad came to the kella at nightfall, and bade me God-speed and to be very prudent; for the tower garrisons are reputed men of violence, as the rest of the Haj service. So came the kellâjy, who surprised to find me still sitting obscurely within, by my baggage, assigned me a cell-chamber. One came then and called him forth to the Pasha; I knew afterward that he was summoned upon my account. About midnight the warning gunshot sounded in the camp, a second was the signal to remove; I heard the last hub-bub of the Haj rising, and in few more moments the solemn jingles of the takhts er-Rûm journeying again in the darkness, with the departing caravan. Few miles lower they pass a *boghrâz*, or strait in the mountains. Their first station is *Zmurrûd* a forsaken kella; in another remove they come to *Sawra* kella, then *Hedîeh* kella, *Sûjwa* kella, *Barraga*, *Oweynat el-Béden*; there the Haj camp is pitched a little before Medina. In every step of the Mecca-bound pilgrims is now heart's rest and religious confidence that they shall see the holy places; they have passed here the midst of the long way. In the morning twilight, I heard a new rumour without, of some wretched nomads, that

with the greediness of unclean birds searched the forsaken
ground of the encampment.

As it was light the Beduins came clamorously flocking into
the tower, and for a day we were overrun by them. Said *Mohammed Aly* the kellâjy 'Wellah, we cannot be sure from hour
to hour; but their humour changing, they might attempt the
kella!' It was thus the same Fejîr Beduins had seized this kella
few years before, when the Haj government established a new
economy upon the pilgrimage road, and would have lessened
the nomads' former surra. The caravan gone by, the Aarab
that were in the kella, with their sheykh *Motlog*, suddenly ran
upon the weak guard, to whom they did not hurt but sent
them in peace to *el-Ally*. Then they broke into the sealed
chambers and pillaged all that might come to their hand, the
Haj and Jurdy soldiers' stores with all that lately brought
down for the victualling of this and the other kellas that stand
under Medáin Sâlih. The tribes that year would hardly suffer
the caravan to pass peaceably, and other kellas were in like
manner surprised and mastered by them; that next below
Medáin, and Sújwa kella were robbed at the same time by the
W. Aly. The Beduw said, they only sought their own; the
custom of surra or payment for right of way, could not now
be broken. A squadron of Syrian cavalry sent down with the
next year's Haj, to protect those towers, was quartered at el-
Ally, but when the caravan was gone by, the Beduins (mostly
W. Aly) went to surround the oasis, and held them besieged
till the second year. I have said to the Beduins, 'If the tower-
keepers shut their plated door, what were all your threatenings
against them?' Arabians have not wit to burst iron-plate with
the brunt of a beam, or by heaping fire-wood to burn the back
timber of the door, nor any public courage to adventure their
miserable lives under defended walls. They have answered me,
'The kella could not be continually shut against us, the Beduin
have many sly shifts; and if not by other means yet by a
thubîha, (gift of a sheep or other beast for slaughter,) we should
not fail sometime to creep in.'

In this kella an old Moor of Fez, *Haj Nejm* was warden (*mo-
hàfuz*); the other tower-keepers were *Haj Hasan* a Moor of

Morocco, who was before of this tower service, and coming in our pilgrimage from Damascus, had been stayed here again, at the entreaty of his countryman Nejm. Then *Abd el-Kâder* (Servitor-of-the-mighty-God), a young man named after the noble Algerian prince, and son of his deceased steward: he growing into fellowship with the muatterîn at Damascus, his 'uncle' (whose venerable authority is absolute over all the Moorish emigration) had relegated the lubber into the main deserts for a year, in charge of Mohammed Aly. A fourth was *Mohammed*, a half Beduin lad, son of a former Damascene kella keeper, by a nomad housewife; and besides, there was only a slave and another poor man that had been sent to keep the water together at the B. Moaddam.

Our few Moors went armed in the tower amongst the treacherous Beduins; Haj Nejm sat, with his blunderbuss crossed upon his knees, amongst his nomad guests, in the coffee chamber. He was feeble and old, and Hasan the only manful sufficient hand amongst them. This stalwart man was singing all the day at his task and smiling to himself with un-abated good humour. Self-minded he was and witty of head to find a shift with any wile, which made all easy to him, yet without his small horizon he was of a barbarous understand-ing; so that Mohammed Aly would cry out upon his strong-headedness, 'Wellah thou art a *Berber*, Hasan!' (The Berbers, often blue-eyed and yellow-haired, a remnant of the former peoples of Barbary.) Twelve years he had been in the East, and might seem to be a man of middle age, but in his own eye his years were fifty and more, 'And wot you why (he would say and laugh again), my heart is ever green.' The Moors are born under wandering stars. Many wearing the white *bernús*, come in every pilgrimage to Mecca; thence they disperse themselves to Syria, to Mesopotamia, and to all the East Arabic world seeking fortune and service. They labour at their old trades in a new land, and those that have none (they have all a humour of arms), will commonly hire themselves as sol-diers. They are hired before other men, for their circumspect acrid nature, to be caretakers of orchards at Damascus, and many private trusts are committed to the bold Moghrebies.

These Western men are distinguished by their harsh ventri-
loquial speech, and foreign voices.

Nejm, now a great while upon this side of the sea, was grown
infirm more than aged; he could not hope to see his Fez again,
that happier soil of which, with a sort of smiling simplicity, he
gossiped continually. He had wandered through the Barbary
states, he knew even the Algerian *sâhara*; at Tunis he had taken
service, then sometime in Egypt far upon the Nile; afterward
he was a soldier in Syria, and later of the Haj-road service, in
the camp at Maan: a fervent Moslem, yet one that had seen
and suffered in the world, he could be tolerant, and I was
kindly received by him. 'The *Engleys* (said he) at *Jebel Tar*
(Gibraltar) were his people's neighbours over the strait.' He
had liever Engleys than Stambûlies, Turks that were corrupted and no good Moslems. Only the last year the Sîr
Amîn had left a keg of wine with them in the kella, till their
coming up again: 'a cursed man (he said) to drink of that
which is forbidden to the Moslemîn!' He was father of two
children, but, daughters, he seemed not to regard them;
female children are a burden of small joy in a poor Moslem
family; for whom the father shall at least receive but a
slender bride-money, when they are divided from his household.

Nature prepared for the lad Mohammed an unhappy age;
vain and timid, the stripling was ambitious to be somewhat,
without virtuous endeavour. A loiterer at his labour and a slug
in the morning, I heard when Mohammed Aly reprehended
him in this manner: 'It is good to rise up, my son (as the day is
dawning), to the hour of morning prayer. It is then the night
angels depart, and the angels of the day arrive, but those that
linger and sleep on still, Satan enters into them. Knowest thou
I had once in my house a serving lad, a Nasrâny, and although
he washed his head with soap and combed out his hair, yet
then his visage always appeared swollen and discoloured,
wellah as a swine; and if you mark them of a morning, you
may see the Nasâra to be all of them as swine.'

Ignorant (*jâhil*) more than ill-given was the young Abd el-
Kâder, and hugely overgrown, so that Hasan said one day,

observing him, 'Abd el-Kâder's costard is as big as the head of our white mule and nothing in it.' Thus they pulled his cox-comb in the kella, till it had done the poor lad's heart good to have blubbered; bye and bye he was dismissed to keep the water with another at B. Moaddam.

Mohammed Aly, (by his surname) *el-Mahjûb*, surveyor of the kellas between Tebûk and el-Medina, was an amiable bloody ruffian, a little broken-headed, his part good partly violent nature had been distempered (as many of their unquiet climbing spirits) in the Turkish school of government; he was without letters. His family had inhabited a mountain country (he said, 'of uncorrupted ancient manners') in Algeria: in the conquest, rather than become subjects of the Nasâra, they em-barked at their own election in French government vessels, to be landed in Syria. There was a tradition amongst their ances-tors, that 'very anciently they occupied all that country about Maan, where also Moses fed the flocks of Jethro the prophet; The B. Israel had dispossessed them.' Entering the military service, he had fought and suffered with the Syrian troops, in a terrible *jehâd* against the Muscovites, in the Caucasus, where he was twice wounded. The shot, it seemed to me, by his own showing, had entered from the backward, and still the old wounds vexed him in ill weather. Afterward, at the head of a small horse troop, he served in Palestine and the lands beyond Jordan, attaching himself to the fortunes of Mohammed Saîd, from whom he had obtained his present office. The man, half ferocious trooper, could speak fair and reasonably in his better mind; then as there are backwaters in every tide, he seemed humane: the best and the worst Moslemîn can dis-course very religiously. He held the valour of the Moghrebies to be incomparable, it were perilous then to contrary him; a tiger he was in his dunghill ill-humour, and had made himself formerly known on this road by his cruelties. Somewhile being lieutenant at Maan, he had hanged (as he vaunted) three men. Then, when it had been committed to him to build a vault over the spring head at the kella Medowwara, and make that water sure from all hostility of the Aarab, he took certain of them prisoners, sheykhs accused of plundering the Haj, and binding them, he fed them every day in the tower with two biscuits, and every day he caused to be ground a measure of meal in an hand-mill (which is of intolerable weight) upon their breasts; until yielding to these extremeties, which they bore sometime with manly fortitude, they had sent for that ransom which he would devour of them. A diseased senile body he was, full of ulcers, and past the middle age, so that he looked not to live long, his visage much like a fiend, dim with the leprosy of the soul and half fond; he shouted when he spoke with a startling voice, as it might have been of the ghrôl: of his dark heart ruled by so weak a head, we had hourly alarms in the lonely kella. Well could he speak (with a certain erudite utterance) to his purpose, in many or in few words. These Orientals study little else, as they sit all day idle at the coffee in their male societies: they learn in this school of infinite human observation to speak to the heart of one another. His tales seasoned with saws, which are the wisdom of the unlearned, we heard for more than two months, they were never ending. He told them so lively to the eye that they could not be bettered, and part were of his own motley experience. Of a licentious military tongue, and now in the shipwreck of a good understanding, with the bestial insane instincts and the like compunctions of a spent humanity, it seemed the jade might have been (if great had been his chance) another Tiberius senex. With all this, he was very devout as only they can be, and in his religion scrupulous; it lay much upon his conscience to name the Nasrâny *Khalîl* and he made shift to call me, for one Khalîl, five times Ibrahîm. He returned always with a wonderful solemnity to his prayers, wherein he found a sweet foretaste of Paradise; this was all the solace here in the deserts of his corrupt mind. A caterpillar himself, he could censure the criminal Ottoman administration, and pinch at all their misdemeanours. At Damascus, he had his name inscribed in the register of French Algerian subjects; he left this hole to creep into, if aught went hard with him, upon the side of the Dowla; and in trouble any that can claim their protection in Turkish countries, are very nimble to run to the foreign consuls.

The nomads have an ill opinion of Turkish Haj government, seeing the tyrannical and brutish behaviour of these
pretended rulers, their paymasters. All townsmen contemn
them again as the most abject of banded robbers. If any nomad
be taken in a fault, the military command 'Away with this
Beduwy' is shouted with the voice of the destroying angel
'and bind him to the gunwheel.' Mohammed Aly was mad, in
his Moorish pride, and of desperate resentment; only the last
year he durst contend here in the deserts, with his Haj Pasha.
In a ground chamber of the kella are sealed government stores
and deposits of the mukowwems' furnitures: with the rest was
sent in by the paymaster-Pasha a bag of reals, of the public
money. When they came again, the Pasha sent his servant to
receive the silver. The man, as he held it in his hand, imagining this purse to have leaked, for the Arabs are always full of
these canine suspicions, began to accuse Mohammed Aly; but
the Moor, pulling out his scimitar, cut down the rash unarmed slave, flung him forth by the heels, and with frantic
maledictions, shut up the iron door after him. The Pasha sent
again, bidding Mohammed Aly come to him and answer for
this outrage: but the Syrian Moor, his heart yet boiling, swore
desperately he would not go until his humour were satisfied. –
'Away and say these words to the Pasha from Mohammed Aly.
If Mohammed Saîd have cannon, so have I artillery upon the
terrace of this kella, – by God Almighty we will hold out to
the last; and let him remember that we are *Moghrârebá*!' This
was a furious playing out friends and playing in mischief, but
he trusted that his old service would assure him with the
robust Pasha; at the worst he would excuse himself, attesting
his wounds suffered in the sacred cause of their religion; and
after all he could complain 'Wellah, his head went not all
times well, and that he was a Moghreby,' that is one of chol-
eric nature and a generous rashness: at the very worst he could
defy them, proving that he was a stranger born and a French
subject. His artillery (and such is wont to be the worth of an
Arabic boast) were two very small rust-eaten pieces, which for
their rudeness, might have been hammered by some nomad
smith: years ago they had been brought from the *Borj*, an

antique tower half a mile distant, towards the monuments, and were said to have served in old nomad warfare between Annezy and *Harb* tribesmen.

Before the departure of the Aarab, came their sheykh Motlog inquiring for me; *Wen-hu wen-hu* 'where is he, this *dowlâny* or government man?' He bounced my door up, and I saw a swarthy Beduin that stood to gaze lowering and strangely on one whom he took to be *gomâny*, an enemy. Mohammed Aly had said to them that I was a Sîr Amîn, some secretary sent down upon a government errand. This was a short illusion for as the Moslems pray openly and Khalîl was not seen to pray, it was soon said that I could not be of the religion. Mohammed Aly was a hater of every other than his own belief and very jealous of the growing despotism in the world of the perilous Nasâra; – thus they muse with a ferocious gloom over the decay of the militant Islam. Yet he could regard me pleasantly, as a philosopher, in whom was an indulgent natural opinion in all matter of religion. – These were the inhabitants of the kella, a tower seventy feet upon a side, square built. Lurid within are these water-stations, and all that I entered are of one fashion of building. In the midst is the well-court, and about it the stable, the forage and store chambers. Stairs lead upon the gallery which runs round above, whereupon in the north and south sides are the rows of small stone dwelling chambers. Staircases lead from this gallery to the terrace roof, where the garrison may suddenly run up in any need to the defence of the kella.

The Poor Derwish

The Beduins had departed. We sat one of these evenings gathered in the small coffee chamber (which is upon the gallery above), about the winter fire of dry acacia timber when between the clatter of the coffee pestle we thought we heard one hailing under the loop-hole! all listened; – an hollow voice called wearily to us. Mohammed Aly shouted down to him in Turkish, which he had learned in his soldier's life: he was answered in the same language. 'Ah,' said the aga withdrawing

his head, 'it is some poor hajjy; up Hasan, and thou run down
Mohammed, open the door': and they hastened with a religious willingness to let the hapless pilgrim in. They led up
to us a poor man of a good presence, somewhat entered in
years; he was almost naked and trembled in the night's cold.
It was a Turkish derwish who had walked hither upon his feet
from his place in Asia Minor, it might be a distance of
600 miles; but though robust, his human sufferance was
too little for the long way. He had sickened a little after
Maan, and the Haj breaking up from Medowwara, left this
weary wight still slumbering in the wilderness; and he had
since trudged through the deserts those 200 miles, on the
traces of the caravan, relieved only at the kellas! The lone and
broken wayfarer could no more overtake the hajjàj, which
removed continually before him by forced marches. Mohammed Aly brought him an Aleppo felt cloth, in which the
poor derwish who had been stripped by Aarab only three
hours before Medáin, might wrap himself from the cold.

Kindly they all now received him and, while his supper was
being made ready, they bade him be comforted, saying, The
next year, and it pleased Ullah, he might fulfil the sacred pilgrimage; now he might remain with them, and they would
find him, in these two and a half months, until the Haj coming
again. But he would not! He had left his home to be very un-
fortunate in strange countries; he should not see the two blissful cities, he was never to return. The palmer sat at our coffee
fire with a devout thankfulness and an honest humility.
Restored to the fraternity of mankind, he showed himself to
be a poor man of very innocent and gentle manners. When we
were glad again, one of the gate-nomads, taking up the music
of the desert, opened his lips to make us mirth, sternly braying
his Beduin song to the grave chord of the rabeyby. This was
Wady of the Fejír Beduins, a comely figure in the firelight company, of a black visage. He had lived a year at Damascus of
late, and was become a town-made cozening villain, under the
natural semblance of worth. Of sheykhly blood and noble easy
countenance, he seemed to be a child of fortune, but the wretch
had not camels; his tent stood therefore continually pitched

before the kella: more than the flies, he haunted the tower coffee chamber, where, rolling his great white eyeballs, he fawned hour by hour with all his white teeth upon Mohammed Aly, assenting with *Ullah Akhbar!* 'God most high,' to all the sapient saws of this great one of the kella.

Lapped in his cloth, the poor derwish sat a day over, in this sweetness of reposing from his past fatigues. The third morrow come, the last of the customary hospitality, they were already weary of him; Mohammed Aly, putting a bundle of meal in his hand and a little water-skin upon his shoulders, brought him forth, and showing the direction bade him follow as he could the footprints of the caravan, and God-speed. Infinite are the miseries of the Haj; religion is a promise of good things to come, to poor folk, and many among them are half destitute persons. This pain, the words of that fatal Arabian, professing himself to be the messenger of Ullah, have imposed upon ten thousands every year of afflicted mankind!

Death by Thirst. This Fatal Ishmaelite!

Beduins soon came in who had seen our derwish slowly travelling upon the lower Haj road: clear was the weather, the winter's sun made hot mid-days, but the season was too chill for such a weary man to lie abroad by night. Weeks after other Beduins arrived from Medina, and we inquired if they had seen aught of our derwish? They hearing how the man was clad, answered 'Ay, billah we saw him lying dead, and the felt was under him; it was by the way side, by Sawra, (not far down,) almost in sight of the kella.' Sorry were his benefactors, that he whom they lately dismissed alive lay now a dead carcase in the wilderness; themselves might so mishap another day in the great deserts. All voices cried at once, 'He perished for thirst!' They supposed he had poured out his water-skin, which must hang wearily on his feeble neck in the hot noons. The sight was not new to the nomads, of wretched passengers fallen down dying upon the pilgrim way and abandoned; they oftentimes (Beduins have said it in my hearing) see the hyenas stand by glaring and gaping to devour them, as ever the breath should be gone out of the warm body. They pass by: – in Beduins is no pious thought of unpaid charity to bury strangers. – Mohammed Aly told me there is no Haj in which some fail not and are left behind to die. They suffer most between the Harameyn, 'where, O Khalîl! the mountains stand walled up to heaven upon either hand!' In the stagnant air there is no covert from the torment of the naked sun: as the breathless *simûm* blows upon them they fall grovelling and are suffocated. There is water by the way, even where the heat is greatest, but the cursed Beduins will not suffer the wayfaring man to drink, except they may have new and new gifts from the Turkish pashas: there is no remedy, nor past this valley of death, is yet an end of mortal evils. The camping ground at Mecca lies too far from the place, the swarm of poor strangers must seek them hired dwelling chambers in the holy city: thus many are commonly stived together in a very narrow room. The most arriving feeble from great journeys, with ill humours increased in their bodies, new and horrible disorders must needs breed among them: – from the Mecca pilgrimage has gone forth many a general pestilence, to the furthest of mankind!

Enormous indeed has been the event of Mohammed's religious faction. The old Semitic currencies in religion were uttered new under that bastard stamp of the (expedite, factious, and liberal) Arabian spirit, and digested to an easy sober rule of human life (a pleasant carnal congruity looking not above men's possibility). Are not Mohammed's saws to-day the mother belief of a tenth part of mankind? What had the world been? if the tongue had not wagged, of this fatal Ishmaelite! Even a thin-witted religion that can array a human multitude, is a main power in the history of the unjust world. Perilous every bond which can unite many of the human millions, for living and dying! Islam and the commonwealth of Jews are as great secret conspiracies, friends only of themselves and to all without of crude iniquitous heart, unfaithful, implacable. – But the pre-Islamic idolatrous religion of the kaaba was cause that the soon ripe Mawmetry rotted not soon again.

Zeyd the Sheykh. The Monuments

Other days passed, Mohammed Aly saying every evening 'on the morrow he would accompany me to the monuments.' These were Turkish promises, I had to deal with one who in his heart already devoured the Nasrâny: in Syria he had admired that curious cupidity of certain Frankish passengers in the purchasing of 'antiquities.' 'What wilt thou give me, said he, to see the monuments? and remember, I only am thy protection in this wilderness. There be some in the kella, that would kill thee except I forbade them: by Almighty God, I tell thee the truth.' I said 'That he set the price of his services, and I would deliver him a bill upon Damascus': – but distant promises will hardly be accepted by any Arab, their world is so faithless and they themselves make little reckoning of the most solemn engagements.

Now came *Zeyd*, a sheykh of the Fejîr Beduins, riding upon a dromedary from the desert, with his gunbearer seated behind him, and the sheykh's young son riding upon his led mare. Zeyd had been to town in Damascus and learned all the craft of the Ottoman manners, to creep by bribes into official men's favours. Two years before when his mare foaled, and it was not a filly, (they hardly esteem the male worth camel-milk,) this nomad fox bestowed his sterile colt upon the Moorish wolf Mohammed Aly; the kellâjy had ridden down on this now strong young stallion from Syria. Zeyd had seen nothing again but glozing proffers: now was this occasion of the Nasrâny, and they both looked that I should pay the shot between them. 'Give Zeyd ten pound, and Zeyd will mount thee, Khalîl, upon his mare, and convey thee round to all the monuments.' The furthest were not two miles from the tower, and the most are within a mile's distance. Zeyd pretended there was I know not what to see besides 'at *Bîr el-Ghrannem* where we must have taken a *rafîk* of *Billî* Aarab.' Only certain it is that they reckon all that to the overthrown country of el-Héjr which lies between Mûbrak en-Nâga and Bîr el-Ghrannem, which is thirty miles nearly; and by the old trade-road, along, there are ruins of villages down even to el-Medina. But the nomads say with one voice, there are not anywhere in these parts *byût* or *bébàn*, that is, chambers in the rock, like to those of el-Héjr or Medáin Sâlih.

Zeÿd had been busy riding round to his tribesmen's tents and had bound them all with the formula, *Jírak* 'I am thy neighbour.' If I refused Zeÿd, I might hire none of them. The lot had fallen, that we should be companions for a long time to come. Zeÿd was a swarthy nearly black sheykh of the desert, of mid stature and middle age, with a hunger-bitten stern visage. So dark a colour is not well seen by the Arabs, who in these uplands are less darkish-brown than ruddy. They think it resembles the ignoble blood of slave races; and therefore even crisp and ringed hair is a deformity in their eyes. We may remember in the Canticles, the paramour excuses the swarthiness of her beautiful looks, 'I am black but comely, ye daughters of Jerusalem, as the booths of the Beduw, as the tentcloths of Solomon'; she magnifies the ruddy whiteness of her beloved. Dark, the privation of light, is the hue of death, (*mawt el-aswad*) and, by similitude, of calamity and evil; the wicked man's heart is accounted black (*kalb el-aswad*). According to this fantasy of theirs, the Judge of all the earth in the last judgement hour will hold an Arabian expedite manner of audit, not staying to parley with every soul in the sea of generations, for the leprosy of evil desert rising in their visages, shall appear manifestly in wicked persons as an horrible blackness. In the gospel speech, the sheep shall be sundered from the goats, – wherein is some comparison of colour – and the just shall shine forth as the sunlight. The Arabs say of an unspotted human life, *kalb-hu-abiâth*, white is his heart: we in like wise say *candid*. Zeÿd uttered his voice in the deepest tones that I have heard of human throat; such a male light Beduin figure some master painter might have portrayed for an Ishmaelite of the desert. Hollow his cheeks, his eyes looked austerely, from the lawless land of famine, where his most nourishment was to drink coffee from the morning, and tobacco; and where the chiefest Beduin virtue is *es-subbor* a courageous forbearing and abiding of hunger. 'Aha wellah, (said Zeÿd,) *el-Aarab fàsidîn* the nomads are dissolute and so are the Dowla': the blight was in his own heart; this Beduish philosopher looked far out upon all human things with a tolerant incredulity. A sheykh among his tribesmen of principal birth, he had yet no honourable estimation; his hospitality was miserable, and that is a reproach to the nomad dwellers in the empty desert. His was a high and liberal understanding becoming a *mejlis* man who had sat in that perfect school of the parliament of the tribe, from his youth, nothing in Zeyd was barbarous and uncivil; his carriage was that haughty grace of the wild creatures. In him I have not seen any spark of fanatical ill-humour. He could speak with me smilingly of his intolerant countrymen; for himself he could well imagine that sufficient is Ullah to the governance of the world, without fond man's meddling. This manly man was not of the adventurous brave, or rather he would put nothing rashly in peril. *Mesquîn* was his policy at home, which resembled a sordid avarice; he was wary as a Beduin more than very far-sighted. Zeyd's friendship was true in the main, and he was not to be feared as an enemy. Zeyd could be generous where it cost him naught, and of his sheykhly indolent prudence, he was not hasty to meddle in any unprofitable matter.

Zeyd (that was his desert guile) had brought five mouths to the kella: this hospitality was burdensome to his hosts, and Mohammed Aly, who thought the jest turned against him, came on the morrow to my chamber with a grave countenance. He asked me 'Did I know that all this corn must be carried down upon camels' backs from Damascus?' I said, not knowing their crafty drifts, that I had not called them; – and he aloud, 'Agree together or else do not detain him, Khalîl; this is a sheykh of Aarab, knowest thou not that every Beduin's heart is with his household, and he has no rest in absence, because of the cattle which he has left in the open wilderness?' I asked, were it not best, before other words, that I see the monuments ? 'It was reasonable,' he said, 'and Zeyd should bring me to the next bébàn.' – 'And Khalîll it is an unheard-of thing, any Christian to be seen in these countries,' (almost at the door of the holy places). I answered, laying my hand upon the rude stones of the kella building, 'But these courses witness for me, raised by Christian men's hands.' – 'That is well spoken, and we are all here become thy friends: Moslem or Nasrâny, Khalîl is now as one of us; wellah, we would not so suffer another. But go now with Zeyd, and afterward we will make an accord with him, and if not I may send you out myself to see the monuments with some of the kella.'

We came in half a mile by those ancient wells, now a watering place of the country Beduins. They are deep as the well in the kella, ten or twelve feet large at the mouth; the brinks are laid square upon a side, as if they had been platforms of the old wheel-work of irrigation. The well-lining of rude stones courses, without mortar, is deeply scored, (who may look upon the like without emotion?) by the soft cords of many nomad generations. Now I had sight at little distance, of a first monument, and another hewn above, like the head of some vast frontispiece, where yet is but a blind door, little entering into the rock, without chamber. This ambitious sculpture, seventy feet wide, is called *Kasr el-Bint* 'the maidens bower.' It is not, as they pretend, inaccessible; for ascending some ancient steps, entailed in the further end of the cliff, my unshod companions have climbed over all the rocky brow. I saw that tall nightmare frontispiece below, of a crystal-line symmetry and solemnity, and battled with the strange half-pinnacles of the Petra monuments; also this rock is the same yellow-grey soft sandstone with gritty veins and small quartz pebbles. *Kasr*, in the plural *kassûr*, has commonly the sense in Arabia of 'stable habitation,' whether clay or stone, and opposite to *beyt shaar*, the hair-cloth booth, or removable house, of the nomads. Thus, even the cottages of clay, seen about outlying seed-grounds in the wilderness, and not continually inhabited, are named kassûr. At *Hâyil* and *er-Riâth* the prince's residence is named el-Kasr, as it were 'the castle.' Kasr is also in some desert villages, a cluster of houses, enclosed in one court wall; thus they say of the village *Semîra* 'she is three kassûr.' Any strong building for defence and security, (such holds are very common in Arabia), is called gella, for kella.

Borj (πύργ-), tower of defence, manifestly a foreign word, I have not heard in Nejd Arabia.

Backward from the Borj rock, we arrived under a principal monument; in the face I saw a table and inscription, and a bird! which are proper to the Héjr frontispiece; the width of sculptured architecture with cornices and columns is twenty-two feet. – I mused what might be the sleeping riddle of those strange crawling letters which I had come so far to seek! The whole is wrought in the rock; a bay has been quarried in the soft cliff, and in the midst is sculptured the temple-like monument. The aspect is Corinthian, the stepped pinnacles – an Asiatic ornament, but here so strange to European eyes – I have seen used in their clay house-building at Hâyil. Flat side-pilasters are as the limbs of this body of architecture; the chapiters of a singular severe design, hollowed and square at once, are as all those before seen at Petra. In the midst of this counterfeited temple-face, is sculptured a stately porch, with the ornaments of architecture. Entering, I found but a rough-hewn cavernous chamber, not high, not responding to the dignity of the frontispiece: (we are in a sepulchre). I saw in this dim room certain long mural niches or *loculi*; all the floor lies full of driven sand. I thought then, with the help of a telescope, I might transcribe the epigraph, faintly appearing in the sun; but the plague of flies at every moment filled my eyes: such clouds of them, said the Arabs, were because no rain had fallen here in the last years.

Sultry was that mid-day winter sun, glancing from the sand, and stagnant the air, under the sun-beaten monuments; those loathsome insects were swarming in the odour of the ancient sepulchres. Zeyd would no further, he said the sun was too hot, he was already weary. We returned through the Borj rocks; and in that passage I saw a few more monuments, which are also remarkable among the frontispieces at el-Héjr: and lying nigh the caravan camp and the kella they are those first visited by any curious hajjies. Under the porch of one of them and over the doorway are sculptured as supporters, some four-footed beast; the like are seen in none other. The side pedestal ornaments upon another are like griffons; these also

are singular. The tablet is here, and in some other, adorned
with a fretwork flower (perhaps pomegranate) of six petals.
Over a third doorway the effigy of a bird is slenderly sculptured upon the tablet, in low relief, the head yet remaining.
Every other sculptured bird of these monuments we see
wrought in high natural relief, standing upon a pedestal,
sculptured upon the frontispiece wall, which springs from the
ridge of the pediment: but among them all, not a head remains; whether it be they were wasted by idle stone-casts of
the generations of herdsmen, or the long course of the weather.
Having now entered many, I perceived that all the monument
chambers were sepulchral. ... The mural loculi in the low
hewn walls of these rudely four-square rooms, are made as
shallow shelves, in length, as they might have been measured
to the human body, from the child to the grown person; yet
their shallowness is such, that they could not serve, I suppose,
to the receipt of the dead. In the rock floors are seen grave-
pits, sunken side by side, full of men's bones, and bones are
strewed upon the sanded floors. A loathsome mummy odour,
in certain monuments, is heavy in the nostrils; we thought our
cloaks smelled villainously when we had stayed within but a
few minutes. In another of these monuments, *Beyt es-Sheykh*, I
saw the sand floor of rotten clouts, shivering in every wind,
and taking them up, I found them to be those dry bones'
grave-clothes!

'Khalîl,' said Mohammed Aly, 'I counsel thee to give Zeyd
three hundred piastres.' I consented, but the sheykh had no
mind to be satisfied with less than a thousand. If I had yielded
then to their fantastic cupidity, the rumour would have raised
the country and made my future travels most dangerous. But
Zeyd departing, I put a little earnest gold into his hand, that
he might not return home scorned; and he promised to come
for me at the time of the returning Haj, to carry me to dwell
with him among the Beduw: Zeyd hoped that my vaccinating
skill might be profitable to himself. The aga had another
thought, he coveted my gun, which was an English cavalry
carbine: a high value is set in these unquiet countries on all

good weapons. 'And so you give me this, Khalîl, I will send you every day with some of the kella till you have seen all you would of the monuments; and I will send you, to see more of these things, to el-Ally: and, further, would you to Ibn Rashîd, I will procure even to send you thither. ...'

... We visited then the western rocks, *K'assûr* or *Kassûr B'theyny*: – this is a name as well of all the Héjr monuments, 'save only the Beyt es-Sâny.' There are many more frontis-pieces in the irregular cliff face and bays of this crag, of the same factitious hewn architecture, not a few with eagles, some are without epitaphs; in some are seen epitaph tablets yet unwritten. Certain frontispieces are seen here nearly wasted away and effaced by the weather.

The crags full of these monuments are 'the Cities of Sâlih.' We were now five hours abroad: my companions, armed with their long matchlocks, hardly suffered me to linger in any place a breathing-while, saying 'It is more than thou canst think a perilous neighbourhood; from any of these rocks and chambers there might start upon us hostile Beduins.' The life of the Arabians is full of suspicion; they turned their heads with continual apprehension, gazing everywhere about them; also Haj Nejm having once shed blood of the Wélad Aly, was ever in dread to be overtaken without his kella. In this plain-bottom where we passed, between cliffs and monuments, are seen beds of strewed potsherds and broken glass. We took up also certain small copper pieces called by the Beduins *himmarît* (perhaps *Himyariát*) of rusted ancient money. Silver pieces and gold are only seldom found by the Arab in ground where the camels have wallowed. A villager of el-Ally thirty years before found in a stone pot, nearly a bushel of old silver coinage. Also two W. Aly tribesmen, one of whom I knew, had found another such treasure in late years. Of the himmarît, some not fully corroded show a stamped Athenian owl, grossly imi-tated from the Greek moneys; they are Himyaric. Potsherds and broken glass, nearly indestructible matter, are found upon all the ancient sites in Arabia: none here now-a-days use these brittle wares, but only wood and copper-tinned vessels. Arabia was then more civil with great trading roads of the ancient world! Arabia of our days has the aspect of a decayed country. All nations trafficked for gold and the sacred incense, to Arabia the Happy: to-day the round world has no need of the daughter of Arabia; she is forsaken and desolate.

Little remains of the old civil generations of el-Héjr, the caravan city; her clay-built streets are again the blown dust in the wilderness. Their story is written for us only in the crabbed scrawlings upon many a wild crag of this sinister neighbourhood, and in the engraved titles of their funeral monuments, now solitary rocks, which the fearful passenger admires, in these desolate mountains. The plots of potsherds may mark old inhabited sites, perhaps a cluster of villages: it is an ordinary manner of Semitic settlements in the Oasis countries that they are founded upon veins of ground-water. A sûk perhaps and these suburbs was Hejra emporium, with palm groves walled about. ...

... We were come last to the *Mahál el-Mejlis* or senate house, here the face of a single crag is hewn to a vast monument more than forty feet wide, of a solemn agreeable simplicity. The great side pilasters are in pairs, which is not seen in any other; notwithstanding this magnificence, the massy frontispiece had remained unperfected. Who was the author of this beginning who lies nearly alone in his huge sepulchral vanity? for all the chamber within is but a little rude cell with one or two grave-places. And doubtless this was his name engrossed in the vast title plate, a single line of such magnitude as there is none other, with deeply engraved cursive characters [now read by the learned interpreters, *For Hail son of Douna* (and) *his descendants*]: The titles could not be read in Mohammed's time, or the prophet without prophecy had not uttered his folly of these caverns, or could not have escaped derision. The unfinished portal with eagle and side ornaments, is left as it was struck out in the block. The great pilasters are not chiselled fully down to the ground; the wild reef yet remains before the monument, channeled into blocks nearly ready to be removed, – in which is seen the manner to quarry of those ancient stone-cutters. Showing me the blocks my rude companions said, 'These were benches of the town councillors.'

The covercles of the sepulchres and the doors of the 'desolate mansions,' have surely been wooden in this country, (where also is no stone for flags) and it is likely they were of acacia or tamarisk timber; which doubtless have been long since consumed at the cheerful watch-fires of the nomads: moreover there should hinder them no religion of the dead in idolatry. Notwithstanding the imitating (Roman) magnificence of these merchants to the Sabeans, there is not a marble plate in all their monuments, nor any strewn marble fragment is seen upon the Héjr plain. It sufficed them to 'write with an iron pen for ever' upon the soft sand-rock of these Arabian mountains. A mortise is seen in the jambs of all doorways, as it might be to receive the bolt of a wooden lock. The frontispieces are often over-scored with the idle wasms of the ancient tribesmen. I mused to see how often they resemble the infantile Himyaric letters.

The Return of the Haj

It was now ascertained that the Haj brought the small-pox among them. This terrible disease and cholera-fever are the destruction of nomad Arabia. In their weakly nourished bodies is only little resistance to any malignant sickness. The pilgrimage caravans, (many from the provinces of Arabia herself,) are as torrents of the cities' infection flowing every year through the waste Peninsula.

The eighth morrow of this long expectation, the Haj, which had journeyed all night, were seen arriving in the plain. The Jurdy troop mounted and galloped with their officers to salute the Pasha. The tent-pitchers came before: in few more minutes they had raised the pilgrims' town of tents, by the Jurdy camp. The jingles sounded again in our ears, measured to the solemn gait of the colossal bearing-camels, of the pageant-like (but now few returning) takhts er-Rûm. The motley multitude of the Haj came riding after. Their straggling trains passed by for half an hour, when the last of the company re-entered their lodgings. Twice every year stands this canvas city of a day, in the Thamudite plain, full of traffic! Cobblers sat at the sûk corners to drive their trade; they had by them raw soles of camels fallen by the way; and with such they clouted shoes for those who fared so far on foot. The Jurdy street of tent-shops was soon enlarged by the new merchants' tents. The price of small commodities is, at this mid-way station, five to eight times the market worth at Damascus. The Jurdy have brought down Syrian olives, leeks and cheese and caravan biscuit. The Jurdy baker was busy with his fire-pit of sticks in the earth and his girdle-pans, *tannûr*, to make fine white flat-bread, for the pennies of the poor pilgrims. The refreshing sweet and sour lemons and helw dates, from el-Ally, I saw very soon sold out. The merchants upon camels from Damascus opened their bales in the tents and set out coffee-cups, iron ware, precious carpets (like gardens of fresh colours and soft as the spring meadows), – fairings for great sheykhs! and clothing stuffs for the poor Beduw. The returning Haj trades-men bring up merchandise from Mecca; now in their tent stalls I saw heaps of coffee from el-Yémen (Arabia the Happy). ...

... I had been in friendly wise commended by the Jurdy officers, and praised by Mohammed Aly to the Pasha; but I did not think it well so early in the busy day to visit him, who of my coming to Medáin Sâlih had formerly conceived a grave displeasure. From M. Aly, both in his better mind and in his angry moments, I had heard all that matter. In the December night of the Haj departure from Medáin, the Turkish Sîr Amîn and Mohammed Saîd Pasha had sent, before they re-moved, to call again M. Aly. 'Wellah, they said to him, hast thou not hidden the Nasrány, to send him secretly to Medina and Mecca?' 'God is my witness, no your lordships, but this man certainly has adventured hither only to see Medáin Sâlih: trust me he shall not pass a step further: in any case I shall know how to let him; but I go to bring him before you: he shall answer for himself.' 'No,' said the Pasha, 'I will not see his face, and I have a dignity to keep.' (It might be when I

44

visited him in Damascus, I had not observed to call the old portly embezzler of public moneys 'Your Magnificence!') Said the Sîr Amîn (of Stambûl), 'Hearken, kellâjy; if this Engleysy should follow us but one footstep further to Medina, thou art to bring me the dog's head.' [Englishmen, who help these barbarians at Constantinople that cannot be taught, they would murder you secretly, and let hounds live, at Medina and Mecca!] The Pasha said to Mohammed Aly, 'Let him remain with you in the kella, and you are to send him round to all the monuments, that no more Franks come hither hereafter. Look to it, that no evil befall this man: for wellah we will require his life at thy hand.' *Sîr Amîn*: 'By Almighty God, except we find him alive at our coming again, we will hang thee, Mohammed Aly, above the door of thine own kella.' Sore adread are they of late to be called in question for the life of European citizens. – M. Aly looked stoutly upon it, and answered to their beards, that 'he would obey his orders, but by High God, he was a Moghreby, and not to be put in awe by living creature.' Now I must ask a boon of the Pasha, namely, that he would commend me to the wild Beduins of the road. When the caravan removed in the morning, I should go forth to wander with the Aarab in the immense wilderness. The Jurdy officers had dissuaded Zeyd, so had even the Pasha himself; but Zeyd hoped to win silver, and they had no power at all with a free Beduin.

The Pasha. Departure with Zeyd

At the first gunfire, before dawn, the Beduins charged their camels and departed. I saw by the stars our course lay much over to the eastward. Because the Aarab are full of all guile which may profit them, I had then almost a doubt of my company, until the light breaking I espied the B.Sókhr Haj-carriers, coming on disorderly with their wild Beduin canticles; the main body of the caravan, far in the rear, was not yet in sight; I saw also the old wheel-ruts of the Jurdy cannon, and knew thereby certainly, that we were in the road. But for more surety, I dismounted to walk; and took an oath of Zeyd, who yesterday had not kept touch, to ride with me before the Pasha. Bye and bye we had sight of the Pasha, riding far in front, with his officers and a few soldiery; it was near Shuk el-Ajûz. I mounted then with Zeyd on his thelûl, (my camel was sick), and we rode to them at a round trot. Zeyd greeted with the noble Beduin simplicity in his deep stern tones, and as a landlord in his own country, 'Peace be with thee.' Mohammed Saîd, hearing the Beduish voice behind him, said only 'Ho'! again, without turning, but looking aside under the sun, he saw and knew me; and immediately with good humour he said to my Beduin companion, – 'I commit him to thee, and (laying the right hand over his heart), have thou a care of him as of mine own eye.' So he said to me, 'Have you ended all at Medáin Sâlih? The epigraphs, are what? believe you there be any in your countries able to read them? And what of the houses? have you not said they were no houses, but sepulchres? But have you not found any treasure? – Good bye.' I delayed yet, I spoke to the Pasha of the sick camel which Zeyd had bought for me: so he said to Zeyd, 'Hearken! thou shalt restore the camel to his owner, and require the money again; – and (he said to me) if this Beduwy do not so I myself will require it of him at Damascus. – (To Zeyd) Where be now your Aarab?' – 'About a day eastward of this, and the face of them is towards Teyma.' The Pasha asked me anew, 'And where are you going?' – 'To Teyma, to Hâyil, I hope also to Kheybar.' The Pasha drew a breath; he misliked my visiting Kheybar, which is in the circuit of Medina: he answered, 'But it is very difficult.' Here Mohammed Tâhir, who came on riding with the Pasha, said friendly, 'He has the vaccination with him, and that will be for his security among the Aarab; I saw it myself.' He added, 'Are all your inscriptions together in the roll which you have committed to me?' I answered immediately, 'All are there, and I trust in God to show them one day to your worships at Damascus.' The Pasha answered gravely, *Insha 'lla* 'if the Lord will,' doubtless his thought was that I might very hardly return from this Arabian adventure. – Afterwards Zeyd, reporting the Pasha's discourse in the nomad tents, put in my mouth so many Beduin *billahs* ('by-Gods'), and never uttered, that I listened to him as one who dreams.

Departing from them, we rode aside from the Haj-road, and went to fill our girby at a pool of sweet rain-water. Then entering eastward in the wild sandstone upland *Borj Selmàn*, we found before us an infinite swarm of locusts, flying together and alighting under the desert bushes, it is their breeding time; the natural office accomplished, it seems they bye and bye perish. As we went fasting, Zeyd found a few wild leeks and small tubers, *thunma* or *sbeydy* which baked are not unlike the potato. He plucked also the twigs of a pleasant-tasting salad bush, *thalúk*, and wild sorrel, and offered me to eat; and taking from his saddle-bags a piece of a barley-cake, he broke and divided it between us. 'This, he said, is of our surra; canst thou eat Beduins' bread, eigh Khalíl?' The upland through which we passed, that they call the Borj Selmàn (an ancient name from the heroic time of the Beny Helál), is a waste land-breadth of gravel and sand, full of sandstone crags. This, said Zeyd, showing me the wild earth with his swarthy hand, is the land of the Beduw. He watched to see if the townling were discouraged, in viewing only their empty desert before him. And he said, 'Hear, O Khalíl; so thou wilt live here with us, thy silver may be sent down to thee year by year with the Haj, and we will give thee a maiden to wife; if any children be born to thee, when thou wouldst go from hence, they shall be as mine own, billah, and remain with me.' – Also of his stock he would give me a camel.

The Nomad Life

We journeyed taking turns to walk and ride, and as Zeyd would changing our mantles, till the late afternoon; he doubted then if we might come to the Aarab in this daylight. They often removing, Zeyd could not tell their camping-ground within a dozen or score miles. One of the last night's Ageylies went along with us; armed with a hammer, he drove my sick camel forward. As we looked for our Aarab we were suddenly in sight of the slow wavering bulks of camels feeding dispersedly under the horizon; the sun nigh setting, they were driven in towards the Beduin camp, *menzil* another hour distant. Come to the herdsmen, we alighted and sat down, and one of the lads receiving our bowl, ran under his nâgas to milk for us. This is *kheyr Ullah* ('the Lord's bounty'), not to be withheld from any wayfaring man, even though the poor owners should go supperless themselves. A little after, my companions inquired, if I felt the worse; 'because, said they, strangers commonly feel a pain after their first drinking camel-milk.' This somewhat harsh thin milk runs presently to hard curds in the stomach.

In approaching the Beduin tents I held back, with the Ageyly, observing the desert courtesy, whilst our host Zeyd preceded us. We found his to be a small summer or 'flitting-tent' which they call *héjra*, 'built' (thus they speak) upon the desert sand. Poor and low it seemed, unbecoming a great sheykh, and there was no gay carpet to spread within: here was not the welfaring which I had known hitherto, of the northern Beduins. Zeyd led me in with his stern smiling; and, a little to my surprise, I must step after him into the women's apartment. These sometime emigrated Beduins, have no suspicion of Nasrânies, whom they have seen in the north, and heard them reputed honest folk, more than the Moslemîn. There he presented me to his young wife: 'Khalîl (said he), here is thy new 'aunt' (*ammatak*, – hostess); and, *Hirfa* this is Khalîl; and see thou take good care of him.' Before the morning the absent tribesmen had returned from the Haj market; the nomads lodged yet one day in the Borj Selmàn: the third to-morrow we removed. The height of this country is nearly 4,500 feet.

The removing of the camp of the Aarab, and driving the cattle with them from one to another pasture ground, is called *ráhla*. In their yesterday's mejlis they have determined whither and how early; or was it left in the sheykh's hand, those in the neighbour booths watch when the day is light, to see if the sheykh's hareem yet strike his tent; and, seeing this, it is the ráhla. The Beduish housewives hasten then to pluck up the tent-pegs, and their booths fall; the tent-cloth is rolled up, the tent-poles are gathered together and bound in a faggot: so they drag out the household stuff, (bestowed in worsted sacks of their own weaving), to load upon the burden-camels. As neighbours see them and the next neighbours see those, all booths are presently cast in the side dispersed menzil. The herdsmen now drive forward; the hareem [plur. of *horma*, woman] mount with their baggage; the men, with only their arms, sword or matchlock, hanging at the saddle-tree behind them, and the long lances in their hands, ride forth upon their thelûls, they follow with the sheykh: – and this is the march of the nomad village. But if the sheykh's tent remain standing and it is already an hour past sun-rising, when their cattle should be dismissed to pasture, the people begin to say, 'Let the beasts go feed then, there will be no ráhla to-day.'

This dawn, about the 16th February, was blustering and chill in that high country. *Shíl*, 'load now!' cried Zeyd; and Hirfa, shivering and sighing, made up their household gear. Sheykhly husbands help not their feeble housewives to truss the baggage; it were an indignity even in the women's eyes. The men sit on, warming themselves over any blazing sticks they have gathered, till the latest moment, and commonly Zeyd made coffee. The bearing-camels are led in and couched between the burdens; only the herdsman helps Hirfa to charge them upon the rude pack-saddles, *hadàj*, a wooden frame of desert acacia timber, the labour of some nomad sâny or Solubby. The underset pad of old tent-cloth, *wittr*, is stuffed with some dry herbage, and all is girded under the camel's belly with a simple cord. Zeyd called to help lift the loads, for they were over-heavy, did it grudgingly, murmuring, 'Was a sheykh a porter to bear burdens?' I also helped them to stay up the weighty half-loads in the sides of the saddles until both were laid even and coupled. Zeyd was a lordling in no contemptible tribe. Such a sheykh should not in men's sight put the hand to any drudgery; he leaves it to his hind. A great sheykh may take upon him part care of his own mare, in the menzil, whilst the hinds are all day herding in the field; yet having led her to the well, if there be any by, of the common tribesmen the sheykh will call him to draw her water.

Nevertheless sheykhs' sons whilst they are children, and later as young men armed, are much abroad with the tribes' cattle and companions with the herdsmen. I have seen Zeyd go out with a grass-hook to cut his mare's forage and bring again a mantlefull on his back, and murmuring, with woe in his black visage, it was Selím his son's duty: and the boy, oftentimes disobedient, he upbraided, calling him his life's torment, *Sheytàn*, only never menacing him, for that were far from a Beduin father's mind.

We removed hardly ten miles, and pitched four hours to the eastward of Dàr el-Hamra. The hareem, busily 'build' their tents; but the men, as they have alighted, are idle, that when nor herding or riding in a foray sit all day at home only lazing and lording. 'The *jowwàr* (Bed. housewives), say they, are for the labour of the household and to be under discipline.' Zeyd, with a footcast in the sand-bank where we had taken shelter from the gusty wind till the *beyts* were standing, had made an hearth; then he kneeled with the Beduin cheerfulness to kindle our gipsy fire. Selím gathered sticks, and we sat down to warm ourselves and roast locusts.

Here we lodged two days, and removed anew five hours eastward through the same sandy moorland, with mild weather, and pitched in the camping-ground *el-Antarîeh*. Sweet and light in these high deserts is the uncorrupt air, but the water is scant and infected with camel urine. Hirfa doled out to me, at Zeyd's commandment, hardly an ounce or two of the precious water every morning, that I might wash 'as the townspeople'. She thought it unthrift to pour out water thus when all day the thirsty tribesmen have not enough to drink. Many times between their waterings, there is not a pint of water left in the greatest sheykhs' tents; and when the good-man bids his housewife fill the bowl to make his guests' coffee, it is answered from their side, 'We have no water.' Too much of a great sheykh's provision is consumed by his mare; the horse, of all cattle in the desert, is most impatient of thirst. Zeyd used oftentimes this fair excuse, (being miserable even in the poor dispense of coffee,) 'There is no water.' Motlog the great sheykh coming one of these mornings to visit me, inquired first: 'Hast thou drunk coffee?'–'Not to-day, they say *there is no water.*' – 'What! he asked, has not Zeyd made you coffee this morning?' for even poor sheykhs will not fail to serve the morrow's cup, each one to his own fellowship. Mot-log knew his cousin Zeyd, and smiled, saying, 'What is this, Zeyd has no water! but, Khalîl, come over to us, and I will make thee coffee.' He led me to his tent, which was not far off, where, sitting at the hearth, and being himself the sheykh of his tribe, he roasted, brayed and boiled, and prepared his cup of hospitality for the Christian stranger. In that place it chanced Zeyd to lose a camel, which had been frayed by wolves. He mounted his mare at the morrow's light, and rode forth with the long shivering horseman's lance upon his shoulder to follow her traces. The day after Zeyd returned to us, driving in his lost beast: he had found her near Birket Moaddam.

The Spring Pasture. The Camp. The Tents

The camels now feeding of the sappy rabîa were *jezzîn* or 'not drinking'. In good spring years they are in these dîras almost two and a half months jezzîn, and not driven to the watering. Then the force of life is spent of the herb lately so fresh upon the ground, and withering under the sun it is dried up. If, after some shower, the great drinkless cattle find rain-water lodged in any hollow rocks, I have seen them slow down their heavy long necks; so they snuff to it, and bathing but the borders of their flaggy lips, blow them out and shake the head again as it were with loathing. The nomads' camels are strong and frolic in these fat weeks of the spring pasture. Now it is they lay up flesh, and grease in their humps, for the languor of the desert summer and the long year. Driven home full-bellied at sunset, they come hugely bouncing in before their herdsmen: the householders, going forth from the booths, lure to them as they run lurching by, with loud *Wolloo-wolloo-wolloo,* and to stay them *Wòh-ho wòh-ho wòh-ho!* they chide any that strikes a tent-cord with *hutch!* The camels are couched every troop beside, about, and the more of them before the booth of their household; there all night they lie ruckling and chawing their huge cuds till the light of the morrow. The Aarab say that their camels never sleep; the weary brute may stretch down his long neck upon the ground, closing awhile his great liquid eyes; but after a space he will right again the great languid carcase and fall to chawing. In this fresh season they rise to graze anew in the moonlight, and roam from the booths of the slumbering Aarab; but fearful by nature, they stray not then very far off. Sometimes wakening after midnight and seeing our camels strayed, I went out to bring them in; but the Beduins said, 'Sleep on, Khalîl, there is no cause; let them go feeding as they will.' They would see them pasture now all they can; but not seldom are they bereaved thus of their cattle by prowling night-robbers. Camels, the only substance of the nomads, are the occasion of all their contending, '*Neshîl*, we load, say they, upon them, and we drink halîb, the milk, of them.' The cows go twelve months with young; now was their time of calving, which falls at the beginning of the rabîa. The nomad year is divided in this sort; *er-rabîa*, spring-time of three months; *el-gâyth*, midsummer, three months; *es-sferry*, fall of the year, three months; *es-shitâ* (pronounce *és-sh'tá*), winter. To be a ready man in this kind of lore, is clerkship with the Beduw, and to have a wayfarer's knowledge of the stars. When they found good pasture the Beduins encamped, and we lodged upon that ground mostly till the third or fourth morrow. The nomads dwelling, the day over, in any place, they say 'el-Aarab *umjemmîn*' (*j* for *k* guttural), or the camp is standing. The herdsmen bring word of the pasture about them, and as the sheykhs determine in the mejlis the people will remove again, it was commonly to twelve or thirteen miles distance; and now their 'face was toward' Teyma.

If the ráhla be short the Beduw march at leisure, the while their beasts feed under them. The sheykhs are riding together in advance, and the hareem come riding in their trains of baggage camels; if aught be amiss the herdsmen are nigh at hand to help them: neighbours will dismount to help neighbours and even a stranger. The great and small cattle are

driven along with their households. You shall see housewives
dismount, and gossips walk on together barefoot (all go here
unshod), and spinning beside their slow-pacing camels. But
say the Beduin husbands, 'We would have the hareem ride always and not weary themselves, for their tasks are many at
home.' The Fukara women alighted an hour before noon, in
the march, to milk their few ewes and goats. Every family and
kindred are seen wayfaring by themselves with their cattle.
The Aarab thus wandering are dispersed widely; and in the
vast uneven ground (the most plain indeed but full of crags),
although many hundreds be on foot together, commonly we
see only those which go next about us. The Beduins coming
near a stead where they will encamp, Zeyd returned to us; and
he thought good there struck down the heel of his tall horseman's lance *shelfa* or *romhh*, stepping it in some sandy desert
bush: this is the standard of Zeyd's fellowship, – they that encamp with him, and are called his people. Hirfa makes her
camel kneel; she will 'build' the booth there: the rest of
Zeyd's kindred and clients coming up, they alight, each family
going a little apart, to pitch their booths about him. This is
'Zeyd's menzil' and the people are Zeyd's Aarab. The bearing-
camels they make to kneel under their burdens with the guttural voice, *ikh-kh-kh!* The stiff neck of any reluctant brute is
gently stricken down with the driving-stick or an hand is imposed upon his heavy halse; any yet resisting is plucked by the
beard; then without more he will fall groaning to his knees.
Their loads discharged, and the pack-saddles lifted, with a
spurn of the master's foot the bearing-camels rise heavily again
and are dismissed to pasture. The housewives spread the tent-
cloths, taking out the corner and side-cords; and finding
some wild stone for a hammer, they beat down their tent pegs
into the ground, and under-setting the tent-stakes or 'pillars'
(*am'dàn*) they heave and stretch the tent-cloth: and now their
booths are standing. The wife enters, and when she has bestowed her stuff, she brings forth the man's breakfast; that is a
bowl of léban, poured from the sour milk-skin, or it is a clot
of dates with a bowl of the desert water: for guest-days it is
dates and buttermilk with a piece of sweet butter. After that

she sits within, rocking upon her knees the *semíla* or sour milk-skin, to make this day's butter.

As Zeyd so is every principal person of these Beduins, the chief of a little menzil by itself: the general encampment is not disposed (as is the custom of the northern Aarab) in any formal circuit. The nomads of these marches pitch up and down in all the 'alighting place' at their own pleasure. The Fejîr or Fukara never wandered in *ferjàn* (*j* for *k* guttural) or nomad hamlets, dispersedly after their kindreds, which is everywhere the nomad manner, for the advantage of pasture; but they journey and encamp always together. And cause was that, with but half-friends and those mostly outraged upon their borders, or wholly enemies, there were too many reckonings required of them; and their country lies open. Zeyd's Aarab were six booths: a divorced wife's tent, mother of his young and only son, was next him; then the tent of another cast-off housewife, mother of a ward of his, *Settàm*, and by whom he had himself a daughter; and besides these (Zeyd had no near kinsfolk), a camel-herd with the old hind his father, of Zeyd's father's time, and the shepherd, with their alliance. Forlorn persons will join themselves to some sheykh's menzil, and there was with us an aged widow, in wretchedness, who played the mother to her dead daughter's fatherless children, a son so deformed that like a beast he crept upon the sand [*ya latíf*, 'oh happy sight!' said this most poor and desolate grandam, with religious irony, in her patient sighing] – and an elf-haired girl wonderfully foul-looking. Boothless, they led their lives under the skies of God, the boy was naked as he came into the desert world. The camel upon which they rode was an oblation of the common charity; but what were their daily food only that God knoweth which feedeth all life's creatures. There is no Beduwy so impious that will chide and bite at such, his own tribesfolk, or mock those whom God has so sorely afflicted; nor any may repulse them wheresoever they will alight in the common wilderness soil. Sometimes there stood a stranger's booth among us, of nomad passengers or an household in exile from the neighbour tribesmen: such will come in to pitch by a sheykh of their acquaintance.

Hirfa ever demanded of her husband toward which part should 'the house' be built. 'Dress the face, Zeyd would answer, to this part,' showing her with his hand the south, for if his booth's face be all day turned to the hot sun there will come in fewer young loitering and parasitical fellows that would be his coffee-drinkers. Since the sheukh, or heads, alone receive their tribe's surra, it is not much that they should be to the arms coffee-hosts. I have seen Zeyd avoid as he saw them approach, or even rise ungraciously upon such men's presenting themselves, (the half of every booth, namely the men's side, is at all times open, and any enters there that will, in the free desert,) and they murmuring he tells them, wellah, his affairs do call him forth, adieu, he must away to the mejlis, go they and seek the coffee elsewhere. But were there any sheykh with them, a coffee lord, Zeyd could not honestly choose but abide and serve them with coffee; and if he be absent himself, yet any sheykhly man coming to a sheykh's tent, coffee must be made for him, except he gently protest, 'billah, he would not drink.' Hirfa, a sheykh's daughter and his nigh kinswoman, was a faithful make to Zeyd in all his sparing policy.

Our menzil, now standing, the men step over to Zeyd's coffee-fire, if the sheykh be not gone forth to the mejlis to drink his mid-day cup there. A few gathered sticks are flung down beside the hearth: with flint and steel one stoops and strikes fire in tinder, he blows and cherishes those seeds of the cheerful flame in some dry camel-dung, sets the burning sherd under dry straws, and powders over more dry camel-dung. As the fire kindles, the sheykh reaches for his *dellàl*, coffee-pots, which are carried in the *fatya*, coffee-gear basket; this people of a nomad life bestow each thing of theirs in a proper *beyt*, it would otherwise be lost in their daily removing. One rises to go fill up the pots at the water-skins, or a bowl of water is handed over the curtain from the woman's side; the pot at the fire, Hirfa reaches over her little palm-full of green coffee-berries. We sit in a half ring about the hearth; there come in perhaps some acquaintance or tribesmen straying between the next menzils. Zeyd prepared coffee at the hours; afterward, when he saw in me little liking of his coffee-water, he went to drink the cup abroad. If he went not to the mejlis, he has hidden himself two or three hours like an owl, or they would say as a dog, in my little close tent, although intolerably heated through the thin canvas in the mid-day sun. It was a mirth to see Zeyd lie and swelter, and in a trouble of mind bid us report to all comers that 'Zeyd was from home': and where his elvish tribesmen were merry as beggars to detect him. *Mukkarîn el-Beduw!* 'the nomads (say the settled Arabs) are full of wily evasions.'

The sheykhs and principal persons assemble at the great sheykh's or another chief tent, when they have alighted upon any new camping-ground; there they drink coffee, the most holding yet the camel-stick, *mishaab, mehjân* or *bakhorra*, as a sceptre, (a usage of the ancient world,) in their hands. The few first questions among them are commonly of the new dispositions of their several menzils: as, '*Rahŷel!* (the sheykh's brother), *fen ahl-ak?* where be thy people (pitched)? – *Eth-Therrŷeh* (the sheykh's son), *fen ahl-ak?* – *Mehsan* (a good simple man, and who had married Zeyd's only sister,) – *Khálaf* and the rest, where be your menzils? – Zeyd is not here! who has seen Zeyd? – and *Mijwel*, where are his Aarab?' for every new march displaces these nomads, and few booths in the shortness of the desert horizon are anywhere in sight. You see the Beduins silent whilst coffee is being made ready, for all their common talk has been uttered an hundred times already, and some sit beating the time away and for pastime limning with their driving-sticks in the idle sand. They walk about with these gay sticks, in the daytime; but where menzils are far asunder, or after nightfall, they carry the sword in their hands: the sword is suspended with a cord from the shoulder. The best metal is the Ajamy, a little bent with a simple crossed hilt (beautiful is the form), wound about with metal wire; next to the Persian they reckon the Indian blade, *el-Hindy*.

In nomad ears this word, Aarab, signifies 'the people.' Beduin passengers when they meet with herdsmen in the desert inquire, *Fen el-Aarab?* 'where is the folk?' Of the multitude of nomad tribes east and west, they say in plural wise, *el-Arbán*. This other word, Beduin, received into all our languages, is in the Arabian speech Beduwy, that is to say inhabitant of the waste, (*bâdia*), in the *Bedaìwy* (*aù* dipth.), but commonly *él-Bèduw*. As we sit, the little cup, of a few black drops, is served twice round. When they have swallowed those boiling sips of coffee-water, and any little news has been related among them, the men rise one after other to go home over the hot sand: all are barefoot, and very rarely any of those Aarab has a pair of sandals. So everyone is come again to his own, they say the mid-day prayers; and when they have breakfasted, they will mostly slumber out the sultry mid-day hours in the housewife's closed apartment. I have asked an honest wife, 'How may your lubbers slug out these long days till evening?' and she answered, demurely smiling, 'How sir, but in solace with the hareem!'

The héjra, or small flitting-tent, laid out by the housewife, with its cords stretched to the pins upon the ground, before the am'dàn or props be set up under, is in this form: to every pair of cords, is a pair of stakes; there are three stakes to every pair of cords in the waist of the tent. Greater booths are stayed by more pairs of waist-cords, and stand upon taller staves. The Aarab tent, which they call the *beyt* (pl. *byût*) *es-shaar*, 'abode, booth, or house of hair,' that is of black worsted or hair-cloth, has, with its pent roof, somewhat the form of a cottage. The tent-stuff, strong and rude, is defended by a list sewed under at the heads of the am'dàn, and may last out, they say, a genertion, only wearing thinner: but when their roof-cloth is threadbare it is a feeble shelter, thrilled by the darting beams of the Arabian sun, and casting only a grey shadow. The Arabian tent strains strongly upon all the staves, and in good holdingground, may resist the boisterous blasts which happen at the crises of the year, especially in some deep mountainous valleys. Even in weak sand the tents are seldom overblown. Yet the cords, *tunb el-beyt*, which are worsted-twist of the women's spinning, oft-times burst: who therefore (as greater sheykhs) can spend silver, will have them of hempen purchased in the town. In all the road tribes, they every year receive rope, with certain clothing and utensils, on account of their Haj surra. The tent-stuff is seamed of narrow lengths of the housewives' rude worsted weaving; the yarn is their own spinning, of the mingled wool of the sheep and camels' and goats' hair together. Thus it is that the cloth is blackish: we read in the Hebrew Scripture, 'Black as the tents of Kedar.' Good webster-wives weave in white borders made of their sheep's wool, or else of their gross-spun cotton yarn (the cotton wool is purchased from Medina or the sea-coast).

When the tent-cloth is stretched upon the stakes, to this roof they hang the tent-curtains, often one long skirt-cloth which becomes the walling of the nomad booth: the selvedges are broached together with wooden skewers. The booth front is commonly left open, to the half at least we have seen, for the *mukaad* or men's sitting-room: the other which is the women's and household side, is sometimes seen closed (when they would not be espied, whether sleeping or cooking,) with a fore-cloth; the woman's part is always separated from the men's apartment by a hanging, commonly not much more than breast or neck high, at the waist-poles of the tent. The mukaad is never fenced in front with a tent-cloth, only in rain they incline the am'dàn and draw down the tent eaves lower. The nomad tents are thus very ill lodging, and the Beduins, clothed no better than the dead, suffer in cold and stormy weather. In winter they sometimes load the back-cloth ground-hem with great stones, and fence their open front at the men's side with dry bushes. The tent side-cloths can be shifted according to the wind and sun: thus the back of the Bediun booth may become in a moment the new front. A good house-wife will bethink herself to unpin and shift the curtain, that her husband's guests may have shadow and the air, or shelter.

Upon the side of the hareem, that is the household apartment, is stored all their husbandry. At the woman's curtain stand the few tent-cloth sacks of their poor baggage, *el-gúsh*: in these is bestowed their corn and rice if they have any: certain lumps of rock-salt, for they will eat nothing insipid; also the housewife's thrift of wool and her spun yarn, – to be a good wool-wife is honourable among Aarab women; and some fathoms perhaps of new calico. There may be with the rest a root of *er'n* or tan wood, the scarlet chips are steeped in water, and in two or three days, between ráhlas, they cure therein their goat-skins for girbies and semílies, besides the leather for watering-buckets, watering-troughs and other nomad gear. The poorest wife will have some box, (commonly a fairing from the town,) in which are laid up her few household medicines, her comb and her mirror, *mèrguba*, her poor inherited ornaments, the ear-rings and nose-ring of silver or even golden (from the former generations); and with these any small things of her husband's, (no pockets are made in their clothing,) which she has in her keeping. But if her good-man be of substance, a sheykh of surra, for his bundle of reals and her few precious things she has a locked coffer painted with vermilion from Medina, which in the ráhla is trussed (also a mark of sheykhly estate) upon her bearing-camel. – Like to this, I have mused, might be that ark of things sacred to the public religion, which was in the nomad life of B. Israel.

Commonly the housewife's key of her box is seen as a glittering pendant, upon her veil backward; and hangs, with her thimble and pincers, (to pluck the thorns out of their bare soles,) by a gay scarlet lace, from the circlet of the head-band. Their clotted dates, if they have any, are stived in heavy pokes of camel-hide, that in the ráhla are seen fluttering upon the bearing-cattle with long thongs of leather. This apparel of fringes and tassels is always to the Semitic humour; of the like we read in Moses, and see them in the antique Jewish sculptures. Of their old camel sack-leather, moisty with the juice of the dates, they cut the best sandals. The full-bellied sweating water-skins are laid, not to fret at the ground, upon fresh spray of broom or other green in the desert; amongst all stands the great brazen pot, *jidda*, tinned within by the nomad smith, or by the artificer in their market village. They boil in it their butter, (when they have any, to make samn,) and their few household messes; they seethe the guest-meal therein in the day of hospitality.

The Aarab *byût shaar* are thus tents of hair-cloth made housewise. The 'houses of hair' accord with that sorry landscape! Tent is the Semitic house: their clay house is built in like manner; a public hall for the men and guests, and an inner woman's and household apartment. Like to this was Moses' adorned house of the nomad God in the wilderness. Also the firmament, in the Hebrew prophet, is a tabernacle of the one household of God's creation. These flitting-houses in the wilderness, dwelt in by robbers, are also sanctuaries of 'God's guests,' *theúf Ullah* the passengers and who they be that haply alight before them. Perilous rovers in the field, the herdsmen of the desert are kings at home, fathers of hospitality to all that seek to them for the night's harbour. 'Be we not all, say the poor nomads, *guests of Ullah*?' Has God given unto them, God's guest shall partake with them thereof: if they will not for God render His own, it should not go well with them. The guest entered, and sitting down amongst them, they observe an honourable silence, asking no untimely questions, (such is school and nurture of the desert,) until we have eaten or drunk somewhat at the least, and by 'the bread and salt' there is peace established between them, for a time (that is counted two nights and the day in the midst, whilst their food is in him). Such is the golden world and the 'assurance of Ullah' in the midst of the wilderness: travelled Beduins are amazed to see the sordid inhospitality of the towns; – but where it were impossible that the nomad custom should hold.

Zeyd's Household: Hirfa

And now to speak of Zeyd's household. He had another wife, but she was fled from him – this is common, in their male tyranny of many marriages – and now dwelt in her mother's tribe, the Bishr; they were pasturing nigh before us in this wilderness. Zeyd rode over to his neighbours, and with pleasant promises, which well he knew to forge and feign, he wooed her home again. A sheykh told me she was beautiful, 'she has egg-great eyes'; but that, when I saw her, was all her pallid beauty. The returned wife would not pitch with us, where jealous Hirfa was, but 'built' her booth with some kindred in another menzil. Zeyd and Hirfa were next cousins; Hirfa was a sheykh's orphan, whom it seems he had taken partly for her few inherited camels. Hirfa was an undergrown thick Beduin lass, her age might be twenty; the golden youth was faded almost to autumn in her childish face, but not un-pleasing; there was a merry wooden laughter always in her mouth, which ended commonly, from the unsatisfied heart, in sighing. 'The woman sighs (says the proverb) who has an ill husband.' Hirfa sighed for motherhood: she had been these two years with an husband and was yet *bint*, as the nomads say, 'in her girlhood'; and she wept inwardly with a Semitic woman's grief. Zeyd and Hirfa were as Isaac and Rebecca; with the Beduin simplicity they sat daily sporting lovingly to-gether before us, for we were all one family and friendly eyes, but oftentimes in the midst Hirfa pouted; then Zeyd would coldly forsake her, and their souls were anew divided. Hirfa in her weary spirit desired some fresh young husband, instead of this palled Zeyd, that she mistrusted could not give her children. Again and again they bade the Christian stranger de-liver judgement of their fruitless marriage, whether it had been lawful, as betwixt brothers' children. Hirfa, a testy little body, of her high birth in sheykhs' booths was a *sheykha* among the hareem, and so even by the men regarded; all the principal sheukh were her nigh kinsmen. In the Arabian small tribes and villages there is a perpetual mingling of kindred blood: to-day after so many generations who may think this Semitic race has been impaired thereby? – but truly we see not few brain-sick and cripples amongst them.

Self-minded, a bold-faced wench, mistress Hirfa cast as she should not a pair of eyes upon their herdsman, a likely young man, whom in her husband's absence she wooed openly and in Zeyd's despite; but he was prudent, and faithful to his sheykh's service. Here, and though bordering the jealous Hejâz and the austere Waháby Nejd, the Fukara women go open-faced, and (where all are kindred) I could never perceive amongst them any jealousy of the husbands. In this tribe of date-eaters, there was not always a well-grown man, besides the sheykh Motlog and his sons, nor any comely woman. Zeyd would tame his little wilful wife; and upon a time he corrected her with the rod in the night.

The comedy of Hirfa and Zeyd was become matter of daily
raillery in the mejlis of the coffee-drinking sheukh their
cousins; where, arriving alone, I might hear them say, 'Eigh!
here comes Khalîl: *márhabba* welcome, O Khalîl; make place
for Khalîl; pass up, Khalîl, and sit thou beside me.' – 'Well
met, Khalîl! but where is thine uncle Zeyd to-day?' – 'Zeyd
is *ʒahlán*, or melancholy; he lies in this mood wilfully slumbering out the day at home': – in the lands of the sun men willingly sleep out their sorrow. 'But tell us, knowst thou was Hirfa
beat? what news to-day? Khalîl, do you love your uncle?' One
said who did not love him (*Khálaf Alláyda* an exile, of the
sheukh of W. Aly), 'Zeyd is not a man, who beats his wife; it
is a *marra*, woman, that will strike a *marra*; do your people so,
Khalîl?' I answered, 'Nay, surely; unless it be some ungracious wretch.' And he, 'It is thus amongst us Beduw, *ayb*,
a shame, wellah.' The wales of Zeyd's driving-stick were ever
in her stubborn little spirit; and at the next alighting from a
ráhla, when she had hastily built the booth and Zeyd was
walked to the mejlis, leaving all, Hirfa ran back embittered
into the wilderness. A devout Beduin of our menzil, he of the
meteors, held awhile her two little hands, beseeching her to
return to her patience; but, a sheykh's daughter, she would
not be held and peevishly she broke from him.

Of a disaffected Beduin wife, such is the public remedy; to
show herself to be alienated from her husband, and ready to
forsake his wedlock and household, thus putting upon him a
common scorn, because he will not dismiss her. There followed after Hirfa, as soon as he heard the tidings, her next
kinsman of her mother's side, one that resembled Hirfa as if
he had been her brother: she was running like an ostrich alone
in the wild desert. An hour passed till he led her home to us,
and left her again sorrowful at her own and Zeyd's tent. 'Ha,
Khalîl,' said he, 'what wilt thou give me now that I have
fetched in thine aunt again, who pours thee out léban and
water? and (showing me his cutlass), Wellah, I have brought
her *bes-seyf* by constraint of the sword.' Zeyd, displeased, now
ranged some nights to his Bishr wife's booth; and jealous
Hirfa, not suffering this new despite, another day, even in the

presence of strangers, Zeyd's guests, fled forth in the gall of her heart from the newly pitched tent when the people alighted at a menzil; Zeyd sat on, as a man aggrieved, only looking after her, but not hindering (in their eyes it had been unseemly, that man's life is free). The fugitive Beduin wife has good leave to run whithersoever she would; she is free as the desert, there is none can detain her. Hirfa hied then to her mother's kindred, and sat down, all sighs, in her aunt's booth; and in what beyt soever a running wife have taken refuge, not her own wedded husband may honestly appear to reclaim his part in her.

The strangers departed, and Zeyd sat by his now desolate booth in long heaviness of mind; but to show any lively resentment, only by occasion of a woman, had been ill nurture and unmanly. He stretched himself upon the sand to sleep out his grief, and slumbered with his head in the scalding sun. The nomads make religion, to observe this mildness and forbearance in the household life! 'God's peace' is in that parcel of the great and terrible wilderness, which is shadowed by every poor herdsman's booth. Bye and bye I shook him and said, 'It is not good to sleep and swoon in the sun.' We went then together to seek coffee at the mejlis, where, some malicious ones smiling at his sadness and new troubled looks, Zeyd had complained in his great, now untoned voice, 'that he had no longer an household, – unless it were that Khalîl (their guest) would fetch Hirfa home.' Every tiding is presently wide blown in all the open tents of a nomad menzil, and there is no idle tale that will not ride upon the tongues, light as leaves, of witless Beduins, to drive the empty hours.

The Woman's Lot. Sons v. Daughters

When I understood in our menzil that this is the guest's honourable office, I went the next afternoon to call Hirfa home to Zeyd's household; where else she had been abashed to return of herself and they to seek her. I found Hirfa a little shamefaced, sitting in the midst of her gossips; old wife-folk that had been friends of her dead mother; they were come together to the aunt's booth to comfort her, and there were the young men her cousins. Sad-faced sat the childless young wife, she was playing fondly with a neighbour's babe. 'Khalîl, she said, must fill her great tobacco pipe, galliûn, or she would not hear my words.' The old wives cried out, 'Thou art Khalîl, to fill all our galliûns (they are great tobacco "bibbers"), and else we will not let Hirfa go.' The young men said they would keep Hirfa, and marry her themselves, and not give her again 'to that wicked Zeyd.'

The tobacco distributed, I took Hirfa by the little Beduish hand (never labouring, they have all these little hands), and bidding her rise, the little peevish housewife answered me, 'But she would not be held, Khalîl must let go her hand.' I said then, 'I will bring thee home, hostess, return with me; and else I must alight to pitch my tent by thee, from the next ráhla.' *Hirfa*: 'That do, Khalîl, and welcome: I and thou will go, – ah! where we shall eat a camel together (she would say a bountiful household), only fill thou again my galliûn.' *The Aunt*: 'And mine, Khalîl; or Hirfa is ours, ay, and we will not let her go.' Having filled the galliûns of them all, I asked if our mistress Hirfa were not now coming. A young cousin said 'I am her father, and Hirfa is mine, Khalîl; no! we will not give her more to Zeyd.' Said her aunt: 'Well, go over, Khalîl; Hirfa follows, and all we (the bevy of old women) accompany her' (to bring her home honourably). Soon after, arriving before my tent door, they called me out to pay them another dole of tobacco: – And Hirfa sat again in her own beyt.

The woman's lot is here unequal concubinage, and in this necessitous life a weary servitude. The possession in her of parents and tutors has been yielded at some price, (in contempt and constraint of her weaker sex,) to an husband, by whom she may be dismissed in what day he shall have no more pleasure in her. It may be, (though seldom among nomads their will is forced,) that those few flowering years of her youth, with her virginity have been yielded to some man of unlikely age. And his heart is not hers alone; but, if not divided already, she must look to divide her marriage in a time to come with other. And certainly as she withers, which is not long to come, or having no fair adventure to bear male children, she will as thing unprofitable be cast off; meanwhile all the house-labour is hers, and with his love will be lost. What oneness of hearts can be betwixt these lemans, whose lots are not faithfully joined? Sweet natural love may bud for a moment, but not abide in so uneven ways. Love is a dovelike confidence, and thereto consents not the woman's heart that is wronged.

Few then are the nomad wives whose years can be long happy in marriage! they are few indeed or nearly none that continue in their first husband's household. Such are commonly mothers of many children, or wedded in needy families, so that the house-fathers are not able to maintain another housewife. But substantial and sheykhly persons will have done betimes with these old wives, and pass to new bride-beds, or they were not Moslemîn; and being rich men they spend cheerfully for new wives as they will spend for the seasonable change of clothing. The cast housewife may be taken up by another worthy man, in favour of some old liking, or pass to the new marriage and household service of some poorer person. The woman's joy and her comfort is to be mother of sons, that at least she may remain a matron in her boy's tent, when even his hard father shall have repudiated her. It was thus with *Ghrobny*, Zeyd's young son Selím's mother. Zeyd, pitying her tears, had found her another husband of poor Khamâla folk, by whom she had now a new babe: but the man dealt unkindly with her; wherefore returning to her young son, she was pitched again as an uncheerful widow to live by Zeyd. A day dawned, and Ghrobny's booth was away! the Arabs stood half laughing and wondering, for it was a poor-spirited creature, that had been a fair woman in her youth, till we understood of Selím she had loaded upon her camel in the night-time and was stolen away to the Khamâly in a distant menzil. The wretch, the day before, coming hither, had kissed her and vowed like a smooth lover to receive her again. But after two days the poor fond woman, and now little pleasing, returned to us with red eyes, to embrace her child, who had remained in the meanwhile confused with his father; and from the next ráhla, the drivelling and desolate wife alighted as before to encamp by Zeyd.

These Aarab say, 'the hareem are twice the men, in number.' If that be so, natural reason should teach that a man may have more wives than one; and I can think that the womankind exceed them. From spring months to spring months, nine months in the year, the most nomad women are languishing with hunger: they bear few children; of two at a birth I have heard no mention among them. They are good mothers, and will suckle the babe very long at their meagre breasts, if they be not again with child. In Zeyd's encampment was a little damsel of four years, not yet weaned; and the mother said, 'We have no goats, there is naught in this waste, and what else might I do for my little bint?' They wash their babies in camel-urine, and think thus to help them from insects: it is acrid, especially when the cattle have browsed of certain alkaline bushes, as the rimth. And in this water they all comb out their long hair, both men and women, yet sometimes thereby bleaching their locks, so that I have seen young men's braided 'horns' grizzled. There is a strange custom, (not only of nomad women, but in the Arabic countries even among Christians, which may seem to remain of the old idolatry among them,) of mothers, their gossips, and even young maidens, visiting married women to kiss with a kind of devotion the *hammam* of the male children.

In all Arabia both men and women, townsfolk and Beduins, where they may come by it, paint the whites of their eyes blue, with *kahl* or antimony; thus Mohammed Ibn Rashîd has his bird-like eyes painted. Not only would they be more lovelooking, in the sight of their women, who have painted them, and that braid their long manly side-locks; but they hold that this sharpens too and will preserve their vision. With long hair shed in the midst, and hanging down at either side in braided horns, and false eyes painted blue, the Arabian man's long head under the coloured kerchief, is in our eyes more than half feminine; and in much they resemble women.

Townswomen of well-faring families, in all the old government of the Waháby are taught the prayers; and there are some

that have learned to read. In the nomad tribes women are seldom seen to pray, except in *ramathán*, the month of bodily
abstinence and devotion: they are few which know the
prayers; I suppose even the half of the men have not learned
them. The Beduwy, in Arabia, passes for as good as a clerk
that can say his formal devotion: the nomads which have much
praying amongst them, are the more ill-natured. Women pray
not as the men, falling upon their faces; but they recite the
form of words with folded arms and kneeling. '*El-entha*, the
female (mild to labour and bringing forth the pastoral riches)
is, of all animals, the better, say the Arabians, save only in
mankind.' Yet this is not an opinion of all Arabs, for the *hurr*,
or dromedary stallion, is preferred for his masculine strength
by the Moors or Western Arabs. Upon the human entha the
Semites cast all their blame. Hers is, they think, a maleficent
nature, and the Aarab complain that 'she has seven lives.' The
Arabs are contrary to womankind, upon whom they would
have God's curse; 'some (say the Beduw) are poisoners of
husbands, and there are many adulteresses.' They, being full
of impotent iniquity themselves, too lightly reproach the
honest housewives, although not without some cause: but
what might not those find to tell all day again of the malignant
inconstancy of husbands? The *horma* they would have under
subjection: admitted (they say) to an equality, the ineptitude
of her evil nature will break forth. They check her all day at
home, and let her never be enfranchised from servitude. If the
sapient king in Jerusalem found never a good woman; many
a better man has found one better than himself. The veil and
the jealous lattice are rather of the obscene Mohammedan
austerity in the towns: among the mild tent-dwellers in the
open wilderness the housewives have a liberty, as where all
are kindred; yet their hareem are now seen in the most Arabian
tribes half veiled. When some asked me, at Zeyd's coffee-fire,
if our hareem went veiled, I answered, 'No! they are open-
faced, there is no need of face-clouts among honest folk; also
I think among you Aarab, they which have their women's
faces veiled, are the most dissolute tribes.' The Beduins are
always glad to hear other tribesmen blamed. It was answered,

'Ay, billah, they are corrupted.' I asked Zeyd, 'Art thou of this opinion?' 'Khalîl – he said in his heart, 'Thou thinkest as the kuffâr' – the face of a wife should be seen of no man besides her own husband.'

The woman's sex is despised by the old nomad and divine law in Moses; for a female birth the days of her purification are doubled, also the estimation of her babe shall be at the half. Did she utter any vow, it is void if her husband say no. But the Semitic mother of a son is in honour. We read: 'Let a man obey his mother and his father,' the Semitic scribe writing his mother first. And commonly it is seen amongst rude Arabs, the grown son has a tender regard toward his mother, that she is his dam, before the teeming love even of his fresh young wife. So the mother's love in the tribes is womanly, tender; and naming her sons she will add some loving superstitious saw, as *el-agal Ullah*, 'The Lord preserve them!' The nomad hareem are delivered as other mothers, with pangs, after a labour of certain hours. It is a fond opinion that the daughters of the desert are as the wild creatures, that suffer not in child-bearing. But her household and nation is migratory; there is no indolent hope before her of comfort and repose. The herb is consumed daily about them, the thirsty cattle are ever advancing to pasture and water, the people is incessantly removing: in the camping-ground of to-day, they cannot perhaps lie upon the morrow. Their bed is a mantle or tent-cloth spread upon the earth; they live indeed in the necessitous simplicity almost of the wild creatures. The nomad woman has therefore, of custom, of necessity! another courage. Are the Aarab in a journey when her time is come? her family halt, and alighting, they build the booth over her. Are the tribesmen encamped? with certain elder women friends she steals forth to be delivered, apart in the wilderness. The nomads about journeying, when it were peril to be left behind, she is gently lifted and seated as any other sick and infirm person in a nest made of her carpet or her tent-cloth wound down upon the camel pack-saddle, to follow riding with them in the ráhla: and that they pass their lives thus nomads feel little fatigue, but rather take rest in riding.

In the *Jahalîat* or 'olden time of heathen ignorance,' there was an horrible custom in the desert, nearly to the generation of Mohammed, to bury maid-children living (which signifies also that the female births among them were more numerous). The woman is not born to manage the sword, but her hand is for the silly distaff, she neither strengthens the ashîra nor is aught to the increase and building of her father's household, but an unprofitable mouth is added to the hungry eaters of a slender substance: and years long he must wear a busy head for the keeping of a maiden; the end of all is an uncertain bride-money (therewith he buys for her again some household stuff, and it is her dower), when she will go forth as a stranger to another house. The father hid himself, in the day of her birth, from his common acquaintance.

When I have questioned the Beduw, had they heard of this by tradition? they have answered, marvelling, 'They could not imagine there had ever been such a cursed custom in the country.' Daughters when past the first amiable infancy are little set by in the Arabic households. The son is beloved by his father, till he be grown, above the wife that bare him before his own soul, and next after the man's own father: and the young child in an household is hardly less beloved of his elder brethren. God has sent a son, and the father cannot contrary him in anything, whilst he is a child. This it is that in time to come may comfort his age, and in his last end honourably bury him; and year by year after, as the nomads in their journeys be come again, offer the sacrifice of the dead and pray over him: so shall his name be yet had in remembrance among the living. Much sooner then, would a man give a buffet to his wife, or twenty, than lay hand-strokes upon the back of the perverse child their son, and turn away the mind of him for ever. In bitterness of a displeasure he will snib his disobedient son with vehement words, but his anger shall pass no further to break the house-peace; after years this child shall be better than himself, and therefore he is one whom he durst not now offend. There be fathers, say the nomads, that rule with the rod. I cannot believe them. A son dying, a father's spirit is long overcast, he is overborne awhile with silent sorrow; but the remembrance of a deceased daughter, unless her life were of any singular worth or goodly promise untimely broken, is not very long enduring. Moslemîn, (this is to say, *The Submitted-to-the-divine-governance-of-the-world,*) the men make no lamentation for the dead; only they say, 'He is gone, the Lord have mercy upon him!'

I found also among these Beduins, that with difficulty they imagine any future life; they pray and they fast as main duties in religion, looking (as the Semitic Patriarchs before them) for the present life's blessing. There is a sacrifice for the dead, which I have seen continued to the third generation. I have seen a sheykh come with devout remembrance, to slaughter his sacrifice and to pray at the heap where his father or his father's father lies buried: and I have seen such to kiss his hand, in passing any time by the place where the sire is sleeping, and breathe out, with almost womanly tenderness, words of blessing and prayer; – and this is surely comfort in one's dying, that he will be long-time so kindly had in his children's mind. In the settled Semitic countries their hareem, and even Christian women, go out at certain days to the graves to weep. I have seen a widow woman lead her fatherless children thither, and they kneeled down together: I saw the mother teach them to weep, and she bewailed her dead with a forced suffocating voice and sobbing, *Ya habîby,* 'Aha! aha! my beloved!' The Aarab children are ruled by entreaties; the nomad girls are often wayward at home, the boys will many times despise the mother's voice. I have known an ill-natured child lay a stick to the back of his good cherishing mother; and asked why she suffered this, she answered, sighing, 'My child is a kafir,' that is, of an heathenish forward nature: this boy was not of the full Beduin blood, his father being Abu Sinûn the Moor. Some asking if our children too were peevish, when they heard from me the old dreadful severity of Moses' law, they exclaimed, 'But many is the ill-natured lad among us that, and he be strong enough, will beat his own father.' The Arabs babble, and here also it were hard to believe them. Savages inure their sons; but Beduin children grow up without instruction of the parents. They learn but in hearing the people's saws, in the worsted tents, where their only censor is the public opinion. There are devout Beduins full, in that religious life of the desert, of natural religion, who may somewhiles reprove them; but the child is never checked for any lying, although the Arabians say 'the lie is shameful.' Their lie is an easy stratagem and one's most ready defence to mislead his enemy. Nature we see to be herself most full of all guile, and this lying mouth is indulged by the Arabian religion.

The Wandering Village. The Coffee Gathering. Motlog

The camels now jezzîn, we wandered without care of great watering places; the people drinking of any small waters of the *suffa*, or ground rock. There are in all this desert mountain soil pit-like places of rock choked with old blown sand. In these sand-pools a water, of the winter rains, is long time preserved, but commonly thick and ill-smelling in the wet sand, and putrefying with rotten fibres of plants and urea of the nomad's cattle, which have been watered here from the beginning. Of such the Aarab (they prefer the thick desert water to pure water) now boiled their daily coffee, which is not then ill-tasting. The worst is that blackish water drawn from pits long forsaken, until they have been voided once; and sooner than drink their water I suffered thirst, and very oft passed the nights half sleepless. Strange are the often forms in this desert of wasted sand-rock, spires, needles, pinnacles, and battled mountains, which are good landmarks. I asked Zeyd, 'Did he know them all?' *Answer*: 'From my childhood, I know as good as every great stone upon all our marches,' that may be over three or four thousand square miles. Mountain (*jebel* in the settled countries) is commonly *thulla* – 'rib,' (and dim. *thulleya,*) with the nomads; – we say *coast* almost in like wise. Any tall peak, berg or monticule, serving for a landmark, they call *towîl*; a headland is *khusshm,* 'naze, snout'; (khusshm is said in Arabia for man's nose). Some hilly mountain-coasts are named *huthb*; *bottîn* in the mouths of the Moahîb Beduins is said of any blunt hilly height. The desert waste is called *khála,* 'the land that is empty'; the soil, *béled.* – And such is desert Arabia.

– But to speak now of the nomad inhabitants and how they lead their lives. El-Beduw *ma yetaabun*, 'toil not' (say they), that is not bodily; but their spirits are made weary with incessant apprehension of their enemies, and their flesh with continual thirst and hunger. The necessitous lives of the Aarab may hardly reach to a virtuous mediocrity; they are constrained to be robbers. 'The life in the desert is better than any, *if there were not the Beduw*,' is said proverbially by oases' Arabians; the poor Beduins they think to be full of iniquity, *melaun el-weyladeyn,* 'of cursed kind, upon both sides, of their father and mother.' Pleasant is the sojourn in the wandering village, in this purest earth and air, with the human fellowship, which is all day met at leisure about the cheerful coffee fire, and amidst a thousand new prospects. Here, where we now alighted, is this day's rest, to-morrow our home will be yonder. The desert day returning from the east, warns the Beduin awake, who rises to his prayers; or it may be, unwitting of the form, he will but murmur toward heaven the supplication of his fearful human nature, and say, 'Ah Lord my God!' and, 'Oh that this day may be fortunate; give Thou that we see not the evil!' Of daily food they have not half enough, and if any head of the cattle be taken! – how many his household yet live? Bye and bye the herdsman is ready, and his beasts are driven far from his sight.

No sweet chittering of birds greets the coming of the desert light, besides man there is no voice in this waste drought. The Beduins, that lay down in their cloaks upon the sandy mother-earth in the open tents, hardly before the middle night, are already up and bestirring themselves. In every coffee-sheykh's tent, there is new fire blown in the hearth, and he sets on his coffee-pots; then snatching a coal in his fingers, he will lay it in his tobacco pipe. The few coffee-beans received from his housewife are roasted and brayed; as all is boiling, he sets out the little cups, *fenjeyl* (for *fenjeyn*) which we saw have been made, for the uningenious Arabs, in the West. When, with a pleasant gravity, he has unbuckled his *gutîa* or cup-box, we see the nomad has not above three or four fenjeyns, wrapt in a rusty clout, with which he scours them busily, as if this should make his cups clean. The roasted beans are pounded amongst Arabs with a magnanimous rattle – and (as all their labour) rhythmical – in brass of the town, or an old wooden mortar, gaily studded with nails, the work of some nomad smith. The water bubbling in the small dellàl, he casts in his fine coffee powder, *el-bunn,* and withdraws the pot to simmer a moment. From a knot in his kerchief he takes then an head of cloves, a piece of cinnamon or other spice, *bahar,* and braying these, he casts their dust in after. Soon he pours out some hot drops to essay his coffee; if the taste be to his liking, making dexterously a nest of all the cups in his hand, with pleasant chattering, he is ready to pour out for the company, and begins upon his right hand; and first, if such be present, to any considerable sheykh and principal persons. The *fenjeyn kahwa* is but four sips: to fill it up to a guest, as in the northern towns, were among Beduins an injury, and of such bitter meaning, 'This drink thou and depart.' Then is often seen a contention in courtesy amongst them, especially in any greater assemblies, who shall drink first. Some man that receives the fenjeyn in his turn, will not drink yet, – he proffers it to one sitting in order under him, as to the more honourable: but the other putting off with his hand will answer *ebbeden,* 'nay, it shall never be, by Ullah! but do thou drink!' Thus licensed, the humble man is dispatched in three sips, and hands up his empty fenjeyn. But if he have much insisted, by this he opens his willingness to be reconciled with one not his friend. That neighbour, seeing the company of coffee-drinkers watching him, may with an honest grace receive the cup, and let it seem not willingly: but an hard man will sometimes rebut the other's gentle proffer.

Some may have taken lower seats than becoming their sheykhly blood, of which the nomads are jealous; entering untimely, they sat down out of order, sooner than trouble all the company. A sheykh, coming late and any business going forward, will often sit far out in the assembly; and show himself a popular person in this kind of honourable humility. The more inward in the booths is the higher place; where also is, with the sheykhs, the seat of a stranger. To sit in the loose circuit without and before the tent, is for the common sort. A tribesman arriving presents himself at that part, or a little lower, where in the eyes of all men his pretension will be well allowed; and in such observances of good nurture, is a nomad man's honour among his tribesmen. And this is nigh all that serves the nomad for a conscience, namely, that which men will hold of him. A poor person approaching from behind, stands obscurely, wrapped in his tattered mantle, with grave ceremonial, until those sitting indolently before him in the sand shall vouchsafe to take notice of him: then they rise unwillingly, and giving back enlarge the coffee-circle to receive him. But if there arrive a sheykh, a coffee-host, a richard amongst them of a few cattle, all the coxcomb companions within will hail him with their pleasant adulation, *taad hennéyi*, 'Step thou up hither.'

The astute Fukara sheukh surpass all men in their coffee-drinking courtesy, and Zeyd himself was more than any large of this gentleman-like imposture; he was full of swaggering complacence and compliments to an humbler person. With what suavity could he encourage, and gently too compel a man, and rising himself yield him parcel of another man's room! In such fashions Zeyd showed himself a bountiful great man, who indeed was the greatest niggard. The cups are drunk twice about, each one sipping after other's lips without misliking; to the great coffee sheykhs the cup may be filled more times, but this is an adulation of the coffee-server. There are some of the Fukara sheukh so delicate Sybarites, that of those three bitter sips, to draw out all their joyance, twisting, turning and tossing again the cup, they could make ten. The coffee-service ended, the grounds are poured out from the small into the great store-pot that is reserved full of warm water: with the bitter lye the nomads will make their next bever, and think they spare coffee.

– This of the greater coffee gatherings: but to speak rather of the small daily company in a private sheykh's menzil, drawn together to the clatter of the good man's *surbût* or coffee-pestle. Grave, with levity, is the indolent nomad man's countenance. As many Beduin heads, so many galliûns or tobacco-pipes, with commonly nothing to put in them. Is any man seen to have a little of the coveted leaf, knotted in his kerchief, he durst not deny to divide it with them, – which if he withheld, yet pretending mirth, the rest would have it from him, perforce. If there be none found among them, they sit raking the old filth out of their galliûns and, with sorry cheer, put the coal upon that, which they have mixed with a little powdered dry camel-dung or some sere herbage: thus they taste at least a savour (such sweetness to them) of tobacco, whereof, when they are any while deprived, I have seen them chop their pipe-stems small for the little tobacco moisture which remained in them; and laying a coal upon this drenched wood they 'drink' in the fume with a last solace. ...

... For the Beduins sitting in the coffee-tent of their menzil, when the sun mounts, it is time to go over to the mejlis, 'sitting,' the congregation or parliament of the tribesmen. There also is the public coffee-drinking, held at Motlog's or some other one of the chief sheykhs' worsted 'houses'; where the great sheykh and the coffee companions may that morrow be assembled: for where their king bee is found, there will the tribesmen assemble together. The mejlis-seekers wending through the wide encampment, inquire of any they meet. 'The mejlis, where? eigh weled! hast thou seen the sheukh sitting?' In this parliament they commune together of the common affairs; they reason of their policy in regard of Ibn Rashîd, the Dowla, the tribes about them. Here is reported what any may have heard of the movement of foemen, or have signs been seen of a ghrazzu: tidings from time to time are brought in of their own or foreign waters; householders tell of the pasture found yesterday by their dispersed herdsmen. Let him speak here who will, the voice of the least is heard among them; he is a tribesman. The mejlis forecast the next journeys of the tribe, whereof a kind of running advice remains in all their minds, which they call *es-shor*; this is often made known to their allies, and is very necessary to any of themselves that are about to take a journey.

This is the Council of the elders and the public tribunal; hither the tribesmen bring their causes at all times, and it is pleaded by the maintainers of both sides with busy clamour;

and everyone may say his word that will. The sheykh meanwhile takes counsel with the sheukh, elder men and more considerable persons; and judgement is given commonly without partiality and always without bribes. This sentence is final. The loser is mulcted in heads of small cattle or camels, which he must pay anon, or go into exile, before the great sheykh send executors to distrain any beasts of his, to the estimation of the debt. The poor Beduins are very unwilling payers, and often think themselves unable at present: thus, in every tribe, some households may be seen of other tribes' exiles.

Their justice is such, that in the opinion of the next governed countries, the Arabs of the wilderness are the justest of mortals. Seldom the judge and elders err, in these small societies of kindred, where the life of every tribesman lies open from his infancy and his state is to all men well known. Even their suits are expedite, as all the other works of the Arabs. Seldom is a matter not heard and resolved in one sitting. Where the accusation is grave and some are found absent that should be witnesses, their cause is held over to another hearing. The nomad justice is mild where the Hebrew law, in this smelling of the settled countries, is crude. In the desert there is no human forfeit, there is nothing even in homicide, if the next to the blood withhold not their assent, which may not be composed, the guilty paying the amends (rated in heads of cattle). The Hebrew law excised the sores in the commonwealth, and the certainty of retaliation must weigh and prick in the mind of evil-doers. The Beduwy has no more to fear before him than a fine afar off; he may escape all if his evil heart sufficeth him, only going from his own kin into perpetual exile.

Towards noon, in days when the camp is standing, as the mejlis is ended, the company begin to disperse. The bare-foot Beduwy returns lonely over the hot sand, and will slumber, in his booth, till vespers, el-assr. The nomads are day-sleepers: some of the Beduins will turn upon their sides to slumber, as if the night were come again, by ten o'clock. But if a man fall asleep, sitting in the coffee circle, it is unbecoming; let him go apart and lie down in the sides of the tent. Is any overcome at unawares amongst them, the rest will shake him and say, 'Up, man! what dost thou here to slumber?' Yet in the midst of their murmuring discourse, and being feeble with fasting, I not seldom fell asleep, upon a sudden, sitting to drink coffee; which weakness of nature they saw in a stranger with wondering piety and humanity! All the Arabs reverence a man's sleeping: he is as it were in trance with God, and a truce of his waking solicitude: in their households they piously withdraw, nor will any lightly molest him, until he waken of himself. Only from el-assr till the sun set, they sleep no more, that such they think were unwholesome. Of their much slumbering, they are more wakeful in the dark night hours, which time in the open wilderness is troubled with alarms; the hounds often bark at the wolf till the morning light, and the habalîs are afoot. Some will talk the mid-day hours away lying out in the next cliff's shadow, or under the thin shade of some gum-acacia tree, or in the sheykh's great tent. At vespers the Beduin bestirs himself; he goes forth again, murmuring some words of pious preparation, to say his afternoon prayer: falling on his knees, he claps his palms upon the sand before him, and rubs them, then drawing them down from the forehead, he washes thus the two sides of his visage, for there is no water. Rising again from his devotion, he walks abroad to look for any new smoke rising, which is a sign of the coffee-fire and cheerful fellowship. A sheykh who would far over the wide encampment, will leap upon his mare's bare back to ride thither. Most officious of the afternoon coffee-hosts was *Burjess*, a rich young sheykh among certain sheukh of W. Aly, malcontents living now with the Fukara; his was the most spacious tent in our encampment. If the mejlis assembled again for any public business, or after a ráhla, the afternoon company was more numerous, many of the shepherds at that hour coming in.

As for the head of the tribe, Motlog, he was a personable strong man and well proportioned, of the middle stature, of middle age, and with a comely Jewish visage; and thereto the Arabian honour of a thick black beard, and he looked forth with a manly assurance under that specious brow of his sheykhly moderation. A fair-spoken man, as they be all in fair

77

weather, full of the inborn Beduin arts when his interest was touched. Simple in his manners, he alone went with no gay camel-stick in his hand and never carried a sword; by which politic urbanity, he covered a superfluous insolence of the nobleman, which became him well. When the mejlis assembled numerous at his booth, he, the great sheykh and host, would sit out with a proud humility among the common people, holding still his looks at the ground; but they were full of unquiet side-glances, as his mind was erect and watching. His authority slumbered, till, there being some just occasion, he ruled with a word the unruly Beduw. A rude son of the desert sat down by me in the mejlis at my first coming, the shepherd of Zeyd's menzil. I asked him in his ear, 'Which of them is Motlog?' *Answer*: 'Yonder is Motlog!' and he added boisterously, to the stranger, 'The man there is our Pasha; for right as the Haj pasha, this Motlog governs the Aarab. When he says 'The ráhla!' we all mount and set forth; and where he alights there we pitch our booths. – Oho, thou Motlog! speak I not well to this Nasrâny? – and, Khalîl, if he would, he might cut off the heads, wellah-billah, of us all.' Motlog lifted his eyes upon us for a moment with half a smile, and then reverted to himself. The sheykh of a nomad tribe is no tyrant; a great sheykh striking a tribesman he should bruise his own honour: man-striking is a very bestiality, in their sight, at home.

The Nomad Milk Supper. Beduin Mares

Pleasant, as the fiery heat of the desert daylight is done, is our homely evening fire. The sun gone down upon a highland steppe of Arabia, whose common altitude is above three thousand feet, the thin dry air is presently refreshed, the sand is soon cold; wherein yet at three fingers depth is left a sunny warmth of the past day's heat until the new sunrise. After a half hour it is the blue night, and clear hoary starlight in which there shines the girdle of the milky way, with a marvellous clarity. As the sun is setting, the nomad housewife brings in a truss of sticks and dry bushes, which she has pulled or hoed with a mattock (a tool they have seldom) in the wilderness;

she casts down this provision by our hearthside, for the sweet smelling evening fire. But to Hirfa, his sheykhly wife, Zeyd had given a little Beduin maid to help her. The housewife has upon her woman's side an hearth apart, which is the cooking-fire. Commonly Hirfa baked then, under the ashes, a bread-cake for the stranger: Zeyd her husband, who is miserable, or for other cause, eats not yet, but only near midnight, as he is come again from the mejlis and would go in to sleep.

At this first evening hour, the Beduw are all *fi ahl-ha,* in their households, to sup of such wretchedness as they may have; there is no more wandering through the wide encampment, and the coming in then of any persons, not strangers, were an unseemly 'ignorance'. The foster-camels lie couched, before the booth of hair: and these Beduins let them lie still an hour, before the milking. The great feeble brutes have wandered all day upon the droughty face of the wilderness; they may hardly crop their fills, in those many hours, of so slender pastures. The mare stands tethered before the booth at the woman's side, where there is not much passage. Such dry wire-grass forage as they find in that waste, is cast down beside her. When the Arabs have eaten their morsel and drunken léban of the flock, the few men of our menzil begin to assemble about the sheykh's hearth, where is some expectation of coffee. The younger or meanest of the company, who is sitting or leaning on his elbow or lies next the faggot, will indolently reach back his hand from time to time for more dry rimth, to cast on the fire, and other sweet resinous twigs, till the flaming light leaps up again in the vast uncheerful darkness. The nomads will not burn the good pasture bushes, *gussha,* even in their enemies' country. It is the bread of the cattle. I have sometimes un-wittingly offended them, until I knew the plants, plucking up and giving to the flames some which grew in the soil nigh my hand; then children and women and the men of little under-standing blamed me, and said wondering, 'It was an heathen-ish deed.'

Glad at the fall of the empty daylight, the householders sit again to make talk, or silent and listless, with the drooping gravity of brute animals. Old men, always weary, and the herdmen, which were all day abroad in the sun, are lying now upon an elbow (this is the right Aarab posture, and which Zeyd would have me learn and use), about the common fire. But the reposing of the common sort at home is to lie heels out backward, about the hearth, as the spokes of a wheel, and flat upon their bellies (which they even think appeases the gnawing of hunger); and a little raising themselves, they discourse staying upon their breasts and two elbows: thus the men of this lean nation will later sleep, spreading only their tattered cloaks under them, upon the wild soil (béled) a posture even reproved by themselves. Béled, we saw in the mouth of the nomads, is the inhabited soil of the open desert and also of the oasis; they say of the dead, 'He is under the béled.' Dîra, the Beduin circuit, is heard also in some oases for their town settlement.—I asked Zeyd, 'Then say ye the béled is our mother?'—'Ay well, and surely, Khalîl; for out of the ground took God man and all return thither.' They asking me of our custom, I said 'You are ground-sitters, but we sit high upon stools like the Tûrk.'—The legs of chair-sitters to hang all day they thought an insufferable fatigue. 'Khalîl says well,' answered Zeyd, who, a sheykh of Aarab, had been in high presence of pashas and government men at Damascus; and he told how he found them sitting in arm-chairs and (they are all cross-leg Orientals) with a leg crossed over the other, a shank or a foot: 'a simple crossed foot is of the under functionaries: but to lap a man's shin, (Zeyd showed us the manner,) he said to be of their principal personages.' The Arabs asked me often, if we sat gathered in this kindly sort about our evening fires? and if neighbours went about to neighbour byût, seeking company of friends and coffee-drinking?

Sitting thus, if there anyone rises, the mare snorts softly, looking that it is he who should now bring her delicious bever of warm camel-milk, and gazing after him, she whinnies with pleasance. There is a foster camel to every nomad marè, since they taste no corn, and the harsh desert stalks could not else sustain her: the horse, not ruminating and losing much moisture by the skin, is a creature very impatient of hunger and thirst. His mare is therefore not a little chargeable to a sheykh in the desert, who must burden oftentimes another camel with her provisions of water. Twice she will drink, and at the hottest of the summer season, even thrice in a daylight; and a camel-load of girbies may hardly water her over two days. Who has wife or horse, after the ancient proverb, may rue, he shall never be in rest, for such brittle possessions are likely to be always ailing. Yet under that serene-climate, where the element is the tent of the world, the Beduw have little other care of their mares; it is unknown in the desert so much as to rub them. They milk first for the mare and then (often in the same vessel) for the nomad household. She stands straining upon her tether, looking toward the pleasant sound of milking: the bowl frothing from the udder is carried to her in the herds-man's hand and she sups through her teeth the sweet warm milk, at a long draught. The milking time for camels is but once in the day, at evening, unless a little be drawn for some sick person or stranger in the morning, or for any wayfaring man in the daytime. The small cattle, *ghrannem* or *dubbush,* are milked at sunset; only in rich spring districts, the housewives may draw their teats again in the morning. The dubbush are milked by their housewives, the milch camels by the men and lads only. Spring is the milky season, when men and beasts (if the winter rain failed not), fare at the best in the wilderness. With small cattle, it lasts only few weeks from the yeaning till the withering of the year be again upon them, when the herb is dried up: but the camel kine are nearly eleven months in milk.

So needful is the supplement of milk to the desert horses, that when, in the dry summer or at some other low times, the camels are driven wide from the standing menzil to be *azab,* absent certain days, that is in quest of pasture, the mare also is led along with them in her master's troop, to drink the foster milk. But if the sheykh have need of his mare then at home, he will nourish her, as he may, without the wet-nurse, mixing at evening a bowl of *mereesy* or dry milk rubbed in water. Mer-eesy is the butter-milk of the flock, dried by boiling to the hard shard, and resembles chalk. It is a drink much to thank God for, in lean times, and in the heat of the year, in the wilderness; in the long dead months when there is no milk, it is every day dearer and hard to be come by. Excellent to take upon journeys, mereesy is gipsy drink and no dainty in the border countries; but in the Arabian oases it is much esteemed to use with their unwholesome date diet, which alone were too heating. Mereesy ('that which rubbed between the palms of the hands, can be mingled with water,') or dry milk, is called by many other names in the provinces of Arabia, as *thiràn* and *bùggila, baggl,* in West Nejd; in the South and towards Mecca, *mùthir*. Butter is the poor nomads' market ware: with this they can buy somewhat in the towns for their household necessities. Having only mereesy in the saddle-bags and water before us every third day on the road, I have not doubted to set out upon long voyages in the khála. Mereesy will remain unaltered till the next season; it is good in the second year, only growing harder. The best were to grind it to flour, as they do in Kasîm; and this stirred, with a little sugar, in a bowl of the desert water is a grateful refreshment after the toil and heat of the desert journey.

A pleasure it is to listen to the cheerful musing Beduin talk, a lesson in the travellers' school of mere humanity, – and there is no land so perilous which by humanity he may not pass, for man is of one mind everywhere, ay, and in their kind, even the brute animals of the same foster earth – a timely vacancy of the busy-idle cares which cloud upon us that would live peaceably in the moral desolation of the world. And pleasant those sounds of the spretting milk under the udders in the Arabs' vessels! food for man and health at a draught in a languishing country. The bowl brought in foaming, the children gather to it, and the guest is often bidden to sup with them, with his fingers, the sweet froth, *orghra* or *roghrwa, irtugh*: or this milk poured into the sour milk-skin and shaken there a moment, the housewife serves it forth again to their suppers, with that now gathered sourness which they think the more refreshing.

The Wandering Solubba

As we went by to the mejlis, 'Yonder (said Zeyd) I shall show thee some of a people of antiquity.' This was a family which then arrived of poor wanderers, *Solubba*. I admired the full-faced shining flesh-beauty of their ragged children, and have always remarked the like as well of the Heteym nomads. These alien and outcast kindreds are of fairer looks than the hunger-bitten Beduw. The Heteym, rich in small cattle, have food enough in the desert, and the Solubba of their hunting and gipsy labour: for they are tinkers of kettles and menders of arms, in the Beduin menzils. They batter out upon the anvil hatchets, *jedûm* (with which shepherds lop down the sweet acacia boughs, to feed their flocks), and grass-hooks for cutting forage, and steels for striking fire with the flint, and the like. They are besides woodworkers, in the desert acacia timber, of rude saddle-trees for the burden-camels, and of the thelûl saddle-frames, of pulley reels, (*mahâl*) for drawing at any deeper wells of the desert, also of rude milk vessels, and other such husbandry: besides, they are cattle surgeons, and in all their trade (only ruder of skill) like the smiths' caste or *Sunna*. The Solubba obey the precept of their patriarch, who forbade them to be cattle-keepers, and bade them live of their hunting in the wilderness, and alight before the Beduin booths, that they might become their guests, and to labour as smiths in the tribes for their living. Having no milch beasts, whereso they ask it at a Beduin tent, the housewife will pour out léban from her semíla, but it is in their own bowl, to the poor Solubba: for Beduins, otherwise little nice, will not willingly drink after Solubbies, that might have eaten of some *futís*, or the thing that is dead of itself. Also the Beduw say of them, 'they eat of vile insects and worms': the last is fable, they eat no such vermin. Rashly the evil tongue of the Beduw rates them as 'kuffâr', because only few Solubbies can say the formal prayers, the Beduins are themselves not better esteemed in the towns. The Solubba show a good humble zeal for the country religion in which they were born, and have no notice of any other; they are tolerant and, in their wretched manner, humane, as they themselves are despised and oppressed persons.

In summer, when the Beduw have no more milk, loading their light tents and household stuff, with what they have gained, upon asses, which are their only cattle, they forsake the

Aarab encampment, and hold on their journey through the wide khála. The Solubby household go then to settle themselves remotely, upon some good well of water, in an unfrequented wilderness, where there is game. They only (of all men) are free of the Arabian deserts to travel whithersoever they would; paying to all men a petty tribute, they are molested by none of them. Home-born, yet have they no citizenship in the Peninsula. No Beduwy, they say, will rob a Solubby, although he met him alone, in the deep of the wilderness, and with the skin of an ostrich in his hand, that is worth a thelûl. But the wayfaring Beduwy would be well content to espy, pitched upon some lone watering, the booth of a Solubby, and hope to eat there of his hunter's pot: and the poor Solubby will make the man good cheer of his venison. They ride even hunting upon ass-back. It is also on these weak brutes, which must drink every second day, (but otherwise the ass is hardly less than the camel a beast of the desert,) that they journey with their families through great waterless regions, where the Beduwy upon his swift and puissant thelûl, three days patient of thirst, may not lightly pass. This dispersed kindred of desert men in Arabia, outgo the herdsmen Beduw in all land-craft, as much as these go before the tardy oases villagers. The Solubba (in all else ignorant wretches,) have inherited a land-lore from sire to son, of the least finding-places of water. They wander upon the immense face of Arabia, from the height of Syria to el-Yémen, beyond *et-Tâif*, and I know not how much further! – and for things within their rat-like understanding, Arabians tell me, it were of them that a man may best inquire.

They must be masters in hunting, that can nourish themselves in a dead land; and where other men may hardly see a footprint of venison, there oftentimes, the poor Solubbies are seething sweet flesh of gazelles and bedûn, and, in certain sand districts, of the antelope; everywhere they know their quarries' paths and flight. It is the Beduw who tell these wonders of them; they say, 'the S'lubba are like herdsmen of the wild game, for when they see a troop they can break them and choose of them as it were a flock, and say, "These we will have

to-day, as for those other heads there, we can take them after
to-morrow." ' – It is human to magnify, and find a pleasant
wonder, this kind of large speaking is a magnanimity of the
Arabs; but out of doubt, the Solubba are admirable wayfarers
and hardy men, keen, as living of their two hands, and the best
sighted of them are very excellent hunters. The Solubba or
Slèyb, besides this proper name of their nation, have some
other which are epithets. West of Hâyil they are more often
called *el-Khlúa* or *Kheluŷ*, 'the desolate,' because they dwell
apart from the *Kabâil*, having no cattle nor fellowship; – a
word which the Beduw say of themselves, when in a journey,
finding no menzil of the Aarab, they must lie down to sleep
'solitaries' in the empty khála. They are called as well in the
despiteful tongue of this country, Kilâb el-Khála, 'hounds of
the wilderness'. *El-Ghrúnemy* is the name of another kindred
of the Slèyb in East Nejd; and it is said, they marry not with
the former. The Arabians commonly suppose them all to be
come of some old kafir kind, or Nasâra.

Visit to Teyma

Wandering and encamping, we had approached Teyma; and
now being hardly a journey distant, some of our people would
go a-marketing thither, and Zeyd with them, to buy provisions:
I should ride also in the company with Zeyd. We set out upon
the morrow, a ragged fellowship, mostly Fehját, of thirty men
and their camels. We passed soon from the sandy highlands to
a most sterile waste of rising grounds and hollows, a rocky
floor, and shingle of ironstone. This is that extreme barrenness
of the desert which lies about Teyma, without blade or bush.
We passed a deep ground, *M'hai*, and rode there by obscure
signs of some ancient settlement, *Jerèyda*, where are seen a few
old circles of flag-stones, pitched edgewise, of eight or nine
yards over, seeming such as might have fenced winter tents of
the antique Aarab, sheltered in this hollow. In the Moallakát,
or elect poems of ancient Arabia, is some mention of round
tents, but the booths of all the Arab nomads are now four-
square only. The company hailed me 'See here! Khalîl, a

village of the *Auellîn*, those of old time.' – 'And what ancients were these?' – 'Some say the Sherarát, others the *Beny Kelàb* or *Chelb*, and theirs, billah, was the Borj Selmàn and the ground *Umsheyrifa*.' Zeyd added: 'This was of the *Ahl Theyma* (not Teyma), and sheykh of them *Aly es-Sweysy* the Yahûdy.' Come upon the highest ground beyond, Zeyd showed me the mountain landmarks, westward *Muntar B. Atîeh*, next *Twoyel Saîda*, *Helaima* before us, in front *el-Ghrenèym*, which is behind the oasis. Some murmured, 'Why did Zeyd show him our landmarks?' – 'I would have Khalîl, said he, become a Beduwy.'

Delightful now was the green sight of Teyma, the haven of our desert; we approached the tall island of palms, enclosed by long clay orchard-walls, fortified with high towers. Teyma is a shallow, loamy, and very fertile old flood-bottom in these high open plains, which lie out from the west of Nejd. Those lighthouse-like turrets, very well built of sun-dried brick, are from the insecure times before the government of Ibn Rashîd, when, as the most Arabian places, Teyma was troubled by the sheykhs' factions, and the town quarters divided by their hereditary enmities. Every well-faring person, when he had fortified his palms with a high clay-brick wall, built his tower upon it; also in every sûk of the town was a clay turret of defence and refuge for the people of that street. In a private danger one withdrew with his family to their walled plantation: in that enclosure, they might labour and eat the fruits, although his old foes held him beleaguered for a year or two. Any enemy approaching by day-light was seen from the watch-tower. Such walling may be thought a weak defence; but for all the fox-like subtlety of Semitic minds, they are of nearly no invention. A powder blast, the running brunt of a palm beam, had broken up this clay resistance; but a child might sooner find, and madmen as soon unite to attempt anything untried. In the Gospel parables, when one had planted a vineyard, he built a tower therein to keep it. The watch-tower in the orchard is yet seen upon all desert borders. We entered between grey orchard walls, overlaid with blossoming boughs of plum trees; of how much amorous contentment to our parched eyes! I read the oasis height 3,400 ft. We dismounted at the head of the first sûk before the *dàr,* house or court of a young man our acquaintance, *Sleymàn,* who in the Haj time had been one of the kella guests at Medáin. Here he lived with his brother, who was Zeyd's date merchant; we were received therefore in friendly wise, and entertained. The hareem led in Hirfa, who had ridden along with us, to their apartment.

As the coffee pestle (which with the mortars, are here of limestone marble, sunna's work, from Jauf,) begins to ring out at the coming of guests; neighbours enter gravely from the sûk, and to every one our sheykh Zeyd arose, large of his friendly greeting, and with the old courtesy took their hands and embraced them.

Teyma is a Nejd colony of Shammar, their fathers came to settle here, by their saying, not above two hundred years past: from which time remain the few lofty palms that are seen grown to fifteen fathoms, by the great well-pit, *Haddàj;* and only few there are, negroes, who durst climb to gather the fruits of them. All their palm kinds have been brought from Jebel Shammar, except the helw, which was fetched from el-Ally. Theirs is even now, in another dîra, the speech of Shammar. Here first we see the slender Nejd figures, elated, bold tongued, of ready specious hospitality, and to the stranger, arriving from the Hejâz, they nearly resemble the Beduins. They go bare-footed, and bravely clad of the Hâyil merchandise from *el-Irâk,* and inhabit clay-built spacious houses, mostly with an upper floor; the windows are open casements for the light and air, their flooring the beaten earth, the rude door is of palm boards, as in all the oases. This open Shammar town was never wasted by plagues, the *burr* or high desert of uncorrupt air lies all round about them from the walls: only Beduins from the dry desert complain here of the night (the evaporation from irrigated soil), which gives them cold in the head, *zikma.* Here are no house-ruins, broken walls and abandoned acres, that are seen in the most Arabian places. Prosperous is this outlying settlement from Nejd, above any which I have seen in my Arabian travels. If anyone here discover an antique well, without the walls, it is his own; and he encloses so much of the waste soil about as may suffice to the watering;

after a ploughing his new acre is fit for sowing and planting of palms, and fifteen years later every stem will be worth a camel. Teyma, till then a free township, surrendered without resistance to the government of Ibn Rashîd. They are skilful husbandmen to use that they have, without any ingenuity: their wells are only the wells of the ancients, which finding again, they have digged them out for themselves: barren of all invention, they sink none, and think themselves unable to bore a last fathom in the soft sandrock which lies at the bottom of the seven-fathom wells. Moslemîn, they say, cannot make such wells, but only Nasâra should be good to like work and Yahûdies. Arabian well-sinkers in stone there are none nearer than Kasîm, and these supine Arabs will call in no foreign workmen. They trust in God for their living, which, say the hearts of these penny-wise men, is better than to put their silver in adventure.

There was none here who asked alms in the street; indeed it is not common to see any destitute persons in West Nejd. I knew in Teyma but one such poor man, helpless, with no great age. In what house he entered at supper time, he might sit down with the rest to eat and welcome, but they grudged that he should carry any morsel away. There were in the town one or two destitute Beduins, who entered to sup and 'to coffee' in which households they would, no man forbidding them. At night they lay down in their cloaks, in what coffee hall they were; or went out to sleep, in the freshing air, upon some of the street clay benches.

A Forced March. Abu Zeyd's Image. The Strayed Mare

In this menzil, because the people must march from the morrow, the booths were struck and their baggage had been made up before they slept. The Beduin families lay abroad under the stars, beside their household stuff and the unshapely full sweating water-skins. The night was cold, at an altitude of 3,600 feet. I saw the nomads stretched upon the sand, wrapped in their mantles: a few have sleeping carpets, *ekîm,* under them, made of black worsted stuff like tent-cloth, but of the finer yarn and better weaving, adorned with a border of chequer-work of white and coloured wool and fringes gaily dyed. The ekîms of Teyma have a name in this country.

It was chill under the stars at this season, marching before the sun in the open wilderness. The children of the poor have not a mantle, only a cotton smock covers their tender bodies; some babes are even seen naked. I found 48° F., and when the sun was fairly up 86°. It was a forced march; the flocks and the herds, *et-tursh*, were driven forth beside us. At a need the Beduw spare not the cattle which are all their wealth, but think they do well to save themselves and their substance, even were it with the marring of some of them; their camel kine great with young were now daily calving. The new-yeaned lambs and kids, the tottering camel-calf of less than five days old, little whelps, which they would rear, of the hounds of the encampment, are laid by the housewives, with their own children, upon the burden camels. Each mother is seen riding upon a camel in the midst of the roll of her tent-cloth or carpet, in the folds lie nested also the young animals; she holds her little children before her. Small children, the aged, the sick, and even bed-rid folk, carried long hours, show no great signs of weariness in camel-riding. Their suffering persons ride seated in a nest of tent-cloth; others, who have been herdsmen, kneel or lie along, not fearing to fall, and seem to repose thus upon the rolling camel's bare back. It is a custom of the desert to travel fasting: however long be the ráhla, the Aarab eat only when they have alighted at the menzil; yet mothers will give their children to drink, or a morsel in their mouths, by the long way.

Journeying in this tedious heat, we saw first, in the after-noon horizon, the high solitary sandstone mountain J. Birrd. 'Yonder thulla,' cried my neighbours in their laughing argot, 'is the *sheykh* of our dîra.' Birrd has a height of nearly 5,000 feet. At the right hand there stretches a line of acacia trees in the wilderness plain, the token of a dry seyl bed, *Gô*, which des-cends, they said, from a day westward of Kheybar, and ends here in the desert. In all this high country, between Teyma and Tebûk and Medáin Sâlih ,there are no wadies. The little latter rain that may fall in the year is but sprinkled in the sand. Still journeying, this March sun which had seen our ráhla, rising, set behind us in a stupendous pavilion of Oriental glories, which is not seldom in these Arabian waste marches, where the atmosphere is never quite unclouded. We saw again the cold starlight before the fainting households alighted under Birrd till the morrow, when they would remove anew; the weary hareem making only a shelter from the night wind of the tent-cloths spread upon two stakes. It was in vain to seek milk of the over-driven cattle with dry udders. This day the nomad village was removed at once more than forty miles. In common times these wandering graziers take their menzils and dismiss the cattle to pasture, before high noon. Hastily, we saw the new day, we removed, and pitched few miles beyond in the Bishr dîra; from hence they reckoned three journeys to Hâyil, the like from Dàr-el-Hamra, a day and a half to Teyma.

A poor woman came weeping to my tent, entreating me to see and divine in my books what were become of her child. The little bare-foot boy was with the sheep, and had been missing after yesterday's long ráhla. The mother was hardly to be persuaded, in her grief, that my books were not cabalistical. I could not persuade the dreary indifference of the Arabs in her menzil to send back some of them, besides the child's father, to seek him: of their own motion they know not any such charity. If the camel of some poor widow woman be strayed, there is no man will ride upon the traces for human kindness, unless she can pay a real. The little herd-boy was found in the end of the encampment, where first he had lighted upon a kinsman's tent.

We removed from thence a little within the high white borders of the Nefûd, marching through a sand country full of last year's plants of the 'rose of Jericho.' These Beduw call them *ch(k)ef Marhab*. *Kef* is the hollow palm, with the fingers clenching upon it. Marhab is in their tradition sheykh of old Jewish Kheybar. We found also the young herb, two velvet green leaves, which has the wholesome smack of cresses, and is good for the nomad cattle. The Aarab alighted afterward in the camping ground *Ghromùl el-Mosubba*; known from far by the landmark of a singular tower-like needle of sand-stone, sixty feet high, the *Towîlan*. The third day we removed from thence, with mist and chill wind blowing, to *J. Chebàd*: from Chebàd we went to the rugged district *el-Jebàl*. After another journey, we came to pitch before the great sandstone mountain chine of Irnàn, in Nejd. Beyond this we advanced southeastward to the rugged coast of *Ybba Moghrair*; the Beduins, removing every second or third day, journeyed seven or eight miles and alighted. I saw about el-Jebâl other circles of rude flag-stones, set edgewise, as those of Jerèyda. In another place certain two cornered wall-enclosures, of few loose courses; they were made upon low rising grounds, and I thought might have been a sort of breastworks; the nomads could give me no account of them, as of things before their time and tradition. East of Ybba Moghrair, we passed the foot of a little antique rude turret in the desert soil. I showed it to some riding next me in the ráhla. 'Works (they answered) remaining from the creation of the world; what profit is there to inquire of them?' 'But all such to be nothing (said Zeyd) in comparison with that he would show me on the morrow, which was a marvel: the effigy of *Abu Zeyd*, a fabulous heroic personage, and dame *Alîa* his wife, portrayed upon some cliff of yonder mountain Ybba Moghrair.'

Wandering in all the waste Arabia, we often see rude trivet stones set by threes together: such are of old nomad pot-fires; and it is a comfortable human token, that some have found to cheer themselves, before us, in land where man's life seems nearly cast away, but at what time is uncertain; for stones, as they were pitched in that forsaken drought, may so continue for ages. The harder and gravel wilderness is seen cross-lined everywhere with old trodden camel paths; these are also from the old generations, and there is not any place of the immense waste, which is not at some time visited in the Aarab's wanderings; and yet whilst we pass no other life, it may be, is in the compass of a hundred miles about us. There is almost no parcel of soil where fuel may not be found, of old camel dung, *jella*, bleaching in the sun; it may lie three years, and a little sand blown upon it, sometime longer. There is another human sign in the wilderness, which mothers look upon; we see almost in every new ráhla, little ovals of stones, which mark the untimely died of the nomads: but grown persons dying in their own dîras, are borne (if it be not too difficult) to the next common burying place.

On the morrow betimes, Zeyd took his mare and his lance, and we set out to visit Abu Zeyd's image, the wonder of the desert. We crossed the sand plain, till the noon was hot over us; and come to the mountain, we rounded it some while in vain: Zeyd could not find the place. White stains, like seamarks, are seen upon certain of those desolate cliffs, they are roosting-places of birds of prey, falcons, buzzards and owls: their great nests of sticks are often seen in wild crags of these sandstone marches. In the waterless soil live many small animals which drink not, as rats and lizards and hares. We heard scritching owls sometimes in the still night; then the nomad wives and children answered them with mocking again *Ymgebâs! Ymgebâs!* The hareem said, 'It is a wailful woman, seeking her lost child through the wilderness, which was turned into this forlorn bird.' Fehjies eat the owl; for which they are laughed to scorn by the Beduw, that are devourers of some other vermin.

We went upon those mountain sides until we were weary. A sheykh's son, a coffee companion from his youth, and here in another dîra, Zeyd could not remember his landmarks. It was high noon; we wandered at random, and, for hunger, and thirst, plucking wild dandelions sprung since some showers in those rocks, we began to break our fast. At length, looking down at a deep place, we espied camels, which went pasturing under the mountain: there we found Fehját herdsmen. The images, they said, were not far before us, they would put us in the way, but first they bade us sit down to refresh ourselves. The poor men then ran for us under the nâga's udders, and drew their milk-skin full of that warm sustenance. – Heaven remember for good the poor charitable nomads. When we had drunk they came along with us, driving the cattle: a little strait

opened further, it was a long inlet in the mountain bosom,
teeming green with incomparable freshness, to our sense, of
rank herbage. At the head of this garden of weeds is an oozy
slumbering pool; and thereabove I perceived the rocks to be
full of scored inscriptions, and Abu Zeyd's yard-high image,
having in his hand the crooked camel stick, bakhorra, or, as
the Aarab say, who cannot judge of portraiture, a sword: beside him, is a lesser, perhaps a female figure, which they call
'Alîa his wife'. It is likely that these old lively shapes were
battered, with a stone, upon the sandstone; they are not as the
squalid scrawling portraiture of the Beduw, but limned round-
ly to the natural with the antique diligence. Here are mostly
short Himyaric legends, written (as is common in these deserts)
from above downwards; the names doubtless, the saws, the
salaams, of many passengers and cameleers of antique generations. *Ybba*, is said for *Abu*, father, in these parts of Arabia
and at Medina; *Moghrair*, is perhaps cave. I bade Zeyd let me
have a milch nâga and abandon me here with Abu Zeyd.
Zeyd answered (with a fable), he had already paid a camel to
Bishr, for license to show me their Abu Zeyd. The Fehját
answered simply, 'A man might not dwell here alone, in the
night time, the demons would affray him.'

As we came again, Zeyd lighted upon a natural sanded
basin among the rocks, under the mountain, and there sounding with his hands to the elbow, he reached to a little stinking
moisture. Zeyd smiled vaingloriously, and cried, 'Ha! we had
discovered a new water. Wellah, here is water a little under
the mire, the hind shall come hither to-morrow and fill our
girbies.' Thereby grew a nightshade weed, now in the berry;
the Beduin man had not seen the like before, and bade me bear
it home to the menzil, to be conned by the hareem: – none of
whom, for all their wise looking, knew it. 'A stranger plant
(said they) in this dîra': it is housewifely amongst them to be
esteemed cunning in drugs and simples. Lower, we came to a
small pool in the rock; the water showed ruddy-brown and
ammoniacal, the going down was stained with old filth of
camels. 'Ay (he said) of this water would we draw for our
coffee, were there none other.' Upon the stone I saw other

Himyaric legends. And here sat two young shepherd lasses; they seeing men approach, had left playing, their little flock wandered near them. Zeyd, a great sheykh, hailed them with the hilarity of the desert, and the ragged maidens answered him in mirth again: they fear none of their tribesmen, and herding maidens may go alone with the flocks far out of seeing of the menzil in the empty wilderness. We looked up and down, but could not espy Zeyd's mare, which, entering the mountain, he had left bound below, the headstall tied back, by the halter, to an hind limb in the nomad manner. Thus, making a leg at every pace, the Beduin mare may graze at large; but cannot wander far. At length, from a high place, we had sight of her, returning upon her traces to the distant camp. 'She is thirsty (said Zeyd), let her alone and she will find the way home': – although the black booths were yet under our horizon. So the nomad horses come again of themselves, and seek their own households, when they would drink water. Daily, when the sun is well risen, the Beduin mare is hop-shackled with iron links, which are opened with a key, and loosed out to feed from her master's tent. The horses wander, seeking each other, if the menzils be not wide scattered, and go on pasturing and sporting together: their sheykhly masters take no more heed of them than of the hounds of the encampment, until high noon, when the mares, returning homeward of themselves, are led in to water. They will go then anew to pasture, or stand shadowing out that hot hour in the master's booth (if it be a great one). They are grazing not far off till the sun is setting, when they draw to their menzils, or are fetched home and tethered for the night.

There hopped before our feet, as we came, a minute brood of second locusts, of a leaden colour, with budding wings like the spring leaves, and born of those gay swarms which, a few weeks before, had passed over and despoiled the desert. After forty days these also would fly as a pestilence, yet more hungry than the former, and fill the atmosphere. We saw a dark sky over the black nomad tents, and I showed Zeyd a shower falling before the westing sun. – 'Would God, he answered, it might reach us!' Their cattle's life in this languishing soil is of a very little rain. The Arabian sky, seldom clear, weeps as the weeping of hypocrites.

We removed from here, and pitched the black booths upon that bleakness of white sand which is, here, the Nefûd, whose edge shows all along upon the brown sandstone desert: a seyl bed, *Terrai*, sharply divides them. The Aarab would next remove to a good well, *el-Hŷza*, in the Nefûd country, where in good years they find the spring of new pasture: but there being little to see upon this border, we returned another day towards the *Helwàn* mountain; in which march I saw other (eight or nine yards large) circles of sandstone flags. Dreary was this Arabian ráhla; from the March skies there soon fell a tempest of cold rain, and, alighting quickly, the Beduin women had hardly breath in the whirling shower to build their booths: – a héjra may be put up in three minutes. In the tents, we sat out the stormy hours upon the moist sand in our stiffened wet mantles; and the windy drops fell through the ragged tilt upon us. In the Nefûd, towards el-Hŷza, are certain booming sand hills, *Rowsa, Deffafîat, Subbîa* and *Irzûm*, such as the sand drift of *J. Nagûs*, by the sea village of *Tor*, in Sinai; the upper sand sliding down under the foot of the passenger, there arises, of the infinite fretting grains, such a giddy loud swelling sound, as when your wetted finger is drawn about the lip of a glass of water, and like that swooning din after the chime of a great bell, or cup of metal. – *Nagûs* is the name of the sounding-board in the belfry of the Greek monastery, whereupon as the sacristan plays with his hammer, the timber yields a pleasant musical note, which calls forth the formal *colieros* to their prayers: another such singing sand drift, *el-Howayrîa*, is in the cliffs (east of the Mezham,) of Medáin Sâlih. . . .

Evening clouds gathered; the sheykhs going homewards had wet mantles. The mare returned of herself through the falling weather, and came and stood at our coffee fire, in half human wise, to dry her soaked skin and warm herself, as one among us. It may be said of the weak nomad horses, that they have no gall. I have seen a mare, stabling herself in the mid-day shadow of the master's booth, that approached the sitters about the coffee hearth and putting down her soft nose the next turned their heads to kiss her, till the sheykh rose to scold his mare away. They are feeble, of the slender and harsh desert forage; and gentle to that hand of man, which is as the mother's teat to them in the wilderness. Wild and dizzy camels are daily seen, but seldom impetuous horses, and perverse never: the most are of the bay colour. The sheykh's hope is in his mare to bear him with advantage upon his enemy, or to save him hastily from the field; it is upon her back he may best take a spoil and outride all who are mounted upon thelûls. Nor she (nor any life, of man or beast, besides the hounds) is ever mishandled amongst them. The mare is not cherished by the master's household, yet her natural dwelling is at the mild nomad tent. She is allied to the beneficent companionship of man; his shape is pleasant to her in the inhospitable khála. The mildness of the Arab's home is that published by their prophet of the divine household; mild-hearted is the koran Ullah, a sovereign Semitic house-father, how indulgent to his people! The same is an adversary, cruel and hard, to an alien people.

Summer Days in the Wilderness. Wild Creatures

Now longwhile our black booths had been built upon the sandy stretches, lying before the swelling white Nefûd side: the lofty coast of Irnàn in front, whose cragged breaches, where is any footing for small herbs nourished of this barren atmosphere, are the harbour of wild goats, which never drink. The summer's night at end, the sun stands up as a crown of hostile flames from that huge covert of inhospitable sandstone bergs; the desert day draws not little and little, but it is noon tide in an hour. The sun, entering as a tyrant upon the waste landscape, darts upon us a torment of fiery beams, not to be remitted till the far-off evening. – No matins here of birds; not a rock partridge-cock, calling with blithesome chuckle over the extreme waterless desolation. Grave is that giddy heat upon the crown of the head; the ears tingle with a flickering shrillness, a subtle crepitation it seems, in the glassiness of this sun-stricken nature: the hot sand-blink is in the eyes, and there is little refreshment to find in the tents' shelter; the worsted booths leak to this fiery rain of sunny light. Mountains looming like dry bones through the thin air, stand far around about us: the savage flank of Ybba Moghrair, the high spire and ruinous stacks of el-Jebàl, Chebàd, the coast of Helwàn! Herds of the weak nomad camels waver dispersedly, seeking pasture in the midst of this hollow fainting country, where but lately the swarming locusts have fretted every green thing. This silent air burning about us, we endure breathless till the assr: when the dazing Arabs in the tents revive after their heavy hours. The lingering day draws down to the sunsetting; the herdsmen, weary of the sun, come again with the cattle, to taste in their menzils the first sweetness of mirth and repose. – The day is done, and there rises the nightly freshness of this purest mountain air: and then to the cheerful song and the cup at the common fire. The moon rises ruddy from that solemn obscurity of jebel like a mighty beacon: – and the morrow will be as this day, days deadly drowned in the sun of the summer wilderness. ...

... The short spring season is the only refreshment of the desert year. Beasts and men swim upon this prosperous tide; the cattle have their fill of sweet pasture, butter-milk is in the booths of the Aarab; but there was little or none in Zeyd's tent. The kids and lambs stand all tied, each little neck in a noose, upon a ground line which is stretched in the nomad booth. At daybreak the bleating younglings are put under the dams, and each mother receives her own, (it is by the scent) – she will put by every other. When the flock is led forth to pasture, the little ones are still bound at home: for following the dams, they would drink dry the dugs, and leave no food for the Arabs. The worsted tent is full all day of small hungry bleatings, until the ghrannem come home at evening, when they are loosed again, and run to drink, butting under their mother's teats, with their wiggle tails; and in these spring weeks, there is little rest for their feebles cries, all night in the booths of the Aarab: the housewives draw what remains of the sweet milk after them. The B.Wáhab tribes of these open highlands, are camel-Beduins; the small cattle are few among them: they have new spring milk when their hinds have calved. The yeaning camel-cow, lying upon her side, is delivered without voice, the fallen calf is big as a grown man: the herdsman stretches out its legs, with all his might; and draws the calf, as dead, before the dam. She smells to her young, rises and stands upon her feet to lick it over. With a great clap of the man's palm upon that horny sole, *zôra*, (which, like a pillar, Nature has set under the camel's breast, to bear up the huge neck,) the calf revives: at three hours end, yet feeble and tottering, and after many falls, it is able to stand reaching up the long neck and feeling for the mother's teat. The next morrow this new born camel will follow to the field with the dam. The cow may be milked immediately, but that which is drawn from her, for a day or two, is purgative. The first voice of the calf is a sheep-like complaint, *bâh-bâh*, loud and well sounding. The fleece is silken soft, the head round and high; and this with a short body, borne arch-wise, and a leaping gait upon so long legs, makes that, a little closing the eyes, you might take them for fledgings of some colossal bird. Till twelve months be out they follow the teat; but when a few weeks old they begin, already, to crop for themselves the tops of the desert bushes; and their necks being not yet of proportionate reach, it is only betwixt the straddled fore legs, that they can feed at the ground. One evening, as I stroked the soft woolly chines of the new-born camels, 'Khalîl! said the hind (coming with a hostile face), see thou do no more so, – they will be hide-bound and not grow well; thou knowest this!' He thought the stranger was about some maleficence; but Zeyd, whose spirit was far from all superstition with an easy smile appeased him, and they were his own camels.

The camel calf at the birth is worth a real, and every month rises as much in value. In some 'weak' households the veal is slaughtered, where they must drink themselves all their camel milk. The bereaved dam wanders, lowing softly, and smelling for her calf; and as she mourns, you shall see her deer-like pupils, say the Arabs, 'standing full of tears.' Other ten days, and her brutish distress is gone over to forgetfulness; she will feed again full at the pasture, and yield her foster milk to the

Aarab. Then three good pints may be drawn from her at morning, and as much to their supper: the udder of these huge frugal animals is not greater than I have seen the dugs of Malta goats. A milch cow with the calf is milked only at evening. Her udder has four teats, which the southern nomads divide thus: two they tie up with a worsted twine and wooden pegs, for themselves, the other they leave to the suckling. The Aarab of the north make their camel udders sure, with a worsted bag-netting. Upon a journey, or when she is thirsting, the nâga's milk is lessened to the half. All their nâgas give not milk alike. Whilst the spring milk is in, the nomads nourish themselves of little else. In poorer households it is all their victual those two months. The Beduins drink no whole-milk, save that of their camels; of their small cattle they drink but the butter-milk. The hareem make butter, busily rocking the (blown) sour milk-skin upon their knees. In the plenteous northern wilderness the semîly is greater; and is hanged to be rocked in the fork of a robust bearing-stake of the nomad tent. As for this milk-diet, I find it, by proof in the Beduin life, to be the best of human food. But in every nomad menzil, there are some stomachs, which may never well bear it; and strong men using this sliding drink-meat feel always an hungry disease in their bodies; though they seem in never so good plight. The Beduins speak thus of the several kinds of milk: 'Goatmilk is sweet, it fattens more than strengthens the body; ewe's milk very sweet, and fattest of all, it is unwholesome to drink whole': so they say, 'it kills people', that is, with the colic. In spite of their saws, I have many times drunk it warm from the dug, with great comfort of languishing fatigue. It is very rich in the best samn: ewe butter-milk 'should be let sour somewhile in the semîly, with other milk, till all be tempered together, and then it is fit to drink.' Camel milk is they think the best of all sustenance, and that most, (as lightly purgative,) of the *bukkra*, or young nâga with her first calf, and the most sober of them add with a Beduish simplicity, 'who drinks and has a jâra he would not abide an hour.' The goat and nâga milk savour of the plants where the cattle are pastured; in some cankered grounds I have found it as wormwood. One

of those Allayda sheykhs called to me in the ráhla, 'Hast thou
not some Damascus *kaak* (biscuit cakes) to give me to eat?
wellah, it is six weeks since I have chewed anything with the
teeth; all our food is now this flood of milk. Seest thou not
what is the Beduins' life; they are like game scattered in all the
wilderness.' Another craved of me a handful of dates; 'with
this milk, only, he felt such a creeping hunger within him.' Of
any dividing food with them the Beduins keep a kindly remembrance; and when they have aught will call thee heartily
again.

The milk-dieted Aarab are glad to take any mouthful of
small game. Besides the desert hare which is often startled in
the ráhlas, before other is the thób; which they call here pleasantly 'Master Hamed, sheykh of wild beasts', and say he is
human, *zillamy*, – this is their elvish smiling and playing – and
in proof they hold up his little five-fingered hands. They eat
not his palms, nor the seven latter thorny rings of sheykh
Hamed's long tail, which, say they, is 'man's flesh'. His pasture is most of the sweet-smelling Nejd bush, *el-arrafej*.
Sprawling wide and flat is the body, ending in a training tail of
even length, where I have counted twenty-three rings. The
colour is blackish and green-speckled, above the pale yellowish
and dull belly: of his skin the nomads make small herdmen's
milk-bottles. The manikin saurian, with the robust hands, digs
his burrow under the hard gravel soil, wherein he lies all the
winter, dreaming. The thób-catcher, finding the hole, and
putting in his long reed armed with an iron hook, draws
Hamed forth. His throat cut, they fling the carcase, whole,
upon the coals; and thus baked they think it a delicate roast.
His capital enemy among beasts, 'which undermines and de-
vours him, is, they say, the *thurbàn*,' I know not whether a living or fabulous animal. The *jerboa*, or spring rat, is a small
white aery creature in the wide waterless deserts, of a pitiful
beauty. These lesser desert creatures lie underground in the
daylight, they never drink. The hedgehog, which they call
kúnfuth, and *abu shauk,* 'father prickles', is eaten in these parts
by Fejîr tribesmen, but by their neighbours disdained, although they be one stock with them of Annezy. Selím brought

in an urchin which he had knocked on the head, he roasted
Prickles in the coals and rent and distributed the morsels, to
every one his part. That which fell to me I put away bye and
bye to the starveling greyhound; but the dog smelling to the
meat rejected it. When another day I told this tale in the next
tribes, they laughed maliciously, that the Fukara should eat
that which the hounds would not of. The porcupine is eaten
by all the nomads, and the *wabbar*. I have seen this thick-bod-
ied beast as much as an heavy hare, and resembling the great
Alpine rat; they go by pairs, or four, six, eight, ten, together.
The wabbar is found under the border of the sandstone mountains, where tender herbs nourish him, and the gum-acacia
leaves, upon which tree he climbs nimbly, holding with his
pad feet without claws; the fore-paws have four toes, the hind-
paws three: the flesh is fat and sweet: they are not seen to sit
upon the hind quarters; the pelt is grey, and like the bear's
coat.

Rarely do any nomad gunners kill the wolf, but if any fall to
their shot he is eaten by the Beduins, (the wolf was eaten in
mediaeval Europe). The Aarab think the flesh medicinal, 'very
good they say for aches in the shins,' which are so common
with them that go bare-legs and bare-footed in all the seasons.
Zeyd had eaten the wolf, but he allowed it to be of dog's kind,
'Eigh, billah (he answered me), the wolf's mother, that is the
hound's aunt.' The fox, *hosseny*, is often taken by their grey-
hounds, and eaten by the Fejîr; the flesh is 'sweet, and next to
the hare.' They will even eat the foul hyena when they may
take her, and say, 'she is good meat.' Of great desert game, but
seldom slain by the shot of these pastoral and tent-dwelling
people, is the bédan of the mountains (the wild goat of Scripture, *pl.* bedûn; with the Kahtân *waúl*, as in Syria). The massy
horns grow to a palm-breadth, I have seen them two and a
half feet long; they grow stretching back upon the chine to
the haunch. The beast at need, as all hunter's relate, will cast
himself down headlong upon them backwards: he is nigh of
kin to the stone-buck of the European Alps.

The gazelle, *ghrazel*, pl. *ghrazlán*, is of the plains; the Arabians say more often *thobby* (the N.T.Tabitha). They are white in

the great sand-plains, and swart-grey upon the black Harra;
these are the roes of the scriptures. There is yet a noble wild
creature of the Arabian deserts, which was hitherto unknown
among us, the *wothŷhi*, or 'wild cow' above mentioned. I saw
later the male and female living at Hâyil; it is an antelope,
Beatrix, akin to the beautiful animals of Africa. It seems that
this is not the 'wild ox' of Moses: but is not this the (Hebr.)
reem, the '*unicorn*' of the Septuagint translators? – Her horns
are such slender rods as from our childhood we have seen pic-
tured 'the horns of the unicorns.' We read in Balaam's parable,
'EL brought them out of Egypt; He hath as it were the
strength of a *reem*': and in Moses' blessing of the tribes,
'Joseph's horns are the *two* horns of reems.' In Job especially,
are shown the headstrong conditions of this *velox* wild creature. 'Will the reem be willing to serve thee – canst thou bind
the reem in thy furrow?' The wounded wothŷhi is perilous
to be approached; this antelope, with a cast of her shape horns,
may strike through a man's body; hunters await therefore the
last moments to run in and cut their quarry's throat. It was a
monkish darkness in natural knowledge to ascribe a single
horn to a double forehead! – and we sin not less by addition,
puttings wings to the pagan images of gods and angels; so
they should have two pairs of fore-limbs! The wothŷhi falls
only to the keenest hunters: the wothŷhies accompany in the
waterless desert by troops of three and five together.

Of vermin, there are many snakes and adders; none of
them eaten by these tribes of nomads. *Jelâmy* is that small
brown lizard of the wilderness which starts from every footstep. Scorpions lurk under the cool stones; I have found them
in my tent, upon my clothing, but never had any hurt. I have
seen many grown persons and children bitten, but the sting is
not perilous; some wise man is called to 'read' over them.
The wounded part throbs with numbness and aching till the
third day, there is not much swelling. Many are the cities,
under this desert sand, of seed-gathering ants; I have measured some watling-street of theirs, eighty-five paces: to speed
once this length and come again, loaded as camels, is these
small busybodies' summer day's journey.

Besides, of the great predatory wild animals, most common is the *thùbba*, hyena; then the *nimmr*, a leopard, brindled black and brown and spotted: little common is the *fáhd*, a wild cat no bigger than the fox; he is red and brown brindled, and spotted. In these Beduins' memory a young fáhd was bred up amongst Bishr, which (they are wonderfully swift footed) had been used by his nomad master to take gazelles. In all the Arabic countries there is a strange superstition of parents, (and this as well among the Christian sects of Syria,) that if any child seem to be sickly, of infirm understanding, or his brethren have died before, they will put upon him a wild beast's name, (especially, wolf, leopard, wolverine,) – that their human fragility may take on as it were a temper of the kind of those animals. Hawks and buzzards are often seen wheeling in the desert sky, and *el-dgab*, which is a small black eagle, and *er-rákham*, the small white carrion eagle, – flying in the air they resemble sea-mews: I have not seen vultures, nor any greater eagle in the deserts (save in Sinai). These are the most of living creatures, and there are few besides in the wilderness of Arabia.

Aarab Children at Play. Circumcision Feasts

The cheerful summer nights are cool from the sunset in these dry uplands. As they have supped, men wander forth to talk with neighbours, coffee drinkers seek the evening cup: in the mejlis coffee company, the Aarab gossip till midnight. Often in our menzil only the herdsman remains at home, who wakens to his rough song the grave chord of the rabeyby.

Some moonlight evenings the children hied by us: boys and girls troop together from the mothers' beyts, and over the sand they leap to play at horses, till they find where they may climb upon some sand-hillock or rock. A chorus of the elder girls assemble hither, that with hand-clapping chant the same and even the same refrain, of a single verse. Little wild boys stripping off their tunics, and flinging down kerchiefs, or that have left all in the mothers' beyts, run out naked; there being only the *haggu* wound about slender loins: this is the plaited leathern ribbon, which is worn, and never left, by all the right Arabians, both men and hareem. Every boy-horse has chosen a mate, his *fáras* or mare; they course hand in hand together, and away, away, every pair skipping after other and are held themselves in chase in the moonlight wilderness. He kicks back to the horses which chevy after them so fast, and escapes again neighing. And this pastime of Aarab children, of pure race, is without strife of envious hearts, an angry voice is not heard, a blow is not struck among them. The nomads are never brutal. This may last for an hour or two: the younger men will sometimes draw to the merry-make where the young maidens be: they frolic like great camels amongst the small ghrannem; but not unclad, nor save with the eyes approach they to that chanting bevy of young damsels; an ill-blooded nature appearing in any young man, he shall have the less estimation among them. After the child's age, these indolent Arabians have not any kind of manly pastime among them. Of Ahl Gibly, or southern nomads, I have not seen horsemen so much as exercise themselves upon their mares. Child's play it were in their eyes, to weary themselves, and be never the better. They have none other sport than to fire off their matchlocks in any household festivals. Herdsmen, they are naturally of the contemplative life: weakly fed, there can be little flushing of gross sanguine spirits in their veins, which might move them to manly games; very rarely is any Beduin robust. Southward of Hâyil I did not see any young woman with the rose blood in her cheeks: even they are of the summer's drought, and palled at their freshest age.

Now in the mild summer is the season of *muzayyins*, the Nomad children's circumcision feasts: the mother's booth is set out with beggarly fringes of scarlet shreds, tufts of mewed ostrich feathers, and such gay gauds as they may borrow or find. Hither a chorus assembles of slender daughters of their neighbours, that should chant at this festival in their best array. A fresh kerchief binds about every damsel's forehead with a feather; she has ear-rings great as bracelets, and wears to-day her nose-ring, *zmèyem*: they are jewels in silver; and a few, as said, from old time are fine gold metal, *thahab el-asfr*. These are ornaments of the Beduin women, hardly seen at other times (in the pierced nostril, they wear for every day a head of cloves), and she has bracelets of beads and metal finger-rings. The thin black tresses loosed to-day and not long, hang down upon their slight shoulders, and shine in the sun, freshly combed out with camel urine. The lasses have borrowed new cloaks, which are the same for man or woman. Making a fairy ring apart, they begin, clapping the palms of their little hands, to trip it round together, chanting ever the same cadence of few words, which is a single verse. Hungered young faces, you might take them for some gipsy daughters; wayward not seldom in their mother's households, now they go playing before men's eyes, with downcast looks and a virginal timidity. But the Aarab raillery is never long silent, and often the young men in this daylight feast, stand jesting about them. Some even pluck roughly at the feathers of the lasses, their own near cousins, in the dance, which durst answer them nothing, but only with reproachful eyes: or laughing loud the weleds have bye and bye divided this gentle bevy among them for their wives; and if a stranger be there, they will bid him choose which one he would marry among them. 'Heigh-ho! what thinkest thou of these maidens of ours, and her, and her, be they not fair-faced?' But the virgins smile not, and if any look up, their wild eyes are seen estranged and pensive. They are like children under the rod, they should keep here a studied demeanour; and for all this they are not Sirens. In that male tyranny of the Mohammedan religion regard is had to a distant maidenly behaviour of the young daughters; and here they dance as the tender candidates for happy marriage, and the blessed motherhood of sons. May their morrow approach! which shall be as this joyful day, whose hap they now sing, wherein a man-child is joined to the religion of Islam; it is better than the day of his birth. The nomad son is circumcised being come to the strength of three full years; and then as the season may serve without any superstition of days, and as the mother shall be able to provide corn or rice enough for her guests' supper. They sometimes put off the surgery till the morrow, in any rough windy weather, or because of the Aarab's ráhla.

The friends of the father will come in to be his guests: some of them have adorned themselves with the gunner's belt and gay baldric, rattling with the many little steel chains and brass powder-cases; and they bear upon their shoulders the long matchlocks. Therewith they would prove their hand to shoot, at the sheep's skull, which the child's *babbu* has sacrificed to the hospitality. Every man kills his sacrifice, as in the ancient world, with his own hands, and the carcase is flayed and brittled with the Arabs' expedition. Nomads are all expert fleshers; the quarters hang now upon some bush or boughs, which wandering in an open wilderness, they have sought perhaps upon a far mountain side. As the sun goes low the meat is cast into the caldron, jidda. The great inwards remain suspended upon their trophy bush. After the flesh, a mess is cooked in the broth of such grain as they have. The sun setting the maidens of the ring-dance disperse: the men now draw apart to their prayers, and in this time the cattle of every household are driven in. The men risen from their prayers, the supper is served in the tent: often thirty men's meat is in that shield-wide wooden platter which is set before them. A little later some will come hither of the young herdsmen returning boisterous from the field; they draw to the merry noise of the muzayyin that feel a lightness in their knees to the dance. A-row, every one his arm upon the next one's shoulder, these laughing weleds stand, full of good humour; and with a shout they foot it forth, reeling and wavering, advancing, recoiling in their chorus together; the while they hoarsely chant the ballad of a single verse. The housewives at the booth clap their palms, and one rising with a rod in her hand, as the dancing men advance, she dances out to meet them; it is the mother by likelihood, and joyously she answers them in her song: whilst they come on bending and tottering a-row together, with their perpetual refrain. They advancing upon her, she dances backward, feinting defence with the rod; her face is turned towards them, who maintain themselves, with that chanted verse of their manly throats, as it were pursuing and pressing upon her. – The nomads imagine even the necessity of circumcision: graziers, they will allege the examples of all cattle, that only in the son of Adam may be found this manner of impediment. When they questioned me I have said, 'You can amend then the work of Ullah!' – 'Of that we speak not, they answered, but only of the expediency.' Questioned, What be the duties of a Moslem? they responded 'That a man fast in the month, and recite his daily prayers'; – making no mention of the circumcision, which they call 'purification.'

The Camel Raid

The 15th of April, after a morning wind, blustering cold from the north-eastward, I found early in the afternoon, with still air and sunshine, the altitude being 4,000 feet, 95° F. in the booth's shelter. The drooping herb withered, the summer drought entering, the wilderness changed colour; the spring was ended. The Beduins removed and lodged in their desolate camps: upon a morrow, when the camels had been driven forth an hour, an alarm was given from the front, of gôm. A herdsman came riding in, who had escaped, upon a thelûl, and told it in the mejlis, 'el-'bil, the camel-herds are taken.' The sheukh rose from the hearth and left their cups with grave startled looks: all went hardily out, and hastily, to find their mares. Hovering haramîyeh had been seen yesterday, and now every man hied to take arms. The people ran, like angry wasps, from the booths: some were matchlock men, some had spears, all were afoot, save the horsemen sheykhs, and hastened forth to requite their enemies, which could not be seen in that short desert horizon: bye and bye only the housewives, children and a few sick and old men were left in the encampment. Some asked me would I not ride to set upon the thieves; for Zeyd's talk had been that Khalîl would foray with them. 'Khalîl (cried the housewives), look for us in your wise books; canst thou not prophesy by them (shûf f'il ghraib): read thou and tell us what seest thou in them of these go-mânies. – A punishment fall upon them! they certainly espied the people's watchfires here last night, and have been lurking behind yonder mountain until the camels were driven out.' – The long morning passed over us, in the cold incertitude of this misadventure.

Motlog had ridden days before to Hâyil to treat with the emir, and left Rahŷel to govern the tribe; a man of perplexed mind in this sudden kind of conjuncture. The armed tribesmen returning after midday, we went to sit in the mejlis and talk over this mishap. I heard no word spoken yet of pursuing; and inquiring of my neighbour, 'Ay, they would mount their thelûls, said he, as soon as the 'bil were come home at evening'; for all the great cattle were not taken, but those which had been driven forth from the north side of the menzil. Celerity is double strokes in warfare, but these Beduins sat still the long day and let the robbers run, to wonder what they were; they all said, 'some Aarab of the North,' for they had seen them armed with pistols. They reasoned whether those should be Sherarát or Howeytát Ibn Jàsy (Beduins from about Maan); or else of the Ruwàlla. 'Hear me, and I shall make it known to you, said Zeyd (who had this vanity among them), what they were. I say then, *es-Sokhûr,* and ye shall find it true.' The few words which had fallen from the foemen's lips were now curiously examined. They had challenged the camel herds, 'What Aarab be ye – ha! the Fejîr?' but this could not suffice to distinguish the *loghrat* of a tribe. The gôm were thirteen horsemen, and twenty riders upon thelûls. In driving off the booty a mare broke loose from them, and she was led into the encampment, but of that nothing could be learned, the nomad sheykhs not using to brand their horses with the tribe's cattle-mark. This mare, by the third day, perished of thirst! that none would pour out to her of their little water. If a tribesman's goat strayed among them, and her owner be not known, none will water her. In the time when I was with them, I saved the lives of a strayed beast or two, persuading some of my patients to give them drink. ...

... Rahŷel's pursuing party was three nights out. The men left in camp being now very few, they came continually together to drink coffee. The affectionate housewives sat abroad all day watching: at mid-afternoon, the fourth after, we heard

the hareem's jubilee, *lullilu!* – but the merry note died away in
their throats when, the longer they looked, they saw those that
came riding in the horizon were leading nothing home with
them. The men rose together, and going forth, they gazed
fixedly. 'What, said they, means this cry of the hareem? for
look, they arrive empty-handed, and every man is riding apart
to alight at his own household!' so returning to their fatal in-
dolence, they re-entered as men that are losers, and sat down
again. 'Some of them, they said, will presently bring us tidings.' Rahŷel soon after dismounted at his tent, pitched near
behind us. – The housewife comes forth as her husband makes
his thelûl kneel; she receives him in silence, unsaddles the
beast, and carries in his gear. The man does not often salute
her openly, nor, if he would to the mejlis, will he speak to his
wife yet; so Rahŷel, without entering his booth, stepped over
to us. – 'Peace be with you!' said he from a dry throat, and
seating himself with a sigh of a weary man, in some sadness,
he told us, 'that in the second day, following the enemy upon
the Nefûd, they came where a wind had blown out the prints,'
and said he, 'So Ullah willed it!' They turned then their beasts'
heads, – they had no list to cast further about, to come again
upon the robbers' traces. 'Ha well! God would have it so!'
responded the indolent Aarab. A weak enemy they thus faintly
let slip through their fingers, for a little wind, though these
were driving with them nearly a tithe of all their camels. But
Rahŷel, to knit up his sorry tale with a good ending, exclaimed, 'Wellah, they had found water at the wells el-Hŷza in
the Nefûd; and as they came again by Teyma, he heard word
that some of the gôm had touched there, and they were of the
Sherarát': – Rahŷel, with his troop, had ridden nearly two
hundred idle miles. 'Bye and bye we shall know (said the
Beduins) which tribesmen robbed our camels; then will we
ghrazzy upon them, and God willing, take as many of them
again.' But the ghrazzus often return empty: a party of Fukara,
'twenty *rikáb*' or wayfaring thelûls, which rode lately upon
the Beny Atîeh, had taken nothing.

Every man leans upon his own hand in the open desert, and
there will none for naught take upon him a public service. The

sheykh may persuade, he cannot compel any man; and if the malcontent will go apart, he cannot detain them. The common body is weak, of members so loosely knit together, and there befalls them many an evil hap, which by a public policy might have been avoided. – 'Why send you not out scouts, (thus I reasoned with Zeyd), which might explore the khála in advance of your pasturing cattle? or cannot you set some watch in the tops of the rocks, for the appearing of an enemy! Why commit yourselves thus to wild hazard, who are living openly in the midst of danger?' When Zeyd gravely repeated my words in the mejlis, the sheykh's son answered readily, 'Ay, and that were very well, if we might put it in practice; but know, Khalîl, there are none of the Beduw will thus adventure themselves by twos and threes together, for fear of the habalîs, we cannot tell where they lie until thou hearest from behind a crag or bush *deh!* and the shot strikes thee.'

The Crater Hill. The Harra

I wished to ascend the great crater-hill Anâz, and look far over this lava country: but if any agreed to accompany me, the sheykh secretly forbad him; Tollog reserved the advantage to himself and his own sons. He supposed I might be good to the discovering of springs or treasure: a Beduwy, he could not otherwise think than that I came to enrich myself, and he would be enriched with me. The Fejîr sheukh, men of more urbane minds, had better understood the Haj officers; but these were men stiff in their opinions, and heavy mountaineers. Tollog, travailing in his heart of all that he had ever heard strange of the Nasâra, inquired of me at the coffee hearth, 'Khalîl, Wellah, is there not a vessel for the air – tell me this, and let the company hear it – in which the Nasrânies may fly?' – 'Very true, Tollog; a great bubble in a silk bag, greater than this booth, and that may float in the air.' *Tollog*: 'But tell us more! is there not a ship which is made to sail under the face of the water, with all her Arabs, and that may rise again?' – 'From whence (I asked) had he this?' – 'Of a son of his uncle (that is a Sbáite) of Syria, who had taken a western woman, very rich, of those lands beyond seas, or he wist not where.'

We removed again, and when we encamped, I looked round from a rising ground, and numbered forty crater hills within our horizon; I went out to visit the nighest of them. To go a mile's way is weariness, over the sharp lava field and beds of wild vulcanic blocks and stones. I passed in haste, before any friendly persons could recall me; so I came to a cone and crater of the smallest here seen, 300 feet in height, of erupted matter, pumice and light rusty cinders, with many sharp ledges of lavas. The hill-side was guttered down by the few yearly showers in long ages. I climbed and entered the crater. Within were sharp walls of slaggy lava, the further part broken down – that was before the bore of out-flowing lavas – and encrusted by the fiery blast of the eruption. Upon the flanks of that hilla, I found a block of red granite, cast up from the head of some Plutonic vein, in the deep of the mountain. Red granite, called by these nomads *hajr el-kra*, in some parts of the Harra lies not far under, they say it is seen near Anâz; and below the Aueyrid mountain. In the Jau, are some antique ruins, built of great blocks of the same mineral: I understand from them that it is the rock of the next lower-lying *Shéfa* country, and of those mighty crested land-marks, appearing in the north-western horizon, mountains of the Teháma, *Wuttid* and *Jowla*. Of the hajr el-kra, the Beduw work out their best quern-stones: they have no tools, but when they choose a block, they hammer incessantly upon it, with another hard stone, till they have beaten it down to that shape they would; and they drill the hole of the pin, beating upon a nail. I found a natural pit under the crater hill of yellow tufa, breathed of old from the vulcanic gulf, and in the great slag-stones about, many common greenish vulcanic crystals (chrysolite).

We look out from every height, upon the Harra, over an iron desolation; what uncouth blackness and lifeless cumber of vulcanic matter! – an hard-set face of nature without a smile for ever, a wilderness of burning and rusty horror of unformed matter. What lonely life would not feel constraint of heart to trespass here! the barren heaven, the nightmare soil! where should he look for comfort? – There is a startled conscience within a man of his *mesquîn* being, and profane, in presence of the divine stature of the elemental world! – this lion-like sleep of cosmogonic forces, in which is swallowed up the gnat of the soul within him, – that short motion and parasitical usurpation which is the weak accident of life in matter. Anâz appeared, riding as it were upon the rocky tempest, at twelve miles distance; – I despaired of coming thither, over so many vulcanic deeps and reefs of lavas, and long scalding reaches of basalt rolling stones.

As we removed again over the Harra, I thought I could not have dreamed of such a direful country; it is like that (a thousand fold) which wearies the eye that looks down from Vesuvius to the south-eastward, where a European will hardly adventure with heavy heart to bewilder his feet; – but that had brought forth, in Arabia, léban and samn to the poor nomads. Where the Aarab alight in some cragged place, some wild bottom, it is our homestead of two or three desert nights and daylights, and there the hideous scars of basalt, the few thorn-tree scrogs and barren broom bushes, wear to our familiar acquaintance, and they become even of our human affections, so that we are unwilling to leave them; – and doubtless the home-born Mahûby is thus affectioned to his foster Harra. They reasoning as simple men, commonly suppose a great part of the world to be thus, lava country; not their children alone, but men and women have inquired of me, 'Is your dîra, Khalîl, Harra or sand plains?'

– Beside the Aarab and their cattle, there is nearly no life upon the Harra. In this pure airy height hardly the flies follow us, which abound even in the waste nomad dîras. There is here but a small black solitary bird of slender form, less than a thrush, with certain white feathers, the *sweydîa*, which is, as our little red-breast, a cheerful neighbour to mankind. Many a time the passenger hears at unawares her short descant ringing upon the waste moors, in perplext desert ways, in the awe and the Titanic ruins of desolate mountains, with a silver sweetness, as it were the voice to his soul of some benign spirit. Of great ground beasts, only wolves prowl in the wind

of our mountain menzils: they are more in number upon the
Harra, and bolder than in the plain dîras. The nights, so serene
in Arabia, were yet fresh at this altitude in the first weeks of
June; even the summer days are here airy. I found one morning, at the sun-rising, 79° F., 90° at the jaila, and about mid-
day 95° in the tent's shadow. This high land is intolerably
cold in winter; Beduin passengers can hardly stand against the
biting blast of it: even the wild beasts have then forsaken
the Harra. The Moahîb at that time retire to the Teháma, and
shelter themselves in the bottom of the Wady Jizzl; where
they find plenty of dry tamarisk timber, *tûrfah*, which will glow
all night in their closed worsted tents: and the Beduins having
but a loose cotton tunic upon their lean bodies, and a wide
mantle, and the most of them lying down without a coverlet,
yet they can say, 'we suffer little then or nothing from the cold.'
In the day-time they comfort themselves with sips of coffee
or milk made hot; the winter mid-day sun is always warm
there.

That we had to drink in the lava country is pool-water,
black, thick and fetid. Commonly after two or three camel
waterings the pool is drawn to the dregs, and that water will
sooner foul than white linen; yet of this the nomads are fain to
fill their girbies and be thankful: – there is none other. But
worse! some will go down to wash themselves, if they see no
sheykh by to forbid them, and will there steep and wring out
their rusty tunics: – and always, where the nomad finds water
enough, there he makes religion to wash the body; in the menzils a man will carry out from the tent a bowl of water, and go
to purify himself in some secret place of the desert. The nomads might cleanse the pools (which now they must needs
abandon at half-water,) from the feculent lees of generations;
they have wit enough, but not public virtue for a common
labour; and the sheykh's authority cannot compel his free
tribesmen. There are found now and then stirring spirits
among them who, betwixt free will and their private advantage, will cleanse some wells which were stopped. ...

The Aueyrid. Eruption of Vesuvius in 1872

... When we look upon the Aueyrid, it were no light task to divine the story of that stupendous physiognomy of nature! A sandstone platform mountain is overlaid, two thousand square miles, to the brink, by a general effusion of lavas: then beyond the vulcanic crust, all around, we see a wasted border of under-cliffs and needles of the sandstone rock, down to the low-lying plains. – It seems thus that the lava floods have preserved the infirm underlying sand-rocks, whilst the old sandstone country was worn down and wasted by most slow decays, in such sort that this Aueyrid mass now stands six hundred fathoms aloft, like a mighty mountain, which was in old time even with the floor of the now low-lying sandstone plains!

Viewing the great thickness of lava floods, we can imagine the very old beginning of the Harra, – those streams upon streams of basalt, which appear in the walls of some wady-breaches of the desolate Aueyrid. Seeing the hillîan are no greater, we may suppose that many of them (as the Avernine *Monte Nuovo*) are the slags and the powder cast up in one strong eruption. The earlier over-streaming lavas are older than the configuration which is now of the land: – we are in an amazement, in a rainless country, to see the lava-basalt pan of the Harra, cleft and opened to a depth of a hundred fathoms to some valley-grounds, as Thirba. Every mass is worn in grooves in the infirmer parts, by aught that moves upon it; but what is this great outwearing of 'stones of iron,' indomitable and almost indestructible matter! We see in the cliff-inscriptions at Medáin, that the thickness of your nail is not wasted from a face of soft sandstone, under this climate, in nearly two thousand years!

Every pasty mass is crazed in the setting; and such kind of chinks we may suppose to be opened in the sandstone frame of this mountain shouldered upon an invading head of the plan-etary lavas; and that, swelling with tremendous violence, the lavas should be infused into many natural clefts, and, by some of them rising to the soil, there break forth with that infinite spitting and spouting of the super-heated fiery vapour of water, entangled and embodied in the lake of molten stone, which, with issue of lavas, is the stupendous elemental rage of a vulcanic eruption. In the year 1872 I was a witness of the great eruption of Vesuvius. Standing from the morning alone upon the top of the mountain, that day in which the great outbreak began, I waded ankle-deep in flour of sulphur upon a burning hollow soil of lava: in the midst was a mammel-like chimney, not long formed, fuming with a light corrosive breath; which to those in the plain had appeared by night as a fiery beacon with trickling lavas. Beyond was a new seat of the weak daily eruption, a pool of molten lava and wherefrom issued all that strong dinning noise and uncouth travail of the mountain; from thence was from time to time tossed aloft, and slung into the air, a swarm of half-molten wreathing missiles. I approached the dreadful ferment, and watched that fiery pool heaving in the sides and welling over, and swimming in the midst as a fount of metal, – and marked how there was cooled at the air a film, like that floating web upon hot milk, a soft drossy scum, which endured but for a moment, – in the next, with terrific blast as of a steam-gun, by the furious breaking in wind of the pent vapours rising from the infernal *magma* beneath, this pan was shot up sheetwise in the air, where, whirling as it rose with rushing sound, the slaggy sheet parted diversely, and I saw it slung out into many great and lesser shreds. The pumy writhen slags fell whissing again in the air, yet soft, from their often half-mile high parabolas, the most were great as bricks, a few were huge crusts as flag-stones. The pool-side spewed down a reeking gutter of lavas.

At afternoon, the weight of molten metal risen in the belly of the volcano hill (which is vulcanic powder wall and old lava veins, and like the plasterer's puddle in his pan of sand,) had eaten away, and leaking at mid-height through the corroded hillsides, there gushed out a cataract of lava. Upon some unhappy persons who approached there fell a spattered fiery shower of vulcanic powder, which in that fearful moment burned through their clothing, and, scorched to death, they lived hardly an hour after. A young man was circumvented and swallowed up in torments by the pursuing foot of lava, whose current was very soon as large as Thames at London Bridge. – The lower lavas rising after from the deep belly of the volcano, and in which is locked a greater expansive violence, way is now blasted to the head of the mountain, and vast outrageous destruction upward is begun.

Before the morrow, the tunnel and cup of the mountain is become a cauldron of lavas, great as a city, whose simmering (a fearful earth-shuddering hubbub) troubles the soil for half a day's journey all round. The upper liquid mineral matter, blasted into the air, and dispersed minutely with the shooting steam, is suddenly cooled to falling powder; the sky of rainy vapour and smoke which hangs so wide over, and enfolds the hideous vulcanic tempest, is overcharged with electricity; the thunders that break forth cannot be heard in that most tremendous dinning. The air is filled many days, for miles round, with heavy rumour, and this fearful bellowing of the mountain. The meteoric powder rains with the wind over a great breadth of country; small cinders fall down about the circuit of the mountain, the glowing up-cast of great slags fall after their weight higher upon the flanks and nearer the mouth of the eruption; and among them are some quarters of strange rocks, which were rent from the underlying frame of the earth (5,000 feet lower), – upon Vesuvius, they are limestone. The eruption seen in the night, from the saddle of the mountain, is a mile-great sheaf-like blast of purple-glowing and red flames belching fearfully and uprolling back smoke from the vulcanic gulf, now half a mile wide. The terrible light of the planetary conflagration is dimmed by the thick veil of vulcanic powder falling; the darkness, the black dust, is such that we cannot see our hands, nor the earth under our feet; we lean upon rocking walls, the mountain incessantly throbs under us: at a mile's distance, in that huge loudness of the elemental strife, one cannot almost hear his own or his neighbour's voice. – Days pass and the hidden subterraneous passions slowly expire, the eruption is at an end.

The vulcanic womb delivered of its superfluous burden, the column of lava is fallen, in the last oscillations, to the hollow roots of the hill; where the fiery force remains under much crusting over and cooling. Massy hardening in any great conduit, to not many fathoms, may be hardly, as we have experience, in two or three generations. If many ages pass of repose, the old vulcanic tunnel, near the floor of the earth, may be then somewhat deeply sealed. As for any pocket of the molten mineral, low seated, as a lake beneath, we cannot suppose it to be set by cooling, in very long space as measured by years of the planet; nor intermeation to cease with the molten magma of the deep of the earth. When the vulcanic outbreak revives, we may suppose such womb of molten metal swelling forth to a new delivery; – it might be incensed by some percolation of sea-water. Slowly must the basaltic stop-rock relent again upon the rising vulcanic heat; or sudden way may be opened by rending upward of the irrepressible elemental force. – Is this word 'lava,' *lâba* in the Arabic, come into our new European languages from the Moorish Italian of Sicily? where the usurping Arabs found so much which they name *lâba*. Laba of the Arabians (where I treat of the great Harras best known to me, the Aueyrid, and the Harrat Kheybar) is not all that which we understand by lava, but is said of the basaltic-massy, the drawn and sharp-set and nearly vitreous kinds: the slags, the drossy, the clinker crusts, cinder and pumice-stone are not called laba. – Thus far of the vulcanic country.

The Fejîr at Teyma. Isa and Zeyd

The Fejîr watered once more at Teyma; I saw the great cattle of our households driven in, and after the watering their burden camels were couched by the booths: for Méshan and the rest would remove in the morning and return to the desert. Among the beasts I found my old nâga, and saw that she was badly galled on the chine; the wound might hardly be healed in fifteen or twenty days, but I must journey to-morrow. I brought nomad friends to look at her, who found that she had been ridden and mishandled, the marks of the saddle-tree cords yet appearing in the hairy hide. It could not be other than the fault of Zeyd's herdman Îsa, a young man, whom I had befriended. So taking him by the beard before them all, I cursed 'the father of this Yahûdy.' The young man, strong and resolute, laid hands upon my shoulders and reviled me for a Nasrâny; but I said, 'Sirrah, thou shouldst have kept her better,' and held him fast by the beard. The tribesmen gathered about us kept silence, even his own family, all being my friends, and they had so good an opinion of my moving only in a just matter. Îsa seeing that his fault was blamed, must suffer this rebuke, so I plucked down the weled's comely head to his breast, and let him go. An effort of strength had been un-becoming, and folly it were to suffer any perturbation for thing that is without remedy; I had passed over his fault, but I thought that to take it hardly was a necessary policy. Also the Arabs would have a man like the pomegranate, a bitter-sweet, mild and affectionate with his friends in security, but tempered with a just anger if the time call him to be a defender in his own or in his neighbour's cause. Isa's father came bye and bye to my tent, and in a demiss voice the old hind acknowledged his son's error; 'Yet, Khalîl, why didst thou lay upon me that re-proach, when we have been thy friends, to name me before the people Yahûdy?' But as old Sâlih saw me smile he smiled again, and took the right hand which I held forth to him.

I found Zeyd, at evening, sitting upon one of the clay benches near the haddàj; he was waiting in the midst of the town, in hope that some acquaintance of the villagers coming by before the sun's going down, might call him to supper. Returning after an hour I found Zeyd yet in the place, his al-most black visage set betwixt the nomad patience of hunger and his lordly disdain of the Teyâmena. Zeyd might have seemed a prosperous man, if he had been liberal, to lay up friendship in heaven and in this world; but the shallow hand must bring forth leanness and faint willing of a man's neigh-bours again. I stayed to speak a word with Zeyd, and saw him draw at last his galliûn, the remedy of hunger; then he called a lad, who issued from the next dàr, to fetch a live coal, and the young villager obeyed him.

In the first hour of this night there fell upon us a tempest of wind and rain. The tall palms rocked, and bowing in all their length to the roaring gusts it seemed they would be rent by the roots. I found shelter with Méshan in the house of Féjr our host; but the flat roof of stalks and rammed earth was soon drenched, and the unwonted wet streamed down inwardly by the walls. Méshan spoke of my setting forth to-morrow with the Bishr, and, calling Féjr to witness, the timid friendly man sought to dissuade me, 'also Zeyd, he said, had forsaken me, who should have commended me to them; it was likely I should see him no more.' – 'Should I wonder at that? – Zeyd has no heart,' they answered both together: 'Ay, billah, Zeyd has no heart,' and repeated *ma láhu kalb*, He has no heart! Féjr was suffering an acute pain of 'the stone', *el-hása* a malady common in these parts, though the country is sand-stone; yet sometimes it may be rather an inflammation, for they think it comes of their going unshod upon the burning soil. When the weather lulled, we went towards our wet tents to sleep out the last night at Teyma.

Journeying with the Bishr

The women of the hauta loaded the tents and their gear, and I saw our Aarab departing before the morning light. Zeyd rode in upon his mare, from the village where he had slept; 'If I would go now with him, he would bring me, he said, to the Bishr and bind them for my better security'; but Zeyd could not dwell, he must follow his Aarab, and I could not be ready in a moment; I saw the Fukara companions no more. A stranger, who passed by, lent me a hand in haste, as I loaded upon my old nâga: and I drove her, still resisting and striving to follow the rest, half a mile about the walls to those Bishr, who by fortune were not so early movers. There, I betook myself to *Hayzàn*, the man who had agreed to conduct me: and of another I bought the frame of a riding-saddle, that I might lay the load upon my wounded camel. They were charging their cattle, and we set forward immediately.

Leaving Teyma on the right hand, we passed forth, between the Érbah peaks and Ghrenéym, to the desert; soon after the bleak border was in sight of the Nefûd, also trending eastward. We journeyed on in rain and thick weather; at four of the afternoon they alighted, in the wet wilderness, at an height of 600 feet above Teyma, and the hungry camels were dismissed to pasture— The Beduin passengers kindled fires, laying on a certain resinous bush, although it be a plant eaten by the cattle, and though full of the drops of the rain, it immediately blazed up. They fenced themselves as they could from the moist wind and the driving showers, building bushes about them; and these they anchored with heavy stones.

We removed at sunrise: the sudden roaring and ruckling hubbub of the Beduins' many camels grudging to be loaded, made me remember the last year's Haj journeys! before ten in the morning, we had Helwàn in front, and clearer weather. The Bishr journeyed a little southward of east, Birrd (Bírd) was visible: at two, afternoon, we alighted, and dismissed the camels to pasture; the height was here as yesterday, nearly 4,000 feet. The rain had ceased and Hayzàn went out hawking. There were two or three men in this company who carried their falcons with them, riding on the saddle peaks, in their hoods and jesses, or sitting upon the master's fist. Sometimes the birds were cast off, as we journeyed, at the few starting small hares of the desert; the hawks' wings were all draggled in the wet: the birds flew without courage wheeling at little height, after a turn or two they soused, and the falconer running in, poor Wat is taken. Thus Hayzàn took a hare every day, he brought me a portion from his pot at evening, and that was much to the comfort of our extenuated bodies. I missed Hannas and his cousin *Rayyàn*, in the way; they had left our journeying Aarab to go to their people encamped more to the southward, above the *Harrat Kheyber*. To-day I was left alone with the Auájy, – somewhat violent dealing and always inhospitable Beduins, but in good hope of the sooner arriving at Hâyil. We sat down to drink coffee with the sheykh, Misshel, who would make it himself. This 'ruler of the seven tribes' roasted, pounded, boiled, and served the cheerful mixture with his own hand. Misshel poured me out but one cup, and to his tribesmen two or three. Because this shrew's deed was in disgrace of my being a Nasrâny I exclaimed, 'Here is billah a great sheykh and little kahwa! Is it the custom of the Auájy, O Misshel, that a guest should sit among you who are all drinking, with his cup empty?' Thus challenged, Misshel poured me out unwillingly, muttering between the teeth some word of his fanatical humour, *yâ fárkah!*

The third day early, we came in sight of J. Irnàn; and I said to my neighbour, 'Ha, Irnàn!' A chiding woman, who was riding within ear-shot, cried out, 'Oh, what hast thou to do with Irnàn?' At half-afternoon we alighted in high ground, upon the rising of Ybba Moghrair, where I found by the instrument, 4,000 feet. Some camels were now seen at a distance, of Aarab *Ibn Mertaad*, allies of theirs. When we were lodged, there came a woman to my tent; who asked for needles and thread (such trifles are acceptable gifts in the khála); but as she would harshly bargain with the weary stranger I bade her begone. She answered, with an ill look, 'Ha! Nasrâny, but ere long we shall take all these things from thee.' I saw, with an aversion (of race), that all these Bishr housewives wore the *berkoa* or heathenish face-clout, above which only the two hollow ill-affected eyes appeared. This desolation of the woman's face was a sign to me that I journeyed now in another country, that is jealous (and Waháby) Nejd; – for even the waste soil of Arabia is full of variety.

The fourth morning from Teyma, we were crossing the high rugged ground of sandstone rocks behind Ybba Moghrair. Strange is the discomfort of rain and raw air in Arabia, when our eyes, wont to be full of the sun, look upon wan mists drooping to the skirts of these bone-dry mountains! wind, with rain, blew strongly through the open wilderness in the night-time. We lodged, at evening, beside some booths of Mertaad Arabs, and I went over bye and bye to their cheerful watch-fires. Where I entered the fire-light before a principal beyt, the householder received me kindly and soon brought me a vast bowl of fresh camel-milk. They asked me no questions, – to keep silence is the host's gentleness, and they had seen my white tent standing before sunset. When I was rising to depart, the man, with a mild gesture, bade me sit still. I saw a sheep led in to be sacrificed; – because Misshel had alighted by them, he would make a great-supper. *Afid* Ibn Mertaad, this good sheykh, told me his Aarab went up in droughty years to the Shimbel, and as far as Palmyra, Keriateyn! I lay down and slumbered in the hospitable security of his worsted tent till his feast was ready, and then they sent and called Misshel and the Auájy sheykhs. Their boiled mutton (so far from the Red Sea coast) was served upon a mess of that other rice-kind, temmn, which is brought from el-Irâk, and is (though they esteem it less) of better savour and sustenance. Misshel, and every man of these Bishr tribesmen, when they rose after supper and had blessed their host, bore away – I had not seen it before – a piece of the meat and a bone, and that was for his housewife journeying with him.

Upon the morrow, the fifth from Teyma, we ascended over the very rugged highlands eastward by a way named the *Derb Zillâj*, where the height was 4,500 feet, and I saw little flower-ets, daughters of the rain, already sprung in the desert. At noon we reached Misshel's menzil of only few tents standing together upon this wide sandstone mountain platform where we now arrived, *el-Kharram*, the altitude is 5,400 feet: the ther-mometer in the open showed 80° F. From hence the long mountain train appeared above the clouds, of Irnàn, in the north, nearly a day distant.

At afternoon there came in two strange tribesmen, that ar-rived from a dîra in the southward near Medina: they said, there was no rain fallen in the Jeheyna dîra, nor in all the country of the W. el-Humth! A bowl of dates was set before them; and the Beduin guests, with the desert comity, bade me [a guest] draw near to eat with them: – Misshel, although I was sitting in his tent, had not bidden the Nasrâny! I took and ate two of the fruits, that there might be 'the bread and salt' be-tween us. I had with me a large Moorish girdle of red woollen; Misshel now said, I should give it him, or else, billah, he would 'take me' and my things for a booty. The girdle of the settled countries, *kúmr*, is coveted by the nomad horsemen, that binding thus the infirmer parts of the body they think a man may put forth his strength the better. 'The girdle, I said, was necessary to me; yet let Misshel give me a strong young camel, and I would give him my old nâga and the girdle.' – This man's camels were many more than two hundred! 'Well then, Misshel answered, he would take me.' – 'See the date-stones in my hand, thou canst not, Misshel, there is now "bread and salt" between us,' – 'But that will not avail thee; what and if to-morrow I drive thee from us, thou and thy old nâga, canst thou find a way in the wilderness and return to el-Héjr?' – 'I know it is four journeys south of west, God visit it upon thee, and I doubt not it may please Ullah, I shall yet come forth.' – 'But all the country is full of habalîs.' – 'Rich Misshel, wouldst thou strip a poor man! but all these threats are idle, I am thy guest.' – They believe the Nasâra to be expert riders, so it was said to me, 'Tomorrow would I meet Misshel on horse-back, and I should be armed with a pistol?' I answered, 'If it must be so, I would do my endeavour.' – 'Nay, in the morning Khalîl shall mount his old nâga (said Misshel again) and ride to Medáin Sâlih'; so with a sturdy smile he gave up the quest, seeing he could not move me. His younger son, who sat dropsical in the father's tent, here said a good word, 'Well, let Khalîl sleep upon it. – and to-morrow they would give me a nâga for the Khuèyra and the girdle.' – In their greediness to spoil the castaway life, whom they will not help forward, the Arabs are viler than any nation!

Hayzàn in the morning bade me prepare to depart, Askar and some companions were setting out for Hâyil, and we might ride with them; he inquired 'Was my old nâga able to run with thelûls?' – 'She is an old camel, and no dromedary.' – 'Then we must ride apart from them.' Hayzàn, when he had received his money, said he could not accompany me himself, '*but this other man,*' whom he feigned to be his brother, besides he named him falsely. – Hard it were to avoid such frauds of the Beduins! Misshel said, 'Well, I warrant him, go in peace.' I made the condition that my bags should be laid upon his thelûl, and I might mount her myself; so we set forward.

This rafîk looked like a wild man: Askar and his fellowship were already in the way before us; we passed by some shallow water-holes that had been newly cleared; I wondered to see

them in this high ground. We came then to the brow, on the
north of the Kharram mountain, here very deep and precipitous to the plain below; in such a difficult place the camels,
holding the fore-legs stiff and plumping from ledge to ledge,
make a shift to climb downward. So, descending, as we could,
painfully to the underlying sand desert, and riding towards a
low sandstone coast, *Abbassîeh*, west of Misma, we bye and
bye overtook Askar's company. Coming nigh the east end of
the mountain, they thought they espied habalîs lurking in the
rocks, 'Heteym of the Nefûd, and foemen,' where landlopers
had been seen the day before. 'Khalîl (said Askar) can your
nâga keep pace with us? we are Beduw, and *nenhash (nahájj)*!
we will hie from any danger upon our thelûls; hasten now the
best thou canst, or we must needs leave thee behind us, so
thou wilt fall alone into the hands of the robbers.' They all put
their light and fresh thelûls to the trot: my old loaded nâga,
and jaded after the long journey from Teyma, fell immediately
behind them, and such was her wooden gait I could not almost suffer it. I saw all would be a vain effort in any peril; the
stars were contrary for this voyage, none of my companions
had any human good in them, but Askar only. My wild rafîk,
whom I had bound at our setting out by the most solemn oath,
'upon the herb stem,' that he would not forsake me, now cried
out, 'Wellah-billah, he would abandon me if I mended not my
pace (which was impossible); he must follow his companions,
and was their rafîk,' so they ran on a mile or two.

The last days' rain had cooled the air; this forenoon was overcast, but the sun sometimes shone out warmly. When with
much ado I came up to my flying fellowship, I said to Askar,
'Were the enemies upon you, would you forsake me who am
your way-fellow?' 'I would, he said, take thee up back-rider
on my thelûl, and we will run one fortune together; Khalîl, I
will not forsake thee.' They were in hope to lodge with Aarab
that night, before we came to the Misma mountain, now before us. The plain was sand, and reefs of sandstone rocks, in
whose hollows were little pools of the sweet rain-water. At
half-afternoon they descried camels very far in front; we
alighted, and some climbed upon the next crags to look out,

who soon reported that those Aarab were rahîl, and they seemed about to encamp. We rode then towards the Misma mountain, till we came to those Beduins; they were but a family of Shammar, faring in the immense solitudes. And doubtless, seeing us, they had felt a cold dread in their loins, for we found them shrunk down in a low ground, with their few camels crouched by them, and the housewife had not built the beyt. They watched us ride by them, with inquiet looks, for there is no amity between Annezy and Shammar. – That which contains their enmities is only the injunction of the Emir. I would have asked these Beduins to let me drink water, for all day we had ridden vehemently without drawing bridle, and the light was now nearly spent; but my companions pricked forward. I bade my rafîk lend me at last his more easy thelûl, that such had been our covenant; but the wild fellow denied me, and would not slack his pace. I was often, whilst they trotted, fallen so far back as to be in danger of losing them out of sight, and always in dread that my worn-out nâga might sink under me, and also cast her young.

At Askar's word, when they saw I might not longer endure the fellow assented to exchange riding with me, and I mounted his dromedary; we entered then at a low gap in the Misma near the eastern end of this long-ranging sandstone reef. My companions looked from the brow, for any black booths of Aarab, in the plain desert beyond to the horizon. One thought he saw tents very far distant, but the rest doubted, and now the sun was setting. We came down by the deep driven sand upon the sides of the mountain, at a windy rush, which seemed like a bird's flight, of the thelûls under us, though in the even any horse may overtake them. The seat upon a good thelûl 'swimming', as say their ancient poets, over sand-ground, is so easy that an inured rider may sometimes hardly feel his saddle. ...

... We had ridden two hours since the sunset, and in this long day's race the best part of fifty miles; and now they consulted together, were it not best to dismount and pass the night as we were? We had not broken our fast to-day, and carried neither food nor water, so confident they were that every night we should sup with Aarab. They agreed to ride somewhat further; and it was not long before we saw a glimpsing of Beduin watch-fires. We drew near them in an hour more, and I heard the evening sounds of a nomad menzil; the monotonous mirth of the children, straying round from the watch-fires and singing at the houses of hair. We arrived so silently, the dogs had not barked. There were two or three booths. When the Aarab perceived us, all voices were hushed: their cheerful fires, where a moment before we saw the people sitting, were suddenly quenched with sand. We were six or seven riders, and they thought we might be an hostile ghrazzu. Alighting in silence, we sat down a little aloof; none of us so much as whispered to his companion by name; for the open desert is full of old debts for blood. At a strange meeting, and yet more at such hours, the nomads are in suspense of mind and mistrust of each other. When, impatient of their mumming, I would have said Salaam! they prayed me be silent. After the whisperers within had sufficiently taken knowledge of our peaceable demeanour, one approaching circumspectly, gave us the word of peace, *Salaam aleyk*, and it was readily answered by us all again, *Aleykom es-salaam*. After this sacrament of the lips between Beduw, there is no more doubt among them of any evil turn. The man led Askar and his fellowship to his beyt, and I went over to another with Nasr my rafîk and a nomad whom we had met riding with his son in the desert beyond Misma. The covered coals were raked up, and we saw the fires again.

What these Aarab were we could not tell, neither knew they what men we were; we have seen the desert people ask no questions of the guest, until he have eaten meat; yet after some little discoursing between them, as of the rain this year, and the pasture, they may each commonly come to guess the other's tribe. When I asked my rough companion 'What tribesmen be these?' he answered in a whisper, 'he knew not yet'; soon after we understood by the voices that they had recognized Askar in the other tent. He was the son of their own high-sheykh; and these Aarab were Wélad Sleyman, a division of

Bishr, though the men's faces were nearly unknown to each other. Our host having walked over to the chief tent to hear the news, we were left with his housewife, and I saw her beginning to bray corn with a bat, in a wooden mortar, a manner not used by the southern Beduw of my former acquaintance; but bruised corn is here as often served for the guest-meal as temmn. The year was now turned to winter in the waste wilderness, they had fenced round their booths from the late bitter rain and wind with dry bushes.

There came in one from the third remaining tent, and supped with us. I wondered, seeing this tribesman, and he wondered to look upon me: he a Beduwy, wearing the Turkey red cap, *tarbûsh*, and an old striped gown *kumbâz*, the use of the civil border countries! When I asked what man he was, he answered that being 'weak' he was gone a soldiering to Sham and had served the Dowla for reals: and now he was come home to the nomad life, with that which he esteemed a pretty bundle of silver. In this the beginning of his prosperity he had bought himself camels, and goats and sheep, he would buy also my old nâga for the price I set upon her, seven reals, to slaughter in the feast for his deceased father. – Where Beduins are soldiery, this seemed to me a new world! Yet afterwards, I have learned that there are tribesmen of Bishr and Harb, Ageyl riders in the great cities. The Beduin who saw in the stranger his own town life at Damascus, was pleased to chat long with me, were it only to say over the names of the chief sûks of the plenteous great city. He should bring his reals in the morning; and, would I stay here, he would provide for my further journey to Hâyil, whither he must go himself shortly. – But when my rafîk called me to mount before the dawn, I could not stay to expect him. Afterwards finding me at Hâyil, he blamed me that I had not awaited him, and inquired for my nâga, which I had already sold at a loss. He told me that at our arriving that night, they had taken their matchlocks to shoot at us; but seeing the great bags on my camel, and hearing my voice, they knew me to be none of the nomads, and that we were not riding in a ghrazzu.

We hasted again over the face of the wilderness to find a

great menzil of Aarab, where my fellowship promised themselves to drink coffee. Sheykhs accustomed to the coffee-tent think it no day of their lives, if they have not sipped kahwa; and riding thus, they smoked tittun in their pipe-heads incessantly. We arrived in the dawning and dismounted, as before, in two fellowships, Askar and his companions going over to the sheykhly coffee-tent: this is their desert courtesy, not to lay a burden upon any household. The people were Shammar, and they received us with their wonted hospitality. Excellent dates (of other savour and colour than those of el-Ally and Teyma) were here set before us, and a vast bowl – that most comfortable refreshment in the wilderness – of their camels' léban. Then we were called to the sheykh's tent, where the sheykh himself, with magnanimous smiles, already prepared coffee. When he heard I was an hakîm, he bade bring in his little ailing grand-daughter. I told the mother that we were but in passage, and my remedy could only little avail her child. The sheykh, turning to my companions, said therefore, 'That I must be some very honest person.' – 'It is thus, Askar answered him, and ye may be sure of him in all.' The sheykh reached me the bowl, and after I had supped a draught, he asked me, 'What countryman I was?' I answered 'An Engleysy,' so he whispered in my ear, 'Engreys! – then a Nasrâny?' I said aloud, 'Ay billah'; the good sheykh gave me a smile again, in which his soul said, 'I will not betray thee.' – The coffee ready, he poured out for me before them all. When my companions had swallowed the scalding second cup, they rose in their unlucky running haste to depart: the sheykh bade me stay a moment to drink a little more of his pleasant milk and strengthen myself.

We rode on in the waste wilderness eastward, here passing out of the Misma district, and having upon the right-hand certain mountains, landmarks of that great watering-place *Baitha Nethîl*. From the Kharram we might have ridden to Hâyil eastward of the mountain *Aija*; but that part they thought would be now empty of the wandering Beduins. This high and open plain, – 3,800 feet, is all strewed with shales as it were of iron-stone; but towards noon I saw we were come in a granite country, and we passed under a small basalt mountain, coal-black and shining. The crags rising from this soil were grey granite; *Ibrân*, a blackish mountain, appeared upon our horizon, some hours distant, ranging to the northward. A little later we came in Nefûd sand and, finding there wild hay, the Beduins alighted, to gather provender. This was to bait their cattle in the time when they should be lying at Hâyil, where the country next about is *mâhal*, a barrenness of soil hardly less than that which lies about Teyma. To make hay were unbecoming in a great sheykh: and whilst the rest were busy, Askar digged with his hands in the sand to the elbow, to sound the depth of the late fallen rain, this being all they might look for till another autumn, and whereof the new year's herb must spring. Showers had lately fallen, sixteen days together; yet we saw almost no sign in the wilderness soil of small freshets. When Askar had put down his bare arm nearly to the shoulder, he took up the old sandy drought; the moisture of the rain had not sunk to a full yard! The seasonable rains are partial in Arabia, which in these latitudes is justly accounted a nearly rainless country. Whilst it rained in the Kharram no showers were fallen in the Jeheyna dîra; and so little fell at Kheybar, a hundred miles distant, that in the new year's months there sprang nearly no rabîa in those lava mountains.

We had not ridden far in this Nefûd, when at half-afternoon we saw a herd of camels moving before us at pasture in their slow dispersed manner; we found beyond where the nomad booths were pitched in an hollow place. Beduins, when encamping few together, choose deep ground, where they are sheltered from the weather, and by day the black beyts are not so soon discerned, nor their watch-fires in the night-time. These also were Shammar, which tribe held all the country now before us to the Jebel villages; – they were scattered by families as in a peaceable country of the Emir's dominion, with many wells about them. Flies swarming here upon the sand, were a sign that we approached the palm settlements. Whenever we came to tents in this country the Aarab immediately asked us of, very earnestly, What of the rain? tell us is there much fallen in the Auájy dîra?' My companions ever answered with the same word, *La tanshud*, 'Ask not of it.' If any questioned them, 'Who was this stranger they brought with them?' the Auájy responded, with what meaning I could not tell, '*El-kheyr Ullah*.' The sheykh in this menzil would have bought my nâga, engaging as well to convey me to Hâyil after a few days in which I should be his guest.

I thought at least we should have rested here this night over; but my companions when they rose from supper took again their thelûls to ride and run, and Nasr with them; they would not tarry a moment for me at the bargain of the nâga. – Better I thought to depart then with these whom I know, and be sure to arrive at Hâyil, than remain behind them in booths of unknown Beduins; besides, we heard that a large Shammar encampment lay not much before us, and a coffee-sheykh: Askar promised to commit me to those Aarab, if he might persuade my rafîk to remain with me. I was broken with this rough riding: the heart every moment leaping to my throat, which torment they call *katu 'l-kalb*, or heart-cutting. They scoured before me all the hours of the day, in their light riding, so that with less than keeping a good will, death at length would have been a welcome deliverance out of present miseries. The Aarab lay pitched under the next mountain; but riding further in the darkness two hours, and not seeing their watch-fires, the Auájy would then have ridden on all that long night, to come the earlier, they said, to Hâyil. They must soon have forsaken me, I could not go much further, and my decrepit nâga fainted under me: bye and bye Askar, overcome by drowsiness, murmured to his companions, 'Let us alight then and sleep.' A watch-fire now appeared upon our right hand, which had been hidden by some unevenness of the ground, but they neglected it, for the present sweetness of sleeping: we alighted, and binding the camels' knees, lay down to rest by our cattle in the sandy desert.

We had not ridden on the morrow an hour when, at sunrising, we descried many black booths of a Beduin encampment, where the Auájy had promised me rest: but as ever the

scalding coffee was past their throats, and they had swallowed
a few of the Shammary's dates, they rose to take their dromedaries again. Such promises of nomads are but sounds in the
air; neither would my wild and brutish rafîk hear my words,
nor could Askar persuade him; 'Wellah, I have no authority,'
said he; and Nasr cried, 'Choose thee, Khalîl, whether thou
wilt sit here or else ride with us; but I go in my company.'
What remained, but to hold the race with them? now to me an
agony, and my nâga was ready to fall under me. As we rode,
'It is plain, said Askar, that Khalîl may not hold out; wilt thou
turn back, Khalîl, to the booths? and doubt not that they will
receive thee.' – 'How receive me? you even now lied to them
at the kahwa, saying ye were not Auájy, and you have not
commended me to them: what when they understand that I
am a Nasrâny? also this Nasr, my rafîk, forsakes me!' – 'We
shall come to-day, they said, to a settlement, and will leave
thee there.' We had neglected to drink at the tents, and riding
very thirsty, when the sun rose high, we had little hope to find
more rain-pools in a sandy wilderness. Afterward espying
some little gleam under the sun far off, they hastened thither,
– but it was a glistening clay bottom, and in the midst a puddle,
which we all forsook. The altitude of this plain is 3,700 feet,
and it seemed to fall before us to J.Ajja which now appeared
as a mighty bank of not very high granite mountain, and
stretching north and south. The soil is granite-sand and grit,
and rolling stones and rotten granite rock. We passed, two
hours before noon, the ruins of a hamlet of one well which had
been forsaken five years before. Askar said, 'The cattle perished after some rainless years for want of pasture, and the few
people died of the small-pox,' – not seldom calamities of the
small out-settlements, in Arabia. When I asked the name of
the place, he answered shortly, *Melûn Tâlibuhu*, which might
mean 'Cursed is everyone that inquireth thereof.'

We found a pool of clear rain in the rock, which, warmed in
the sun, seemed to us sweeter than milk. There we satisfied
our thirst, and led our beasts to drink, which had run an
hundred and thirty miles without pasture or water, since the
Kharram. His companions before we mounted went to cut

a little more dry grass, and Askar said to me, 'Khalîl, the people where we are going are jealous. Let them not see thee writing, for be sure they will take it amiss; but wouldst thou write, write covertly, and put away these leaves of books. Thou wast hitherto with the Beduw, and the Beduw have known thee what thou art; but, hearest thou? they are not like good-hearted, in yonder villages!' We rode again an hour or two and saw the green heads of palms, under the mountain, of a small village, where, they said, five or six families dwelt, *Jefeyfa*. Upon the north I saw *J. Tâly*, a solitary granitic mountain on the wilderness horizon. My company, always far in advance, were now ridden out of my sight. I let them pass, I could no longer follow them, not doubting that with these landmarks before me I should shortly come to the inhabited. There I lighted upon a deep-beaten path, – such are worn in the hard desert soil, near settlements which lie upon common ways, by the generations of nomad passengers. I went on foot, leading my fainting camel at a slow pace, till I espied the first heads of palms, and green lines of the plantations of Môgug. At length I descried Nasr returning out of the distance to meet me. At the entering of the place my jaded camel fell down bellowing, this a little delayed us; but Nasr raised and driving her with cruel blows, we entered Môgug about an hour and a half after noon.

I wondered to see the village full of ruins and that many of their palms were dead and sere, till I learned that Môg(k)ug(k) had been wasted by the plague a few years before. Their house-building is no more the neat clay-brick work which we see at Teyma, but earthen walls in layers, with some cores of hard sun-dried brick laid athwart in them; the soil is here granitic. The crumbling aspect of the place made me think of certain oases which I had seen years before in the Algerian Sáhara. Their ground-water is luke-warm, as in all the Arabian country, and of a corrupt savour; the site is feverish, their dates are scaly, dry, and not well-tasting. We went towards the sheykh's kahwa, where the companions had preceded us, and met with the good sheykh who was coming forth to meet me. He led me friendly by the hand, and bade his man straw down green garden stalks for our camels. When we were seated in the coffee-room there entered many of the villagers, who without showing any altered countenance – it might be for some well-said word of Askar beforehand – seemed to regard me favourably. Seeing all so well disposed, I laid before the sheykh my quarrel with Nasr, and was supported by Askar, he allowing that my nâga could not go forward.

Even now they would mount immediately, and ride all night to be at Hâyil ere day. 'He would go in their company, said Nasr, and if I could not ride with them, he must forsake me here.' The sheykh of Môgug ruled that since the camel could not proceed, Nasr, who had taken wages, must remain with me, or leaving so much of his money as might pay another man (to convey me to Hâyil) he might depart freely. The elf, having, by the sheykh's judgement, to disburse a real, chose rather to remain with me. Askar and his fellowship rose again hastily from the dates and water, to ride to Hâyil. This long way from the Kharram they had ridden in a continued running, carrying with them neither food nor water-skins, nor coffee: they trusted to their good eyesight to find every day the Aarab. All were young men in the heat of their blood, that rode in a sort of boast of their fresh endurance and ability. I asked Askar, wherefore this haste, and why they did not in any place take a little repose. *Answer*: 'That we may be the sooner at home again; and to stay at the menzils by the way were unbecoming (*ayb*).' When they were gone, the villagers sitting in the kahwa – they were Shammar – blamed my companions as *Annezy!* These narrow jealousies of neighbours often furthered me, as I journeyed without favour in this vast land of Arabia.

Here I first saw Bagdad wares, from the sûk at Hâyil: the men of Môgug no longer kindled the galliûns with flint and steel, but with the world-wide Vienna *Zündhölzer*, – we were in the world again! Dim was their rudely-built coffee-hall, and less cleanly than hospitable; the earthen floor where we sat was littered with old date-stones of the common service to daily guests. The villagers were of a kindly humour; and pleased themselves in conversing with the stranger, so far as their short notice might stretch, of foreign countries and religions: they lamented that the heathen yet resisted the truth, and more especially the Nasâra, in whom was a well of the arts, and learning. They reached me from time to time their peaceable galliûns. I thought the taste of their bitter green tobacco, in this extremity of fatigue, of incomparable sweetness, and there was a comfortable repose in those civil voices after the wild malignity of the Bishr tongues. A young man asked me, 'Could I read? – had I any books?'; He was of Môgug, and their schoolmaster. I put in his hand a geography written in the Arabic tongue by a learned American missionary of Bey-rût. – The young man perused and hung his head over it in the dull chamber, with such a thirsty affection of letters, as might in a happier land have ripened in the large fields of learning: at last closing the book, when the sun was going down, he laid it on his head in token how highly he esteemed it, – an Oriental gesture which I have not seen again in Arabia, where is so little (or nothing) of '*Orientalism*'. He asked me, 'Might he buy the book? – (and because I said nay) might he take it home then to read in the night? which I granted.

A tall dark man entered the kahwa, I saw he was a stranger from the north, of a proud carriage and very well clad. Coldly he saluted the company, and sat down: he arrived from *Gofar* where he had mounted this morning. The dates were set before him, and looking round when he remembered one or two sitting here, with whom he had met in former years, he greeted them and, rising solemnly, kissed and asked of their welfare. He was a Shammary of Irâk; his Beduin dîra lay 250 miles from hence. Long and enviously he looked upon me, as I sat with my kerchief cast back in the heat, then he inquired, 'Who is he? – eigh! a Nasrâny, say ye! and I knew it: this is one, O people! who has some dangerous project, and ye cannot tell what; this man is one of the Frankish nation!' I answered, 'It is known to all who sit here, that I am an Engleysy, and should I be ashamed of that? what man art thou, and wherefore in these parts?' – 'I am at Hâyil for the Emir's business! –

wellah he said, turning to the company, he can be none other than a spy, one come to search out the country! tell me what is reported of this man; if he question the Aarab, and does he write their answers?' – A villager said, 'Years before one had been here, a stranger, who named himself a Moslem, but he could guess, he was such as Khalîl, and he had written what-soever he inquired of them.'

The villagers sat on with little care of *Nasr's* talk (that was also his name), misliking, perhaps, the northern man's lofty looks, and besides they were well persuaded of me. The sheykh answered him, 'If there be any fault in Khalîl, he is going to Hâyil, and let the Emir look to it.' Nasr, seeing the company was not for him, laid down his hostile looks and be-gan to discourse friendly with me. At evening we were called out to a house in the village; a large supper was set before us, of boiled mutton and temmn, and we ate together.

Nasr told me the northern horses abound in his dîra; he had five mares, though he was not a sheykh, and his camels were many; for their wilderness is not like these extreme southern countries, but full of the bounty of Ullah. As he saw my clothing worn and rent – so long had I led my life in the khála – he bade me go better clad before the Emir at Hâyil, and be very circumspect to give no cause, even of a word that might be taken amiss, amongst a people light and heady, soon angry, and [in which lies all the hardship of travelling in Arabia] un-used to the sight of a stranger. Here first in Nejd I heard the *nûn* in the ending of nouns pronounced indefinitely, it is like an Attic sweetness in the Arabian tongue, and savours at the first hearing of self-pleasing, but is with them a natural erudi-tion. The sultry evening closed in with a storm of lightning and rain; these were the last days of October. In this small village might be hardly 150 souls.

Upon the morrow we stayed to drink the early kahwa; and then riding over a last miles of the plain, with blue and red granite rocks, to the steep sides of Ajja, I saw a passage before us in a cleft which opens through the midst of the mountain, eighteen long miles to the plain beyond; this strait is named, *Ría es-Self*. The way at first is steep and rugged; about nine o'clock we went by a cold spring, which tumbled from the cliff above! – I have not seen another falling water in the waterless Arabia. There we filled our girby, and the Arabs, stripping off their clothing, ran to wash themselves; – the nomads, at every opportunity of water, will plash like sparrows. Not much further are rude ground-walls of an ancient dam, and in a bay of the mountain unhusbanded palms of the Beduins; there was some tillage in time past. At the highest of the rîa, I found 5,100 feet.

A poor Beduwy had joined our company in the plain, he came, driving an ass, along with us, and was glad when I reached him an handful of Teyma dates to his breakfast. Later, at a turn of the rock, there met us three rough-looking tribesmen of Shammar, coming on in hot haste, with arms in their hands. These man stayed us; and whilst we stood, as the Arabs will, to hear and tell tidings, they eyed me like fiends. They understanding, perhaps, from some of Askar's malicious fellowship, of the Nasrâny's passing to-day by the rîa, had a mind to assail me. Now seeing themselves evenly matched, they said to him of the ass, and who was their tribesman, 'Turn thou and let us kill him!' – 'God forbid it (the poor man answered them), he is my fellow!' They grinning savagely then with all their teeth, passed from us. 'Now Khalîl! (said Nasr,) hast thou seen? – and this that I told thee, the peril of lonely riding through their country! these are the cursed Shammar, and, had we been by ourselves, they would have set upon thee, – Ullah curse the Shammar!' – 'Have we not in the last days tasted of their hospitality?' – 'Well, I tell thee they are fairfaced and good to the guest in the beyts, but if they meet a solitary man, *kh'lúy*, in the khála, and none is by to see it, they will kill him! and those were murderers we saw now, lurkers behind rocks, to cut off any whom they may find without defence.'

There is but the Emir's peace and no love between Bishr and Shammar. Not many years before, a bitter quarrel for the rights of the principal water station of their deserts, Baitha Nethîl, had divided these nigh dwellers. Baitha Nethîl is in the Bishr borders, and they could not suffer it patiently, that Sham-

mar came down to water there, and in that were supported by
the Emir Talâl. For this they forsook even their own dîra, and
migrating northward, wandered in the wilderness of their
Annezy kindred in Syria, and there remained two or three
years: but, because they were new comers in those strange
marches, many foraying enemies lifted their cattle; – and the
Bishr returned to their own country and the Emir.

– In the midst of the rîa the granite mountain recedes upon
the north side and there are low domes of plutonic basalt,
which resemble cones of volcanoes. We heard there a galloping tumult behind us, and a great shuffling of camels' feet over
the gritty rocks; it was a loose troop of *ajlâb*, or 'fetched',
dromedaries, the drove of a camel-broker. The drovers went
to sell them 'in Jebel Shammar.' These tribesmen were Bisr,
and in their company our apprehensions were ended. A driving lad cried to me, 'Hast thou not some kaak (biscuit cake of
Damascus) to give me? in all this day's going and running I
have tasted nothing.' It was late in the afternoon when we
came forth, and as I looked down over the plain of Gofar, the
oasis greenness of palms lay a little before us. The sun was
setting, and Nasr showed me the two-horned basalt mountain,
Sumrâ Hâyil, which stands a little behind the village capital,
upon the northward. Gofar, written Káfar, and in the mouth
of the nomads Jiffar, lies, like Môgug, enclosed by orchard
walling from the desert. In the plain before the town, I read
the altitude 4,300 feet. We entered by a broad empty way, between long walls, where we saw no one, nor the houses of the
place. It was sunset, when the Arabian villagers go in to their
suppers. There met us only a woman, – loathly to look upon!
for the feminine face was blotted out by the sordid veil-clout;
in our eyes, an heathenish Asiatic villany! and the gentle
blooded Arabian race, in the matter of the hareem, are become
churls. – Beginning at Káfar, all their women's faces, which
God created for the cheerfulness of the human world, are
turned to this jealous horror; and there is nothing seen of
their wimpled wives, in sorry garments, but the hands! We
dismounted by a mosque at the *munâkh*, or couching place of
strangers' camels, where all passengers alight and are received

to supper: the public charge for hospitality is here (upon a common way) very great, for, by the Arabian custom, wayfarers depart at afternoon, and those who ride from Hâyil to the southward pass only that first short stage, to sleep at Gofar.

Arriving with the drovers, we were bidden in together to sup of their scaly lean dates and water; dates, even the best, are accounted no evening fare to set before strangers. He who served us made his excuses, saying that the householder was in Hâyil. The citizens of Gofar, *Beny Temîm*, are not praised for hospitality, which were sooner to find in Hâyil, inhabited by Shammar. Nasr my rafîk, who had showed himself more treatable since the others' departure, afterwards began to blame the passers-by in the street, because none had bidden me to coffee and to sleep in their houses, saying, 'Would they leave an honourable person to lodge in the open ways!' Nasr strawed down equally, of his store of dry provender, to his thelûl and to my poor nâga; then he made dough of some barley-meal I had bought at Môgug and kneaded it with dates, and thrusting this paste into her mouth by handfuls, he fed my weary beast. There we lay down by our cattle, to pass this starry night, in the dust of their village street.

We mounted at break of day: Nasr would be at Hâyil in time to go to breakfast in the guest-hall, with Askar and his fellowship. I wondered, to see that all that side of Gofar town, towards Hâyil, was ruinous, and the once fruitful orchard-grounds were now like the soil of the empty desert, – and tall stems, yet standing in their ranks, of sere and dead palms. We rode by cavernous labyrinths of clay-building under broken house-walling, whose timbers had been taken away, and over sunken paths of the draught-camels, where their wells now lay abandoned. When I asked, 'What is this?' Nasr answered, *Béled mât*, 'a died-out place.' The villagers had perished, as those of Môgug, in a plague which came upon them seven years before. Now their wells were fallen in, which must be sunk in this settlement to more than twenty-five fathoms. The owners of the ground, after the pestilence, lacked strength to labour, and had retired to the inner oasis.

Beyond Gofar orchard walls is that extreme barrenness of desert plain (máhal) which lies before Hâyil; the soil, a sharp granite-grit, is spread out between the desolate mountains Ajja and *Selma*, barren as a sea-strand and lifeless as the dust of our streets; and yet therein are hamlets and villages, upon veins of ground-water. It is a mountain ground where almost nothing may spring of itself, but irrigated it will yield barley and wheat, and the other Nejd grains. Though their palms grow high they bear only small and hot and therefore less wholesome kinds of date-berries. We found hardly a blade or a bush besides the senna plant, flowering with yellow pea-like blossoms. The few goats of the town must be driven far back under the coast of Ajja to find pasture. After two hours Nasr said, 'Hâyil is little further, we are here at the mid-way; women and children go between Hâyil and Gofar before their (noon) breakfast.' Thus the road may be eleven miles nearly. Hâyil was yet hidden by the brow of the desert, – everywhere the horizon seemed to me very near in Nomad Arabia. Between these towns is a trodden path; and now we met those coming out from Hâyil. They were hareem and children on foot, and some men riding upon asses: 'Ha! (said a fellow, and then another, and another, to Nasr) why dost thou bring him?' – So I knew that the Nasrâny's coming had been published in Hâyil! and Nasr hearing their words began to be aghast. 'What, he said, if his head should be taken off!' – 'And Khalîl, where is the tobacco-bag? and reach me that galliûn, for billah, my head turns.' We had ridden a mile further, when I espied two horsemen galloping towards us in a great dust. I began to muse, were these hot riders some cruel messengers of the Emir, chevying out from Hâyil upon my account? – The name of Nasrâny was yet an execration in this country, and even among nomads a man will say to another, 'Dost thou take me for a Nasrâny! that I should do such [iniquitous] thing.' – Already the cavaliers were upon us, and as only may riders of the mild Arabian mares, they reined up suddenly abreast of us, their garments flying before them in the still air; and one of them shouted in a harsh voice to Nasr (who answered nothing, for he was afraid), 'All that baggage is whose,

ha?' – so they rode on from us as before; I sat drooping upon
my camel with fatigue, and had not much regarded what men
they were.

Arrival at Hâyil: Audience of the Emir

We saw afterward some high building with battled towers.
These well-built and stately Nejd turrets of clay-brick are
shaped like our light-houses; and, said Nasr, who since Telâl's
time had not been to Hâyil, 'That is the Emir's summer residence.' As we approached Hâyil I saw that the walls extended
backward, making of the town a vast enclosure of palms.
Upon our right hand I saw a long grove of palms in the desert,
closed by high walls; upon the left lies another outlying in the
wilderness and larger, which Abeyd planted for the inherit-
ance of his children. Now appeared as it were suspended above
the town, the whitened donjon of the *Kasr*, – such clay buildings they whiten with jiss. We rode by that summer residence
which stands at the way-side; in the tower, they say, is
mounted a small piece of artillery. Under the summer-house
wall is a new conduit, by which there flows out irrigation water
to a public tank, and townswomen come hither to fetch water.
This, which they call *mâ es-Sáma*, is reckoned the best water
in the town; from all their other wells the water comes up
with some savour of salty and bitter minerals, 'which (though
never so slight) is an occasion of fever.' We alighted, and at
my bidding a woman took down the great (metal) water-pan
upon her head to give us to drink. Nasr spoke to me not to
mount anew; he said we had certain low gateways to pass.
That was but guile of the wild Beduwy, who with his long
matted locks seemed less man than satyr or werwolf. They are
in dread to be cried down for a word, and even mishandled in
the towns; his wit was therefore not to bring in the Nasrâny
riding at the (proud) height of his camel.

I went on walking by the short outer street, and came to the
rude two-leaved gateway (which is closed by night) of the
inner sûk of Hâyil. There I saw the face of an old acquaintance
who awaited me, – Abd el-Azîz, he who was conductor of Ibn

Rashîd's gift-mare, now twelve months past, to the kella at el-Héjr. I greeted him, and he greeted me, asking kindly of my health, and bade me enter. He went before me, by another way, to bring the tiding to the Emir, and I passed on, walking through the public sûk, full of tradesmen and Beduw at this hour, and I saw many in the small dark Arab shops, busy about their buying and selling. Where we came by the throng of men and camels, the people hardly noted the stranger; some only turned to look after us. A little further there stepped out a well-clad merchant, with a saffron-dye beard, who in the Arabian guise took me by the hand, and led me some steps forward, only to inquire cautelously of the stranger 'From whence I came?' A few saffron beards are seen at Hâyil; in his last years Abeyd ibn Rashîd had turned his grey hairs to saffron beard. It is the Persian manner, and I may put that to my good fortune, being a traveller of the English colour, in Arabia. The welfaring men stain their eyes with kahl; and of these bird-like Arabians it is the male sex which is bright-feathered and adorned. Near the sûk's end is their corn market, and where are sold camel-loads of fire-wood, and wild hay from the wilderness. Lower I saw veiled women-sellers under a porch with baskets where they sit daily from the sunrise to sell dates and pumpkins; and some of them sell poor ornaments from the north, for the hareem.

We came into the long-square public place, *el-Méshab*, which is before the castle, *el-Kasr*. Under the next porch, which is a refuge of poor Beduin passengers, Nasr crouched my camel, hastily, and setting down the bags, he withdrew from me; the poor nomad was afraid. Abd el-Azîz, coming again from the Kasr, asked me why was I sitting in that place? he sat down by me to inquire again of my health. He seemed to wish the stranger well, but in that to have a fear of blame, – had he not also encouraged my coming hither? He left me and entered the Kasr gate, to speak anew with the Emir. Abd el-Azîz, in the rest a worthy man, was timid and ungenerous, the end of life to them all is the least displeasure of Ibn Rashîd, and he was a servant of the Emir. A certain public seat is appointed him, under the Prince's private kahwa upon the Méshab, where he

sat in attendance with his company at every mejlis. The people
in the square had not yet observed the Nasrâny, and I sat on
three-quarters of an hour, in the midst of Hâyil; – in the meanwhile they debated perhaps of my life within yonder earthen
walls of the castle. I thought the Arabian curiosity and avarice
would procure me a respite: at least I hoped that someone
would call me in from this pain of famine to breakfast.

In the further end of the Méshab were troops of couched
thelûls; they were of Beduin fellowships which arrived daily,
to treat of their affairs with the Emir. Certain of the Beduw
now gathered about me, who wondered to see the stranger
sitting under this porch. I saw also some personage that issued
from the castle gate under a clay tower, in goodly fresh apparel, walking upon his stick of office, and he approached me.
This was *Mufarrij, rájul el-Mothif*, or marshal of the Prince's
guest-hall, a foreigner, as are so many at Hâyil of those that
serve the Emir. His town was Aneyza in Kasîm (which he had
forsaken upon a horrible misadventure, afterwards to be related). The comely steward came to bid the stranger in to
breakfast; but first he led me and my nâga through the Méshab
and allotted me a lodging, the last in the row of guest-chambers, *makhzans*, which are in the long side of this public place
in front of the Kasr: then he brought me in by the castle-gate,
to the great coffee-hall, which is of the guests, and the castle
service of the Emir. At this hour – long after all had breakfasted and gone forth – it was empty, but they sent for the
coffee-server. I admired the noble proportions of this clay hall,
as before of the huge Kasr; the lofty walls, painted in device
with ochrè and jiss, and the rank of tall pillars, which in the
midst upheld the simple flat roof, of ethel timbers and palm-
stalk matwork, goodly stained and varnished with the smoke
of the daily hospitality. Under the walls are benches of clay
overspread with Bagdad carpets. By the entry stands a mighty
copper-tinned basin or 'sea' of water, with a chained cup
(daily replenished by the hareem of the public kitchen from
the mâ es-Sáma); from thence the coffee-server draws, and he
may drink who thirsts. In the upper end of this princely kahwa
are two fire-pits, like shallow graves, where desert bushes are

burned in colder weather; they lack good fuel, and fire is blown commonly under the giant coffee-pots in a clay hearth like a smith's furnace. I was soon called out by Mufarrij to the guest-hall, *mothif*; this guest-house is made within the castle buildings, a square court cloistered, and upon the cloisters is a gallery. Guests pass in by the Prince's artillery, which are five or six small pieces of cannon; the iron is old, the wood is ruinous.

The Beduins eat below, but principal sheykhs and their fellowships in the galleries; Mufarrij led me upstairs, to a place where a carpet was belittered with old date-stones. Here I sat down and dates were brought me, – the worst dates of their desert world – in a metal standish, thick with greasy dust; they left me to eat, but I chose still to fast. Such is the Arabian Ruler's morning cheer to his guests – they are Beduw – and unlike the desert cleanness of the most Arabian villages, where there is water enough. Till they should call me away I walked in the galleries, where small white house-doves of Irâk were flittering, and so tame that I took them in my hands. I found these clay-floor galleries eighty feet long; they are borne upon five round pillars with rude shark's-tooth chapiters. Mafurrij appearing again we returned to the kahwa where coffee was now ready. A young man soon entered shining in silken clothing, and he began to question me. This Arabian cockney was the Prince's secretary, his few words sounded disdainfully: 'I say, eigh! what art thou? – whence comest thou, and wherefore hast thou come?' I answered after the nomad sort, 'Weled I can but answer one question at once; let me hear what is thy first request': he showed himself a little out of countenance at a poor man's liberal speech, and some friendly voice whispered to me, 'Treat him with more regard, for this is *Nasr*.' So said this Nasr, 'Up! the Emir calls thee': and we went out towards the Prince's quarters.

There is made a long gallery under the body of the clay castle-building, next the outer wall upon the Méshab; by this we passed, and at the midst is an iron-plated door, kept by a young Galla slave within; and there we knocked. The door opens into a small inner court, where a few of the Emir's men-

at-arms sit in attendance upon him; at the south side is his
chamber. We went through and entered from the doorway of
his open chamber into a dim light, for their windows are but
casements to the air, and no glass panes are seen in all Nejd.
The ruler Mohammed – a younger son of Abdullah ibn Rashîd
the first prince of Shammar, and the fourth Emir since his
father – was lying half along upon his elbow, with leaning-
cushions under him, by his fire-pit side, where a fire of the
desert bushes was burning before him. I saluted him '*Salaam
aleyk*, Peace be with thee'; he lifted the right hand to his head,
the manner he had seen in the border countries, but made me
no answer; – their hostile opinion that none out of the saving
religion may give the word of God's peace! He wore the long
braided hair-locks for whose beauty he is commended in the
desert as 'a fresh young man.' His skin is more than commonly tawny, and even yellowish; lean of flesh and hollow as
the Nejders, he is of middle height: his is a shallow Nejd
visage, and Mohammed's bird-like looks are like the looks of
one survived out of much disease of the world, – and what
likelihood was there formerly that he should ever be the Emir?

'Sit down!' he said. Mohammed, who under the former
Princes was conductor of the 'Persian' Haj, had visited the
cities of Mesopotamia, and seen the manners of the Dowla. –
The chief of the guard led me to the stranger's seat. In the
midst of a long carpet spread under the clay wall, between my
place and the Emir, sat some personage leaning upon cushions;
he was, I heard, a kinsman of Ibn Rashîd, a venerable man of
age and mild countenance. The Emir questioned me, 'From
whence comest thou, and what is the purpose of thy voyage?'
– 'I am arrived from Teyma, and el-Héjr, and I came down from
Syria to visit Medáin Sâlih.' '*Rájul sadúk*, wellah! a man to
trust (exclaimed that old sheykh). This is not like him who
came hither, thou canst remember Mohammed in what year,
but one that tells us all things plainly.' *Emir*: 'And now from
Teyma, well! and what sawest thou at Teyma – anything?' –
'Teyma is a pleasant place of palms in a good air.' – 'Your
name?' – 'Khalîl.' – 'Ha! and you have been with the Beduw,
eigh Khalîl, what doest thou think of the Beduw? *Of the Beduw*

there are none good: – thou wast with which Beduins?' – 'The
Fukara, the Moahîb, the Sehamma beyond the Harra.' – 'And
what dost thou think of the Fejîr, and of their sheykhs? Motlog, he is not good?' – 'The Fukara are not unlike their name,
their neighbours call them Yahûd Kheybar.' The Emir, half
wondering and smiling, took up my words (as will the
Arabians) and repeated them to those present: 'He says they
are the Yahûd Kheybar! and well, Khalîl, how did the Aarab
deal with thee? they milked for thee, they showed thee hospitality?' – 'Their milk is too little for themselves.' The Emir
mused and looked down, for he had heard that I wandered
with the Beduins to drink camel milk. 'Ha! and the Moahîb,
he asked, are they good? and Tollog, is he good?' – The Emir
waited that I should say nay, for Tollog was an old enemy or
'rebel' of theirs. – 'The man was very good to me, I think he
is a worthy Beduin person.' To this he said, '*Hmm hmm!* – and
the Sehamma, who is their sheykh?' – 'Mahanna and Fóthil.'
– 'And how many byût are they?'

He said now, 'Have you anything with you (to sell)? and
what is thy calling?' – 'I have medicines with me, I am an
hakîm.' – 'What medicines? *kanakîna* (quinine)?' – 'This I
have of the best.' – 'And what besides?' – 'I have this and
that, but the names are many; also I have some very good *chai*,
which I will present to thee, Emir!' – 'We have chai here,
from Bagdad; no, no, we have enough.' [Afterward it was
said to me, in another place, – 'He would not accept thy chai
though it were never so good: Ibn Rashîd will eat or drink of
nothing which is not prepared for him by a certain slave of his;
he lives continually in dread to be poisoned.'] *Emir*: 'Well!
thou curest what diseases? canst thou cure the mejnûn?' (the
troubled, by the jân, in their understanding): – the Emir has
some afflicted cousins in the family of Abeyd, and in his heart
might be his brother Telâl's sorrowful remembrance. I answered, '*El-mejnûn hu mejnûn*, who is a fool by nature, he is a
fool indeed.' The Emir repeated this wisdom after me, and
solemnly assenting with his head, he said to those present, '*Hu
sâdik*, he said truth!' Some courtiers answered him '*Fî tarîk*,
but there is a way in this also.' The Aarab suppose there is a

tarîk, if a man might find it, a God-given way, to come to what end he will. – 'And tell me, which beasts thou sawest in the wilderness?' – 'Hares and gazelles, I am not a hunter.' – 'Is the hare unlawful meat! – you eat it? (he would know thus if I were truly a Christian). And the swine you eat?' I said, 'There is a strange beast in the Sherarát wilderness, which they call wild ox or wothŷhi, and I have some horns of it from Teyma.' – 'Wouldst thou see the wothŷhi? we have one of them here, and will show it thee.' Finally he said, 'Dost thou "drink" smoke?' The use of tobacco, not yet seen in the Nejd streets but tolerated within doors, is they think unbecoming in persons of more than the common people's dignity and religion. Mohammed himself and Hamûd his cousin were formerly honest brothers of the galliûn; but come up to estimation, they had forsaken their solace of the aromatic Hameydy. The Emir said further, 'So you are Mesîhy?' – that was a generous word! he would not call me by the reproachful name of Nasrâny; also the Emir, they say, 'has a Christian woman among his wives.' – Christians of the Arabic tongue in the great border lands name themselves *Mesíhiyûn*.

He bade Nasr read in a great historical book which lay upon a shelf, bound in red (*Akhbâru-'d-Dúal wa athâru-'l-Uwwal*), what was written therein of the prophet *Isa ibn Miriam*; – and the secretary read it aloud. The Mohammedan author tells us of the person, the colour, the human lineaments of Jesus, 'son of the virgin'; and the manner of his prophetic life, how he walked with his disciples in the land of Israel, and that his wont was to rest in that place where the sun went down upon him. The Emir listened sternly to this tale, and impatiently. – 'And well, well! but what could move thee (he said) to take such a journey?' I responded suddenly, '*El-elûm!* the liberal sciences'; but the sense of this plural is, in Nejd and in the Beduin talk, *tidings*. The Ruler answered hastily, 'And it is for this thou art come hither!' It was difficult to show him what I intended by the sciences, for they have no experience of ways so sequestered from the common mouth-labours of mankind. He said then, 'And this language, didst thou learn it among the Beduw, readest thou *Araby*?' – He bade Nasr bring the book, and put it in Khalîl's hands, Mohammed rose himself from his place, [he is said to be very well read in the Arabic letters, and a gentle poet though, in the dispatch of present affairs of state, he is too busy-headed to be longer a prentice in unprofitable learning] – and with the impatient half-childish curiosity of the Arabians, the Emir Ibn Rashîd himself came over and sat down beside me. – 'Where shall I read?' – 'Begin anywhere at a chapter, – there!' and he pointed with his finger. So I read the place, '*The king* (such an one) *slew all his brethren and kindred.*' It was *Sheytàn* that I had lighted upon such a bloody text; the Emir was visibly moved! and, with the quick feeling of the Arabs, he knew that I regarded him as a murderous man. 'Not there! he said hastily, but read here! – out of this chapter above' (beating the place with his finger); so I read again some passage. *Emir*: 'Ha, well! I see thou canst read a little,' so rising he went again to his place. Afterward he said, 'And whither wouldst thou go now?' – 'To Bagdad.' – 'Very well, we will send thee to Bagdad,' and with this word the Emir rose and those about him to go forth into his palm grounds, where he would show me the 'wild kine'.

Nasr then came with a letter-envelope in his hand, and asked me to read the superscription. 'Well, I said, this is not Arabic!' – 'Ay, and therefore we wish thee to read it.' – 'From whom had ye this letter?' – 'From a Nasrâny, who came from the Haurân hither, and *this we took from him.*' Upon the seal I found in Greek letters *Patriarchate of Damascus,* and the legend about it was in Latin, *Go ye into all the world and preach this gospel to every creature.* They were stooping to put on their sandals, and awaited a moment to hear my response; and when I recited aloud the sense *Ukhruju fî kulli el-âlam* ... the venerable sheykh said piously to the Emir: 'Mohammed, hearest thou this? – and they be the words of the Messîah!'

All they that were in his chamber now followed abroad with the Emir; these being his courtier friends and attendance. Besides the old sheykh, the captain of the guard, and Nasr, there was not any man of good countenance amongst them. They of the palace and the Prince's men wear the city gown, but go ungirded. Mohammed the Emir appeared to me, when we came into the light, like a somewhat undergrown and hard-favoured Beduwy of the poorer sort; but he walked loftily and with somewhat unquiet glancing looks. At the irrigation well, nigh his castle walls, he paused, and showing me with his hand the shrill running wheel-work, he asked suddenly, 'Had I seen such gear?' – 'How many fathoms have ye here?' – 'Fifteen.' He said truly his princely word, though I thought it was not so, – for what could it profit them to draw upon the land from so great depths? I walked on with Mohammed and the old sheykh, till we came to his plantation, enclosed in the castle wall; it seemed to me not well maintained. The Emir stayed at a castor-oil plant (there was not another in Hâyil) to ask 'What is that?' He questioned me, between impatient authority and the untaught curiosity of Arabians, of his plants and trees,– palms and lemons, and the thick-rinded citron; then he showed me a seedling of the excellent pot-herb *bâmiya* and thyme, and single roots of other herbs and salads. All such green things they eat not! so unlike is the diet of Nejd Arabia to the common use in the Arabic border countries.

Gazelles were running in the further walled grounds; the Emir stood and pointed with his finger, 'There (he said) is the wothŷhi!' This was a male of a year and a half, no bigger than a great white goat; he lay sick under a fig-tree. *Emir*: – 'But look yonder, where is a better, and that is the cow.' – 'Stand back for fear of her horns! the courtiers said about me, do not approach her.' One went out with a bunch of date twigs to the perilous beast, and stroked her; her horns were like sharp rods, set upright, the length I suppose of twenty-seven inches. I saw her, about five yards off, less than a small ass; the hide was ash-coloured going over to a clear yellow, there was a slight rising near the root of her neck, and no hump, her smooth long tail ended in a bunch. She might indeed be said 'to resemble a little cow'; but very finely moulded was this creature of the waterless wilderness, to that fiery alacrity of their wild limbs. '*Uktub-ha!* write, that is portray, her!' exclaimed the Emir. As we returned, he chatted with me pleasantly; at last he said 'Where are thy sandals?' – 'Little wonder if you see me unshod and my clothing rent, it is a year since

I am with the Beduw in the khála.' – 'And though he go without soles (answered the kind old sheykh), it is not amiss, for thus went even the prophets of Ullah.' – This venerable man was, I heard, the Emir's mother's brother: he showed me that mild and benevolent countenance, which the Arabs bear for those to whom they wish a good adventure.

The Emir in his spirituous humour, and haughty familiar manners, was much like a great sheykh of the Aarab. In him is the mark of a former contrary fortune, with some sign perhaps of a natural baseness of mind; Mohammed was now 'fully forty years old,' but he looked less. We came again into the Kasr yard, where the wood is stored, and there are two-leaved drooping gates upon the Méshab; here is the further end of that gallery under the castle, by which we had entered. The passage is closed by an iron-plated door; the plates (in their indigence of the arts) are the shield-like iron pans (*tannûr*) upon which the town housewives bake their girdle bread. – But see the just retribution of tyrants! they fear most that make all men afraid. Where is – the sweetest of human things – their repose? for that which they have gotten from many by their power, they know by the many to be required of them again! There the Emir dismissed the Nasrâny, with a friendly gesture, and bade one accompany me to my beyt or lodging.

Hamûd and Mohammed. The Public Day. The Desert Soil

When this day's sun was setting, Mufarrij called me to the Mothîf gallery, where a supper-dish was set before me of mutton and temmn. When I came again into the coffee-hall, as the cup went round there began to be questioning among the Beduin guests and those of the castle service, of my religion. I returned early to my beyt, and then I was called away by his servants to see one, whom they named 'The Great Sheykh.' – 'Who was, I asked, that great sheykh?' they answered '*El-Emir!*' So they brought me to a dàr, which was nearly next by, and this is named Kahwat Abeyd. They knocked and a Galla slave opened the door. We passed in by a short entry, which smelled cheerfully of rose-water, to that which seemed to my eyes full of the desert a goodly hall-chamber. The Oriental rooms are enclosures of the air, without moveables, and their only ornaments are the carpets for sitting-places, here laid upon the three sides of the upper end, with pillowed places for 'the Emir' and his next kinsman. All was clay, the floor is beaten clay, the clay walls I saw were coloured in ochre; the sitters were principal persons of the town, a Beduin sheykh or two, and men of the princely service; and bright seemed the civil clothing of these fortunate Arabs. – They had said *'The Emir!'* and in the chief place I saw a great noble figure half lying along upon his elbow! – but had I not seen the Prince Ibn Rashîd himself this morning? If the common sort of Arabs may see a stranger bewildered among them it is much to their knavish pleasure.

This personage was *Hamûd*, heir, although not the eldest son, of his father Abeyd; for *Fáhd*, the elder, was *khíbel*, of a troubled understanding, but otherwise of a good and upright behaviour; the poor gentleman was always much my friend. – The princely Hamûd has bound his soul by oath to his cousin the Emir, to live and to die with him; their fathers were brethren and, as none remain of age of the Prince's house, Hamûd ibn Rashîd is next after Mohammed in authority, is his deputy at home, fights by his side in the field, and he bears the style of Emir. Hamûd is the Ruler's companion in all daily service and counsel. – The son of Abeyd made me a pleasant countenance, and bade me be seated at his right hand, and when he saw I was very weary, he bade me stretch the legs out easily, and sit without any ceremony.

Hamûd spoke friendly to the Nasrâny stranger; I saw he was of goodly stature, with painted eyes, hair shed [as we use to see in the images of Christ] and hanging down from the midst in tresses, and with little beard. His is a pleasant man-like countenance, he dissembles cheerfully a slight crick in the neck, and turns it to a grace, he seems to lean forward. In our talk he inquired of those marvellous things of the Nasâra, the telegraph, 'and glass, was made of what? also they had heard

to be in our Christian countries a palace of crystal; and Baris
(Paris) a city builded all of crystal; also what thing was rock
oil,' of which there stood a lamp burning on a stool before
them: it is now used in the principal houses of Hâyil, and they
have a saying that the oil is made from human urine. He wondered when I told them it is drawn from wells in the New World;
he had heard of that *Dínya el-jedída*, and inquired to which
quarter it lay, and beyond what seas. He asked me of my medicines, and then he said, 'Lean towards me, I would inquire of
thee.' Hamûd whispered, under the wing of his perfumed
kerchief, 'Hast thou no medicine, that may enable a man?' I
answered immediately, 'No, by thy life.' – 'No, by my life!' he
repeated, turning again, and smiled over to the audience, and
laughed cheerfully, 'ha! ha!' – for some crabbed soul might
misdeem that he had whispered of poison. Also that common
oath of the desert, 'By thy life,' is blamed among these half-
Wahábies. Hamûd said, with the same smiling demeanour,
'Seest thou here those two horsemen which met with thee
upon the road?' – 'I cannot tell, for I was most weary.' – 'Ay,
he said with the Arabian humanity, thou wast very weary; ask
him!' Hamûd showed me with his finger a personage, one of
the saffron-beards of Hâyil, who sat leaning upon cushions, in
the place next by him, as next in dignity to himself. This was a
dull-witted man, *Sleymàn*, and his cousin. I asked him, 'Was
it thou?' but he, only smiling, answered nothing. *Hamûd*:
'Look well! were they like us? be we not the two horsemen? –
It was a match, Khalîl, to try which were the better breathed
of our two mares; how seest thou? the horses of the Engleys
are better, or our Nejd horses?' – Hamûd now rising to go to
rest (his house is in another part), we all rose with him. In that
house – it stands by the public birket which is fed from the
irrigation of this kahwa palm-yard – are his children, a wife
and her mother, and his younger brothers; but, as a prince of
the blood, he has a lodging for himself (where he sleeps) within the castle building. The Hâyil Princes are clad as the nomads, but fresh and cleanly and in the best stuffs; their long
wide tunic is, here in the town, washed white as a surplice, and
upon their shoulders is the Aarab mantle of finer Bagdad

woollen, or of the black cloth of Europe. They wear the haggu upon their bodies, as in all nomad Arabia.

I was but ill-housed in my narrow, dark, and unswept cell: – they told me, a Yahûdy also, at his first coming, had lodged there before me! This was a Bagdad Jew, now a prosperous Moslem dwelling at Hâyil and married, and continually increasing with the benediction of the son-in-law of Laban; the man had a good house in the town, and a shop in the sûk, where he sold clothing and dates and coffee to the nomads: his Hâyil wife had borne him two children. The gaping people cried upon me, 'Confess thou likewise, Khalîl, "There is one God, and His apostle Mohammed," and thine shall be an equal fortune, which the Emir himself will provide.' From the morrow's light, there was a gathering of sick and idle townsmen to the Nasrâny's door, where they sat out long hours bibble-babbling, and left me no moment of repose. They asked for medicines, promising, 'If they found them good remedies they would pay me, but not now.' When I answered they might pay me the first cost for the drugs, this discouraged them; and nothing can be devised to content their knavish meaning. I said at length, 'None of you come here to chaffer with me, for I will not hear you,' and putting my door to upon them, I went out. As I sat at my threshold in the cool of the afternoon, Hamûd went by with his friends; he stayed to greet me, and bade me come to supper, and showed me his sword, which he carries loosely in his hand with the baldric, like the nomads, saying, 'What thinkest thou of it?' – they suppose that every son of the Nasâra should be schooled in metal-craft. As I drew his large and heavy blade out of the scabbard – the steel was not Damascened – Hamûd added, 'It is Engleys' (of the best Christian countries' work): he had this sabre from Ibn Saûd, and 'paid for it one thousand reals.' 'It seems to be excellent,' I said to him, and he repeated the words smiling in their manner, 'It is excellent.' The sword is valued by the Arabians as the surest weapon; they all covet to have swords of the finest temper.

At sunset came a slave from Abeyd's coffee-hall to lead me to supper. Hamûd sups there when he is not called to eat with the Emir; his elder son *Mâjid*, and the boy's tutor, eat with him; and after them, the same dish is set before the men of his household. His simple diet is of great nourishment, boiled mutton upon a mess of temmn, with butter, seasoned with onions, and a kind of curry. When the slave has poured water upon our hands, from a metal ewer, over a laver, we sit down square-legged about the great brazen tinned dish upon the carpet floor. 'Mudd yédak, Reach forth thine hand' is the Arabs' bidding, and with 'Bismillah, In the name of God,' they begin to eat with their fingers. They sit at meat not above eight or ten minutes, when they are fully satisfied; the slave now proffers the bowl, and they drink a little water; so rising they say 'El-hamd illah, The Lord be praised,' and go apart to rinse the mouth, and wash their hands: – the slave lad brought us grated soap. So they return to their places refreshed, and the cheerful cup is served round; but the coffee-server – for the fear of princes – tasted before Hamûd. There is no banqueting among them. Arabians would not be able to believe, that the food-creatures of the three inhabited elements (in some happier lands) may hardly sustain an human entrail; and men's sitting to drink away their understanding must seem to them a very horrible heathenish living. Here are no inordinate expenses of the palace, no homicide largesses to smooth favourites of the spoil of the lean people. Soon after the sunrising, the Shammar princes breakfasted of girdle-bread and butter with a draught of milk; at noon a dish of dates is set before them; at sunset they sup as we have now seen: Prince and people, they are all alike soberly dieted. The devil is not in their dish; all the riot and wantonness of their human nature lies in the Mohammedan luxury of hareem. – I remember to have heard, from some one who knew him, of the diet of the late Sultan of Islam, Abd el-Azîz, otherwise reproached for his insatiable luxury. Only one dish – which his mother had tasted and sealed – was set before him, and that was the Turks' every day pilaw (which they say came in with Tamerlane) of boiled rice and mutton; he abstained (for a cause which may be divined) from coffee and tobacco. I heard Hamûd say he had killed the sheep in my honour; but commonly his supper mutton is bought in the sûk. ...

...The Prince Mohammed goes but once at el-assr to prayers in the great mesjid; he prays in an oratory within the castle, or standing formally in his own chamber. And else so many times to issue from the palace to their public devotion, were a tediousness to himself and to his servitors, and to the townspeople, for all fear when they see him, since he bears the tyrant's sword. And Mohammed fears! – the sword which has entered this princely house 'shall never depart from them – so the Arab muse – until they be destroyed.' He cut down all the high heads of his kindred about him, leaving only Hamûd; the younger sort are growing to age; and Mohammed must see many dreams of dread, and for all his strong security, is ever looking for the retribution of mankind. Should he trust himself to pass the Méshab oftentimes daily at certain hours? – but many have miscarried thus. Both Hamûd and the Emir Mohammed affect popular manners: Hamûd with an easy frankness, and that smiling countenance which seems not too far distant from the speech of the common people; Mohammed with some softening, where he may securely, of his princely asperity, and sowing his pleasant word between; he is a man very subtle witted, and of an acrid understanding. Mohammed as he comes abroad casts his unquiet eyes like a falcon; he walks, with somewhat the strut of a stage-player, in advance of his chamber-followers, and men-at-arms. When Hamûd is with him, the Princes walk before the rout. The townspeople (however this be deemed impossible) say 'they *love him and fear him*' : – they praise the prince under whose sufficient hand they fare the better, and live securely, and see all prosper about them; but they dread the sharpness, so much fleshed already, of the Ruler's sword.

The evening after, Mohammed sent for me to his apartment: the clay walls are stained with ochre. When I said to the Emir, I was an Englishman, this he had not understood before! he was now pleasant and easy. There sat with him a great swarthy man, Sâlih, (I heard he was of the nomads,) who watched me with fanatical and cruel eyes, saying at length in a fierce sinister voice, 'Lookest thou to see thy land again?' –

'All things, I answered, are in the power of Ullah.' – 'Nay,
nay, Sâlih! exclaimed the Emir, and Khalîl has said very well,
that all things are in the hand of Ullah.' Mohammed then asked
me nearly Hamûd's questions. 'The telegraph is what? and we
have seen it (at Bagdad in time of his old conductorship of the
"Persian" pilgrims): but canst thou not make known to us
the working, which is wonderful?' – 'It is a trepidation –
therewith we may make certain signs – engendered in the
corrosion of metals, by strong medicines like vinegar,' *Emir*:
'Then it is an operation of medicine, canst thou not declare
it?' – 'If we may suppose a man laid head and heels between
Hâyil and Stambûl, of such stature that he touched them both;
if one burned his feet at Hâyil, should he not feel it at the instant in his head, which is at Stambûl?' – 'And glass is what?'
He asked also of petroleum; and of the New Continent, where
it lay, and whether within 'the Ocean'. He listened coldly to
my tale of the finding of the New Land over the great seas,
and inquired, 'Were no people dwelling in the country when
it was discovered?' At length he asked me, 'How did I see
Hâyil? and the market street, was it well? but ah (he answered
himself) it is a *sûk Aarab!*' little in comparison with the chief
cities of the world. He asked 'Had I heard of J. Shammar in
my own country?' The ruler was pleased to understand that
the Nasâra were not gaping after his desert provinces; but it
displeased the vain-glory of the man that of all this troublous
tide of human things under his governance, nearly no rumour
was come to our ears in a distant land. Hamûd asked me of
another while the like question, and added, 'What! have ye
never heard of Ibn Saûd the Waháby!' When I had sat two
hours, and it might be ten o'clock, the Emir said to the captain of the guard, who is groom of his chamber, 'It is time to
shut the doors'; and I departed.

In the early days of my being in Hâyil, if I walked through
their sûk, children and the ignorant and poor Beduw flocked
to me, and I passed as the cuckoo with his cloud of wondering
small birds, until some citizen of more authority delivered me,
saying to them, 'Wellah, thus to molest the stranger would be
displeasing to the Emir!' Daily some worthy persons called

me to coffee and to breakfast; the most of them sought counsel of the hakîm for their diseases, few were moved by mere hospitality, for their conscience bids them show no goodness to an adversary of the saving religion; but a Moslem coming to Hâyil, or even a Frankish stranger easily bending and assenting to them, might find the Shammar townspeople hospitable, and they are accounted such.

And first I was called to one *Ghrânim*, the Prince's jeweller, and his brother *Ghruneym*. They were rich men, of the smiths' caste, formerly of Jauf, where are some of the best sânies, for their work in metal, wood, and stone, in nomad Arabia. Abeyd at the taking of the place found these men the best of their craft, and he brought them perforce to Hâyil. They are continually busied to labour for the princes, in the making and embellishing of sword-hilts with silver and gold wire, and the inlaying of gun-stocks with glittering scales of the same. All the best sword-blades and matchlocks, taken (from the Beduw) in Ibn Rashîd's forays, are sent to them to be remounted, and are then laid up in the castle armoury. Of these, some very good Persian and Indian blades are put in the hands of the Emir's men-at-arms. In his youth, Ghrânim had wandered in his metal trade about the Haurân, and now he asked me of the sheykhs of the Druses, such and such whom he had known, were they yet alive. The man was fanatical, his understanding was in his hands, and his meditations were not always of the wise in the world: so daily meeting me, Ghrânim said before other words, 'Khalîl, I am thine enemy!' and in the end he would proffer his friendly counsels. – He had made this new clay house and adorned it with all his smith's art. Upon the earthen walls, stained with ochre, were devices of birds and flowers, and koran versets in white daubing of jiss, – which is found everywhere in the desert sand: the most houses at Hâyil are very well built, though the matter be rude. He had built a double wall with a casement in each, to let the light pass, and not the weather. I saw no sooty smith's forge within, but Ghrânim was sitting freshly clad at his labour, in his best chamber; his floor was spread with fine matting, and the sitting places were Bagdad carpets. His brother Ghruneym called away the hakîm to his own house to breakfast: he was hindered in his craft by sickness and the Emir oft-times threatened to forsake him. His son showed me an army rifle [from India] whereupon I found the Tower mark; the sights – they not understanding their use! – had been taken away.

The Jew-Moslem – he had received the name *Abdullah*, 'the Lord's servitor,' and the neophyte surname *el-Moslemanny* – came to bid me to coffee. His companion asked me, 'Did my nation love the Yahûd?' 'We inquire not, I answered, of men's religions, so they be good subjects.' We came to the Jew's gate, and entered his house; the walls within were pleasantly stained with ochre, and over-written with white flowerets and religious versets, in daubing of gypsum. I read: 'THERE IS NO POWER BUT OF GOD'; and in the apostate's entry, instead of Moses' words, was scored up in great letters the Mohammedan testimony, 'There is none other god than (very) God, and Mohammed is the apostle of (very) God.' Abdullah was a well-grown man of Bagdad with the pleasant elated countenance of the Moslemîn, save for that mark (with peace be it spoken) which God has set upon the Hebrew lineaments. Whilst his companion was absent a moment, he asked me under his breath 'Had I with me any –' (I could not hear what). – 'What sayest thou?' '*Brandi*, you do not know this (English Persian Gulf word) – brandi?' His fellow entering, it might be his wife's brother, Abdullah said now in a loud voice, 'Would I become a Moslem, his house should be mine along with him.' He had whispered besides a word in my ear – 'I have a thing to say to thee, but not at this time.' It was seven years since this Bagdad Jew arrived at Hâyil. After the days of hospitality he went to Abeyd saying, he would make profession of the religion of Islam 'upon his hand'; – and Abeyd accepted the Jew's words upon his formal hand full of old bloodshed and violence. The princely family had endowed the Moslemanny at his conversion with 'a thousand reals,' and the Emir licensed him to live at Hâyil, where buying and selling, – and Abdullah knew the old art, – he was now a thriving tradesman. I had heard of him at Teyma, and that 'he read in such books as those they saw me have': yet I found him a man without instruction, – doubtless he read Hebrew, yet now he denied it.

A merchant in the town, *Jâr Ullah*, brought me a great foreign folio. It was a tome printed at Amsterdam in the last century, in Hebrew letters! so I said to him, 'Carry it to Abdullah, this is the Jews' language.' – 'Abdullah tells me he knows it not.' – This book was brought hither years before from the salvage of a Bagdad caravan, that had perished of thirst in the way to Syria. Their dalîl, 'because Ullah had troubled his mind,' led them astray in the wilderness; the caravaners could not find the wells, and only few that had more strength saved themselves, riding at adventure and happily lighting upon Beduins. The nomads fetched away what they would of the fallen-down camel-loads, 'for a month and more.' There were certain books found amongst them, a few only of such unprofitable wares had been brought in to Hâyil.

It was boasted to me that the Jew-born Abdullah was most happy here; 'many letters had been sent to him by his parents, with the largest proffers if he would return, but he always refused to receive them.' He had forsaken the Law and the Promises; – but a man who is moved by the affections of human nature, may not so lightly pass from all that in which he has been cherished and bred up in the world!

Jâr Ullah invited me to his spacious house, which stands in the upper street near the Gofar gate: he was a principal corn-merchant. One *Nasr*, a fanatical Harb-Beduwy of the *rajajîl*, meeting with us in the way, and *Aneybar* coming by then, we were all bidden in together: our worthy host, otherwise a little fanatical, made us an excellent breakfast. Aneybar was a *Hábashy*, a home-born Galla in Abdullah ibn Rashîd's household, and therefore to be accounted slave-brother of Telâl, Metaab and Mohammed: also his name is of the lord's house, Ibn Rashîd. This libertine was a principal personage in Hâyil, in affairs of state-trust under the Emirs since Telâl's time. The man was of a lively clear understanding, and courtly manners, yet in his breast was the timid soul-not-his-own of a slave: bred in this land, he had that suddenness of speech and the

suspicious-mindedness of the Arabians. – When I came again
to Hâyil Aneybar had the disposing of my life; – it was a fair
chance, to-day, that I broke bread with him!

Hamûd bade me again to supper, and as I was washing,
'How white (said one) is his skin!' Hamûd answered in a
whisper, 'It is the leprosy.' – 'Praised be God, I exclaimed,
there are no lepers in my land.' – 'Eigh! said Hamûd (a little
out of countenance, because I overheard his words), is it so?
eigh! eigh! (for he found nothing better to say, and he added
after me) the Lord be praised.' Another said, 'Wellah in Bagdad I have seen a maiden thus white, with yellow hair, that
you might say she were Khalîl's daughter.' – 'But tell me (said
the son of Abeyd), do the better sort in your country never
buy the Circass women? – or how is it among you to be the
son of a bought-woman, and even of a bond-woman, I say it
is not-convenient in your eyes?' – When it seemed the bar-
baric man would have me to be, for that uncommon whiteness, the son of a Circass bond-woman, I responded with some
warmth, 'To buy human flesh is not so much as named in my
country: as for all who deal in slaves we are appointed by God
to their undoing. We hunt the cursed slave-sail upon all seas,
as you hunt the hyena.' Hamûd was a little troubled, because I
showed him some flaws in their manners, some heathenish
shadows in his religion where there was no spot in ours, and
had vaunted our naval hostility, (whereby they all have dam-
age in their purses, to the ends of the Mohammedan world). –
'And Khalîl, the Nasâra eat swine's flesh?' – 'Ay billah, and
that is not much unlike the meat of the wabar which ye eat, or
of the porcupine. Do not the Beduw eat wolves and the hyena,
the fox, the thób, and the spring-rat? – owls, kites, the carrion
eagle? but I would taste of none such.' Hamûd answered, with
his easy humanity, 'My meaning was not to say, Khalîl, that
for any filth or sickliness of the meat we abstain from swine's
flesh, but because the Néby has bidden us'; and turning to
Sleymàn, he said, 'I remember *Abdullah*, he that came to
Hâyil in Telâl's time, and cured *Bunder*, told my father that the
swine's flesh is very good meat.' – 'And what (asked that

heavy head, now finding the tongue to utter his scurvy soul) is the wedlock of the Nasâra? as the horse covers the mare it is said [in all Nejd] the Nasâra be engendered, – wellah like the hounds!'

And though they eat no profane flesh, yet some at Hâyil drink the blood of the grape, *mâ el-enab*, the juice fermented of the fruit of the vines of their orchards, here ripened in the midsummer season. Mâjid told me, that it is prepared in his father's household; the boy asked me if I had none such, and that was by likelihood his father's request. The Moslemîn, in their religious luxury, extremely covet the forbidden drink, imagining it should enable them with their wives.

When coffee was served at Hamûd's, I always sat wondering that to me only the cup was not poured; this evening, as the servitor passed by with the pot and the cups, I made him a sign, and he immediately poured for me. Another day Mâjid, who sat next me, exclaimed, 'Drinkest thou no kahwa, Khalîl?' As I answered, 'Be sure I drink it,' the cup was poured out to me, – Hamûd looked up towards us, as if he would have said something. I could suppose it had been a friendly charge of his, to make me the more easy. In the Mohammedan countries a man's secret death is often on the fenjeyn kahwa. The Emir where he enters a house is not served with coffee, nor is coffee served to any in the Prince's apartment, but the Prince called for a cup when he desired it; such horrible apprehensions are in their daily lives!...

... To speak now of the public day at Hâyil: it is near two hours after sunrise, when the Emir comes forth publicly to the Méshab to hold his morning mejlis, which is like the mejlis of the nomads. The great sheykh sits openly with the sheukh before the people; the Prince's mejlis is likewise the public tribunal, he sitting as president and judge amongst them. A bench of clay is made all along under the Kasr wall of the Méshab, in face of the mesjid, to the tower-gate; in the midst, raised as much as a degree and in the same clay-work (whereupon in their austere simplicity no carpet is spread), is the high settle of the Emir, with a single step beneath, upon which sits his clerk or secretary Nasr, at the Prince's feet. Hamûd's seat (such another clay settle and step, but a little lower) is that made nigh the castle door. A like ranging bank and high settle are seen under the opposite mesjid walls, where the sheukh sit in the afternoon shadow, holding the second mejlis, at el-assr. Upon the side, in fact of the Emir, sits always the kâdy, or man of the religious law; of which sort there is more than one at Hâyil, who in any difficult process may record to the Emir the words, and expound the sense, of the koran scripture. At either side of the Prince sit sheykhly men, and court companions; the Prince's slaves stand before them; at the sides of the sheukh, upon the long clay bank, sit the chiefs of the public service and their companies; and mingled with them all, beginning from the next highest place after the Prince, there sit any visiting Beduins after their dignities. – You see men sitting as the bent of a bow before all this mejlis, in the dust of the Méshab, the *rajajíl*, leaning upon their swords and scabbards, commonly to the number of one hundred and fifty; they are the men-at-arms, executors of the terrible Emir, and riders in his ghrazzus; they sit here (before the tyrant) in the place of the people in the nomads' mejlis. The mejlis at Hâyil is thus daily a muster of this mixed body of swordsmen, many of whom in other hours of the day are civilly occupied in the town. Into that armed circuit suitors enter with the accused and suppliants, and in a word all who have any question (not of state), or appear to answer in public audience before the Emir; and he hears their causes, to every one shortly defining justice: and what judgements issue from the Prince's mouth are instantly executed. In the month of my being at Hâyil might be daily numbered sitting at the mejlis with the Emir about four hundred persons.

The Emir is thus brought nigh to the people, and he is acquainted with the most of their affairs. Mohammed's judgement and popular wisdom is the better, that he has sometime himself tasted of adversity. He is a judge with an indulgent equity, like a sheykh in the Beduin commonwealths, and just with a crude severity: I have never heard anyone speak against the Emir's true administration of justice. When I asked if there were no handling of bribes at Hâyil, by those who are nigh the Prince's ear, it was answered, 'Nay.' The Byzantine corruption cannot enter into the eternal and noble simplicity of this people's (airy) life, in the poor nomad country; but (we have seen) the art is not unknown to the subtle-headed Shammar princes, who thereby help themselves with the neighbour Turkish governments. Some also of Ibn Rashîd's Aarab, tribesmen of the Medina dîras, have seen the evil custom: a tale was told me of one of them who brought a bribe to advance his cause at Hâyil, and when his matter was about to be examined he privily put ten reals into the kâdy's hand. But the kâdy rising, with his stick laid load upon the guilty Beduin's shoulders until he was weary, and then he led him over to the Prince, sitting in his stall, who gave him many more blows himself, and commanded his slaves to beat him. The mejlis is seldom sitting above twenty minutes, and commonly there is little to hear, so that the Prince being unwell for some days (his ordinary suffering of headache and bile), I have seen it intermitted; – and after that the causes of seven days were dispatched in a morning's sitting! The mejlis rising and dispersing, as the Prince is up, they say *Thâr el-Emir!* – and then, what for the fluttering of hundreds of gay cotton kerchiefs in the Méshab, we seem to see a fall of butterflies. The town Arabians go clean and honourably clad; but the Beduins are ragged and even naked in their wandering villages.

The Emir walks commonly from the mejlis, with his companions of the chamber, to a house of his at the upper end of the Méshab, where they drink coffee, and sit awhile: and from thence he goes with a small attendance of his rajajîl to visit the stud; there are thirty of the Prince's mares in the town, tethered in a ground next the clay castle, and nearly in face of the Kahwat Abeyd. After this the Emir dismisses his men, saying to them, 'Ye may go, *eyyâl*,' and re-enters the Kasr; or sometimes with Hamûd and his chamber friends he walks abroad to breathe the air, it may be to his summer residence by the mâ es-Sáma, or to Abeyd's plantation: or he makes but a passage through the sûk to visit someone in the town, as Ghrânim the smith, to see how his orders are executed; – and so he returned to the castle, when if he have any business with Beduins, or men from his villages, and messengers awaiting him, they will be admitted to his presence. It is a busy pensive life to be the ruler at Hâyil, and his witty head was always full of the perplexity of this world's affairs. Theirs is a very subtle Asiatic policy. In it is not the clement fallacy of the (Christian) Occident, to build so much as a rush upon the natural goodness (fondly imagined to be) in any man's breast; for it is certain they do account most basely of all men, and esteem without remorse every human spirit to be a dunghill solitude by itself. Their (feline) prudence is for the time rather than seeing very far off, and always savours of the impotent suddenness of the Arab impatience. He rules as the hawk among buzzards, with eyes and claws in a land of ravin, yet in general not cruelly, for that would weaken him. An Arab stays not in long questioning, tedious knots are in peril to be resolved by the sword. Sometimes the Prince Ibn Rashîd rides to take the air on horseback, upon a white mare, and undergrown, as are the Nejd horses in their own country, nor very fairly shaped. I was sitting one after-sunset upon the clay benching at the castle-gate when the Prince himself arrived, riding alone: I stood up to salute the Emir and his horse startled, seeing in the dusk my large white kerchief. Mohammed rode with stirrups, he urged his mare once, but she not obeying, the witty Arab ceded to his unreasonable beast; and lightly dismounting the Emir led in and delivered her to the first-coming hand of his castle service.

Beduin companies arrived every day for their affairs with the Prince, and to every such company or *rubba* is allotted a makhzan, and they are public guests (commonly till the third day) in the town. Besides the tribesmen his tributaries, I have seen at Hâyil many foreign Beduins as *Thuffîr* and *Meteyr*, that were friendly Aarab without his confederacy and dominion, yet from whom Ibn Rashîd is wont to receive some yearly presents. Moreover there arrived tribesmen of the free Northern Annezy, and of Northern Shammar, and certain migrated Kahtân now wandering in el-Kasîm.

An hour before the morning's mejlis the common business of the day is begun in the oasis. The inhabitants are husbandmen, tradesmen (mostly strangers) in the sûk, the *rajajîl es-sheukh,* and not many household slaves. When the sun is risen, the husbandmen go out to labour. In an hour the sûk is opened: the *dellâls,* running brokers of all that is put to sale, new or old, whether clothing or arms, cry up and down the street, and spread their wares to all whom they meet, and entering the shops as they go with this illiberal noise, they sell to the highest bidders; and thus upon an early day I sold my nâga the Khuèyra. I measured their sûk, which is between the Méshab and the inner gate towards Gofar, two hundred paces; upon both sides are the shops, small ware-rooms built backward, into which the light enters by the doorway, – they are in number about one hundred and thirty, all held and hired of the Emir. The butchers' market was in a court next without the upper gate of the sûk: there excellent mutton was hastily sold for an hour after sunrise, at less than two-pence a pound, and a small leg cost sixpence, in a time when nine shillings was paid for a live sheep at Hâyil, and for a goat hardly six shillings. So I have seen Beduins turn back with their small cattle, rather than sell them here at so low prices: – they would drive them down then, nearly three hundred miles more, to market at Medina! where the present value of sheep they heard to be as much again as in the Jebel. The butchers' trade, though all the nomads are slaughterers, is not of persons of liberal condition in the townships of Nejd.

Mufarrij towards evening walks again in the Méshab: he comes forth at the castle gate, or sends a servant of the kitchen, as often as the courses of guests rise, to call in other Beduin rubbas to the public supper, which is but a lean dish of boiled temmn seconds and barley, anointed with a very little samn. Mufarrij bids them in his comely-wise, with due discretion and observance of their sheykhly or common condition, of their being here more or less welcome to the Emir, and the alliance or enmities of tribesmen. Also I, the Nasrâny, was daily called to supper in the gallery; and this for two reasons I accepted, – I was infirm, so that the labour had been grievous to me if I must cook anything for myself, and I had not fuel, and where there was no chimney, I should have been suffocated in my makhzan by the smoke, also whilst I ate bread and salt in the Mothîf I was, I thought, in less danger of any sudden tyranny of the Emir; but the Mothîf breakfast I forsook, since I might have the best dates in the market for a little money. If I had been able to dispend freely, I had sojourned more agreeably at Hâyil; it was now a year since my coming to Arabia, and there remained but little in my purse to be husbanded for the greatest necessities.

In the Jebel villages the guest is bidden with: *summ!* or the like is said when the meat is put before him. This may be rather *'smm* for *ism*, in *b'ismi 'llah* or bismillah, 'in God's name.' But when I first heard this summ! as a boy of the Mothîf set down the dish of temmn before me, I thought he had said (in malice) *simm*, which is 'poison', and the child was not less amazed, when with the suddenness of the Arabs I prayed Ullah to curse his parentage: – in this uncertainty whether he had said poison I supped of their mess, for if they would so deal with me I thought I might not escape them. From supping, the Beduins resort in their rubbas to the public kahwa: after the guests' supper the rajajîl are served in like manner by messes, in the court of the Mothîf; there they eat also at noon their lean collation of the date-tribute, in like manner as the public guests. The sorry dates and corn of the public kitchen have been received on account of the government tax of the Emir, from his several hamlets and villages; the best of all is reserved for the households of the sheykhly families. As the public supper is ended, you may see many poor women, and some children, waiting to enter, with their bowls, at the gate of the Kasr. These are they to whom the Emir has granted an evening ration, of that which is left, for themselves, and for other wretched persons. There were daily served in the Mothîf to the guests, and the rajajîl, 180 messes of barley-bread and temmn of second quality, each might be three and a quarter pints; there was a certain allowance of samn. This samn for the public hospitality is taken from the Emir's Beduins, so much from every beyt, to be paid at an old rate, that is only sometimes seen in the spring, two shillings for three pints, which cost now in Hâyil a real. A camel or smaller beast is killed, and a little flesh meat is served to the first-called guests, once in eight or ten days. When the Prince is absent, there come no Beduins to Hâyil, and then (I have seen) there are no guests. So I have computed may be disbursed for the yearly expenses of the Prince's guest-house, about £1,500 sterling.

– Now in the public kahwa the evening coffee is made and served round. As often as I sat with them the mixed rubbas of Beduins observed towards me the tolerant behaviour which is used in their tents; – and here were we not all guests together of the Emir? The princely coffee-hall is open, soon after the dawn prayers, to these bibbers of the morning cup; the door is shut again, when all are gone forth about the time of the first mejlis. It is opened afresh, and coffee is served again after vespers. To every guest the cup is filled twice and a third is offered, when, if he would not drink, a Beduwy of the Nejd tribes will say shortly, with the desert courtesy, *Káramak Ullah*, 'the Lord requite thee.' The door of the kahwa is shut for the night as the coffee-drivelling Beduw are gone forth to the last prayers in the mesjid. After that time, the rude two-leaved gates of this (the Prince's) quarter and the market street are shut, – not to be opened again 'for prayer nor for hire' till the morrow's light; and Beduins arriving late must lodge without: – but the rest of Hâyil lies open, which is all that built towards Gofar, and the mountain Ajja.

The Emir Mohammed rode out one half-afternoon with the companions of his chamber and attendance to visit *ed-dubbush*, his live wealth in the desert. The Nejd prince is a very rich cattle-master, so that if you will believe them he possesses 'forty thousand' camels. His stud of good Nejd blood, and as *Aly el-Ayid* told me, (an honest man, and my neighbour, who was beforetime in the stud service, – he had conducted horses for the former Emirs to the Pashas of Egypt,) some three hundred mares, and an hundred horses, with many foals and fillies. After others' telling Ibn Rashîd has four hundred free and bond soldiery, two hundred mares of the blood, one hundred horses; they are herded apart in the deserts; and he has 'an hundred bond-servants' (living with their families in booths of hair-cloth, as the nomads), to keep them. Another told me the Emir's stud is divided in troops of fifty or sixty, all mares or all horses together; the foals and fillies after the weaning are herded likewise by themselves. The troops are dispersed in the wilderness, now here, now there, near or far off, – according to the yearly springing of the wild herbage. The Emir's horses are grazed in nomad wise; the fore-feet hop-shackled, they are dismissed to range from the morning. Barley or other grain they taste not; they are led home to the booths, and tethered at evening, and drink the night's milk of the she-camels, their foster mothers. – So that it may seem the West Nejd Prince possesses horses and camels to the value of about a quarter of a million pounds sterling; and that has been gotten in two generations of the spoil of the poor Beduw. He has besides great private riches laid up in metal, but his public taxes are carried into the government treasury, *beyt el-mâl*, and bestowed in sacks and in pits. He possesses much in land, and not only in Hâyil, but he has great plantations also at Jauf, and in some other conquered oases. – I saw Mohammed mount at the castle gate upon a tall dromedary, bravely caparisoned. In the few days of this his peaceable sojourn in the khála, the Prince lodged with his company in booths like the Beduins. He left Hamûd in Hâyil, to hold the now small daily mejlis; – the sons of Abeyd sits not then in the Prince's settle, but in his own lower seat by the tower.

Hamûd sent for me in his afternoon leisure: 'Mohammed is gone, he said, and we remain to become friends.' He showed me now his cheap Gulf watches, of which he wore two upon his breast, and so does his son Mâjid who has a curious mind in such newels, – it was said he could clean watches! and that Hamûd possessed not so few as an hundred, and the Emir many more than he. Hamûd asked me if these were not 'Engleys', he would say 'of the best Nasâra work.' He was greedy to understand of me if I brought many gay things in my deep saddle-bags of the fine workmanship of the Nasâra: he would give for them, he promised me with a barbarous emphasis,

FULÛS! 'silver scales' or money, which the miserable Arab people believe that all men do cherish as the blood of their own lives. I found Hamûd lying along as the nomads, idle and yawning, in the plantation of Abeyd's kahwa, which, as said, extends behind the makhzans to his family house in the town (that is not indeed one of the best). In this palm-ground he has many gazelles, which feed of vetches daily littered down to them, but they were shy of man's approach: there I saw also a bédan-buck. This robust wild goat of the mountain would follow a man and even pursue him, and come without fear into the kahwa. The beast is of greater bulk and strength than any he-goat, with thick short hair; his colour purple ruddle or nearly as that blushing before the sunset of dark mountains....

...Mâjid, the elder of Hamûd's children, was a boy of fifteen years, small for his age, of a feminine beauty, the son (the Emirs also match with the nomads) of a Beduin woman. There accompanied him always a dissolute young man, one Aly, who had four wives and was attached to Hamûd's service. This lovely pair continually invaded me in my beyt, with the infantile curiosity of Arabs, intent to lay their knavish fingers upon any foreign thing of the Nasâra, – and such they hoped to find in my much baggage; and lighting upon aught Mâjid and his villainous fellow Aly had it away perforce. – When I considered that they might thus come upon my pistol and instruments, I wrested the things from their iniquitous fingers, and reminded them of the honest example of the nomads, whom they despise. Mâjid answered me with a childish wantonness: 'But thou, Khalîl, art in our power, and the Emir can cut off thy head at his pleasure!' One day as I heard them at the door, I cast the coverlet over my loose things, and sat upon it, but nothing could be hidden from their impudence, with *bethr-ak! bethr-ak!* 'by thy leave'; – it happened that they found me sitting upon the koran. 'Ha! said they now with fanatical bitterness, he is sitting upon the koran!' – this tale was presently carried in Mâjid's mouth to the castle; and the elf Mâjid returned to tell me that the Emir had been much displeased.

Mâjid showed himself to be of an affectionate temper, with

the easy fortunate disposition of his father, and often child-
ishly exulting, but in his nature too self-loving and tyrannical.
He would strike at the poorer children with his stick as he
passed by them in the street and cry, 'Ullah curse thy father!'
they not daring to resent the injury or resist him, – the best of
the *eyyâl es-sheukh*; for thus are called the children of the
princely house. For his age he was corrupt of heart and cove-
tous; but they are all brought up by slaves! If he ever come to
be the Prince, I muse it will be an evil day for Hâyil, except,
with good mind enough to amend, he grow up to a more
humane understanding. Mâjid, full of facility and the felicity
of the Arabs, with a persuading smile, affected to treat me always according to his father's benevolence, naming me 'his
dear friend'; and yet he felt that I had a cold insight into his
ambitious meaning. So much of the peddling Semite was in
him, that he played huckster and bargained for my nâga at the
lowest price, imagining to have the double for her (when she
would be a milch cow with the calf) in the coming spring: this
I readily yielded, but 'nay, said then the young princeling, except that I would give him her harness too,' (which was worth
a third more). – I have many times mused what could be their
estimation of honour! They think they do that well enough in
the world which succeeds to them; human deeds imitating our
dream of the divine ways are beautiful words of their poets,
and otherwise unknown to these Orientals.

As I walked through their clean and well-built clay town I
thought it were pleasant to live here, – save for the awe of the
Ruler and their lives disquieted to ride in the yearly forays of
the Emir: yet what discomfort to our eyes is that squalor of
the desert soil which lies about them! Hâyil for the unlikeli-
hood of the site is town rather than oasis, or it is, as it were, an
oasis made *ghrósb*, perforce. The circuit for their plantations
are not very wide, may be nearly an hour; the town lies as far
distant from the Ajja cliffs (there named *el-M'nîf*). Their town,
fenced from the wholesome northern air by the bergs *Sumrâ
Hâyil*, is very breathless in the long summer months. The
Sumrâ, of plutonic basalt, poured forth (it may be seen in face
of the Méshed gate) upon the half-buried grey-red granite of

Ajja, is two members which stand a little beyond the town, in a half moon, and the seyl bed of Hâyil, which comes they say from Gofar, passes out between them. That upon the west is lower; the eastern part rises to a height of 500 feet, upon the crest are cairns; and there was formerly the look-out station, when Hâyil was weaker.

The higher Samrâ, *Umm Arkab*, is steep, and I hired one morning an ass, *jâhash*, for eightpence to ride thither. The thick strewed stones upon this berg, are of the same rusty black basalt which they call *hurrî* or *hurra*, heavy and hard as iron, and ringing like bell-metal. Samrâ in the nomadic speech of Nejd is any rusty black berg of hard stone in the desert: and in the great plutonic country from hence to Mecca the samrâs are always basalt. The same, when any bushes grow upon it, is called *házm*, and házm is such a vulcanic hill upon the Harras. I saw from the cairns that Hâyil is placed at the midst in a long plain, which is named *Sâhilat el-Khammashîeh*, and lies between the M'nîf of Ajja (which may rise in the highest above the plain to 1,500 feet), and that low broken hilly train, by which the Sâhilat is bounded along, two leagues eastward, toward Selma, *J.Fittij*; and under us north-eastward from Hâyil is seen *el-Khreyma*, a great possession of young palms, – the Emir's; and there are springs, they say, which water them!...

...In returning home towards the northern gate, I visited a ruined suburb *Wâsit* 'middle' (building), which by the seyl and her fields only is divided from Hâyil town. There were few years ago in the street, now ruins, 'forty kahwas', that is forty welfaring households receiving their friends daily to coffee.

Wâsit to-day is ruins without inhabitant; her people (as those in the ruined quarter of Gofar and in ruined Môgug) died seven years before in the plague, *wába*. I saw their earthen house-walls unroofed and now ready to fall, for the timbers had been taken away: the fields and the wells lay abandoned. The owners and heirs of the soil had so long left the waterer's labour that the palm-trees were dead and sere: few palms yet showed in their rusty crowns any languishing greenness. Before I left Hâyil I saw those lifeless stems cut down, and the earth laid out anew in seed-plots. There died in Wâsit 300 persons; in Hâyil, 'one or two perished in every household (that were seven hundred or eight hundred); but now, the Lord be praised, the children were sprung up and nearly filled the rooms.' Of the well-dieted princely and sheykhly families there died no man! Beduins that visited Hâyil in time of the pestilence perished sooner than towns-folk; yet the contagion was lighter in the desert and never prevailed in their menzils as a mortal sickness. The disease seized upon the head and bowels; some died the same day, some lingered awhile longer. Signs in the plague-struck were a black spot which appeared upon the nose, and a discolouring of the nails; the sufferings were nearly those of cholera. After the pest a malignant fever afflicted the country two years, when the feeble survivors loading the dead upon asses (for they had more strength to carry out piously themselves) were weary to bury....

...After Wâsit, in a waste, which lies between the town walls and the low crags of the Sumrâ, is the wide grave-yard of Hâyil. Poor and rich whose world is ended, lie there alike indigently together in the desert earth which once fostered them, and unless it be for the sites here or there, we see small or no difference of burial. Telâl and Abeyd were laid among them. The first grave is a little heap whose rude head-stone is a wild block from the basalt hill, and the last is like it, and such is every grave; you shall hardly see a scratched epitaph, where so much is written as the name which was a name. In the bor-der Semitic countries is a long superstition of the grave; here is but the simple nomad guise, without other last loving care or adornment. At a side in the mákbara is the grave-heap of Abeyd, a man of so much might and glory in his days: now these but are a long remembrance; he lies a yard under the squalid gravel in his shirt, and upon his stone is rudely scored, with a nail, this only word, *Abeyd bin-Rashîd*. When I ques-tioned Mâjid, 'And did his grandsire, the old man Abeyd, lie now so simply in the earth?' my words sounded coldly and strange in his ears; since in this land of dearth, where no piece of money is laid out upon thing not to their lives' need, they are nearly of the Wife of Bath's opinion, 'it were but waste to bury him preciously,' – whom otherwise they follow in her luxury. When one is dead, they say, *khálas!* 'he is ended,' and they wisely dismiss this last sorrowful case of all men's days without extreme mourning.

Between the mákbara and the town gate is seen a small menzil of resident nomads. They are pensioners of the palace; and notwithstanding their appearance of misery some of them are kin to the princely house. Their Beduin booths are fenced from the backward with earthen walling, and certain of them have a chamber (kasr) roofed with a tent-cloth, or low tower of the same clay building. They are Shammar, whose few cattle are with their tribesfolk in the wilderness; in the spring months they also remove thither, and refresh themselves in the short season of milk. As I went by, a woman called me from a ragged booth, the widest among them: 'had I a medicine for her sore eyes?' She told me in her talk that her sister had been a wife of Metaab, and she was 'aunt' of Mohammed now Emir. Her sons fled in the troubled times and lived yet in the northern dîras. When she named the Emir she spoke in a whisper, looking always towards the Kasr, as if she dreaded the wings of the air might carry her word into the Prince's hearing. Her grown daughter stood by us, braying temmn in a great wooden mortar, and I wondered to see her unveiled; perhaps she was not married, and Moslems have no jealous opinion of a Nasrâny. The comely maiden's cheeks glowed at her labour; such little flesh colour I had not seen before in a nomad woman, so lean and bloodless they all are, but she was a stalwart one bred in the plenteous northern dîras. I counted their tents, thirty; nearer the Gofar gate were other fifteen booths of half-resident Shammar, pitched without clay building.

A Third Audience. The House of Ibn Rashîd.
Its Dominion

A week passed and then the Emir Mohammed came again from the wilderness: the next afternoon he called for me after the mejlis. His usher found me slumbering in my makhzan;

worn and broken in this long year of famine and fatigues, I
was fallen into a great languor. The Prince's man roused me
with haste and violence in their vernile manner: 'Stand up
thou and come off; the Emir calls thee'; and because I stayed
to take the kerchief and mantle, even this, when we entered
the audience, was laid against me, the slave saying to the Emir
that 'Khalîl had not been willing to follow him!'

Mohammed had gone over from the mejlis with the rajajîl
to Abeyd's kahwa. The Emir sat now in Hamûd's place, and
Hamûd where Sleymàn daily sat. The light scimitar, with
golden hilt, that Mohammed carries loose in his hand, was
leaned up to the wall beside him; the blade is said to be of
some extremely fine temper. He sat as an Arabian, in his loose
cotton tunic, mantle and kerchief, with naked shanks and feet,
his sandals, which he had put off at the carpet, were set out
before him. I saluted the Emir, *Salaam aleyk.* – No answer: then
I greeted Hamûd and Sleymàn, now of friendly acquaintance,
in the same words, and with *aleykom es-salaam* they hailed me
smiling comfortably again. One showed me to a place where I
should sit down before the Emir, who said shortly 'From
whence?' – 'From my makhzan.' – 'And what found I there
to do all the day, ha! and what had I seen in the time of my
being at Hâyil, was it well?' When the Prince said, 'Khalîl!' I
should have responded in their manner *Aunak* or *Labbeyk* or
Tawîl el-Ummr, 'O Long-of-age! and what is thy sweet will?'
but feeling as an European among these light-tongued Asiatics
and full of mortal weariness, I kept silence. So the Emir, who
had not responded to my salutation, turned abruptly to ask
Hamûd and Sleymàn: *Mâ yarûdd?* 'how! he returns not one's
word who speaks with him?' Hamûd responded kindly for
me, 'He could not tell, it might be Khalîl is tired.' I answered
after the pause, 'I am lately arrived in this place, but *aghrûty,*
I suppose it is very well.' The Emir opened his great feminine
Arab eyes upon me as if he wondered at the not flattering
plainness of my speech; and he said suddenly, with an emphasis, before the company, 'Ay, I think so indeed, it is very well!
– and what think you Khalîl, it is a good air?' – 'I think so,
but the flies are very thick.' – 'Hmm, the flies are very thick!

and went you in the pilgrimage to the Holy City (Jerusalem)?'
– 'Twice or thrice, and to *J.Tôr*, where is the mountain of our
Lord Mûsa.' – Some among them said to the Emir, 'We have
heard that monks of the Nasâra dwell there, their habitation
is built like a castle in the midst of the khála, and the entry
is by a window upon the wall; and who would come in there
must be drawn up by a wheelwork and ropes.' The Emir
asked, 'And have they riches?' – 'They have a revenue of
alms.' The Emir rose, and taking his sandals, all the people
stood up with him, – he beckoned them to be seated still, and
went out to the plantation. In the time of his absence there was
silence in all the company; when he returned he sat down
again without ceremony. The Prince, who would discern my
mind in my answers, asked me, 'Were dates good or else bad?'
and I answered '*battâl, battâl*, very bad.' – 'Bread is better?
and what in your tongue is bread?' he repeated to himself the
name which he had heard in Turkish, and he knew it in the
Persian; Mohammed, formerly conductor of the pilgrimage,
can also speak in that language.

The Emir spoke to me with the light impatient gestures of
Arabs not too well pleased, and who play the first parts, – a
sudden shooting of the brows, and that shallow extending of
the head from the neck, which are of the bird-like inhabitants
of nomadic Nejd, and whilst at their every inept word's end
they expect thy answer. The Emir was favourably minded toward me, but the company of malignant young fanatics always
about him, continually traduced the Nasrâny. Mohammed
now Prince was as much better than they, as he was of an
higher understanding. When to some new question of the
Emir I confirmed my answer in the Beduin wise, By his life,
hayâtak, he said to Hamûd, 'Seest thou? Khalîl has learned to
speak (Arabic) among the Annezy, he says *aghrûty*.' –'And
what might I say, O el-Muhafûth? I speak as I heard it of the
Beduw.' The Prince would not that I should question him of
grammar, but hearing me name him so justly by his title,
Warden (which is nearly that in our history of Protector), he
said mildly, 'Well, swear By the life of Ullah!' (The other,
since they are become so clear-sighted with the Waháby, is an

oath savouring of idolatry.) I answered somewhat out of the Prince's season, ' – and thus even the nomads use, in a greater occasion, but they say, *By the life of thee*, in a little matter.' As the Prince could not draw from me any smooth words of courtiers, Hamûd and Sleymàn hastened, with their fair speech, to help forth the matter and excuse me. 'Certainly, they said, Khalîl is not very well to-day, eigh, the poor man! he looks sick indeed!' – And I passed the most daylight hours, stretched weakly upon the unswept floor of my makhzan, when the malignants told the Emir I was writing up his béled; so there oft-times came in spies from the Castle, who opened upon me suddenly, to see in what manner the Nasrâny were busied. – *Emir*: 'And thy medicines are what? hast thou *tiryâk?*' [thus our fathers said treacle, θηριακ-, the antidote of therine poisons). In an extreme faintness, I was now almost falling into a slumber, and my attention beginning to waver I could but say, – 'What is tiryâk? – I remember, but I have it not, by God there is no such thing.' *Sleymàn*: 'Khalîl has plenty of salts Engleys (magnesia) – hast thou not, Khalîl?' At this dull sally, and the Arabian Emir being so much in thought of poison, I could not forbear to smile, – an offence before rulers. Sleymàn then beginning to call me to give account in that presence of the New Continent, he would I should say, if we had not dates there, but the 'Long-of-Days' rose abruptly and haughtily, – so rose all the rest with him, and they departed.

A word now of the princely family and of the state of J. Shammar: and first of the tragedies in the house of Ibn Rashîd. Telâl returning from er-Riâth (whither he was accustomed, as holding of the Wahâby, to go every year with a present of horses) fell sick, *musky,* poisoned, it was said, in his cup, in East Nejd. His health decayed, and the Prince fell into a sort of melancholy frenzy. Telâl sent to Bagdad for a certain Persian hakîm. The hakîm journeyed down to Hâyil, and when he had visited the Prince, he gave his judgement unadvisedly: 'This sickness is not unto death, it is rather a long disease which must waste thy understanding.' – Telâl answered, 'Aha, shall I be a fool? – wellah *mejnûn! wa ana el-*HAKÎM, and I being the Ruler?' And because his high heart might not longer endure to live in the common pity, one day when he had shut himself in his chamber, he set his pistols against his manly breast, and fired them and ended. So Metaab, his brother, became Emir at Hâyil, as the elder of the princely house inheriting Abdullah their father's dignity: Telâl's children were (legally) passed by, of whom the eldest, Bunder, afterwards by his murderous deed Emir, was then a young man of seventeen years. Metaab I have often heard praised as a man of mild demeanour, and not common understanding; he was princely and popular at once, as the most of his house, politic, such as the great sheukh el-Aarab, and a fortunate governor. Metaab sat not fully two years, – always in the ambitious misliking of his nephew Bunder, a raw and strong-headed young man. Bunder conspiring with his next brother, Bedr, against their uncle, the ungracious young men determined to kill him.

They knew that their uncle wore upon his arm 'an amulet which assured his life from lead,' therefore the young parricides found means to cast a silver bullet. – Metaab sat in his fatal hour with his friends and the men-at-arms before him in the afternoon mejlis, which is held, as said, upon the further side of the Méshab, twenty-five paces over in face of the Kasr. – Bunder and Bedr were secretly gone up from the apartments within to the head of the castle wall, where is a terrace and parapet. Bunder pointing down his matchlock through a small trap in the wall, fired first; and very likely his hand wavered when all hanged upon that shot, for his ball went a little awry and razed the thick head-band of a great Beduin sheykh *Ibn Shalàn*, chief of the strong and not unfriendly Annezy tribe er-Ruwàlla in the north, who that day arrived from his dîra, to visit Prince Ibn Rashîd. Ibn Shalàn, hearing the shot sing about his ears, started up, and (cried he) putting a hand to his head, 'Akhs, Mohafûth, wouldst thou murder me!' The Prince, who sat on, and would not save himself by an unseemly flight, answered the sheykh with a constant mild face, 'Fear not; thou wilt see that the shot was levelled at myself.' A second shot struck the Emir in the breast, which was Bedr's.

Bunder being now Prince, sat not a full year out, and could

not prosper: in his time, was that plague which so greatly
wasted the country. Mohammed who is now Emir, when his
brother Metaab was fallen, fled to er-Riâth, where he lived
awhile. The Waháby prince, Abdullah Ibn Saûd, was a mean
to reconcile them, and Bunder, by letters, promising peace,
invited his uncle to return home. So Mohammed came, and
receiving his old office, was governor again of the Bagdad Haj
caravan. Mohammed went by with the convoy returning from
Mecca to Mesopotamia, and there he was to take up the year's
provision of temmn for the Mothîf (if you would believe
them, a thousand camel-loads, – 150 tons!). Mohammed finding only Thuffîr Aarab at el-Méshed, hired camels of them
with promise of safe-conduct going and returning, in the es-
tates of Ibn Rashîd; for they were Beduw from without, and
not friendly with the Jebel. The journey is two weeks' marches
of the nomads for loaded camels. – Mohammed approaching
Hâyil, sent before him to salute the Emir saying, 'Mohammed
greets thee, and has brought down thy purveyance of temmn
for the Mothîf.' – 'Ha! is Mohammed come? answered
Bunder, – he shall not enter Hâyil.' Then Bunder, Bedr, and
Hamûd rode forth, these three together, to meet Mohammed;
and at Bunder's commandment the town gates behind them
were shut.

Mohammed sat upon his thelûl, when they met with him, as
he had ridden down from the north, and said Bunder, 'Mohammed, what Beduw hast thou brought to Hâyil? – the
Thuffîr! and yet thou knowest them to be gôm with us!'
Mohammed: 'Wellah, yâ el-Mohafûth, I have brought them *bî
wéjhy*, under my countenance! (and in the Arabian guise he
stroked down his visage to the beard) – because I found none
other for the carriage of your temmn.' Whilst Bunder lowered
upon him, Hamûd, who was in covenant with his cousin
Mohammed, made him a sign that his life was in doubt, – by
drawing (it is told) the forefinger upon his gullet. Mohammed
spoke to one of the town who came by on horseback, 'Ho
there! lend me thy mare awhile,' making as though he would
go and see to the entry and unloading of his caravan. Mohammed, when he was settled on horseback, drew over to the

young Prince and caught Bunder's 'horns', and with his other
hand he took the crooked broad dagger, which upon a journey
they wear at the belt. – '*La ameymy, la ameymy*, do it not, do it
not, little 'nuncle mine!' exclaimed Bunder in the horror and
anguish of death. Mohammed answered with a deadly stern
voice, 'Wherefore didst thou kill thine uncle?' *wa hu fî batn-ak*,
and he is in thy belly (thou hast devoured him, dignity, life,
and all),' and with a murderous hand-cast he struck the blade
into his nephew's bowels! – There remained no choice to
Mohammed, when he had received the sign, he must slay his
elder brother's son, or himself be lost; for if he should fly, how
might he have outgone the godless young parricides? his
thelûl was weary, he was weary himself; and he must forsake
the Thuffîr, to whom his princely word had been plighted. –
Devouring is the impotent ambition to rule, of all Arabians
who are born near the sheykhly state. Mohammed had been a
loyal private man under Metaab; his brother fallen, what remained but to avenge him? and the garland should be his own.

Bunder slain, he must cut off kindred, which else would endanger him. The iniquity of fortune executed these crimes by
Mohammed's hand, rather than his own execrable ambition. –
These are the tragedies of the house of Ibn Rashîd! their beginning was from Telâl, the murderer of himself: the fault of
one extends far round, such is the cursed nature of evil, as the
rundles of a stone dashed into water, trouble all the pool.
There are some who say, that Hamûd made Bunder's dying
sure with a pistol-shot, – he might do this, because his lot was
bound up in Mohammed's life: but trustworthy persons in
Hâyil have assured me that Hamûd had no violent hand in it.
– Hamûd turning his horse's head, galloped to town and commanded to 'keep the gates close, and let no man pass out or
enter for any cause'; and riding in to the Méshab he cried:
'Hearken, all of you! a Rashîdy has slain a Rashîdy, – there is
no word for any of you to say! let no man raise his voice or
make stir, upon pain of my hewing off his head wellah with
this sword.'

In Hâyil there was a long silence, the subject people shrunk
in from the streets to their houses! Beduins in the town were

aghast, inhabitants of the khála, to which no man 'may set doors and bars,' seeing the gates of Hâyil to be shut round about them.

An horrible slaughter was begun in the Kasr, for Mohammed commanded that all the children of Telâl should be put to death, and the four children of his own sister, widow of one *el-Jabbár* of the house *Ibn Aly* (that, till Abdullah won all, were formerly at strife with the Rashîdy family for the sheykhship of Hâyil, – and of them was Mohammed's own mother). Their uncle's bloody command was fulfilled, and the bleeding warm corpses, deceived of their young lives, were carried out the same hour to the burial; there died with them also the slaves, their equals in age, brought up in their father's households, – their servile brethren, that else would be, at any time, willing instruments to avenge them.

All Hâyil trembled that day till evening and the long night till morning, when Mohammed, standing in the Méshab with a drawn sword, called to those who sat timidly on the clay banks, – the most were Beduins – 'Yâ Moslemîn! I had not so dealt with them, but because I was afraid for this! (he clapped the left palm to the side of his neck), and as they went about to kill me, *ana sabáktahum*, I have prevented them.' Afterward he said: – 'And they which killed my brother Metaab, think ye they had spared me?' 'And hearing his voice, we sat (an eyewitness, of the Meteyr, told me) astonished, every one seeing the black death before him.' – Then Mohammed sat down in the Emir's place as Muhafûth. By and by some of the principal persons at Hâyil came into the Méshab bending to this new lord of their lives, and giving him joy of his seized authority. Thus 'out dock in nettle,' Bunder away, Mohammed began to rule; and never was the government, they say, in more sufficient handling.

– Bedr had started away upon his mare for bitter-sweet life to the waste wilderness: he fled at assr. On the morrow, fainting with hunger and thirst, and the suffered desolation of mind and weariness, he shot away his spent horse, and climbed upon a mountain. – From thence he might look far out over the horror of the world, become to him a vast dying place!

Mohammed had sent horsemen to scour the khála, and take him; and when they found Bedr in the rocks they would not listen to his lamentable petitions: they killed him there without remedy, and hastily loading his body they came again the same day to Hâyil. The chief of them as he entered, all heated, to Mohammed, exclaimed joyfully, 'Wellah, O Muhafûth, I bring thee glad tidings! it may please thee come with me whereas I will show thee Bedr lies dead; this hand did it, and so perish all the enemies of the Emir!' But Mohammed looked grimly upon the man, and cried, 'Who commanded thee to kill him? I commanded thee, son of an hound? when, thou cursed one? Ullah curse thy father, akhs! hast thou slain Bedr?' and, drawing his sword, he fetched him a clean back-stroke upon the neck-bone, and swapt off at once (they pretend) the miserable man's head. Mohammed used an old bitter policy of tyrants, by which they hope to make their perplexed causes seem the more honest in the thick eyesight of the common people. 'How happened it, I asked, that Bedr, who must know the wilderness far about, since the princely children accompany the ghrazzus, had not ridden hardily in some way of escape? Could not his mare have borne him an hundred miles? – a man of sober courage, in an extremity, might have endured, until he had passed the dominion of Ibn Rashîd, and entered into the first free town of el-Kasîm.' It was answered, 'The young man was confused in so great a calamity, and jâhil, of an inept humour, and there was none to deliver him.'

Hamûd and Mohammed allied together, there was danger between them and Telâl's sons; and if they had not forestalled Bunder and Bedr, they had paid it with their lives. The massacres were surely contrary to the clement nature of the strong man Hamûd. Hamûd, who for his pleasant equal countenance, in the people's eyes, has deserved to be named by his fellow citizens *Azîz*, 'a beloved', is for all that, when contraried out of friendship, a lordly man of outrageous incontinent tongue and jabbâr, as his father was; and doubtless he would be a high-handed Nimrod in any instant peril. Besides, it is thus that Arabs deal with Arabs; there are none more pestilent, and ungenerous enemies. Hamûd out of hospitality, is as all the Arabs of a somewhat miserable humour, and I have heard it uttered at Hâyil, 'Hamûd *khâra*!' that is draffe or worse. These are vile terms of the Hejâz, spread from the dens of savage life, under criminal governors, in the Holy Cities; and not of those schools of speaking well and of comely manners, which are the kahwa in the Arabian oases and the mejlis in the open khála. – A fearful necessity was laid upon Mohammed: for save by these murders of his own nigh blood, he could not have sat in any daily assurance. Mohammed is childless, and ajjr, a man barren in himself; the loyal Hamûd el-Abeyd has many children.

His instant dangers being thus dispersed, Mohammed set himself to the work of government, to win the opinion of his proper merit; and affecting popular manners, he is easier of his dispense than was formerly Telâl. Never Prince used his authority, where not resisted, with more stern moderation at home, but he is pitiless in the excision of any unsound parts of the commonwealth. When Jauf fell to him again by the mutiny of the few Moghrâreba left in garrison, it is said, he commanded to cut off the right hands of many that were gone over to the faith of the Dowla. Yet Jauf had not been a full generation under the Jebel; for Mohammed himself, then a young man, was with his uncle Abeyd at the taking of it, and he was wounded then by a ball in the foot which lodged in the bone; – the shot had lately been taken from him in Hâyil by a Persian hâkim, come down, for the purpose, from Mesopotamia.

As for any bounty in such Arabian Princes, it is rather good laid out by them to usury. They are easy to lose a pound to-day, which within a while may return with ten in his mouth. The Arabs say, 'Ibn Rashîd uses to deal with every man *aly aklu*, according to his understanding.' Fortune was to Mohammed's youth contrary, a bloody chance has made him Ruler. In his government he bears with that which may not be soon amended; he cannot by force only bridle the slippery wills of the nomads; and though his heart swell secretly, he receives all with his fair-weather countenance, and to friendly discourse; and of few words, in wisely questioning them, he discerns their minds. Motlog, sheykh of the Fejîr, whom he misliked, he sends home smiling; and the Prince will levy his next year's *mîry* from the Fukara, without those tribesmen's unwillingness. The principal men of Teyma, his good outlying town, whose well was fallen, depart from him with rewards. Mohammed smooths the minds of the common people; if any rude Beduin lad call to him in the street, or from the mejlis (they are all arrant beggers), 'Aha! el-Muhafûth, God give thee long life! as truly as I came hither, in such a rubba, and wellah am naked,' he will graciously dismiss him with '*bismillah*, in God's name! go with such an one, and he will give thee garments,' – that is a tunic worth two shillings at Hâyil, a coarse worsted cloak of nine shillings, a kerchief of sixpence; and since they are purchased in the gross at Bagdad, and brought down upon the Emir's own camels, they may cost him not ten shillings.

What is the state and authority for which these bitter Arabians contended? Ibn Rashîd is master, as I can understand, of some thirty oases, of which there are five good desert towns: Sh'kâky, Jauf, Hâyil, Gofar, Teyma, with a population together of 12,000 to 13,000 souls: others are good villages, as *el-Kasr*, *Môgug*, *Aly*, *Mustajidda*, *Feyd*, *er-Rautha*, *Semîra*, *el-Hâyat*, and more, with hardly 5,000 persons. There are, besides the oases, many outlying hamlets in the desert of Jebel Shammar inhabited by a family or two or three households, that are colonists from the next villages; in the best may be a score of houses, in the least are not ten inhabitants; such are *Jefeyfa*, *el-Agella*, *el-Gussa*, *Biddîa*, *Haleyfa*, *Thùrghrod*, *Makhaûl*, *Otheym*. Some among them are but granges, which lie forsaken, after the April harvest is carried, until the autumn sowing and the new months of irrigation: but the palm hamlets have stable inhabitants, as Biddîa, Thùrghrod. So the settled population of Jebel Shammar may be hardly 20,000 souls: add to these the tributary nomads, Beny Wáhab, – the Fejîr, 800, and half tribe of Wélad Aly in the south, 1,600 – say together 2,500; then Bishr in the south, say 3,000, or they are less; northern Harb in the obedience of Ibn Rashîd, say 2,000; southern Shammar, hardly 2,000; midland Heteym, say 1,500; Sherarát, say, 2,500; and besides them no more. In all, say 14,000 persons or less: and the sum of stable and nomad dwellers may be not much better than 30,000 souls. ...

The Prince Mohammed is pitiless in battle, he shoots with an European rifle; Hamûd, of ponderous strength, is seen raging in arms by the Emir's side, and, if need were, since they are sworn together to the death, he would cover him with his body. The princes, descended from their thelûls, and sitting upon horseback in their 'David shirts of mail', are among the forefighters, and the wings of the men-at-arms, shooting against the enemy, close them upon either hand. The Emir's battle bears down the poor Beduw, by weight and numbers; for the rajajîl, and his riders of the villages, used to the civil life, hear the words of command, and can maintain themselves in a body together. But the bird-witted Beduins whom in their herding life, have no thought of martial exercises, may hardly gather, in the day of battle, under their sheukh, but like screaming hawks they fight dispersedly, tilting hither and thither, every man with less regard of the common than of his private interest, and that is to catch a beggarly booty: the poor nomads acknowledge themselves to be betrayed by tóma, the greediness of gain. Thus their resistance is weak, and woe to the broken and turned to flight! None of the Emir's enemies are taken to quarter until they be destroyed: and cruel are the mercies of the rajajîl and the dire-hearted slaves of Ibn Rashîd. I have known when some miserable tribesmen made prisoners were cast by the Emir's band into their own well-pits: – the Arabians take no captives. The battles with nomads are commonly fought in the summer, about their principal water-stations, where they are long lodged in great standing camps.

Thus the Beduins say 'It is Ibn Rashîd that weakens the Beduw!' Their resistance broken, he receives them among his confederate tributaries, and delivers them from all their enemies from his side. A part of the public spoil is divided to the rajajîl, and every man's is that commonly upon which he first laid his hand. Ibrahîm the Algerian, one of them who often came to speak with me of his West Country, said that to every man of the Emir's rajajîl are delivered three or four reals at the setting out, that he may buy himself wheat, dates and ammunition; and there is carried with them sometimes as much as four camel loads of powder and lead from Hâyil, which is partly for the Beduw that will join him by the way.

But to circumscribe the principality or dominion in the deserts of Ibn Rashîd: – his borders in the North are the Ruwàlla, northern Shammar and Thuffîr marches, nomad tribes friendly to the Jebel, but not his tributaries. Upon the East his limits are at the dominion of Boreyda, which we shall see is a principality of many good villages in the Nefûd of Kasîm, as el-Ayûn, Khubbera, er-Russ, but with no subject Beduw. The princely house of Hâyil is by marriage allied to that usurping peasant *Weled Mahanna* tyrant of Boreyda, and they are accorded together against the East, that is Aneyza, and the now decayed power of the Waháby beyond the mountain. In the South, having lost Kheybar, his limits are at about an hundred miles from el-Medina; the deserts of his dominion are bounded westwards by the great Haj-way from Syria, – if we leave out the B.Atîeh – and all the next territory of the Sherarát is subject to him, which ascends to J. Sherra and so turns about by the *W. Sirhân* to his good northern towns of Jauf and Sh'kâky and their suburbs. In a word, all that is Ibn Rashîd's desert country lying between Jauf, el-Kasîm and the Derb el-Haj; north and south some ninety leagues over, and between east and west it may be 170 leagues over. And the whole he keeps continually subdued to him with a force (by their own saying) of about 500 thelûl riders, his rajajîl and villagers; for who may assemble in equal numbers out of the dead wilderness, or what were twice so many wild Beduins, the half being almost without arms, to resist him?

The Coffee Server's Violence

A fire was kindled morning and evening in the great kahwa, and I went there to warm myself with the Beduins. One evening before almost anyone came in, I approached to warm myself at the fire-pit. – 'Away! (cried the coffee-server, who was of a very splenetic fanatical humour) and leave the fire to the guests that will presently arrive.' Some Beduins entered and sat down by me. 'I say, go back!' cries the coffee-keeper. 'A moment, man, and I am warm; be we not all the Prince's guests?' Some of the Beduw said in my ear: 'It were better to remove, not to give them an occasion.' That káhwajy daily showed his rancour, breaking into my talk with the Beduw, as when someone asked me 'Whither wilt thou next, Khalîl?' – 'May it please Ullah (cries the coffee-server) to jehennem!' I have heard he was one of servile condition from Aneyza in Kasîm; but being daily worshipfully saluted by guesting Beduin sheykhs, he was come to some solemn opinion of himself. To cede to the tyranny of a servant might, I thought, hearten other fanatics' audacity in Hâyil. The coffee-server, with a frenetic voice, cried to a Beduwy sitting by, 'Reach me that camel-stick,' (which the nomads have always in their hands,) and having snatched it from him, the slave struck me with all his decrepit force. The Beduins had risen round me with troubled looks, – they might feel that they were not themselves safe; none of these were sheykhs, that durst say any word, only they beckoned me to withdraw with them, and sit down with them at a little distance. It had been perilous to defend myself among dastards; for it it were told in the town that the Nasrâny laid heavy hands on a Moslem, then the wild fire had kindled in many hearts to avenge him. The Emir must therefore hear of the mátter and do justice, or so long as I remained in Hâyil every shrew would think he had as good leave to insult me. I passed by the gallery to the Emir's apartment, and knocking on the iron door, I heard the slave-boy who kept it within say to the guard that it was Khalîl the Nasrâny. The Emir sent out Nasr to inquire my business, and I went to sit in the Méshab. Later someone coming from the Kasr who had been with the Emir, said that the Emir sent for the coffee-server immediately, and said to him, 'Why! Ullah curse thy father, hast thou struck the Nasrâny?' – 'Wellah, O el-Muhafûth (the trembling wretch answered) I touched him not!' – so he feared the Emir, who said then to some of the guard 'Beat him!' – but Hamûd rose and going over to Mohammed, he kissed his cousin's hand, asking him, for his sake, to spare the coffee-server, 'who was a *mesquin* (meskîn).' 'Go káhwajy, said the Emir, and if I hear any more there shall nothing save thee, but thou shalt lose thy office.' Because I forsook the coffee-hall, the second coffee-server came many times to my makhzan, and wooed me to return among them; but I responded, 'Where the guests of the Emir are not safe from outrage –!'

Departure from Hâyil. The Kheybar Journey

I thought no more of Bagdad, but of Kheybar; already I stayed too long in Hâyil. At evening I went to Abeyd's kahwa to speak with Hamûd; he was bowing then in the beginning of his private devotion, and I sat down silently, awaiting his leisure. The son of Abeyd at the end of the first bout looked up, and nodding cheerfully, inquired, 'Khalîl, is there need, wouldst thou anything immediately?' – 'There is nothing, the Lord be praised.' – 'Then I shall soon have ended.' As Hamûd sat again in his place, I said, 'I saw the child Feysal's health returning, I desired to depart, and would he send me to Kheybar?' Hamûd answered, 'If I wished it.' – 'But why, Khalîl, to Kheybar, what is there at Kheybar? go not to Kheybar, thou mayest die of fever at Kheybar; and they are not our friends, Khalîl, I am afraid of that journey for thee.' I answered, 'I must needs adventure thither, I would see the antiquities of the Yahûd, as I have seen el-Héjr.' – 'Well, I will find some means to send thee; but the fever is deadly, go not thither, eigh Khalîl! lest thou die there.' – Since I had passed the great Aueyrid I desired to discover also the Harrat Kheybar, such another vulcanic Arabian country, and wherein I heard to be the heads of the W. er-Rummah, which westward of the Tueyk mountains is the dry waterway of all northern Arabia. This great valley which descends from the heads above el-Hâyat and Howeyat to the Euphrates valley at ez-Zbeyer, a suburb of Bosra, has a winding course of 'fifty camel marches.'

Hamûd, then stretching out his manly great arm, bade me try his pulse; the strokes of his heart-blood were greater than

I had felt any man's among the Arabians, the man was strong as a champion. When they hold out their forearms to the hakîm, they think he may well perceive all their health; I was cried down when I said it was imposture. 'Yesterday a Persian medicaster in the Haj was called to the Kasr to feel the Emir's pulse. The Persian said, 'Have you not a pain, Sir, in the left knee?' the Prince responded, 'Ay I feel a pain there by God!' – and no man knew it!'...

... Afterwards, I met with Imbârak. 'Wouldst thou (he said) to Kheybar? there are some Annezy here, who will convey thee.' When I heard their menzils were in the Kharram, and that they could only carry me again to Misshel, and were to depart immediately: I said that I could not so soon be ready to take a long journey, and must call in the debts for medicines. 'We will gather them for thee; but longer we cannot suffer thee to remain in our country: if thou wouldst go to Kheybar, we will send thee to Kheybar or to el-Kasîm, we will send thee to el-Kasîm.' – 'To Kheybar, yet warn me a day or two beforehand, that I may be ready.'

The morning next but one after, I was drinking kahwa with those of ew-Riâth, when a young man entered out of breath, he came, he said, to call me from Imbârak. Imbârak when I met him, said, 'We have found some Heteym who will convey thee to Kheybar.' – 'And when would they depart?' – 'To-morrow or the morning after.' But he sent for me in an hour to say he had given them handsel, and I must set out immediately. 'Why didst thou deceive me with *to-morrow*?' – 'Put up thy things and mount.' – 'But will you send me with Heteym!' – 'Ay, ay, give me the key of the makhzan and make up, for thou art to mount immediately.' – 'And I cannot speak with the Emir?' – '*Ukhlus!* have done, delay not, or wellah! the Emir will send, to take off thy head.' – 'Is this driving me into the desert to make me away, covertly?' – 'Nay, nothing will happen to thee.' – 'Now well let me first see Hamûd.' There came then a slave of Hamûd, bringing in his hand four reals, which he said his 'uncle' sent to me. So there came Zeyd, the Moghreby porter of the Kasr; I had shown him a good turn by the gift of medicines, but now quoth the burly villain, 'Thou hast no heart (understanding) if thou wouldst resist Imbârak; for this is the captain and there ride behind him 500 men.'

I delayed to give the wooden key of my door, fearing lest if they had flung the things forth my aneroid had been broken, or if they searched them my pistol had been taken; also I doubted whether the captain of the guard (who at every moment laid hand to the hilt of his sword) had not some secret commission to slay the Nasrâny there within. His slaves already came about me, some plucked my clothes, some thrust me forward; they would drive me perforce to the makhzan. – 'Is the makhzan thine or ours, Khalîl?' – 'But Imbârak, I no longer trust thee: bear my word to the Emir, "I came from the Dowla, send me back to the Dowla."' The Arab swordsman with *fugh!* spat in my face. 'Heaven send thee confusion that art not ashamed to spit in a man's face.' – 'Khalîl, I did it because thou saidst "I will not trust thee."' I saw the Moghreby porter go and break open my makhzan door, bursting the clay mortice of the wooden lock. The slaves plucking me savagely again, I let go the loose Arab upper garments in their hands, and stood before the wondering wretches in my shirt. 'A shame! I said to them, and thou Imbârak *dakhîl-ak*, defend me from their insolence.' As Imbârak heard 'dakhîl-ak,' he snatched a camel-stick from one who stood by, and beat them back and drove them from me.

They left me in the makhzan and I quickly put my things in order, and took my arms secretly. Fáhd now came by, going to Abeyd's kahwa: I said to him, 'Fáhd, I will enter with thee, for here I am in doubt, and where is Hamûd?' The poor man answered friendly, 'Hamûd is not yet abroad, but it will not be long, Khalîl, before he come.' – *Imbârak*: 'Wellah, I say the Emir will send immediately to cut off thy head! '*Mâjid* (who passed us at the same time, going towards Abeyd's kahwa); 'Eigh! Imbârak, will the Emir do so indeed?' and the boy smiled with a child's dishonest curiosity of an atrocious spectacle. As I walked on with Fáhd, Imbârak retired from us, and passed through the Kasr gate, perhaps then he went to the Emir. Fáhd sighed, as we were beyond the door, and 'Khalîl, please Ullah, said the poor man, it may yet fall out well, and Hamûd will very soon be here.' I had not sat long, when they came to tell me, 'the Emir desired to see me.' I said, 'Do not deceive me, it is but Imbârak who knocks.' *Fáhd*: 'Nay, go Khalîl, it is the Emir.'

When I went out, I found it was Imbârak, who with the old menaces, called upon me to mount immediately. 'I will first, I answered, see Hamûd': so he left me. The door had been shut behind me, I returned to the makhzan, and saw my baggage was safe; and Fáhd coming by again, 'Hamûd, he said, is now in the house,' and at my request he sent back a servant to let me in. After a little, Hamûd entering, greeted me, and took me by the hand. I asked, 'Was this done at the commandment of the Emir?' *Hamûd*: 'By God, Khalîl, I can do nothing with the Emir; *hu yáhkam aleyna* he rules over us all.' – 'Some books of mine, and other things, were brought here.' – 'Ha! the eyyâl have taken them from thy makhzan, they shall be restored.' When I spoke of a knavish theft of his man Aly – he was gone now on pilgrimage – Hamûd exclaimed: 'The Lord take away his breath!' – He were not an Arab if he had proffered to make good his man's larceny. 'What intended you by that money you lately sent me?' – 'My liberality, Khalîl, why didst thou refuse it?' – 'Is it for medicine and a month's daily care of thy child, who is now restored to health?' – 'It was for this I offered it, and we have plenty of quinine; wilt thou buy an handful of me for two reals?' He was washing to go to the mid-day public prayer, and whilst the strong man stayed to speak with me it was late. 'There is a thing, Hamûd.' – 'What is that, Khalîl?' and he looked up cheerfully. 'Help me in this trouble, for that bread and salt which is between us.' – 'And what can I do? Mohammed rules us all.' – 'Well, speak to Imbârak to do nothing till the hour of the afternoon mejlis, when I may speak with the Emir.' – 'I will say this to him,' and Hamûd went to the mesjid.

After the prayer I met the Prince himself in the Méshab; he walks, as said, in an insolent cluster of young fanatics, and a half score of his swordsmen close behind them. – Whenever I had encountered the Emir and his company of late, in the streets, I thought he had answered my greeting with a strutting look. Now, as he came on with his stare, I said, without a salutation, *Arûth*, 'I depart.' '*Rûhh*, So go,' answered Mohammed. 'Shall I come in to speak with thee?' – '*Meshghrûl!* we are too busy.'

When at length the afternoon mejlis was sitting, I crossed through them and approached the Emir, who sat enforcing himself to look gallantly before the people; and he talked then with some great sheykh of the Beduw, who was seated next him. Mohammed Ibn Rashîd looked towards me, I thought with displeasure and somewhat a base countenance, which is of evil augury among the Arabs. 'What (he said) is thy matter?' – 'I am about to depart, but I would it were with assurance. To-day I was mishandled in this place, in a manner which had made me afraid. Thy slaves drew me hither and thither, and have rent my clothing; it was by the setting on of Imbârak, who stands here: he also threatened me, and even spat in my face.' The Emir inquired, under his voice, of Imbârak, 'what had he done,' who answered, excusing himself. I added, 'And now he would compel me to go with Heteym; and I foresee only mischance.' 'Nay (said the Emir, striking his breast), fear not; but ours be the care for thy safety, and we will give thee a passport,' – and he said to Nasr, his secretary, who sat at his feet – 'Write him a schedule of safe-conduct.'

I said, 'I brought thee from my country an excellent telescope.' The cost had been three or four pounds; and I thought, 'if Ibn Rashîd receive my gift, I might ask of him a camel': but when he said: 'We have many, and have no need,' I answered the Emir with a frank word of the desert, *weysh aad*, as one might say, 'What odds!' Mohammed Ibn Rashîd shrunk back in his seat, as if I had disparaged his dignity before the people; but recovering himself, he said, with better looks and a friendly voice, 'Sit down.' Mohammed is not ungenerous, he might remember in the stranger his own evil times. Nasr having ended his writing, upon a small square of paper, handed it up to the Emir, who perused it, and daubing his Arabic copper seal in the ink, he sealed it with the print of his name. I asked Nasr, 'Read me what is written herein,' and he read, 'That all unto whose hands this bill may come, who owe obedience to Ibn Rashîd, know it is the will of the Emir that no one *yaarud aley*, should do any offence to, this Nasrâny.' Ibn Rashîd rising at the moment, the mejlis rose with him and dispersed. I asked, as the Emir was going, 'When shall I depart?' – 'At thy pleasure.' – 'To-morrow?' – 'Nay, to-day.' He had turned the back, and was crossing the Méshab.

'Mount!' cries Imbârak: but, when he heard I had not broken my fast he led me through the Kasr, to the Mothif and to a room behind, which is the public kitchen, to ask the cooks what was ready. Here they all kindly welcomed me, and Mufarrij would give me dates, flour and samn for the way, the accustomed provision from the Emir, but I would not receive them. The kitchen is a poor hall, with a clay floor, in which is a pool and conduit. The temmn and barley is boiled in four or five coppers: other three stand there for flesh days (which are not many), and they are so great that in one of them may be seethed the brittled meat of a camel. So simple is this palace kitchen of nomadic Arabia, a country in which he is feasting who is not hungry! The kitchen servants were one poor man, perhaps of servile condition, a patient of mine, and five or six women under him; besides there were boys, bearers of the metal trays of victual for the guests' suppers. – When I returned to the Méshab, a nomad was come with his camel to load my baggage: yet first he entreated Imbârak to take back his real of earnest-money and let him go. The Emir had ordered four reals to be given for this voyage, whether I would or no, and I accepted it in lieu of that which was robbed from my makhzan; also I accepted the four reals from Hamûd for medicines.

'Imbârak, swear, I said as we walked together to the sûk, where the nomads would mount, that you are not sending me to the death.' – 'No, by Ullah, and Khalîl nothing I trust will happen to thee.' – 'And after two journeys in the desert will the Aarab any more observe the word of Ibn Rashîd?' – 'We rule over them! – and he said to the nomads, Ye are to carry him to *Kâsim ibn Barâk* (a great sheykh of the midland Heteym, his byût were pitched seventy miles to the southward), and he will send him to Kheybar.' – The seller of drugs from Medina, a good liberal Hejâz man, as are many of that partly Arabian city, came out, as we passed his shop, to bid me God speed, 'Thou mayest be sure, he said, that there is no treachery, but understand that the people (of Hâyil and Nejd) are Beduw.' – 'O thou (said the nomad to me) make haste along with us out of Hâyil, stand not, nor return upon thy footsteps, for then they will kill thee.'

Because I would not that his camel should kneel, but had climbed upon the overloaded beast's neck standing, the poor pleased nomad cried out, 'Lend me a grip of thy five!' that is the five fingers. A young man, Ibrahîm, one of the Emir's men – his shop was in the end of the town, and I had dealt with him – seeing us go by, came out to bid me farewell, and brought me forward. He spoke sternly to the nomads that they should have a care for me, and threatened them, that 'If anything befell me, the Emir would have their heads.' Come to the Mâ es-Sáma, I reached down my water-skin to one of the men, bidding him go fill it. 'Fill the kafir's girby! nay, said he, alight, Nasrâwy, and fill it thyself.' Ibrahîm then went to fill it, and hanged the water at my saddle-bow. We passed forth and the sun was now set. My companions were three, – the poor owner of my camel, a timid smiling man, and his fanatic neighbour, who called me always the Nasrâwy (and not Nasrâny), and another and older Heteymy, a somewhat strong-headed holder of his own counsel, and speaking the truth uprightly. So short is the twilight that the night closed suddenly upon our march, with a welcome silence and solitude, after the tumult of the town. When I responded to all the questions of my nomad company with the courtesy of the desert, 'Oh! wherefore, cried they, did those Hâyil persecute him? Wellah the people of Hâyil are the true Nasâra!' We held on our dark way three and a half hours till we came before Gofar; there we alighted and lay down in the wilderness.

When the morrow was light we went to an outlying kasr, a chamber or two built of clay-brick, without the oasis, where dwelt a poor family of their acquaintance. We were in the end of November (the 21st by my reckoning); the nights were now

cold at this altitude of 4,000 feet. The poor people set dates
before us and made coffee; they were neither settlers upon the
soil nor nomads, but Beduw. Weak and broken in the nomad's
life, and forsaking the calamities of the desert, they had become 'dwellers in clay' at one of the Jebel villages, and
Seyadîn or traffickers to the Aarab. They buy dates and corn in
harvest time, to sell later to the *hubts* or passing market parties
of nomad tribesmen. When spring is come they forsake the
clay-walls and, loading their merchandise upon asses, go forth
to trade among the Aarab. Thus they wander months long,
till their lading is sold; and when the hot summer is in they
will return with their humble gains of samn and silver to the
oasis. From them my companions took up part of their winter
provision of dates, for somewhat less the market price in
Hâyil. These poor folk, disherited of the world, spoke to me
with human kindness; there was not a word in their talk of the
Mohammed fanaticism. The women, of their own thought,
took from my shoulders and mended my mantle which had
been rent yesterday at Hâyil; and the house-father put in my
hand his own driving-stick made of an almond rod. Whilst I
sat with them, my companions went about their other business. Bye and bye there came in a butcher from Hâyil. (I had
bought of him three pounds of mutton one morning, for
fourpence), and with a loud good humour he praised the
Nasrâny in that simple company.

The men were not ready till an hour past midday; then they
loaded their dates and we departed. Beyond Gofar we journeyed upon a plain of granite grit; the long Ajja mountain
trended with our course upon the right hand. At five we
alighted and I boiled them some temmn which I carried, but
the sun suddenly setting upon us, they skipt up laughing to
patter their prayers, and began to pray as they could, with
quaking ribs; and they panted yet with their elvish mirth –
Some wood-gatherers of Hâyil went by us. The double head
of the Sumrâ Hâyil was still in sight at a distance of twenty-five
miles. Remounting we passed in the darkness the walls and
palms of el-Kasr, thirteen miles from Gofar, under the cliffs of
Ajja; an hour further we alighted in the desert to sleep. I saw

in the morning the granite flanks of Ajja strangely blotted, as it were with the shadows of clouds, by the running down of erupted basalts; and there are certain black domes upon the crest in the likeness of volcanoes. Two hours later we were in a granitic mountain ground *el-Mukhtelif.* Ajja upon the right hand now stands far off and extends not much further. We met here with a young man of el-Kasr riding upon his thelûl in quest of a strayed well-camel. Rock-partridges were everywhere calling and flying in this high granite country, smelling in the sun of the (resinous) sweetness of southernwood.

About four in the afternoon we went by an outlying hamlet *Biddîa,* in the midst of the plain, but encompassed by lesser mountains of granite and basalt. This small settlement, which lies thirty-five miles W. of S. from el-Kasr, was begun not many years ago by projectors from Môgug; there are only two wells and four households. When I asked my companions of the place, they fell a coughing and laughing, and made me signs that only coughs and rheums there abounded. – A party of Shammar riding on dromedaries overtook us. They had heard of Khalîl and spoke friendly, saying that there lay a menzil of their Aarab not far before us (where we might sup and sleep). And we heard from them these happy tidings of the wilderness in front, 'The small cattle have yeaned, and the Aarab have plenty of léban; they pour out (to drink) till the noon day!' One of them cried to me: 'But why goest thou in the company of these dogs?' – he would say 'Heteymies.'

A great white snake, *hánash,* lay sleeping in the path: and the peevish owner put it to the malice of the Nasrâny that I had not sooner seen the worm, and struck away his camel, which was nearly treading on it; and with his lance he beat in pieces the poisonous vermin. When the daylight was almost spent my companions climbed upon every height to look for the black booths of the Aarab. The sun set and we journeyed on in the night, hoping to espy the Beduin tent-fires. Three hours later we halted and lay down, weary and supperless, to sleep in the khála. The night was chill and we could not slumber; the land-height was here 4,000 feet.

We loaded and departed before dawn. Soon after the day broke we met with Shammar Aarab removing. Great are their flocks in their dîra, all of sheep, and their camels are a multitude trooping over the plain. Two herdsmen crossed to us to hear tidings: 'What news, they shouted, from the villages? how many sahs to the real?' – Then, perceiving what I was, one of them who had a lance lifted it and said to the other, 'Stand back, and he would slay me.' 'Nay do not so! wellah! (exclaimed my rafîks), for this (man) is in the safeguard of Ibn Rashîd, and we must billah convey him, upon our necks, to Ch(K)âsim Ibn Barák.' Heteymies in presence of high-handed Shammar, they would have made no manly resistance; and my going with these rafîks was nearly the same as to wander alone, save that they were eyes to me in the desert.

In the slow march of the over-loaded camels I went much on foot; the fanatic who cried Nasrâwy Nasrâwy! complained that he could not walk, he must ride himself upon my hired camel. Though weary I would not contradict them, lest in remembering Hâyil they should become my adversaries. I saw the blown sand of the desert lie in high drifts upon the mountain sides which encompassed us; they are granite with some basalt bergs. – We were come at unawares to a menzil of Shammar. Their sheykh hastened from his booth to meet us, a wild looking carl, and he had not a kerchief, but only the woollen head-cord *maasub* wound about his tufted locks. He required of me dokhân; but I told them I had none, the tobacco-bag with flint and steel had fallen from my camel a little before. – 'Give us tobacco (cried he), and come down and drink kahwa with us, and if no we will *nô'kh* (make kneel) thy camel, and take it perforce.' – 'How (I said), ye believe not in God! I tell you I have none by God, it is *aŷib* (a shame) man to molest a stranger, and that only for a pipe of tobacco.' Then he let me pass, but they made me swear solemnly again that I had none indeed.

As we journeyed in the afternoon and were come into Heteym country we met with a sheykhly man riding upon his thelûl: he would see what pasture was sprung hereabout in the wilderness. The rafîks knew him, and the man said he would carry me to Kheybar himself, for tôma (gain). This was one whom I should see soon again, *Eyâda ibn Ajjuèyn*, an Heteymy sheykh. My rafîks counselled me to go with him: 'He is a worthy man, they said, and one with whom I might safely adventure.' – The first movements of the Arabs from their heart, are the best, and the least interested, and could the event be foreseen it were often great prudence to accept them; but I considered the Emir's words, – that I should go to Kâsim ibn Barák sheykh of the Beny Rashîd 'who would send me to Kheybar,' and his menzil was not now far off. This Kâsim or Châsim, or *Jâsim*, they pronounce the name diversely, according to their tribes' loghrat, my companions said was a great sheykh, 'and one like to be to Ibn Rashîd' in his country.

The sun set as we came to the first Heteym booths, and there the rafîks unloaded. Kâsim's beyt we heard was built under a brow yonder, and I mounted again with my rafîk Sâlih, upon his empty camel, to ride thither. And in the way said Sâlih, 'When we arrive see that thou get down lightly; so the Aarab will hold of thee the more as one inured to the desert life.' Kâsim's tent was but a héjra, small and rent; I saw his mare tied there, and within were only the hareem. One of them went to call the sheykh, and Sâlih hastily put down my bags: he remounted, and without leave-taking would have ridden away; but seizing his camel by the beard I made the beast kneel again, 'My rafîk, why abandon me thus? but Sâlih thou shalt deliver all the Emir's message to Kâsim'; – we saw him coming to us from a neighbour beyt.

Kâsim was a slender young man, almost at the middle age. At first he said that he could not receive me. 'How! (he asked), had the Emir sent this stranger to him, to send him on to Kheybar, when he was at feud with those of Kheybar!' Then he reproached Sâlih who would have 'forsaken me at strange tents.' – I considered how desperate a thing it were, to be abandoned in the midst of the wilderness of Arabia, where we dread to meet with unknown mankind more than with wild beasts! 'You, Kâsim, have heard the word of Ibn Rashîd, and if it cannot be fulfilled at least I have alighted at thy beyt and

am weary; here, I said, let me rest this night, *wa ana dakhîlak*,
and I enter under thy roof.'

He now led me into his booth and bade me repose: then
turning all his vehement displeasure against Sâlih, he laid
hands on him and flung him forth – these are violences of the
Heteym – and snatched his mantle from him. 'Away with
thee! he cried, but thy camel shall remain with me, whereupon
I may send this stranger to Kheybar; Ullah curse thy father,
O thou that forsakedst thy rafîk to cast him upon Aarab.'
Sâlih took all in patience, for the nomads when they are overborne make no resistance. Kâsim set his sword to Sâlih's
throat, that he should avow to him all things without any
falsity, and first what tribesman he was. Sâlih now acknowledged himself to be of *Bejaida*, that is a sub-tribe of Bishr; he
was therefore of Annezy, but leading his life with Noâmsy
Heteymies he passed for an Heteymy. Many poor families both
of Annezy and Harb join themselves to that humbler but more
thriving nomad lot, which is better assured from enemies; only
they mingle not in wedlock with the Heteym. So Kâsim let
Sâlih go, and called to kindle the fire, and took up himself a
lapful of his mare's provender and littered it down to Sâlih's
camel; so he came again and seated himself in the tent with the
hypochondriacal humour of a sickly person. 'Who is there,
said he, will go now and seek us kahwa that we may make a
cup for this stranger? – thy name?' – 'Khalîl.' – 'Well, say
Khalîl, what shall I do in this case, for wellah, I cannot tell;
betwixt us and those of Kheybar and the Dowla there is only
debate and cutting of throats: how then says the Emir, that I
must send thee to Kheybar?' – Neighbours came in to drink
coffee, and one answered, 'If Khalîl give four reals I will set
him down, billah, at the edge of the palms of Kheybar and be
gone.' *Kâsim*: 'But Khalîl says rightly he were then as much
without Kheybar as before.'

The coffee-drinkers showed me a good countenance; 'Eigh!
Khalîl (said Kâsim), hadst thou complained to me that the
man forsook thee, he who came with thee, wellah I would have
cut off his head and cast it on this fire: accursed be all the *Anúz*
[nation of Annezy].' – 'Well, if Kheybar be too difficult, you

may send me to Hannas sheykh of the Noâmsy; I heard he is encamped not far off, and he will receive me friendly.' – 'We shall see in the morning.' A scarce dish of boiled temmn without samn, and a little old rotten léban was set before me, – the smallest cheer I had seen under worsted booths; they had no fresh milk because their camel troops were âzab, or separated from the menzil, and pasturing towards Baitha Nethîl, westward.

The night closed in darkly over us, with thick clouds and falling weather, it lightened at once upon three sides without thunder. The nomad people said, '*It is the angels!*' – their word made me muse of the nomads' vision in the field of Bethlehem. 'The storm, they murmured, is over the Wady er-Rummah,' – which they told me lay but half a thelûl journey from hence. They marvelled that I should know the name of this great Wady of middle Nejd: the head, they said, is near el-Hâyat, in their dîra, one thelûl day distant, – that may be over plain ground forty-five to seventy miles. The cold rain fell by drops upon us through the worn tent-cloth: and when it was late said Kâsim, 'Sleep thou, but I must wake with my eyes upon his camel there, all night, lest that Annezy (man) come to steal it away.'

When I rose with the dawn Kâsim was making up the fire; 'Good morrow! he said: well, I will send thee to Hannas; and the man shall convey thee that came with thee.' – 'He betrayed me yesterday, will he not betray me to-day? he might even forsake me in the khála.– But I will make him swear so that he shall be afraid.' Women came to me hearing I was a mudowwy with baggl or dry milk shards, to buy medicines; and they said it was a provision for my journey. Kâsim's sister came among the rest and sat down beside me. Kâsim, she said, was vexed with the rîhh or ague-cake, and what medicine had I? These women's veil is a blue calico clout suspended over the lower face; her eyes were wonderfully great, and though lean and pale, I judged that she was very beautiful and gracious; she leaned delicately to examine my drugs with the practised hands of a wise woman in simples. When she could find no medicine that she knew, she said, with a gentle sweet voice,

'Give then what thou wilt, Khalîl, only that which may be effectual.' Although so fair, and the great sheykh's sister, yet no man of the Beduins would have wedded with her; because the Heteym 'are not of the stock' of the Aarab.

Now came Sâlih, and when he saw his camel restored to him, he was full of joy, and promised all that Kâsim would; and he swore mighty oaths to convey me straightway to Hannas. We mounted and rode forth; but as we were going I drew bridle and bound Sâlih by that solemn oath of the desert, *aly el-aûd wa Rubb el-mabûd*, that he would perform all these things: if he would not swear, I would ride no further with him. But Sâlih looking back and trembling cried, 'I do swear it, billah, I swear it, only let us hasten and come to our rafîks, who have awaited us at the next tents.'

We set out anew with them, and quoth Sâlih, 'I was never in such fear in my life, as when Châsim set his sword to my neck!' We marched an hour and a half and approached another Heteym menzil of many beyts: as we passed by Sâlih went aside to them to inquire the tidings. Not far beyond we came upon a brow, where two lone booths stood. My companions said the (overloaded) camels were broken, they would discharge them there to pasture an hour. When we were come to the place they halted.

In the first tent was an old wife: she bye and bye brought out to us, where we sat a little aloof, a bowl of milk shards and samn, and then, that which is of most comfort in the droughty heat, a great bowl of her butter-milk. 'Canst thou eat this fare? said Sâlih, – the Heteym have much of it, they are good and hospitable.' The men rose after their breakfast and loaded upon the camels, – but not my bags! – and drove forth. I spoke to the elder Heteymy, who was a worthy man, but knitting the shoulders and turning up his palms he answered gravely, 'What can I do? it is Sâlih's matter, wellah, I may not meddle in it; but thou have no fear, for these are good people, and amongst them there will no evil befall thee.' 'Also Eyâda ibn Ajjuèyn, said Sâlih, is at little distance.' – 'But where is thy oath, man?' The third fanatic fellow answered for him, 'His oath is not binding, which was made to a Nasrâwy!' – 'But what of the Emir? and Kâsim is not yet far off.' *Sâlih*: 'As for Kâsim we curse both his father and his mother; but thou be not troubled, the Heteym are good folk and this will end well.' – To contend with them were little worth; they might then have published it that I was a Nasrâny, I was as good quit of such rafîks, – here were but two women – and they parted.

– 'It is true, quoth the old wife, that Eyâda is near, yesterday I heard their dogs bark.' In the second tent was but her sick daughter-in-law; their men were out herding. The old wife looked somewhat grim when the hubt had forsaken me; afterwards she came where I sat alone, and said, 'Be not sorrowful! *ana khâlatak*, for I am thy mother's sister.' Soon after that she went out to bear word to the men in the wilderness of this chance. Near by that place I found the border of a brown vulcanic flood, a kind of trachytic basalt: when the sun was setting I walked out of sight, – lest seeing the stranger not praying at the hour I had been too soon known to them.

Not much after the husband came home, a deaf man with the name of happy augury *Thaifullah*: kindly he welcomed me, and behind him came three grown sons driving-in their camels; and a great flock of sheep and goats followed them with many lambs and kids. I saw that (notwithstanding their Heteym appearance of poverty) they must be welfaring persons. Thaifullah, as we sat about the evening fire, brought me in a bowl of the evening milk, made hot; – 'We have nothing, he said, here to eat, no dates, no rice, no bread, but drink this which the Lord provideth, though it be a poor supper.' I blessed him and said it was the best of all nourishment. 'Ay, thus boiled, he answered, it enters into the bones.' When he heard how my rafîks forsook me to-day he exclaimed, 'Billah if he had been there, he had cut off their heads.' That poor man was very honourable; he would hardly fill his galliûn once with a little tittun that I had found in the depth of my bags, although it be so great a solace to them; neither suffered he his young men to receive any from the (forlorn) guest whom the Lord had committed to them, to-day. These were simple, pious and not (formal) praying Arabs, having in their mouths no cavilling questions of religion, but they were full of the godly humanity of the wilderness. 'He would carry me in the morning (said my kind host) to Eyâda ibn Ajjuèyn, who would send me to Kheybar.'

It was dim night, and the drooping clouds broke over us with lightning and rain. I said to Thaifullah, 'God sends his blessing again upon the earth.' – 'Ay verily,' he answered devoutly, and kissed his pious hand towards the flashing tempest and murmured the praises of Ullah. – How good! seemed to me, how peaceable! this little plot of the nomad earth under the dripping curtains of a worsted booth, in comparison with Hâyil town!

When the morning rose the women milked their small cattle; and we sat on whilst the old housewife rocked her blown-up milk-skin upon her knees till the butter came; they find it in a clot at the mouth of the semîly. I saw soon that little butter seething on the fire, to be turned into samn, and they called me to sup the pleasant milk-skim with my fingers. They throw in now a little meal, which brings down the milkiness; and the samn or clarified butter may be poured off. The sediment of the meal thus drenched with milky butter is served to the guest; and it is the most pleasant sweet-meat of the poor nomad life. Afterward the good old woman brought me the samn (all that her flocks had yielded this morning), in a little skin (it might be less than a small pint): this was her gift, she said; and would I leave with them some fever medicine? I gave her doses of quinine. She brought forth a large bowl of butter-milk; and when we had drunk a good draught Thaifullah laid my bags upon a camel of his. We mounted, and rode southward over the khála.

We journeyed an hour and approached Eyâda's menzil, the worsted booths were pitched in a shelving hollow overlooking a wide waste landscape to the south: I saw a vast blackness beyond, – that was another Harra (the *Harrat Kheybar*) – and rosy mountains of granite. Sandstones, lying as a tongue between the crystalline mountains and overlaid by lavas, reach

southward to Kheybar. – 'When we come to the tents thus
and thus shalt thou speak to them, said Thaifullah: say thou
art a mudowwy arrived from Hâyil, and that thou wouldst go
over to Kheybar; and for two reals thou shalt find some man
who will convey thee thither.'

We alighted and Thaifullah commended me to Eyâda; I was
(he said) a skilful mudowwy, – so he took his camel again and
departed. This was that Heteymy sheykh whom I had two days
before seen chevying in the wilderness: – he might have understood then (from some saying of the fanatic) that I was not a
right Moslem, for now when I saluted him and said I would go
to Kheybar with him, he received me roughly. He was a
sturdy carl, and with such ill-blooded looks as I have remarked
in the Fehját, which are also of Heteym. *Eyâda*: 'Well, I said
it yesterday, but I cannot send thee to Kheybar.' – Some men
were sitting before his tent – 'Ho! which of you, he said, will
convey the man to Kheybar, and receive from him what –?
three reals.' One answered, 'I will carry him, if he give me this
money.' I promised, and he went to make ready; but returning
he said, 'Give me four reals, – I have a debt, and this would
help me in it.' *Eyâda*: 'Give him four, and go with him.' I consented, so the sheykh warranted me that the man would not
forsake his rafîk, as did those of the other day. 'Nay, trust me,
this is *Ghroceyb*, a sheykh, and a valorous man.' – 'Swear, O
Ghroceyb, by the life of this stem of grass, that thou wilt not
forsake me, thy rafîk, until thou hast brought me to Kheybar!'
– 'I swear to bring thee thither, but I be dead.' *Eyâda*: 'He has
a thelûl too, that can flee like a bird.' *Ghroceyb*: 'See how the
sun is already mounted! let us pass the day here, and to-
morrow we will set forward.' – 'Nay, but to-day,' answered
the sheykh, shortly, so that I wondered at his inhospitable
humour and Ghroceyb at this strangeness. The sheykh did not
bid me into his tent, but he brought out to us a great bowl of
butter-milk. The hareem now came about me, bringing their
little bowls of dry milk shards, and they clamoured for medicines. I have found no Beduins so willing as the Heteym to buy
of the mudowwy. After my departure, when they had proved
my medicines, they said that Khalîl was a faithful man; and

their good report helped me months later, at my coming by this country again.

Ghroceyb told me that from hence to Baitha Nethîl was half a (thelûl) journey, to Hâyil three, to Teyma four, to el-Ally four and a half; and we should have three nights out to Kheybar. When we had trotted a mile, a yearling calf of the thelûl, that was grazing in the desert before us, ran with their side-long slinging gait (the two legs upon a side leaping together) to meet the dam, and followed us lowing, – the mother an-swered with sobs in her vast throat; but Ghroceyb dismounted and chased the weanling away. We rode upon a plain of sand. Nigh before us appeared that great craggy blackness – the Harra, and thereupon certain swart hills and crests, *el-Hélly*: I perceived them to be crater-hills of volcanoes! A long-ranging inconsiderable mountain, *Bothra*, trended with our course upon the left hand, which I could not doubt to be granitic. Ghroceyb encouraged his thelûl with a pleasant *gluck!* with the tongue under the palate, – I had not heard it before; and there is a diversity of cattle-calls in the several tribes of the Arabian khála.

We entered upon that black Harra. The lava field is now cast into great waves and troughs, and now it is a labyrinth of lava crags and short lava sand-plains. – This is another member of the vulcanic country of West Arabia, which with few con-siderable breaches, extends from Tebûk through 7° of latitude to the borders of Mecca.

We found clayey water, in a cavern (after the late showers), and Ghroceyb alighted to fill our girby. At half-afternoon we saw a goatherd loitering among the wild lavas. The lad was an Heteymy, he knew Ghroceyb, and showed us where the beyts were pitched, in a deep place not far off. Here Ghroceyb came to his own kindred; and we alighted at the tent of his brother. The cragged Harra face is there 4,300 feet above sea-level. Their hareem were veiled like those of Kâsim's encampment, and they wore a braided forelock hanging upon their foreheads. In the evening we were regaled with a caldron of temmn, and the host poured us out a whole skinful of thick butter-milk. ...

... In the early morning Ghroceyb milked our thelûl and brought me this warm bever; and after that, in the fatigue of the long way to be passed almost without her tasting herbage, her udder would be dried up, and the Beduwy fetched in a hurr to cover her; [at such times doubtless in the hope that she may bear a female]. We were called away to breakfast in another booth where they set before us dates fried in samn, and bowls of butter-milk. All was horrid lava-field far before us, and we should be 'two nights out without Aarab,' and the third at Kheybar.

Gloomy were these days of drooping grey clouds in the golden-aired Arabia. We journeyed quickly by the camel paths (*jiddar* pl. *jiddrân*) worn, since ages, in the rolling cinders and wilderness of horrid lavas. Hither come Bishr and Heteym nomads in the early year with their cattle, to seek that rabîa which may be sprung among the lava clefts and pits and little bottoms of vulcanic sand. Before noon we were among the black hills (*billiân*) which I had viewed before us since yesterday; they are cones and craters of spent volcanoes. Our path lay under the highest *hilly*, which might be of four hundred or five hundred feet. Some are two-headed, – it is where a side of the crater is broken down. Others are seen ribbed, that is they are guttered down from the head. *All is here as we have seen in the Harrat el-Aueyrid.* We passed over a smooth plain of cinders; and, at the roots of another hilly, I saw yellowish soft tufa lying under the scaly crags of lavas. From hence we had sight of the Kharram, a day distant to the westward; lying beyond the Harra in a yellow border of Nefûd; the white sand lay in long drifts upon the high flanks of the mountain.

There was now much ponded rain upon these vulcanic highlands; and in a place I heard the heavy din of falling water! We came to a cold new tarn, and it seemed a fenny mountain lake under the setting sun! from this strange desert water issued a wild brook with the rushing noise of a mill-race. Having gone all the daylight, we drew bridle in a covert place, where we might adventure to kindle our fire. My rafîk was never come so far in this sea of lava, but he knew the great landmarks, He went about to pull an armful of the scanty herbage in the crevices, for his fasting thelûl; I gathered dry stems to set under our pot, poured in water and began our boiling, which was but of temmn. When Ghroceyb came again I bid him mind the cooking; but said he, 'What can I do? I, billah, understand it not.' – 'Yet I never saw the nomad who could not shift for himself upon a journey.' – 'I eat that which the hareem prepare and have never put my hand to it.' – He had brought for himself only two or three handfuls of dry milk shards! in Ghroceyb was the ague-cake of old fever, and he could eat little or nothing. In this place I found the greatest height which I had passed hitherto in Arabia, nearly 6,000 feet. And here I have since understood to be the division of waters between the great wady bottoms of northern Arabia; namely the W. er-Rummah descending from the Harra to the north-eastward, and the W. el-Humth. This night was mild, and sheltered in the wild lavas, as between walls, we were warm till the morning.

We mounted in the morrow twilight; but long after day-break the heavens seemed shut over us, as a tomb, with gloomy clouds. We were engaged in the horrid lava beds; and were very oftentimes at fault among sharp shelves, or finding before us precipitous places. The vulcanic field is a stony flood which has stiffened; long rolling heads, like horse-manes, of those slaggy waves ride and over-ride the rest: and as they are risen they stand petrified, many being sharply split length-wise, and the hollow laps are partly fallen down in vast shells and in ruinous heaps as of massy masonry. The lava is not seldom wreathed as it were bunches of cords; the crests are seen also of sharp glassy lavas, *lâba* (in the plural *lúb*); lâba is all that which has a likeness to molten metal. – That this soil was ever drowned with burning mineral, or of burning moun-tains, the Aarab have no tradition. As we rode further I saw certain golden-red crags standing above the black horror of lavas; they were sandstone spires touched by the scattered beams of the morning sun. In the sheltered lava bottoms, where grow gum-acacias, we often startled *gatta* fowl ('sand-grouse'); they are dry-fleshed birds and not very good to eat, say the nomads. There is many times seen upon the lava fields a glistering under the sun as of distant water; it is but dry clay glazed over with salt.

Ghroceyb spread forth his hands devoutly; he knew not the formal prayers, but wearied the irrational element with the lowings of his human spirit in this perilous passage. 'Give, Lord, that we see not the evil! and oh that this be not the day of our deaths and the loss of the thelûl!' My rafîk knew not that I was armed. Ghroceyb, bearing his long matchlock, led on afoot betwixt running and walking, ever watching for a way before the thelûl, and gazing wide for dread of any traversing enemies. Upon a time turning suddenly he surprised me as I wrote with a pencil [a reading of the aneroid]. 'Is it well, O Khalîl? quoth my rafîk, how seest thou (in your magical art of letters), is there good or else evil toward? canst thou not write something (a strong spell) for this need?' Then seeing me ride on careless and slumbering for weariness he took comfort. My pistol of six chambers gave me this confidence in Arabia, for must we contend for our lives I thought it might suffice to defend me and my company, and Ghroceyb was a brave companion. Ghroceyb's long piece must weigh heavily upon the strenuous man's sick shoulders, and I spoke to him to hang it at the saddle-bow of me his rafîk; to this he consented, 'so I did not loop the shoulder-cord about the peak; it must hang simply, he said, that in any appearance of danger he might take it again at the instant.'

Two hours after the sunrise we passed the Harra borders, and came without this lava field upon soil of sandstone. The vulcanic country which we had crossed in seventeen hours is named Harrat *el-Ethnân*, of the great crater-hill of that name *J. Ethnân*; the dîra is of the Noâmsa Heteym. We came in an hour by a descending plain of red sand-rock, to a deep cleft, *es-Shotb*, where we drove down the dromedary at short steps, upon the shelves and ledges. In the bottom were gum-acacias, and a tree which I knew not, it has leaves somewhat like the mountain ash. 'The name of it is *thirru*, it has not any use that we know,' said Ghroceyb. Beyond the grove were some thin effluxions of lava run down upon the sandstone soil, from the vulcanic field above. By noon we had passed the sand-rock and came again upon the main Harra beyond, which is all one eastward with the former Harra; and there we went by a few low craters. The whole – which is the *Harrat Kheybar* – lies between north-west and south-east four days in length; and that may be, since it reaches to within a thelûl journey of Medina, an hundred great miles. The width is little in comparison, and at the midst it may be passed in a day.

Ghroceyb now said: 'But wouldst thou needs go to Kheybar? – *tûahi*, hearest thou? shall I not rather carry thee to el-Hâyat? – My rafîk was in dread of going to Kheybar, the Dowla being there: those criminals-in-office (I understood it later) might have named him an enemy and seized the poor nomad's thelûl, and cast him into prison; but el-Hâyat was yet a free village in the jurisdiction of Ibn Rashîd. Ghroceyb I knew afterward to be an homicide, and there lay upon him a grievous debt for blood; it was therefore he had ridden for four reals with me in this painful voyage. From Eyâda's menzil we might have put the Harra upon our left hand, and passed by easy sand-plains [where I journeyed in the spring] under the granite mountains; but Ghroceyb would not, for in the open there had been more peril than in this cragged way of the Harra.

An hour from the Shotb I found the altitude to be 5,000 feet. Before mid-afternoon upon our right hand, beyond the flanks of the Harra and the low underlying sand-plain, appeared a world of wild ranging mountains *Jebâl Hejjûr*, twenty-five miles distant, in dîrat of the Wélad Aly. We went all day as fugitives in this vulcanic country. Sunset comes soon in winter and then we halted, in a low clay bottom with tall acacias and yellow ponds of rain water. Ghroceyb hopshackled her with a cord and loosed out the two days' fasting thelûl to browse the green branches. There we cooked a little temmn; and then laid ourselves down upon the fenny soil and stones in a mizzling night-rain to slumber.

When the day began to spring we set forward, and passed over a brook running out from ponded water in the lava-field. The weather was clearer, the melting skies lifted about us. The vulcanic country is from henceforward plain, and always descending and full of jiddrân. Before and below our path, we had now in sight the sharp three-headed mountain, *Atwa*, that stands beside Kheybar: Ghroceyb greeted the landmark with joy. 'Beyond Atwa was but a night out, he said, for thelûl riders to Medina.' Upon our left hand a distant part of the Harra, *Harrat el-Abyad*, showed white under the sun and full of hilliân. Ghroceyb said, 'The hills are whitish, the lava-field lies about them; the white stone is burned-like, and heavy as metal.' Others say 'The heads only of the hilliân are white stone, the rest is black lava.' – Those white hills might be limestone, which, we know, lies next above the Hisma sand-rock.

Already we saw the flies of the oasis: Kheybar was yet covered from sight by the great descending limb of the Harra; we felt the air every moment warmer and, for us, faint and breathless. All this country side to Jebâl Hejjûr seyls down by the wady grounds *el-Khâfutha* and *Gumm'ra* to the Wady el-Humth. Ghroceyb showed me a wolf's footprints in the vulcanic sand. At the half-afternoon we were near Kheybar, which lay in the deep yonder, and was yet hidden from us. Then we came upon the fresh traces of a ghrazzu: they had passed down towards Kheybar. We rode in the same jiddar behind them! – the footprints were of two mares and two camels. Ghroceyb made me presently a sign to halt; he came and took his gun in silence, struck fire to the match and ran out to reconnoitre. He stayed behind a covet of lavas, from whence he returned to tell me he saw two horsemen and two *ráduffa* (radîfs), upon thelûls, riding at a long gunshot before us: they had not seen us. And now, blowing his match, he inquired very earnestly, 'Were I able with him to resist them?' – Contrary to the will of Ghroceyb I had stayed this day, at noon, ten minutes, to take some refreshment: but for this we had met with them as they came crossing from the westward, and it is too likely that blood had been shed between us. We stood awhile to give them ground, and when they were hidden by the unequal lava-field, we passed slowly forward. The sun was now going low in the west, – and we would be at Kheybar this night ere the village gate should be shut.

Locusts alighted by our path, and I saw aloft an infinite flight of them drifted over in the evening wind. Ghroceyb asked again, 'If I were afraid of the Dowla.' – 'Am I not a Dowlany? they are my friends.' – 'Wellah, *yâ sámy*, my namesake, couldst thou deliver me and quit the thelûl, if they should take me?' – 'Doubt not; they of the Dowla are of my part.'

Now we descended into a large bottom ground in the lavafield, *el-Húrda*, full of green corn: – that corn I saw ripen before my departure from Kheybar! Here Ghroceyb dreaded to meet with the ghrazzu, – the robbers might be grazing their mares in the green corn of the settlement. Where we came by suânies, wild doves flew up with great rattling of wings, from the wells of water. I thought these should be the fields of Kheybar, and spoke to Ghroceyb to carry me to the *Jériat Wélad Aly*. There are three villages, named after the land-inheriting Annezy tribes, *Jériat Bishr* (that is Kheybar proper), *Jériat W. Aly*, at the distance of half a mile, and at two miles the hamlet *Jériat el-Fejîr*, – Jériat is said for kériat in the loghrat of these nomads.

Ghroceyb saw only my untimely delay, whilst he dreaded for his thelûl, and was looking at every new turn that we should encounter the enemies who had ridden down before us. I drew bridle, and bade my rafîk – he stepped always a little before me on foot – promise to bring me to none other than the Wélad Aly village. My visiting Kheybar, which they reckon in '*The Apostle's Country*,' was likely to be a perilous adventure; and I might be murdered to-night in the tumult if it went ill with me: but at the W. Aly hamlet I should have become the guest of the clients of Motlog and Méhsan, great sheykhs of that tribe. Ghroceyb saw me halt, as a man beside himself! and he came hastily, to snatch the thelûl's halter; then he desperately turned his matchlock against me, and cried, 'Akhs! why would I compel him to do me a mischief?' – 'Thou canst not kill thy rafîk! now promise me and go forward.' He promised, but falsely. – Months after I heard he had told his friends, when he was at home again, that 'he had found the stranger a good rafîk, only in the journey's end, as we were about entering Kheybar, I would have taken his thelûl!'

We passed the corn-fields of the Húrda without new alarms, and came upon the basalt neck of the Harra about the oasis' valleys, which is called *el-figgera* (in the pl. *el-fuggar*) Kheybar. Ghroceyb mounted with me, and he made the thelûl run swiftly, for the light was now failing. I saw ruins upon the figgera of old dry building and ring-walls: some are little yards of the loose basalt blocks, which the Beduw use to dry their dates in the sun, before stiving the fruit in their sacks. After a mile, we came to a brow, and I saw a palm forest in a green valley of Kheybar below us, but the village not yet. The sun set as we went down by a steep path. At the left hand was an empty watch-tower, one of seven lately built by the now occupying Medina government, upon this side, to check the hostile Annezy [Bishr and Fejîr]. This human landmark seemed to be more inhuman than all the Harra behind us; for now I remembered Medáin Sâlih and the danger of the long unpaid, and sometimes to be dreaded, Turkish soldiery. How pleasant then seemed to me the sunny drought of the wilderness, how blessed the security of the worsted booths in the wandering villages! These forts are garrisoned in the summer and autumn season.

We came through palm-groves in a valley bottom, *W. Jellâs*, named after that old division of Annezy, which having long since forsaken Kheybar, are at this day – we have seen – with the Ruwàlla in the north. The deep ground is mire and rushes and stagnant water, and there sunk upon our spirits a sickly fenny vapour. In the midst we passed a brook running in a bed of green cresses. Foul was the abandoned soil upon either hand, with only few awry and undergrown stems of palms. The squalid ground is whitish with crusts of bitter salt-warp, *summakha* [written *subbakha*], and stained with filthy rust: whence their fable, that 'this earth purges herself of the much blood of the Yahûd, that was spilt in the conquest of Kheybar.' The thelûl which found no foot-hold under her sliding soles, often halted for fear. We came up between rough walling, built of basalt stones, and rotten palm-stocks, and clots of black clay. – How strange are these dank Kheybar valleys in the waterless Arabia! A heavy presentiment of evil lay upon my heart as we rode in this deadly drowned atmosphere.

We ascended on firm ground to the entering of Kheybar, that is Jériat Bishr, under the long basalt crag of the ancient citadel *el-Húsn*. In the falling ground upon the left hand stands an antique four-square building of stone, which is the old mesjid from the time, they say, of Mohammed; and in the precinct lie buried the *Ashab-en-Néby*, – those few primitive Moslemîn, partisans and acquaintance of the living 'apostle', that fell in the (poor) winning of Kheybar.

At the village gate a negro woman met us in the twilight, of whom I inquired, whether *Bou* (*Abu*) *Ras* were in the town? – I had heard of him from the Moghrebies in Hâyil as a safe man: he was a Moghreby negro trader settled in those parts; also I hoped to become his guest. But he was gone from the place, since the entrance of the (tyrannical) Dowla – being now, as they say, *shebbaan*, or having gotten his suffisance of their poor riches, – to live yet under the free Nejd government at el-Hâyat. – She answered timidly, bidding the strangers a good evening, 'She could not tell, and that she knew nothing.'

Kheybar, Abdullah and the Nejûmy

We passed the gates made of rude palm boarding into the street of the Hejâz negro village, and alighted in the dusk before the house of an acquaintance of Ghroceyb. The host, hearing us busy at the door of his lower house, looked down from the casement and asked in the rasping negro voice what men we were? Ghroceyb called to him, and then he came down with his brother to receive the guests. They took my bags upon their shoulders, and led us up by some clay stairs to their dwelling-house, which is, as at el-Ally, an upper chamber, here called *suffa*. The lower floor, in these damp oases, is a place where they leave the orchard tools, and a stable for their few goats which are driven in for the night. This householder was named *Abdel-Hâdy*, 'Servitor of Him who leadeth in the way of Truth,' a young man under the middle age, of fine negro lineaments. – These negro-like Arabians are not seldom comely.

Our host's upper room was open at the street side with long

casements, *tâga*, to the floor; his roof was but a loose strawing of palm stalks, and above is the house terrace of beaten clay, to which you ascend [they say *erkâ!*] by a ladder of two or three palm beams, with steps hacked in them. Abd el-Hâdy's was one of the better cottages, for he was a substantial man. Kheybar is as it were an African village in the Hejâz. Abd el-Hâdy spread his carpet and bade us welcome, and set before us Kheybar dates, which are yellow, small and stived together; they are gathered ere fully ripe [their Beduin partners' impatience, and distrust of each other!] and have a drug-like or fenny savour, but are 'cooler' than the most dates of the country and not unwholesome. After these days' efforts in the Harra we could not eat; we asked for water to quench our burning thirst. They hang their sweating girbies at the stairhead, and under them is made a hole in the flooring, that the drip may fall through. The water, drawn, they said, from the spring head under the basalt, tasted of the ditch; it might be sulphurous. We had left our thelûl kneebound in the street.

Many persons, when they heard say that strangers had arrived, came up all this evening to visit us; – the villagers were black men. Ghroceyb told them his tale of the ghrazzu; and the negroes answered. 'Wellah! except we sally in the morning to look for them –!' They feared for the outlying corn lands, and lest any beasts of theirs should be taken. There came with the rest a tall and swarthy white man, of a soldierly countenance, bearing a lantern and his yard-long tobacco-pipe: I saw he was of the mixed inhabitants of the cities. He sat silent with hollow eyes and smoked tobacco, often glancing at us; then he passed the *chibûk* to me and inquired the news. He was not friendly with Abd el-Hâdy, and waived our host's second cup. The white man sat on smoking mildly, with his lantern burning; after an hour he went forth [and this was to denounce us, to the ruffian lieutenant at Kheybar]. My rafîk told me in a whisper, 'That was *Ahmed*; he has been a soldier and is now a tradesman at Kheybar.' – His brother was *Mohammed en-Nejûmy*, he who from the morrow became the generous defender of my adversity at Kheybar: they were citizens of Medina. It was near midnight when the last coffee-drinkers departed; then I whispered to Ghroceyb: 'Will they serve supper, or is it not time to sleep?' 'My namesake, I think they have killed for thee; I saw them bring up a sheep, to the terrace, long ago.' – 'Who is the sheykh of the village?' – 'This Abd el-Hâdy is their sheykh, and thou wilt find him a good man.' My rafîk lied like a (guileful) nomad, to excuse his not carrying me to the W. Aly village.

Our host and his brother now at length descended from the house-top, bearing a vast metal tray of the seethed flesh upon a mess of thùra (it may be a sort of millet): since the locusts had destroyed their spring corn, this was the only bread-stuff left to them at Kheybar.

The new day's light beginning to rise Ghroceyb went down to the street in haste; 'Farewell, he said, and was there any difference between us forgive it, Khalîl'; and taking my right hand (and afraid perchance of the stranger's malediction) he stooped and kissed it. Hâdy, our host's brother, mounted also upon the croup of his thelûl; this strong-bodied young negro with a long matchlock upon his shoulder rode forth in his bare tunic, girded only with the *házam* or gunner's belt. Upon the baldric are little metal pipes, with their powder charges and upon the girdle leather pouches for shot, flint and steel and a hook whereupon a man – they go commonly barefoot – will hang his sandals. The házams are adorned with copper studs and beset with little rattling chains; there are some young men who may be seen continually *muházamîn*, girded and vain-glorious with these little tinkling ornaments of war. It is commonly said of tribes well provided with fire-arms 'They have many muházamîn.' – Hâdy rode to find the traces of the ghrazzu of yesterday.

Some of the villagers came up to me immediately to inquire for medicines: they were full of tedious words; and all was to beg of me and buy none. I left them sitting and went out to see the place, for this was Kheybar.

Our host sent his son to guide me; the boy led down by a lane and called me to enter a doorway and see a spring. I went in: – it was a mesjid! and I withdrew hastily. The father (who had instructed the child beforehand), hearing from him when we came again that I had left the place without praying, went down and shut his street door. He returned and took his pistol from the wall, saying, 'Let us go out together and he would show me round the town.' When we were in the street he led me by an orchard path out of the place.

We came by a walled path through the palms into an open space of rush-grass and black vulcanic sand, *es-Sefsáfa*: there he showed me the head of a stream which welled strongly from under the figgera. The water is tepid and sulphurous as at el-Ally, and I saw in it little green-back and silver-bellied fishes: – all fish are named *hút* by the Arabians. 'Here, he said, is the (summer) menzil of the Dowla, in this ground stand the askars' tents.' We sat down, and gazing into my face he asked me, 'Were I afraid of the Dowla?' 'Is the Dowla better or Ibn Rashîd's government?' – 'The Dowla delivered us from the Beduw, – but is more burdenous.'

We passed through a burial ground of black vulcanic mould and salt-warp: the squalid grave-heaps are marked with head-stones of wild basalt. That funeral earth is chapped and ghast-ly, bulging over her enwombed corses, like a garden soil, in springtime, which is pushed by the new-aspiring plants. All is horror at Kheybar! – nothing there which does not fill a stranger's eye with discomfort.

– 'Look, he said, this is the spring of our Lord Aly! – I saw a lukewarm pool and running head of water. – Here our Lord Aly [Fatima's husband] killed *Márhab*, smiting off his head; and his blade cleft that rock, which thou seest there divided to the earth': – so we came beyond. – 'And here, he said, is Aly's mesjid' [already mentioned]. The building is homely, in courses of the wild basalt blocks: it is certainly ancient. Here also the village children are daily taught their letters, by the sheykh of the religion.

When we had made the circuit, 'Let us go, he said, to the *Emir*.' So the villager named the aga or lieutenant of a score of Ageyl from Medina. Those thelûl riders were formerly Nejd Arabians; but now, because the Dowla's wages are so long in coming, the quick-spirited Nejders have forsaken that sorry service. The Ageyl are a mixed crew of a few Nejders (villagers, mostly of el-Kasîm, and poor Nomads), and of Gallas, Turks, Albanians, Egyptians, Kurdies and Negroes. The Ageyl at Kheybar now rode upon their feet: some of their thelûls were dead, those that remained were at pasture (far off) with the nomads. They all drew daily rations of corn for their thelûls alive and dead; and how else might the poor wretches live? who had not touched a cross of their pay (save of a month or twain) these two years. A few of the government armed men at Kheybar were zabtîyah, men of the police service. – 'The Aga is a Kurdy,' quoth Abd el-Hâdy.

We ascended, in a side street, to a suffa, which was the soldiers' coffee-room: swords and muskets were hanging upon pegs in the clay walls. Soon after some of them entered; they were all dark-coloured Gallas, girded (as townsmen) in their white tunics. They came in with guns from some trial of their skill, and welcomed us in their (Medina) manner, and sat down to make coffee. I wondered whilst we drank together that they asked me no questions! We rose soon and departed. As we stepped down the clay stair, I heard a hoarse voice saying among them, 'I see well, he is *adu* (an enemy)'; – and I heard answered, 'But let him alone awhile.'

It was time I thought to make myself known. When I asked where was the Kurdy Aga? my host exclaimed, 'You did not see him! he sat at the midst of the hearth.' That was *Abdullah es-Siruân*, chief of the Medina crew of soldiery: his father was 'a Kurdy', but he was a black man with Galla looks, of the younger middle age, – the son of a (Galla) bond-woman. I was new to discern this Hejâz world, and the town manner of the Harameyn. In the street I saw two white faces coming out of a doorway; they were infirm soldiery, and the men, who walked leaning upon long staves of palm-stalks, seemed of a ghastly pallor in the dreadful blackness of all things at Kheybar: they came to join hands with me, a white man, and passed on without speaking. One of them with a hoary beard was an Albanian, *Muharram*; the other was an Egyptian. When we were again at home Abd el-Hâdy locked his street door; and coming above stairs, 'Tell me, said he, art thou a Moslem?

and if no I will lay thy things upon a cow and send thee to a place of safety.' – 'Host, I am of the Engleys; my nation, thou mayest have heard say, is friendly with the Dowla, and I am of them whom ye name the Nasâra.'

Abd el-Hâdy went out in the afternoon and left his street-door open! There came up presently *Sâlem* a Beduin Agely, to inquire for medicines, and a Galla with his arms, *Sirûr*; – he it was who had named me adu. – 'Half a real for the fever doses!' (salts and quinine), quoth Sâlem. The Galla murmured, 'But soon it would be seen that I should give them for nothing'; and he added, 'This man has little understanding of the world, for he discerns not persons: ho! what countryman art thou?' – 'I dwell at Damascus.' – 'Ha! and that is my country, but thou dost not speak perfectly Araby; I am thinking we shall have here a Nasrâny; oho! What brings thee hither?' – 'I would see the old Jews' country.' – 'The Jews' country! but this is *dîrat er-Rasûl*, the apostle's country': so they forsook me. And Abd el-Hâdy returning, 'What, said he, shall we do? for wellah all the people is persuaded that thou art no Moslem.' – 'Do they take me for an enemy! and the aga. ...?' – 'Ah! he is *jabbàr*, a hateful tyrant.' My host went forth, and Sirûr came up anew; – he was sent by the aga. 'What was I?' he de-manded. – 'An Englesy, of those that favour the Dowla.' – 'Then a Nasrâny; sully aly en-Néby, – come on!' and with another of the Ageyl the brutal black Galla began to thrust me to the stairs. Some villagers who arrived saying that this was the police, I consented to go with them. 'Well, bring him (said the bystanders), but not with violence.' – 'Tell me, before we go further, will ye kill me without the house?' I had secretly taken my pistol under my tunic, at the first alarm.

At the end of the next street one was sitting on a clay bench to judge me, – that dark-coloured Abyssinian 'Kurdy', whom I heard to be the soldier's aga. A rout of villagers came on be-hind us, but without cries. – In what land, I thought, am I now arrived! and who are these that take me (because of Christ's sweet name!) for an enemy of mankind? – Sirûr cried, in his bellowing voice, to him on the clay bench, 'I have detected him, – a Nasrâny!' I said, 'What is this! I am an Engleysy, and

being of a friendly nation, why am I dealt with thus?' 'By
Ullah, he answered, I was afraid to-day, are thou indeed an
Engleysy, art thou not a Muskôvy?' – 'I have said it already!'
– 'But I believe it not, and how may I trust thee?' – 'When I
have answered, here at Kheybar, *I am a Nasrâny*, should I not
be true in the rest?' – 'He says well; go back, Abd el-Hâdy,
and fetch his baggage, and see that there be nothing left behind.' The street was full of mire after the late rain; so I spoke
to Abdullah, and he rising led to an open place in the clay
village which is called *es-Saheyn*, 'the little pan.' – 'By God
(added Abdullah es-Siruân, – the man was illiterate), if any
books should be found with thee, or the what-they-call-them,
– charts of countries, thou shalt never see them more: they
must all be sent to the Pasha at Medina. But hast thou not an
instrument, – ah! and I might now think of the name, – I have
it! the air-measure? – And from whence comest thou?' – 'From
Hâyil; I have here also a passport from Ibn Rashîd.' Abdullah
gave it to a boy who learned in the day school, – for few of the
grown villagers, and none of those who stood by, knew their
letters. *Abdullah*: 'Call me here the sheykh *Sâlih*, to read and
write for us.' A palm-leaf mat was brought out from one of
the houses and cast before us upon a clay bench; I sat down
upon it with Abdullah. – A throng of the black villagers stood
gazing before us.

So Sâlih arrived, the sheykh of this negro village – an elder
man, who walked lame – with a long brass inkstand, and a
leaf of great paper in his hand. *Siruân*: 'Sâlih, thou art to write
all these things in order. [My great camel-bags were brought
and set down before him]. Now have out the things one by
one; and as I call them over, write, sheykh Sâlih. Begin: a
camel-bridle, a girby, bags of dates, hard milk and temmn; –
what is this?' – 'A medicine box.' – 'Open it!' As I lifted the
lid all the black people shrunk back and stopped their nostrils.
Sirûr took in his hands that which came uppermost, a square
compass, – it had been bound in a cloth. 'Let it be untied!'
quoth Abdullah. The fellow turning it in his hand, said, 'Auh!
this is *sabûny*,' (a square of Syrian soap), so Abdullah, to my
great comfort, let it pass. But Abd el-Hâdy espying somewhat

stretched forth his hand suddenly, and took up a comb; 'Ha!
ha!' cries my host (who till now had kindly harboured me;
but his lately good mind was turned already to fanatical rancour – the village named him *Abu Summakh*, 'Father Jangles')
'what is this perilous instrument, – ha! Nasrâny? Abdullah,
let him give account of it; and judge thou if it be not some gin
devised by them against the Moslemîn!'

Next came up a great tin, which I opened before them: it
was full of tea, my only refreshment. 'Well, this you may
shut again,' said Abdullah. Next was a bundle of books. 'Aha!
exclaimed the great man, the former things – hast thou written
them, sheykh Sâlih? – were of no account, but the books! –
thou shalt never have them again.' Then they lighted upon the
brass reel of a tape measure. 'Ha!' he cries, 'tell me, and see
thou speak the truth (*alemny b'es sahîhh*), is not this the sky-
measure?' 'Here, I said to him, I have a paper, which is a
circular passport from the Wàly of Syria.' – 'Then read it,
sheykh Sâlih.' Sâlih pored over the written document awhile;
– 'I have perused it, he answered, but may perceive only the
names, because it is written in *Turki*, [the tongue was Arabic,
but engrossed in the florid Persian manner!], and here at the
foot is the seal of the Pasha,' – and he read his name. 'Ho! ho!
(cries Sirûr) that Pasha was long ago; and he is dead, I know
it well.' – A sigh of bodily weariness that would have rest
broke from me. 'Wherefore thus? exclaimed the pious scelerat
Abdullah, only stay thee upon *el-Mowla* (the Lord thy God).'

– To my final confusion, they fetched up from the sack's
bottom the empty pistol case! – in that weapon was all my
hope. 'Aha! a pistol case! cried many voices, and, casting their
bitter eyes upon me, oh thou! where is the pistol?' I answered
nothing; – in this moment of suspense, one exclaimed, 'It is
plain that Ibn Rashîd has taken it from him.' – 'Ay, answered
the black villagers about me, he has given it to Ibn Rashîd;
Ibn Rashîd has taken it from him, trust us, Abdullah.' – A
pistol among them is always preciously preserved in a gay
holster; and they could not imagine that I should wear a naked
pistol under my bare shirt. After this I thought 'Will they
search my person?' – but that is regarded amongst them as an

extreme outrage; and there were here too many witnesses. He
seemed to assent to their words, but I saw he rolled it in his
turbid mind, 'what was become of the Nasrâny's pistol?' The
heavy weapon, worn continually suspended from the neck,
not a little molested me; and I could not put off my Arab cloak
(which covered it) in the sultry days. – So he said, 'Hast thou
money with thee! and we may be sure thou hast some. Tell
us plainly, where is it, and do not hide it; this will be better
for thee, – and, that I may be friends with thee! also it must
be written in the paper; and tell us hast thou anything else? –
mark ye O people, I would not that a needle of this man's be
lost!' – 'Reach me that tin where you saw the tea: in the midst
is my purse, – and in it, you see, are six liras!' The thief
counted them, with much liking, in his black palm; then
shutting up the purse he put it in his own bosom, saying,
'Sâlih, write down these six liras Fransâwy. I have taken
them for their better keeping; and his bags will be under key
in my own house.'

There came over to me Ahmed, whom I had seen last evening; he had been sitting with the old tranquillity amongst the
lookers-on, and in the time of this inquisition he nodded
many times to me friendly. '*Mâ aleyk, mâ aleyk,* take comfort,
he said, there shall no evil happen to thee.' – *Abdullah*: 'Abd
el-Hâdy, let him return to lodge with thee; also he can cure
the sick.' The negro answered, 'I receive again the kafîr! –
Only let him say the testimony and I will receive him will-
lingly.' – 'Then he must lodge with the soldiery; thou *Amân*
– a Galla Agely – take him to your chamber: Khalîl may have
his provisions with him and his box of medicines.'

I saw the large manly presence standing erect in the backward of the throng – for he had lately arrived – of a very
swarthy Arabian; he was sheykhly clad, and carried the sword,
and I guessed he might be some chief man of the irregular
soldiery. Now he came to me, and dropping (in their sudden
manner) upon the hams of the legs, he sat before me with the
confident smiling humour of a strong man; and spoke to me
pleasantly. I wondered to see his swarthiness, – yet such are

commonly the Arabians in the Hejâz – and he not less to see a man so 'white and red.' This was Mohammed en-Nejûmy, Ahmed's brother, who from the morrow became to me as a father at Kheybar. 'Go now, said Abdullah, with the soldier.' – 'Mâ aleyk, mâ aleyk,' added some of the better-disposed bystanders. *Abdullah*: 'You will remain here a few days, whilst I send a post to the Pasha (of Medina) with the books and papers.' – 'Ho! ye people, bellows Sirûr, we will send to the Pasha; and if the Pasha's word be to cut his head off, we will chop off thy head Nasrâny.' 'Trouble not thyself, said some yet standing by, for this fellow's talk, – he is a brute.' Hated was the Galla bully in the town, who was valiant only with their hareem, and had been found *khòaf*, a skulking coward, in the late warfare.

So I came with Amân to the small suffa which he inhabited with a comrade, in the next house. They were both *Habûsh*, further-Abyssinians, that is of the land of the Gallas. Lithe figures they are commonly, with a feminine grace and fine lineaments; their hue is a yellow-brown, deep brown or blackish, and that according to their native districts, – so wide is the country. They have sweet voices and speak not one Galla tongue alike, so that the speech of distant tribes is hardly understood between them. Amân could not well understand his comrade's talk (therefore they spoke together in Arabic), but he spoke nearly one language, with Sirûr. Amân taught me many of his Galla words; but to-day I remember no more than *bîsàn*, water. Though brought slaves to the Hejâz in their childhood they forget not there their country language: so many are now the Gallas in Mecca and Medina, that *Hábashy* is currently spoken from house to house. Some of the beautiful Galla bondwomen become wives in the citizen families, even of the great, others are nurses and house servants; and the Arab town children are bred up amongst them. – The poor fellows bade me be of good comfort, and all would now end well, after a little patience: one set bread before me, and went out to borrow dates for their guest. They said, 'As for this negro people, they are not men but oxen, apes, sick of the devil and niggards.' – These Semite-like Africans vehemently

disdain the Sudân, or negro slave-race. 'Great God!' I have
heard them say at Kheybar, 'can those woolly polls be of the
children of Adam?'

We heard Mohammed en-Nejûmy upon the clay stairs. He
said, 'It is the first time I ever came here, but for thy sake I
come.' At night-fall we went forth together, lighting our way
with flaming palm-branches, to the soldiers' kahwa. Abdullah,
whom my purse had enriched to-day, beckoned me to sit beside him. Their talk took a good turn, and Mohammed en-
Nejûmy pronounced the famous formula: *kull wâhed aly dínu*,
'every man in his own religion!' – and he made his gloss, 'this
is to say the Yahûdy in his law, the Nasrâny in his law and the
Moslem in his law; aye, and the kafir may be a good faithful
man in his belief.' The Nejûmy was an heroic figure, he sat
with his sword upon his knees, bowing and assenting, at every
word, to the black villain Abdullah: this is their Turkish town
courtesy. Sometimes (having heard from me that I understood
no Turkish) they spoke together in that language. Mohammed
answered, after every clement saw of the black lieutenant, the
pious praise [though it sounded like an irony], *Ullah yubèyith
wejh-ak,* 'the Lord whiten thy visage (in the day of doom)!'
There was some feminine fall in the strong man's voice, – and
where is any little savour of the mother's blood in right manly
worth, it is a pleasant grace. He was not altogether like the
Arabs, for he loved to speak in jesting-wise, with kindly
mirth: though they be full of knavish humour, I never saw
among the Arabians a merry man!

Mohammed and Ahmed were sons of a Kurdy sutler at
Medina; and their mother was an Harb woman of the Ferrâ,
a palm settlement of that Beduin nation in the Hejâz, betwixt
the Harameyn. We drunk round the soldiers' coffee; yet here
was not the cheerful security of the booths of hair, but town
constraint and Turkish tyranny, and the Egyptian plague of
vermin. They bye and bye were accorded in their sober cups
that the Nasâra might pass everywhere freely, only they may
not visit the Harameyn: and some said, 'Be there not many
of Khalîl's religion at Jidda? the way is passed by riders in one
night-time from Mecca' [many in the Hejâz pronounce *Mekky*].

Abdullah said at last, 'Wellah, Khalîl is an honest man, he speaks frankly, and I love him.' I was soon weary, and he sent his bondman to light me back to my lodging. Hearing some rumour, I looked back, and saw that the barefoot negro came dancing behind me in the street with his drawn sword.

Abdullah said to me at the morning coffee, that I might walk freely in the village; and the black hypocrite inquired 'had I rested well?' When it was evening, he said, 'Rise, we will go and drink coffee at the house of a good man.' We went out, and some of his soldiers lighted us with flaming palm leaves to the cottage of one *Ibrahîm el-kâdy*. Whilst we sat in his suffa, there came up many of the principal villagers. Ibrahîm set his best dates before us, made up the fire, and began to prepare kahwa, and he brought the village governor his kerchief full of their green tobacco. ...

There was an honest vainglory in Amm Mohammed to show himself a citizen and a loyal man, and to be seen in company with the officers of the Dowla: the *quondam* trooper maintained a horse at Kheybar, chiefly that in the months of the military occupation he might ride, like a sheykhly person, with those great ones. Now he foresaw the brave time when he should bid the Medina officers to this ground, which would be his herb-garden; where sitting dangle-legs upon our terrace wall, they should partake of his summer fruits. Mohammed was of a metal which I have seen in all countries: strong men and large-bodied, yet infirm soon, with sweet and clear, almost feminine, voices. He was of a mild and cheerful temper, confident, tolerant, kind, inwardly God-fearing, lightly moved: his heart was full of a pleasant humour of humanity. Loving mankind he was a peacemaker, not selfish of his own, true and blithe in friendship, of a ready and provident wit, both simple and sly, eluding enmities; – an easy nature passing overall hard and perplexed matter, content with the natural course of the world, manly and hardy, but not long-breathed in any enterprise.

Kheybar Wells. The Deliverance from Kheybar. The Rafîks

The few weeks of winter had passed by, and the teeming spring heat was come, in which all things renew themselves: the hamîm month would soon be upon us, when my languishing life, which the Nejûmy compared to a flickering lamp-wick, was likely (he said) to fail at Kheybar. Two months already I had endured this black captivity of Abdullah; the third moon was now rising in her horns, which I hoped in Heaven would see me finally delivered. The autumn green corn was grown to the yellowing ear; another score of days – so the Lord delivered them from the locust – and they would gather in their wheat-harvest.

I desired to leave them richer in water at Kheybar. Twenty paces wide of the strong Sefsáfa spring was a knot of tall rushes; there I hoped to find a new fountain of water. The next land-holders hearkened gladly to my saw, for water is mother of corn and dates, in the oases; and the sheykh's brother responded that to-morrow he would bring eyyâl to open the ground. – Under the first spade-stroke we found wet earth, and oozing joints of the basalt rock: then they left their labour, saying we should not speed, because it was begun on a Sunday. They remembered also my words that, in case we found a spring of water, they should give me a milch cow. On the morrow a greater working party assembled. It might be they were in doubt of the cow and would let the work lie until the Nasrâny's departure, for they struck but a stroke or two in my broken ground; and then went, with crowbars, to try their strength about the old well-head, and see if they might not enlarge it. The iron bit in the flaws of the rock; and stiffly straining and leaning, many together, upon their crowbars, they sprung and rent up the intractable basalt. Others who looked on, whilst the labourers took breath, would bear a hand in it: among them the Nejûmy showed his manly pith and stirred a mighty quarter of basalt. When it came to mid-day they forsook their day's labour. Three forenoons they wrought thus with the zeal of novices: in the second they sacrificed a goat, and sprinkled her blood upon the rock. I had not seen Arabs labour thus in fellowship. In the Arabs are indigent corroded minds full of speech-wisdom; in the negroes' more prosperous bodies are hearts more robust. They also fired the rock, and by the third day the labourers had drawn out so many huge stones: now the old well-head was become like a great bath of tepid water, and they began to call it el-hammàm. We had struck a side vein, which increased the old current of water by half as much again, – a benefit for ever to the husbandmen of the valley.

The tepid springs of Kheybar savour upon the tongue of sulphur, with a milky smoothness, save the *Ayn er-Reyih*, which is tasteless. Yellow frogs inhabit these springs, besides the little silver-green fishes. Green filmy webs of water-weed are wrapped about the channels of the lukewarm brooks, in which lie little black turreted snails, like those of W.Thirba and el-Ally [and Palmyra]. I took up the straws of caddis-worms and showed them to Amm Mohammed: he considered the building of those shell-pipes made without hands, and said; 'Oh the marvellous works of God; they are perfect without end! and well thou sayest, "that the Kheyâbara are not housed as these little vermin!"'

I had nearly outworn the spite of fortune at Kheybar; and might now spend the sunny hours, without fear, sitting by the spring Ayn er-Reyih, a pleasant place little without the palms, and where only the eye has any comfort in all the blackness of Kheybar. Oh, what bliss to the thirsty soul is in that sweet light water, welling soft and warm as milk, (86° F.) from the rock! And I heard the subtle harmony of Nature, which the profane cannot hear, in that happy stillness and solitude. Small bright dragon-flies, azure, dun and vermilion, sported over the cistern water ruffled by a morning breath from the figgera, and hemmed in the solemn lava rock. The silver fishes glance beneath, and white shells lie at the bottom of this water world. I have watched there the young of the thób shining like scaly glass and speckled: this fairest of saurians lay sunning, at the brink, upon a stone; and oft-times moving upon them and shooting out the tongue he snatched his prey of flies without ever missing. – Glad were we when Jummàr had filled our girby of this sweet water.

One afternoon when I went to present myself to the village tyrant, I saw six carrion beasts, that had been thelûls, couched before Abdullah's door! the brutes stretched their long necks faintly upon the ground, and their mangy chines were humpless. Such could be none other than some unpaid soldiers' jades from Medina; and I withdrew hastily to the Nejûmy. – Certain Ageylies had been sent by the Pasha; and the men had ridden the seventy miles hither in five days! – Such being the Ageyl, whose forays formerly – some of them have boasted to me – 'made the world cold!' they are now not seldom worsted by the tribesmen of the desert. In a late expedition of theirs from Medina, we heard that 'forty were fallen, their baggage had been taken, and the rest hardly saved themselves.' – I went back to learn their tidings, and meeting with Abdullah in the street, he said, 'Good news, Khalîl! thy books are come again, and the Pasha writes, "send him to Ibn Rashîd." '

On the morrow, Abdullah summoned me; he sat at coffee in our neighbour Hamdàn's house.—'This letter is for thee, said he, (giving me a paper) from the Pasha's own hand.' And opening the sheet, which was folded in our manner, I found a letter from the Pasha of Medina! written [imperfectly], as follows, in the French language; with the date of the Christian year, and signed in the end with his name. – *Sâbry.*

(*Ad literam.*)   Le 11 janvier 1878
                                                            (Medine)

D'aprés l'avertissement de l'autorité local, nous sommes saché votre arrivée à Khaiber, à cette occasion je suis obligé de faire venir les lettres de recommendation et les autres papiers à votre charge.

En étudiant à peine possible les livres de compte, les papiers volants et les cartes, enfin parmi ceux qui sont arrivaient-ici, jai disserné que votre idée de voyage, corriger la carte, de savoir les conditions d'état, et de trouver les monuments antiques de l'Arabie centrale dans le but de publier au monde.

je suis bien satisfaisant à votre etude utile pour l'univers dans ce point, et c'est un bon parti pour vous aussi; mais vous avez connu certainement jusqu' aujourd'hui parmi aux alantours des populations que vous trouvé, il y a tant des Bedouins témeraire, tant que vous avez le recommendion de quelque personnages, je ne regarde que ce votre voyage est dangereux parmi les Bédouins sus-indiqué; c'est pour cela je m'oblige de vous informé à votre retour à un moment plutôt possible auprès de Cheïh d'Ibni-Réchite à l'abri de tout danger, et vous trouvrez ci-join tous vos les lettres qu'il était chez-nous, et la recommendation au dite Cheïh de ma part, et de là prenez le chemin dans ces joirs à votre destination.

SABRI

'And now, I said to Abdullah, where is that money which pertains to me, – six lira!' The black village governor startled, changed his Turkish countenance, and looking felly, he said 'We will see to it.' The six Ageylies had ridden from Medina, by the Pasha's order, only to bring up my books, and they treated me with regard. They brought word, that the Pasha would send other twenty-five Ageylies to Hâyil for this cause. The chief of the six, a Waháby of East Nejd, was a travelled man, without fanaticism; he offered himself to accompany me whithersoever I would, and he knew, he said, all the ways, in those parts and far southward in Arabia.

The day after when nothing had been restored to me, I found Abdullah drinking coffee in sheykh Sâlih's house. 'Why I said, hast thou not restored my things?' – 'I will restore them at thy departure.' – 'Have you any right to detain them?' 'Say no more (exclaimed the villain, who had spent my money) – a Nasrâny to speak to me thus! – or I will give thee a buffet.' – 'If thou strike me, it will be at thy peril. My hosts, how may this lieutenant of a dozen soldiery rule a village, who cannot rule himself? one who neither regards the word of the Pasha of Medina, nor fears the Sultàn, nor dreads Ullah himself. Sâlih the sheykh of Kheybar, hear how this coward threatens to strike a guest in thy house; and will ye suffer it my hosts?' – Abdullah rose and struck me brutally in the face. – 'Sâlih, I said to them, and you that sit here, are you free men? I am one man, infirm and a stranger, who have suffered so long, and unjustly, – you have all seen it! at this slave's hands, that it might have whitened my beard: if I should hereafter remember to

226

complain of him, it is likely he will lose his office.' Auwad, the
kâdy who was a friend, and sat by me, began some conciliating
speech. 'Abdullah, he said, was to blame: Khalîl was also to
blame. There is danger in such differences; let there be no
more said betwixt you both.' *Abdullah*: 'Now, shall I send thee
to prison?' – 'I tell thee, that I am not under thy jurisdiction'; and I rose to leave them. 'Sit down,' he cries, and
brutally snatched my cloak, 'and this askar – he looked
through the casement and called up one of his men that passed
by – shall lead thee to prison.' I went down with him, and,
passing Amm Mohammed's entry, I went in there, and the
fellow left me.

The door was locked, but the Beduin housewife, hearing
my voice, ran down to open: when I had spoken of the matter,
she left me sitting in the house, and, taking the key with her,
the good woman ran to call her husband who was in the palms.
Mohammed returned presently, and we went out to the plantations together; but finding the chief of the riders from Medina,
in the street, I told him, 'since I could not be safe here that I
would ride with them to the gate of the city. It were no new
thing that an Englishman should come thither; was there not
a cistern, without the northern gate, named *Birket el-Engleysy*?'

Mohammed asked 'What had the Pasha written? he would
hear me read his letter in the Nasrâny language': and he stood
to listen with great admiration. '*Pitta-pitta-pitta!* is such
their speech? laughed he; and this was his new mirth in the
next coffee meetings. But I found the good man weak as water
in the end of these evils: he had I know not what secret understanding now with the enemy Abdullah, and, contrary to his
former words, he was unwilling that I should receive my
things until my departure! The Ageylies stayed other days,
and Abdullah was weary of entertaining them. I gave the
Waháby a letter to the Pasha; which, as soon as they came
again to town, he delivered. ...

... We beat the pad-footed thelûl over the fenny ground,
and the last brooks and plashes. And then I came up from the
pestilent Kheybar wadiàn, and the intolerable captivity of the

Dowla, to a blissful free air on the brow of the Harra! In the next hour we went by many of the vaults, of wild basalt stones which I have supposed to be barrows. After ten miles' march we saw a nomad woman standing far off upon a lava rock, and two booths of Heteym. My Beduin rafîks showed me the heads of a mountain southward, *el-Baîtha*, that they said stands a little short of Medina.

It was afternoon, we halted and loosed out the thelûl to pasture, and sat down till it should be evening. When the sun was setting we walked towards the tents: but the broken-headed Eyâd left me with Hamed and his loaded thelûl, and went with Merjàn to guest it at the other beyt. The house-holder of the booth where I was, came home with the flocks and camels; he was a beardless young man. They brought us buttermilk, and we heard the voice of a negress calling in the woman's apartment, *Hamed! yâ Hamô!* She was from the vil-lage, and was staying with these nomad friends in the desert, to refresh herself with léban. It was presently dark, but the young man went abroad again with the ass to bring in water. He returned after two hours and, without my knowledge, they sacrificed a goat: it was for this he had fetched water. The young Heteymy called me – the adulation of an abject race – *Towîl el-amr*.

After the hospitality Eyâd entered, 'Khalîl, he said, hast thou reserved no morsels for me that am thy rafîk?' – 'Would a rafîk have forsaken me?' He now counselled to hold a more westerly course, according to the tidings they had heard in the other tent, 'that we might come every day to menzils of the Aarab, and find milk and refreshment; whereas, if I visited el-Hâyat, all the way northward to Hâyil from thence was now bare of Beduins.' – I should thus miss el-Hâyat, and had no provisions: also I assented to them in evil hour! it had been better to have yielded nothing to such treacherous rafîks.

We departed at sunrise, having upon our right hand, in the 'White Harra' (el-Abiath) a distant mountain, which they like-wise named *el-Baîtha* [other than that in the Hejâz, nigh Medina]. In that jebel, quoth my rafîks, are the highest *shdebân* (seylstrands) of W. er-Rummah; but all on this side seyls down to the (great Hejâz) Wady el-Humth. We passed by sharp glassy lavas; '– *loub*', said my companions. A pair of great lapwing-like fowls, *habâra*, fluttered before us; I have seldom seen them in the deserts [and only at this season]: they have whitish and dun-speckled feathers. Their eggs (brown and rose, black speckled) I have found in May, laid two together upon the bare wilderness gravel [near Maan]; they were great as turkey-eggs, and well tasting: the birds might be a kind of bustards. 'Their flesh is nesh as cotton between the teeth,' quoth the Bishr Sybarite Eyâd. Merjàn and Eyâd lured to them, whistling; they drew off their long gun-leathers, and stole under the habâras; but as Beduins will not cast away lead in the air, they returned bye and bye as they went. I never saw the Arabs' gunning help them to any game; only the Nejûmy used to shoot at (and he could strike down) flying partridges.

From hence the vulcanic field about us was a wilderness of sharp lava stones, where few or no cattle paths [Bishr, *jadda*] appeared; and nomads go on foot among the rocking blocks unwillingly. A heavy toppling stone split the horny thickness of Hamed's great toe. I alighted that he might ride; but the negro borrowed a knife and, with a savage resolution, shred away his flesh, and went on walking. In the evening halt, he seared the bloody wound, and said, it would be well enough, for the next marches. As we journeyed the March wind blustered up against us from the north; and the dry herbage and scudding stems of sere desert bushes, were driven before the blast. Our way was uncertain, and without shelter or water; the height of this lava-plain is 3,400 feet. Merjàn – the lad was tormented with a throbbing ague-cake (*táhal*), after the Kheybar fever, shouted in the afternoon that he saw a flock; and then all beside his patience he shrieked back curses, because we did not follow him: the flock was but a troop of gazelles. '*Fen el-Aarab*, they said at last, the nomads where? – *neffera!* deceitful words; but this is the manner of the Heteymàn! they misled us last night, Ullah send them confusion.' The negro had drunk out nearly all in my small water-skin: towards evening he untied the neck and would have made a full end of it himself at a draught; but I said to him, 'Nay, for we have gone and thirsted all the day, and no man shall have more than other.' The Beduins cried out upon him, 'And thinkest thou that we be in the Saheyn? this is the khála and no swaggering-place of the Kheyâbara.' Finally, when the sun set, we found a hollow ground and sídr trees to bear off the night wind, which blew so fast and pierced our slender clothing; they rent down the sere white arms of a dead acacia, for our evening fire. Then kneading flour of the little water which remained to us, we made hasty bread under the embers. The March night was cold.

We departed when the day dawned, and held under the sandstone mountain *Gurs*: and oh, joy! this sun being fairly risen, the abhorred land-marks of Kheybar appeared no more. We passed other vaulted cells and old dry walling upon the waste Harra, and an ancient burying-place. 'See, said Eyâd, these graves of the auellîn, how they lie heaped over with stones!' We marched in the vulcanic field – 'a land whose stones are iron,' and always fasting, till the mid-afternoon, when we found in some black sand-beds footprints of camels. At first my rafîks said the traces were of a ráhla five to ten days old; but taking up the jella, they thought it might be of five days ago. The droppings led us over the Harra north-west-ward, towards the outlying plutonic coasts of J. Hejjûr. – Footprints in the desert are slowly blotted by insensible wind causing the sand corns to slide; they might otherwise remain perfectly until the next rain. – In a monument lately opened in Egypt, fresh prints of the workmen's soles were found in the fine powder of the floor; and they were of an hundred men's ages past! The Beduins went to an hollow ground, to seek a little ponded rain, and there they filled the girby. That water was full of wiggling white vermin; and we drank – giving God thanks – through a lap of our kerchiefs. [We may see the flaggy hare-lips of the camel fenced with a border of bristles bent inwardly; and through this brush the brute strains all that he drinks of the foul desert waters!] The Beduin rafîks climbed upon every high rock to look for the nomads: we went on till the sun set, and then alighted in a low ground with acacia trees

and bushes; there we found a dàr of the nomads lately forsaken. We were here nigh the borders of the Harra. ...

We halted an hour after the stars were shining, in a low
place, under a solitary great bush; and couched the thelûl before us, to shelter our bodies from the chill night wind, now
rising to a hurricane, which pierced through their light Hejâz
clothing. The Beduin rafîks, to comfort themselves with fire,
forgot their daylight fears: they felt round in the darkness for
a few sticks. And digging there with my hands, I found jella
in the sand, – it was the old mûbrak, or night lair, of a camel;
and doubtless some former passenger had alighted to sleep at
our inn of this great desert bush: the beast's dung had been
buried by the wind, two or three years. Merjàn gathered his
mantle full: the precious fuel soon glowed with a red heat in
our sandy hearth, and I boiled tea, which they had not tasted
till now.

The windy cold lasted all night, the blast was outrageous.
Hardly at dawn could they, with stiffened fingers, kindle a
new fire: the rafîks sat on, – there was not warmth in their
half naked bodies to march against this wild wind. – A puff
whirling about our bush scattered the dying embers, 'Akhs!
cries Eyâd, the sot, *Ullah yulâan abu ha'l hubûb*, condemn the
father of this blustering blast: and he added, *Ullah yusullat aly
ha'l hattab*, God punish this firewood.' We rose at last; and the
Beduin rafîks bathed their bodies yet a moment in the heat,
spreading their loose tunics over the dying embers. The baff-
ling March blast raged in our teeth, carrying the sandy grit into
our eyes. The companions staggered forward on foot, – we
marched north-eastward: after two hours, they halted to
kindle another fire. I saw the sky always overcast with thin
clouds. Before noon the storm abated; and the wind chopping
round blew mildly in the afternoon, from the contrary part!
We approached then the black border of the Harra, under the
high crater-hill Ethnàn. Ethnàn stands solitary, in a field of
sharp cinder-like and rifted lavas; the nomads say that this
great *hilla* is inaccessible. Sometimes, after winter rain, they
see a light reeking vapour about the volcano head: and the

like is seen in winter mornings over certain rifts in the Harra,
– 'the smell of it is like the breath of warm water.' This was
confirmed to me by Amm Mohammed.

In that part there is a (land-mark) valley-ground which lies
through the Harra towards el-Hâyat, *W. Mukheyat*. My small
waterskin might hardly satisfy the thirst of three men in one
summer's march, and this was the second journey; we drank
therefore only a little towards the afternoon, and had nothing
to eat. But my mind was full to see so many seamed, guttered
and naked cinder-hills of craters in the horrid black lavas before us. The sense of this word hilla, hillaya, is according to
Amm Mohammed, 'that which appears evidently,' – and he
told me, there is a kind of dates of that name at Medina. Eyâd
said thus, '*Halla* is the Harra-hill of black powder and slaggy
matter; *hellayey* is a little Harra-hill; *hillî* or *hellowat* (others say
hilliân) are the Harra-hills together.' – We marched towards
the same hillies which I had passed with Ghroceyb. When the
sun was near setting the rafîks descried, and greeted (devoutly)
the new moon. ...

The Treacherous Rafîks

At daybreak we departed from Gofar: this by my reckoning
was the first week in April. Eyâd loosed out our sick thelûl to
pasture; and they drove her slowly forward in the desert plain
till the sun went down behind Ajja, when we halted under
bergs of grey granite. These rocks are fretted into bosses and
caves more than the granite of Sinai: the heads of the granite
crags are commonly trap rock. Eyâd, kindling a fire, heated
his iron ramrod, and branded their mangy thelûl. – I had gone
all day on foot; and the Ageylies threatened every hour to cast
down my bags, though now light as Merjàn's temmn, which
she also carried. We marched four miles further, and espied a
camp fire; and coming to the place we found a ruckling troop
of camels couched for the night, in the open khála. The herd-
lad and his brother sat sheltering in the hollow bank of a seyl,
and a watch-fire of sticks was burning before them. The
hounds of the Aarab follow not with the herds, the lads could

not see beyond their fire-light, and our *salaam* startled them:
then falling on our knees we sat down by them, – and with
that word we were acquainted. The lads made some of their
nâgas stand up, and they milked full bowls and frothing over
for us. We heard a night-fowl shriek, where we had left our
bags with the thelûl: my rafîks rose and ran back with their
sticks, for the bird (which they called *sirrûk*, a thief) might,
they said, steal something. When we had thus supped, we lay
down upon the pleasant seyl sand to sleep.

As the new day lightened we set forward. A little further we
saw a flock of some great sea-fowl grazing before us, upon
their tall shanks in the wilderness. – I mused that (here in Nejd)
they were but a long flight on their great waggle wings from
the far seabord; a morrow's sun might see them beyond this
burning dust of Arabia! At first my light-headed rafîks mis-
took them for sheep-flocks, although only black fleeces be
seen in these parts of Nejd: then having kindled their gun-
matches, they went creeping out to approach them; but bye
and bye I saw the great fowl flag their wings over the wide
desert, and the gunners returning. – I asked 'from whence are
these birds?' – 'Wellah from Mecca' [that is from the middle
Red Sea bord].

This soil was waste gravel, baked hard in the everlasting
drought, and glowing under the soles of our bare feet; the air
was like a flame in the sun. An infirm traveller were best to
ride always in the climate of Arabia: now by the cruelty of my
companions, I went always on foot; and they themselves
would ride. And marching in haste, I must keep them in view,
or else they had forsaken the Nasrâny: my plight was such
that I thought, after a few days of such efforts, I should rest
for ever. So it drew to the burning midst of the afternoon,
when, what for the throes in my chest, I thought that the
heart would burst. The hot blood at length spouted from my
nostrils: I called to the rafîks who went riding together before
me to halt, that I might lie down awhile, but they would not
hear. Then I took up stones, to receive the dropping gore, lest
I should come with a bloody shirt to the next Aarab: besides
it might work some alteration in my rafîks' envenomed

spirits! – in this haste there fell blood on my hands. When I overtook them, they seeing my bloody hands drew bridle in astonishment! *Merjàn*: 'Now is not this a kafîr!' – 'Are ye not more than kafirs, that abandon the rafîk in the way?' They passed on now more slowly, and I went by the side of the thelûl. – 'If, I added, ye abandon the rafîk, what honourable man will hereafter receive you into their tents?' Merjàn answered, 'There is keeping of faith betwixt the Moselmîn, but not with an enemy of Ullah!'

They halted bye and bye and Eyâd dismounted: Merjàn who was still sitting upon the thelûl's back struck fire with a flint: I thought it might be for their galliûns, since they had bought a little sweet hameydy, with my money, at Hâyil: but Eyâd kindled the cord of his matchlock. I said, 'This is what?' They answered, 'A hare!' – 'Where is your hare? I say, show me this hare!' Eyâd had yet to put priming to the eye of his piece: they stumbled in their words, and remained confused. I said to them, 'Did I seem to you like this hare? by the life of Him who created us, in what instant you show me a gun's mouth, I will lay dead your hare's carcases upon this earth: put out the match!' he did so. The cool of the evening approached; we marched on slowly in silence, and doubtless they rolled it in their hollow hearts what might signify that vehement word of the Nasrâny. 'Look, I said to them, *rizelleyn*! you two vile dastards, I tell you plainly, that in what moment you drive me to an extremity ye are but dead dogs; and I will take this carrion thelûl!'

My adventure in such too unhappy case had been nearly desperate; nigher than the Syrian borders I saw no certain relief. Syria were a great mark to shoot at, and terribly far off; and yet upon a good thelûl, fresh watered – for extremities make men bold, and the often escaping from dangers – I had not despaired to come forth; and one watering in the midway, – if I might once find water, had saved both thelûl and rider. – Or should I ride towards Teyma; 200 miles from hence? – But seeing the great landmarks from this side, how might I know them again! – and if I found any Aarab westward, yet these would be Bishr, the men's tribesmen. Should

I ride eastward in unknown dîras? or hold over the fearful Nefûd sand billows to seek the Sherarát? Whithersoever I rode I was likely to faint before I came to any human relief; and might not strange Aarab sooner kill the stranger, seeing one arrive thus, than receive me? My eyes were dim with the suffered ophthalmia, and not knowing where to look for them, how in the vastness of the desert landscape should I descry any Aarab? If I came by the mercy of God to any wells, I might drink drop by drop, by some artifice, but not water the thelûl.

Taking up stones I chafed my blood-stained hands, hoping to wash them when we should come to the Aarab; but this was the time of the spring pasture, when the great cattle are jezzîn, and oft-times the nomads have no water by them, because there is léban to drink. Eyâd thought the game turned against him! when we came to a menzil, I might complain of them and he would have a scorn. – 'Watch, said he, and when any camel stales, run thou and rinse the hands: for wellah seeing blood on thy hands, there will none of the Aarab eat with thee.' – The urine of camels has been sometimes even drunk by town caravaners in their impatience of thirst. I knew certain of the Medânite tradesmen to the Sherarát, who coming up at mid-summer from the W. Sirhàn, and finding the pool dry (above Maan) where they looked to have watered, filled their bowl thus, and let in it a little blood from the camel's ear. I have told the tale to some Beduins; who answered me, 'But to drink this could not help a man, wellah he would die the sooner, it must so wring his bowels.'

It was evening, and now we went again by el-Agella. When the sun was setting, we saw another camel troop not far off. The herdsmen trotting round upon some of their lighter beasts were driving-in the great cattle to a sheltered place between two hills; for this night closed starless over our heads with falling weather. When we came to them the young men had halted their camels and were hissing to them to kneel, – *ikh-kh-kh!* The great brutes fall stiffly, with a sob, upon one or both their knees, and under-doubling the crooked hind legs

they sit ponderously down upon their haunches. Then shuffling forward one and the other fore-knee, with a grating of
the harsh gravel under their vast carcase-weight, they settle
themselves, and with these pains are at rest: the fore bulk-
weight is sustained upon the *zôra*; so they lie still and chaw
their cud, till the morning sun. The camel leaves a strange
(reptile-like) print (of his knees, of the zôra and of the sharp
hind quarters), which may be seen in the hard wilderness soil
after even a year or two. The smell of the camel is muskish
and a little dog-like, the hinder parts being crusted with urine;
yet is the camel more beautiful in our eyes than the gazelles,
because man sees in this creature his whole welfare, in the
khála.

The good herding lads milked for us largely: we drunk deep
and far into the night; and of every sup is made ere morning
sweet blood, light flesh and stiff sinews. The rain beat on our
backs as we sat about their watch-fire of sticks on the pure
sand of the desert; it lightened and thundered. When we were
weary we went apart, where we had left our bags, and lay
down in our cloaks, in the night wind and rain. I lay so long
musing of the morrow, that my companions might think me
sleeping. They rested in the shelter of the next crag, where I
heard them say – my quick hearing helping me in these dangers
like the keen eyesight of the nomads – that later in the night
they would lift their things on the thelûl and be gone. I let
them turn over to sleep: then I rose and went to the place
where the fire had been.

The herdsmen lay sleeping in the rain; and I thought I
would tell the good lads my trouble. Their sister was herding
with them, but in presence of strange menfolk she had sat all
this evening obscurely in the rain, and far from the cheerful
fire. Now she was warming herself at the dying embers, and
cast a little cry as she saw me coming, for all is fear in the
desert. 'Peace! I said to her, and I would speak with her
brethren.' She took the elder by the shoulder, and rolling him,
he wakened immediately, for in this weather he was not well
asleep. They all sat up, and the young men, rubbing their faces
asked, 'Oh, what –? and wherefore would not the stranger let

them rest, and why was I not gone to sleep with my rafîks?' These were manly lads but rude; they had not discerned that I was so much a stranger. I told them, that those with me were Annezy, Ageylies, who had money to carry me to Kheybar; but their purpose was to forsake me, and perhaps they would abandon me this night.' – 'Look you (said they, holding their mouths for yawning), we are poor young serving men, and have not much understanding in such things; but if we see them do thee a wrong, we will be for thee. Go now and lie down again, lest they miss thee; and fear nothing, for we are nigh thee.'

About two hours before the day Eyâd and Merjàn rose, whispering, and they loaded the things on the couching thelûl; then with a little spurn they raised her silently. 'Lead out (I heard Eyâd whisper), and we will come again for the guns.' I lay still, and when they were passed forth a few steps I rose to disappoint them: I went with their two matchlocks in my hands to the herdsmen's place, and awaked the lads. The treacherous rafîks returning in the dark could not find their arms: then they came over where I sat now with the herdsmen. – 'Ah! said they, Khalîl had of them an unjust suspicion; they did but remove a little to find shelter, for where they lay the wind and rain annoyed them.' Their filed tongues prevailed with the poor herding lads, whose careless stars were unused to these nice cases; and heartless in the rain, they consented with the stronger part, – that Khalîl had misconstrued the others' simple meaning. 'Well, take, they said, your matchlocks, and go sleep again, all of you; and be content Khalîl. And do ye give him no more occasion, said these upland judges: – and wellah we have not napped all this long night!'

I went forward with the Ageylies, when we saw the morning light; Eyâd rode. We had not gone a mile when he threatened to abandon me there in the khála; he now threatened openly to shoot me, and raised his camel-stick to strike me; but I laid hand on the thelûl's bridle, and for such another word, I said, I would give him a fall. Merjàn had no part in this violence; he walked wide of us, for being of various humour, in the last hour he had fallen out with Eyâd. ... – 'Well, Khalîl, let be now, said Eyâd, and I swear to thee a menzil of the Aarab is not far off, if the herding lads told us truly.'

Departure for Boreyda. The Arrival. The Nasrâny is Robbed. The Lame Emir sets out for Aneyza

The same morning came two Beduins with camel-loads of temmn; which the men had brought down for Tollog and Motlog, from el-Irâk! They were of Shammar and carriers in Ibn Rashîd's Haj caravan. I wondered how after long journeying they had found our booths: they told me, that since passing Hâyil they had inquired us out, in this sort, – 'Where is Ibn Náhal?' – *Answer*: 'We heard of him in the S.E. country. – Some say he is gone over to the Ateyba marches. – When last we had word of him, he was in such part. – He went lately towards Seleyma. – You shall find his Aarab between such and such landmarks. – He is grazing about Genna.' Whilst they were unloading, a Beduin stranger, but known in this ferîj, arrived upon his camel after an absence: he had lately ridden westward 130 miles, to visit Bishr, amongst whom he had been bred up; but now he dwelt with Harb. The man was of Shammar, and had a forsaken wife living as a widow in our menzil: he came to visit their little son. Motlog counselled me to engage the honest man for the journey to Kasîm. We called him: – He answered, 'Wellah, he feared to pass so open a country, where he might lose his camel to some foraying Ateybân; but Motlog persuaded him, saying he could buy with his wages a load of dates (so cheap in el-Kasîm) to bring home to his household. He proffered to carry me to *el-Buk-kerîeh*: but we agreed for five reals that he should carry me to Boreyda. 'Mount, *érkub!*' quoth the man, whose name was *Hàmed*; he loaded my things, and climbed behind me, – and we rode forth. 'Ullah bring thee to thy journey's end! said Tollog; Ullah, give that you see not the evil!'

The sun was three hours high: we passed over a basalt coast, and descended to another ferîj; in which was Hàmed's beyt. There he took his water-skin, and a few handfuls of

mereesy – all his provision for riding other 450 miles – and
to his housewife he said no more than this: 'Woman, I go
with the stranger to Boreyda.' She obeyed silently; and commonly a Beduwy in departing bids not his wife farewell: –
'Hearest thou? (said Hàmed again), follow with these Aarab
until my coming home!' Then he took their little son in his
arms and kissed him.

... Now I saw the greater dunes of the Nefûd; such are
called *tâus* and *nef'd* (pl. *anfàd*) by Beduins: and *adanàt* and
kethîb (pl. *kethbàn*) are words heard in Kasîm. 'Not far beyond
the dunes on our right hand (towards Aneyza) lies the W. er-
Rummah,' said Hàmed. We journeyed an hour and a half, and
came upon a brow of the Nefûd, as the sun was going down.
And from hence appeared a dream-like spectacle! – a great
clay town built in this waste sand with enclosing walls and
towers and streets and houses! and there beside a bluish dark
wood of ethel trees, upon high dunes! This is Boreyda! and that
square minaret, in the town, is of their great mesjid. I saw, as
it were, Jerusalem in the desert! [as we look down from the
mount of Olives]. The last upshot sun-beams enlightened
the dim clay city in glorious manner, and pierced into that
dull pageant of tamarisk trees. I asked my rafîk, 'Where are
their palms?' He answered, 'Not in this part, they lie beyond
yonder great dune towards the Wady (er-Rummah).'

Hàmed: 'And whilst we were in the way, if at any time I
have displeased thee, forgive it me; and say hast thou found
me a good rafîk? Khalîl, thou seest Boreyda! and to-day I am
to leave thee in this place. And when thou art in any of their
villages, say not, "I (am) a Nasrâny," for then they will utterly
hate thee; but pray as they, so long as thou shalt sojourn in the
country, and in nothing let it be seen that thou art not of the
Moslemîn: do thus, that they may bear thee also goodwill, and
further thee. Look not to find these townlings mild-hearted
like the Beduw! but conform thyself to them; or they will not
suffer thee to abide long time among them. I do counsel thee
for the best – I may not compel thee! say thou art a *mudowwy*,
and tell them what remedies thou hast, and for which diseases:

this also must be thine art to live by. Thou hast suffered for this name of Nasrâny, and what has that profited thee? only say now, if thou canst, "I (am a) Musslim." '

We met with some persons of the town, without their walls, taking the evening air; and as we went by, they questioned my Beduwy rafîk: among them I noted a sinister Galla swordsman of the Emir. Hàmed answered, 'We were going to the Emir's hostel.' They said, 'It is far, and the sun is now set; were it not better for you to alight at such an house? that stands a little within the gate, and lodge there this night; and you may go to the Emir in the morning.' We rode from them and passed the town gate: their clay wall [vulg. *ajjidât*] is new, and not two feet thick. We found no man in the glooming streets; the people were gone home to sup, and the shops in the sûk were shut for the night: their town houses of (sandy) clay are low-built and crumbling. The camel paced under us with shuffling steps in the silent and forsaken ways: we went by the unpaved public place, *mejlis*; which I saw worn hollow by the townspeople's feet! and there is the great clay mesjid and high-built minaret. Hàmed drew bridle at the yard of the Emir's hostel, *Munôkh es-Sheukh.*

The porter bore back the rude gates; and we rode in and dismounted. The journey from er-Rauth had been nearly twenty-five miles. It was not long, before a kitchen lad bade us, 'rise and say God's name.' He led through dim cloistered courts; from whence we mounted by great clay stairs to supper. The degrees were worn down in the midst, to a gutter, and we stumbled dangerously in the gloom. We passed by a gallery and terraces above, which put me in mind of our convent buildings: the boy brought us on without light to the end of a colonnade, where we felt a ruinous floor under us. And there he fetched our supper, a churlish wheaten mess, boiled in water (a sort of Arabian *búrghrol*,) without samn: we were guests of the peasant Emir of Boreyda. It is the evening meal in Kasîm, but should be prepared with a little milk and butter; in good houses this búrghrol, cooked in the broth and commonly mixed with temmn, is served with boiled mutton. — When we had eaten and washed, we must feel the way back

in the dark, in danger of breaking our necks, which were more
than the supper's worth. – And now Hàmed bade me his short
Beduin *adieux*: he mounted his camel; and I was easy to see
my rafîk safely past the (tyrant's) gates. The moon was rising;
he would ride out of the town, and lodge in one of the villages.

I asked now to visit 'the Emir,' – Hásan's brother, whom
he had left deputy in Boreyda; it was answered, 'The hour is
late, and the Emir is in another part of the town: – *el-bâkir!* in
the morning.' The porter, the coffee server, a swordsman, and
other servitors of the guest-house gathered about me: the
yard gates were shut, and they would not suffer me to go forth.
Whilst I sat upon a clay bench, in the little moonlight, I was
startled from my weariness by the abhorred voice of their bar-
baric religion! the muéthin crying from the minaret to the
latter prayer. – 'Ah! I mused, my little provident memory!
what a mischance! why I had sat on thus late, and no Emir,
and none here to deliver me, till the morning?' I asked quickly,
'Where was the sleeping place?' Those hyenas responded,
with a sort of smothered derision, 'Would I not pray along
with them, ere I went to rest?' – they shoved me to a room in
the dark hostel building, which had been used for a small
kahwa.

All was silent within and sounding as a chapel. I groped,
and felt clay pillars, and trod on ashes of an hearth: and lay
down there upon the hard earthen floor. My pistol was in the
bottom of my bags, which the porter had locked up in another
place: I found my pen-knife, and thought in my heart, they
should not go away with whole skins, if any would do me a
mischief; yet I hoped the night might pass quietly. I had not
slumbered an hour when I heard footsteps, of some one feeling
through the floor; 'Up, said a voice, and follow me, thou art
called before the sheykhs to the coffee hall': – he went before,
and I followed by the sound; and found persons sitting at
coffee, who seemed to be of the Emir's guard. They bade me
be seated, and one reached me a cup: then they questioned
me, 'Art not thou the Nasrány that was lately at Hâyil? thou
wast there with some of Annezy; and Aneybar sent thee away

241

upon their *jurraba* (mangy thelûl): they were to convey thee to Kheybar?' – 'I am he.' – 'Why then didst thou not go to Kheybar?' – 'You have said it, – because the thelûl was jurraba; those Beduins could not carry me thither, which Aneybar well knew, but the slave would not hear: – tell me, how knowest thou this?' – 'I was in Hâyil, and I saw thee there. Did not Aneybar forbid thy going to Kasîm?' – 'I heard his false words, that ye were enemies, his forbidding I did not hear; how could the slave forbid me to travel, beyond the borders of Ibn Rashîd?' – At this they laughed and tossed their shallow heads, and I saw some of their teeth, – a good sign! The inquisitors added, with their impatient tyranny, 'What are the papers with thee, ha! go and fetch them; for those will we have instantly, and carry them to the Emir, – and (to a lad) go thou with the Nasrâny.'

The porter unlocked a store-closet where my bags lay. I drew out the box of medicines; but my weary hands seemed slow to the bird-witted wretches that had followed me. The worst of them, a Kahtâny, struck me with his fist, and reviled and threatened the Nasrâny. 'Out, they cried, with all thy papers!' and snatched them from my hands: 'We go with these, they said now, to the Emir.' They passed out; the gates were shut after them: and I was left alone in the court. The scelerat remained who had struck me: he came to me presently with his hand on his sword, and murmured, 'Thou kafîr! say *La îlah îll' Ullah*;' and there came another and another. I sat upon the clay bench in the moonlight, and answered them, 'To-morrow I will hear you; and not now, for I am most weary.'

Then they plucked at my breast (for money)! I rose, and they all swarmed about me.– The porter had said a word in my ear, 'If thou hast any silver commit it to me, for these will rob thee': but now I saw he was one of them himself! All the miscreants being upon me, I thought I might exclaim, '*Haramîeh*, thieves! ho! honest neighbours!' and see what came of it; but the hour was late, and this part of the town solitary.– None answered to my voice, and if any heard me, doubtless their hearts would shrink within them; for the Arabs [inhabiting a country weakly governed and full of alarms] are commonly dastards. When I cried *thieves*! I saw my tormentors stand a little aghast: 'Shout not (they said hoarsely) or by Ullah – !' So I understood that this assailing me was of their own ribald malice, and shouted on; and when I began to move my arms, they were such cowards that, though I was infirm, I might, I perceived, with a short effort have delivered myself from them: yet this had been worse – for then they would return with weapons; and I was enclosed by walls, and could not escape out of the town. Six were the vile crew struggling with me: I thought it best to shout on *haramîeh*! and make ever some little resistance, to delay the time. I hoped every moment that the officer would return from the Emir. Now my light purse was in their brutish hands; and that which most troubled me, the aneroid barometer. – it seemed to them a watch in the starlight! The Kahtâny snatched and burst the cord by which the delicate instrument was suspended from my neck; and ran away with it like a hound with a good bone in his mouth. They had plucked off my mantle and kerchief; and finally the villains left me standing alone in a pair of slops: then they hied all together to the door where my bags lay. But I thought they would not immediately find my pistol in the dark; and so it was.

– Now the Emir's man stood again at the gate, beating and calling loudly to be admitted: and the porter went like a truant to open. 'What has happened?' quoth the officer who entered. 'They have stripped the Nasrâny.' – 'Who has done this?' 'It was the Kahtâny, in the beginning.' 'And this fellow, I answered, was one of the nimblest of them!' The rest had fled into the hostel building, when the Emir's man came in. 'Oh, the shame! (quoth the officer) that one is robbed in the Kasr of the Emir; and he a man who bears letters from the Sooltân, what have you done? the Lord curse you all togèther.' 'Let them, I said, bring my clothes, although they have rent them.' – 'Others shall be given thee by the Emir.' The lurkers came forth at his call from their dark corners; and he bade them, 'Bring the stranger his clothes: – and all, he said to me,

that they have robbed shall be restored, upon pain of cutting
off the hand; wellah the hand of anyone with whom is found
aught shall be laid in thy bags for the thing that was stolen. I
came to lead thee to a lodging prepared for thee; but I must
now return to the Emir: – and (naming them) thou, and thou,
and thou, do no more thus, to bring on you the displeasure
of the Emir.' They answered, 'We had not done it, but he refused to say, *La îlah ill' Ullah*.' – 'This is their falsehood! – for
to please them I said it four of five times; and hearken! I will
say it again, La îlah, ill' Ullah.' – *Officer*: ' I go, and shall be
back anon.' – 'Leave me no more among robbers.' – 'Fear
not, none of them will do anything further against you'; and
he bade the porter close the gates behind him.

He returned soon: and commanded those wretches, from
the Emir, 'upon pain of the hand,' to restore all that they had
robbed from the Nasrâny; he bade also the porter make a fire
in the porch to give us light. The Kahtâny swordsman, who
had been the ringleader of them – he was one of the Emir's
band – adjured me to give a true account of the money which
was in my purse: 'for my words might endanger his hand;
and if I said but the sooth the Lord would show me mercy.' –
'Dost thou think, Miserable, that a Christian man should be
such as thyself!' – 'Here, is the purse, quoth the officer; how
much money should be therein? take it, and count thy *derâhim*
($\delta\rho\alpha\chi\mu$).' I found their barbarous hands had been in it; for
there remained only a few pence! 'Such and such lacks.' –
Officer: 'Oh! ye who have taken the man's money, go and fetch
it, and the Lord curse you.' The swordsman went; and came
back with the money, – two French gold pieces of 20 francs:
all that remained to me in this bitter world. *Officer*: 'Say now,
is this all thy *fulûs*?' – 'That is all.' – 'Is there any more?'
'No!' – The Kahtâny showed me his thanks with a wondering
brutish visage. *Officer*: 'And what more?' – 'Such and such.'
The wretches went, and came again with the small things and
what else they had time, after stripping me (it was by good
fortune but a moment), to steal from my bags. *Officer*: 'Look
now, hast thou all, is there anything missing?' – 'Yes, my
watch' (the aneroid, which after the pistol was my most care

in Arabia); but they exclaimed, 'What watch! no, we have restored all to him already.' *Officer*: 'Oh, you liars, you cursed ones, you thieves, bring this man his watch! or the (guilty) hand is forfeited to the Emir.' It was fetched with delays; and of this they made restitution with the most unwillingness: the metal gilt might seem to them fine gold. – To my comfort, I found on the morrow that the instrument was uninjured: I might yet mark in it the height of a fathom.

He said now, 'It was late, and I should pass the night here.' – 'Lend me a sword, if I must sleep in this cursed place; and if any set upon me again, should I spare him?' – 'There is no more danger, and as for these they shall be locked in the coffee-hall till the morning': and he led away the offenders. – The officer had brought my papers: only the safe-conduct of Aneybar was not among them!

When the day broke the Emir's officer – whose name was Jeyber – returned to me: I asked anew to visit the Emir. Jeyber answered, he must first go and speak with him. When he came again, he laid my bags on his infirm shoulders saying, he would bring me to my lodging. He led me through an outlying street; and turned into a vast ruinous yard, before a great building – now old and crumbling, that had been the Emir's palace in former days [the house walls here of loam may hardly stand above one hundred years]. We ascended by hollow clay stairs to a great hall above; where two women, his housewives, were sitting. Jeyber, tenant of all the rotten palace, was a tribesman of Kahtân. In the end was a further room, which he gave me for my lodging. 'I am weary, and thou more, said he; a cup of kahwa will do us both good': Jeyber sat down at his hearth to prepare the morrow's coffee.

In that there came up some principal persons of the town; clad in the (heavy) Mesopotamian wise. A great number of the well-faring sort in Boreyda are *jemmamîl*, camel masters trading in the caravans. They are wheat carriers in Mesopotamia; they bring down clothing and temmn to Nejd; they load dates and corn of Kasîm (when the prices serve) for el-Medina. In autumn they carry samn, which they have taken up from the country Nomads, to Mecca; and from thence they draw coffee.

These burly Arabian citizens resemble peasants! they were travelled men; but I found in them an implacable fanaticism.

Jeyber said when they were gone, 'Now shall we visit the Emir?' We went forth; and he brought me through a street to a place, before the Prince's house. A sordid fellow was sitting there, like Job, in the dust of the street: two or three more sate with him, – he might be thirty-five years of age. I inquired, 'Where was Abdullah the Emir?' They said 'He is the Emir!' – ' Jeyber (I whispered), is this the Emir?' – 'It is he.' I asked the man, 'Art thou Weled Mahanna?' He answered, 'Ay.' 'Is it (I said) a custom here, that strangers are robbed in the midst of your town? I had eaten of your bread and salt; and your servants set upon me in your yard.' – 'They were Beduw that robbed you.' – 'But I have lived with the Beduw; and was never robbed in a menzil: I never lost any thing in a host's tent. Thou sayest they were Beduins; but they were the Emir's men!' – *Abdullah*: 'I say they were Kahtân all of them.' He asked to see my 'watch'. 'That I have not with me; but here is a telescope!' He put this to his eyes and returned it. I said, 'I give it thee; but thou wilt give me other clothing for my clothing which the Emir's servants have rent.' – He would not receive my gift, the peasant would not make the Nasrâny amends; and I had not money to buy more. 'Today, said he, you depart.' – 'Whither?' – 'To Aneyza; and there are certain cameleers – they left us yesterday, that are going to *Siddûs*: they will convey thee thither.' ... But this was Abdullah's guile, he fabled with me of cameleers to Siddûs: and then he cries, '*Min yeshîl*, who will convey the Nasrâny on his camel to *eh-Wady*?' – which I afterwards knew to signify the palms at the *Wady er-Rummah*: I said to him, 'I would rest this day, I was too weary for riding.' Abdullah granted (albeit unwillingly); for all the Arabians [inhabitants of a weary land] tender human infirmities. – 'Well, as thou wilt; and that may suffice thee.' ...

... The mid-day heat was come; and he went to slumber in a further part of the waste building. I had reposed somewhile, in my chamber, when a creaking of the old door, painted in

vermilion, startled me! – and a sluttish young woman entered.
I asked, wherefore had she broken my rest? Her answer was
like some old biblical talk; *Tekhálliny aném fî hothnak?* Suffer
me to sleep in thy bosom.' – Who could have sent this lurid
quean? the Arabs are the basest of enemies, – hoped they to
find an occasion to accuse the Nasrâny? But the kind damsel
was not daunted; for when I chided she stood to rate the
stranger: saying, with the loathly voice of misery, 'Aha! the
cursed Nasrâny! and I was about to be slain, by faithful men;
that were in the way, sent from the Emir, to do it! and I might
not now escape them.' – I rose and put this baggage forth,
and fastened the door. – But I wondered at her words, and
mused that only for the name of a Religion, (O Chimæra of
human self-love, malice and fear!) I was fallen daily into such
mischiefs, in Arabia. – Now Jeyber came again from napping;
and his hareem related to him the adventure: Jeyber left us
saying, he must go to the Emir.

Soon after this we heard people of the town flocking about
our house, and clamouring under the casements, which opened
backward upon a street, and throwing up stones! and some
noisy persons had broken into the great front yard! – The stair
was immediately full of them; and they bounced at our door
which the women had barred. – 'Alas, said the hareem, wring-
ing their hands, what can we do now? for the riotous people
will kill thee; and Jeyber is away.' One of them was a townswoman, the other was a Beduwîa: both were good towards the
guest. I sat down saying to them, 'My sisters, you must defend
the house with your tongues.' – They were ready; and the
townswoman looking out backward chided them that made
this hubbub in the street. 'Ha! uncivil people; who be they
that throw up stones into the apartment of the hareem? akhs!
what would ye? – ye seek what? God send a sorrow upon you!
– Oh! ye seek Khalîl the Nasrâny? but here is not Khalîl; ye
fools, he is not here: away with you. Go! I say, for shame, and
Ullah curse you.' – And she that kept the door cried to them
that were without, 'Aha! what is your will? – akhs! who are
these that beat like to break our door? O ye devil-sick and
shameless young men! Khalîl is not here; he went forth, go

and seek the Nasrâny, go! We have told you Khalîl went
forth, we know not whither, – akhs! [they knocked now on
the door with stones.] Oh you shameless fellows! would ye
break through folks' doors, to the hareem? Ullah send a very
pestilence upon you all; and for this the Emir will punish you.'
Whilst she was speaking there was a confused thrusting and
shuffling of feet without the door; the strokes of their sticks
and stones sounded hideously upon the wood. – The faithful
women's tongues yet delayed them! and I put my hope in the
stars, that Jeyber would return with speed. But if the besiegers
burst in to rend me in pieces, should I spare the foremost of
them? The hareem cried on, 'Why beat thus, ye cursed people?
– akhs! will ye beat down our door indeed?'

At length came Jeyber again; and in the name of the Emir
he drove them all forth, and locked them out of his yard. –
When he entered, he shrunk up his shoulders and said to me,
'They are clamouring to the Emir for thy death! "No Nasrâny,
they say, ever entered Boreyda": there is this outcry in the
town, and Abdullah is for favouring the people! – I have now
pleaded with him. If, please Ullah, we may pass this night in
safety, to-morrow when my thelûl shall be come – and I have
sent for her – I will convey thee by solitary lanes out of the
place; and bring thee to Aneyza.' – As we were speaking, we
heard those townspeople swarming anew in his court! the
foremost mounted again upon our stairs, – and the door was
open. But Jeyber, threatening grievous punishment of the
Emir, drove them down once more; and out of his yard.
When he returned, he asked his housewives, with looks of
mistrust, who it was had undone the gate (from within)?
which he had left barred! He said, he must go out again, to
speak with Abdullah; but should not be long absent. I would
not let him pass, till he had promised me to lock his gates, and
carry the (wooden) key with him. There remained only this
poor soul, and the timber of an old door, betwixt me, a lonely
alien, and the fanatical wildness of this townspeople. When
he came again he said the town was quiet: Abdullah, at his
intercession, had forbidden to make more ado, the riotous
were gone home; and he had left the gate open. ...

Jeyber returned all doubtful and pensive! 'The people, he said, were clamouring again to Abdullah; who answered them, that they might deal with me as they would: he had told them already, that they might have slain the Nasrâny in the desert; but it could not be done in the town.' Jeyber asked me now, 'Would I forsake my bags, and flee secretly from Boreyda on foot?' I answered 'No! – and tell me sooth, Jeyber! hast thou no mind to betray me?' He promised as he was a faithful man that he would not. 'Well, what is the present danger?' – 'I hope no more, for this night, at least in my house.' – 'How may I pass the streets in the morning?' – 'We will pass them; the peril is not so much in the town as of their pursuing.' – 'How many horsemen be there in Boreyda, a score?' – 'Ay, and more.' – 'Go quickly and tell Abdullah, Khalîl says I am *rájol Dowla,* one who is safe-guarded (my papers declare it) by the government of the Sooltàn: if an evil betide me (a guest) among you, it might draw some trouble upon yourselves. For were it to be suffered that a traveller, under the imperial protection, and only passing by your town, should be done to death, for the name of a religion, which is tolerated by the Sooltàn? Neither let them think themselves secure here, in the midst of deserts; for "*long is the arm of the Dowla!*" Remember Jidda, and Damascus! and the guilty punished, by commandment of the Sooltàn!' Jeyber answered, 'He would go and speak these words to Abdullah.'

Jeyber returned with better looks, saying that Abdullah allowed my words: and had commanded that none should any more molest the Nasrâny; and promised him, that no evil should befall me this night. *Jeyber*: 'We be now in peace, blessed be the Lord! go in and rest, Khalîl; to be ready betimes.'

I was ready ere the break of day; and thought it an hundred years till I should be out of Boreyda. At sunrise Jeyber sat down to prepare coffee; and yet made no haste! the promised thelûl was not come. – 'And when will thy thelûl be here?' – 'At some time before noon.' – 'How then may we come to Aneyza to-night?' – 'I have told thee, that Aneyza is not far off.' My host also asked for remedies for his old infirmities. – 'At Aneyza!' – 'Nay, but now; for I would leave them here.' When he had received his medicines, Jeyber began to make it strange of his thelûl-riding to Aneyza. I thought an host would not forswear himself; but all their life is passed in fraud and deceit. – In this came up the Kahtâny who had been ring-leader in the former night's trouble; and sat down before his tribesman's hearth; where he was wont to drink the morrow's cup. Jeyber would have me believe that the fellow had been swinged yesterday before Abdullah: I saw no such signs in him. The wretch who had lately injured me would now have maintained my cause! I said to Jeyber's Beduin jâra, who sat with us, 'Tell me, is not he possessed by a jin?' The young man answered for himself, 'Ay Khalîl, I am somewhiles a little lunatic.' He had come to ask the Nasrâny for medicines, – in which surely he had not trusted one of his own religion.

– A limping footfall sounded on the palace stairs: it was the lame Emir Abdullah who entered! leaning on his staff. Sordid was the (peasant) princeling's tunic and kerchief: he sat down at the hearth, and Jeyber prepared fresh coffee. Abdullah said, – showing me a poor man standing by the door and that came in with him; 'This is he that will carry thee on his camel to Aneyza; rise! and bring out thy things.' – 'Jeyber promises to convey me upon his thelûl.' But now my host (who had but fabled) excused himself, saying, 'he would follow us, when his thelûl were come.' Abdullah gave the cameleer his wages, the quarter of a mejîdy, eleven pence. The man took my bags upon his shoulders, and brought me by a lonely street to a camel couched before his clay cottage. We mounted and rode by lanes out of the town.

The Nasrâny, Forsaken, Finds a Bread-and-Salt Friend and Enters Aneyza

We saw a nomad child keeping sheep: and I asked my rafîk, 'When should we come to Aneyza?' – 'By the sunsetting.' I found the land-height to be not more than 2,500 feet. When we had ridden slowly three hours, we fell again into the road,

by some great-grown tamarisks. '*Negîl*, quoth Hásan, we wil'
alight here and rest out the hot mid-day hours.' I saw trenches
dug under those trees by locust hunters. I asked, 'Is it far
now?' – 'Aneyza is not far off.' – 'Tell me truth rafîk, art thou
carrying me to Aneyza' – 'Thou believest not; see here!' (he
drew me out a bundle of letters – and yet they seemed worn
and old). 'All these, he said, are merchants' letters which I am
to deliver to-day in Aneyza; and to fetch the goods from
thence.' – And had I not seen him accept the young franklin's
letter for Aneyza! Hásan found somewhat in my words, for
he did not halt; we might be come ten miles from Boreyda.
The soil shelved before us; and under the next tamarisks I saw
a little oozing water. We were presently in a wady bottom, not
a stone-cast over; and in crossing we plashed through trickling water! I asked, 'What bed is this?' – *Answer*: 'EL WADY'
– that is, we were in (the midst of) the Wady er-Rummah. We
came up by oozing (brackish) water to a palm wood unen-
closed, where are grave-like pits of a fathom digged beside
young palm-sets to the ground water. The plants are watered
by hand a year or two, till they have put down roots to the
saltish ground moisture.

It is nearly a mile to pass through this palm wood, where
only few (older) stems are seen grown aloft above the rest;
because such outlying possessions are first to the destruction
in every warfare. I saw through the trees an high-built court
wall, wherein the husbandmen may shelter themselves in any
alarms; and Hásan showed me, in an open ground, where Ibn
Rashîd's tents stood two years ago, when he came with Weled
Mahanna against Aneyza. We met only two negro labourers;
and beyond the palms the road is again in the Nefûd. Little
further at our right hand, were some first enclosed properties;
and we drew bridle at a stone trough, a sebîl, set by the land-
owner in his clay wall, with a channel from his suânies: the
trough was dry, for none now passed by that way to or from
Boreyda. We heard creaking of well-wheels and voices of
harvesters in a field. 'Here, said Hásan, as he put down my
bags, is the place of repose: rest in the shadow of this wall,
whilst I go to water the camel. And where is the girby? that I

may bring thee to drink; you might be thirsty before evening, when it will be time to enter the town, – thus says Abdullah; and now open thy eyes, for fear of the Beduw.' I let the man go, but made him leave his spear with me.

When he came again with the waterskin, Hásan said he had loosed out the camel to pasture; 'and wellah Khalîl I must go after her, for see! the beast has strayed. Reach me my romh, and I will run to turn her, or she will be gone far out in the Nefûd.' – 'Go, but the spear remains with me.' 'Ullah! doubt not thy rafîk, should I go unarmed? give me my lance, and I will be back to thee in a moment.' I thought, that if the man were faithless and I compelled him to carry me into Aneyza, he might have cried out to the fanatical townspeople: 'This is a Nasrâny!' – 'Our camel will be gone, do not delay me.' – 'Wilt thou then forsake me here?' – 'No wellah, by this beard!' I cast this lance upon the sand, which taking up, he said, 'Whilst I am out, if thou have need of anything, go about the corner of the wall yonder; so thou wilt see a palm ground, and men working. Rest now in the shadow, and make thyself a little mereesy, for thou art fasting; and cover these bags! let no man see them. Aneyza is but a little beyond that *ádan* there; thou mayest see the town from thence, I will run now, and return.' I let him pass, and Hásan, hieing after his camel, was hidden by the sand billows. I thought soon, I would see what were become of him, and casting away my mantle I ran barefoot in the Nefûd; and from a sand dune I espied Hásan riding forth upon his camel – for he had forsaken me! he fetched a circuit to go about the Wady palms homeward. I knew then that I was betrayed by the secret commission of Abdullah, and remembered his word, 'Who will carry the Nasrâny *to the Wady*?'

This was the cruellest fortune which had befallen me in Arabia! to be abandoned here without a chief town, in the midst of fanatical Nejd. I had but eight reals left, which might hardly more than carry me in one course to the nearest coast. I returned and armed myself; and rent my maps in small pieces, – lest for such I should be called in question, amongst lettered citizens.

A negro man and wife came then from the palms, carrying firewood towards Aneyza: they had seen us pass, and asked me simply, 'Where is thy companion and the camel?' – After this I went on under the clay walling towards the sound of suânies; and saw a palm ground and an orchard house. The door was shut fast: I found another beyond; and through the chinks I looked in, and espied the owner driving, – a plain natured face. I pushed up his gate and entered at a venture with, 'Peace be with thee'; and called for a drink of water. The goodman stayed a little to see the stranger! then he bade his young daughter fetch the bowl, and held up his camels to speak with me. 'Drink if thou wilt, said he, but we have no good water.' The taste was bitter and unwholesome; but even this cup of water would be a bond between us.

I asked him to lend me a camel or an ass, to carry my things to the town, and I would pay the hire. I told further how I came hither, – with a cameleer from Boreyda; who whilst I rested in the heat had forsaken me nigh his gate: that I was an hakîm, and if there were any sick in this place I had medicines to relieve them. – 'Well, bide till my lad return with a camel: – I go (he said to his daughter) with this man; here! have my stick and drive, and let not the camels stand. – What be they, O stranger, and where leftest thou thy things? come! thou shouldst not have left them out of sight and unguarded; how, if we should not find them –?' – They were safe; and taking the great bags on my shoulders, I tottered back over the Nefûd to the good man's gate; rejoicing inwardly, that I might now bear all I possessed in the world. He bade me sit down there (without), whilst he went to fetch an ass. – 'Wilt thou pay a piastre and a half (threepence)?' There came now three or four grave elder men from the plantations, and they were going in at the next gate to drink their afternoon kahwa. The good-man stayed them and said, 'This is a stranger, – he cannot remain here, and we cannot receive him in our house; he asks for carriage to the town.' They answered, he should do well to fetch the ass and send me to Aneyza. 'And what art thou? (they said to me) – we go in now to coffee; has anyone heard the íthin?' *Another*: 'They have cried to prayers in the town, but we cannot always hear it; – for is not the sun gone down to the âssr? then pray we here together.' They took their stand devoutly, and my host joined himself to the row; they called me also, 'Come and pray, come!' – 'I have prayed already.' They marvelled at my words; and so fell to their formal reciting and prostrations. When they rose, my host came to me with troubled looks: – 'Thou dost not pray, hmm!' said he; and I saw by those grave men's countenance, they were persuaded that I could be no right Moslem. 'Well send him forward,' quoth the chief of them, and they entered the gate.

My bags were laid now upon an ass. We departed: and little beyond the first *ádan*, as Hásan had foretold me, was the beginning of cornfields; and palms and fruit trees appeared, and some houses of outlying orchards. – My companion said [he was afraid!] 'It is far to the town, and I cannot go there tonight; but I will leave thee with one yonder who is *ibn juâd*, a son of bounty; and in the morning he will send thee to Aneyza.' – We came on by a wide road and unwalled, till he drew up his ass at a rude gateway; there was an orchard house, and he knocked loud and called, *'Ibrahîm!'* An old father came to the gate, who opened it to the half and stayed – seeing my clothes rent (by the thieves at Boreyda)! and not knowing what strange person I might be: – but he guessed I was some runaway soldier from the Harameyn or el-Yémen, as there had certain passed by Aneyza of late. He of the ass spoke for me; and then that housefather received me. They brought in my bags to his clay house; and he locked them in a store closet; so without speaking he beckoned with his hand, and led me out in his orchard, to the 'diwán' (their clean sanded sitting-place in the field); and there left me.

Pleasant was the sight of their tilled ground with corn stubbles and green plots of vetches, *jet*, the well-camels' provender; and borders of a dye-plant, whose yellow blossoms are used by the townswomen to stain the partings of their hair. When this sun was nigh setting, I remembered their unlucky prayer-hour! and passed hastily to the further side of their palms; but I was not hidden by the clear-set rows of trees: when I came again in the twilight, they demanded of me, 'Why

I prayed not? and wherefore had I not been with them at the prayers?' Then they said over the names of the four orthodox sects of Islam, and questioned with me, 'To which of them pertainest thou; or be'st thou (of some heterodox belief) a *râfuthy*?' – a word which they pronounced with enmity. I made no answer, and they remained in some astonishment. They brought me, to sup, boiled wheat in a bowl and another of their well water; there was no greater hospitality in that plain household. I feared the dampish (oasis) air and asked, where was the coffee chamber. *Answer*: 'Here is no kahwa, and we drink none.' They sat in silence, and looked heavily upon the stranger, who had not prayed.

He who brought me the bowl (not one of them) was a manly young man, of no common behaviour; and he showed in his words an excellent understanding. I bade him sup with me. –'I have supped.' – 'Yet eat a morsel, for the bread and salt between us': he did so. After that, when the rest were away, I told him what I was, and asked him of the town. 'Well, he said, thou art here to-night; and little remains to Aneyza, where they will bring thee in the morning; I think there is no danger – Zâmil is a good man: besides thou art only passing by them. Say to the Emir to-morrow, in the people's hearing, "I am a soldier from *Béled-el-Asîr*" (a good province in el-Yémen, which the Turks had lately occupied).' – Whilst we were speaking, the last íthin sounded from the town! I rose hastily; but the three or four young men, sons of Ibrahîm, were come again, and began to range themselves to pray! they called us, and they called to me the stranger with insistance, to take our places with them. I answered: 'I am over-weary, I will go to sleep.' – *The bread-and-salt Friend*: 'Ay-ay, the stranger says well, he is come from a journey; show him the place without more, where he may lie down.' – 'I would sleep in the house, and not here abroad.' – 'But first let him pray; ho! thou, come and pray, come!' – *The Friend*: 'Let him alone, and show the weary man to his rest.' – 'There is but the woodhouse.' – 'Well then to the wood-house, and let him sleep immediately.' One of them went with me, and brought me to a threshold: the floor was sunk a foot or two, and I fell in a dark place full of sweet tamarisk boughs. After their praying came all the brethren: they sat before the door in the feeble moonlight, and murmured, 'I had not prayed! – and could this be a Musslim?' But I played the sleeper; and after watching half an hour they left me. How new to us is this religiosity, in rude young men of the people! but the Semetic religion – so cold, and a strange plant, in the (idolatrous) soil of Europe, is like to a blood passion, in the people of Moses and Mohammed.

An hour before day I heard one of these brethren creeping in – it was to espy if the stranger would say the dawning prayers! When the morrow was light all the brethren stood before the door; and they cried to me, *Ma sulleyt*, 'Thou didst not say the prayer!' – 'Friends, I prayed.' – 'Where washed you then?' – This I had not considered, for I was not of the dissembler's craft. Another brother came to call me; and he led me up the house stairs to a small, clean room: where he spread matting on the clay floor, and set before me a dish of very good dates, with a bowl of whey: and bade me breakfast, with their homely word, *fúk er-ríg* 'Loose the fasting spittle': (the Bed. say *ríj*, for *rík*). 'Drink!' said he, and lifted to my hands his hospitable bowl. – After that he brought the ass and loaded my bags, to carry them into the town. We went on in the same walled road, and passed a ruinous open gate of Aneyza. Much of the town wall was there in sight; which is but a thin shell, with many wide breaches. Such clay walling might be repaired in few days, and Aneyza can never be taken by famine; for the wide town walls enclose their palm grounds: the people, at this time, were looking for war with Boreyda....

After Meeting Zâmil the Emir, the Nasrâny Gains a Friend in Abdulláh El-Kenneyny

Some principal persons went by again, returning from their friends' houses.– One of them approached me, and said, 'Hast thou a knowledge of medicine?' The tremulous figure of the speaker, with some drawing of his face, put me in mind of the Algerine Mohammed Aly, at Medáin Sâlih! But he that stood here was a gentle son of Temîm, whose good star went before me from this day to the end of my voyage in Arabia! Taking my hand in his hand, which is a kind manner of the Arabs, he said, 'Wilt thou visit my sick mother?'

He led me to his house gate not far distant; and entering himself by a side door he came round to open for me: I found within a large coffee-hall, spread with well-wrought grass matting, which is fetched hither from *el-Hása*. The walls were pargetted with fretwork of jis, such as I had seen at Boreyda. A Persian tapet spread before his fire-pit was the guests' sitting place; and he sat down himself behind the hearth to make me coffee. This was *Abdullah el-Kenneyny*, the fortunate son of a good but poor house. He had gone forth a young man from Aneyza; and after the first hazards of fortune, was grown to be one of the most considerable foreign merchants. His traffic was in corn, at Bosra, and he lived willingly abroad; for his heart was not filled in Aneyza, where he despised the Waháby straitness and fanaticism. In these days leaving his merchandise at Bosra to the care of his brother (Sâlih, who they told me little resembles him), Abdullah was come to pass a leisure year at home; where he hoped to refresh his infirm health in the air of the Nefûd.

When I looked in this man's face he smiled kindly. – 'And art thou, said he, Engleysy? but wherefore tell the people so, in this wild fanatical country? I have spent many years in foreign lands, I have dwelt at Bombay, which is under government of the Engleys: thou canst say thus to me, but say it not to the ignorant and foolish people; – what simplicity is this! and incredible to me, in a man of *Europa*. For are we here in a government country? no, but in land of the Aarab, where the name of the Nasâra is an execration. A Nasrâny they think to be a son of the Evil One, and (therefore) deserving of death: an half of this townspeople are Wahábies.' – 'Should I not speak truth, as well here as in mine own country?' *Abdullah*: 'We have a tongue to further us and our friends, and to illude our enemies; and indeed the more times the lie is better than the sooth. – Or dreadest thou, that Ullah would visit it upon thee, if thou assentedst to them in appearance? Is there not in everything the good and evil?' [even in lying and

257

dissembling.] – 'I am this second year, in a perilous country, and have no scathe. Thou hast heard the proverb, "Truth may walk through the world unarmed."' – 'But the Engleys are not thus! nay, I have seen them full of policy: in the late warfare between Abdullah and Saûd ibn Saûd, their Resident on the Gulf sent hundreds of sacks of rice, secretly, to Saûd [the wrongful part; and for such Abdullah the Waháby abhors the English name.] – I see you will not be persuaded! yet I hope that your life may be preserved: but they will not suffer you to dwell amongst them! you will be driven from place to place.' – 'This seemed to me a good peaceable town, and are the people so illiberal?' – 'As many among them, as have travelled, are liberal; but the rest no. Now shall we go to my mother?'

Abdullah led me into an inner room, from whence we ascended to the floor above. He had bought this great new (clay) house the year before, for a thousand reals, or nearly £200 sterling. The loam brickwork at Aneyza is good, and such house-walls may stand above one hundred years. ...

... In Abdullah's upper storey were many good chambers, but bare to our eyes, since they have few more moveables than the Beduw: all the husbandry of his great town house might have been carried on the backs of three camels! In the Arabic countries the use of bed-furniture is unknown; they lie on the floor, and the wellborn and welfaring have no more than some thin cotton quilt spread under them, and a coverlet: I saw only a few chests, in which they bestow their clothing. Their houses in this land of sunny warmth, are lighted by open loopholes made high upon the lofty walls. But Abdullah was not so simply housed as Bosra; for there – in the great world's side, the Arab merchants' halls are garnished with chairs: and the Aneyza *tájir* sat (like the rest) upon a *takht* or carpeted settle in his counting-house.

He brought me to a room where I saw his old mother, sitting on the floor; and clad – so are all the Arabian women, only in a calico smock dipped in indigo. She covered her old visage, as we entered, with a veil! Abdullah smile to me, and looked to see 'a man of Europa' smile. 'My mother, said he, I bring thee el-hakîm; say what aileth thee, and let him see thine eyes': and with a gentle hand he folded down her veil. 'Oh! said she, my head; and all this side so aches that I cannot sleep, my son.' Abdullah might be a man of forty; yet his mother was abashed, that a strange man must look upon her old blear eyes. – We returned to the coffee room perfect friends. 'My mother, said he, is aged and suffering, and I suffer to see her: if thou canst help us, that will be a great comfort to me.'

Abdullah added, 'I am even now in amazement! that, in such a country, you openly avow yourself to be an Englishman; but how may you pass even one day in safety! You have lived hitherto with the Beduw; ay, but it is otherwise in the townships.' – 'In such hazards there is nothing, I suppose, more prudent than a wise folly.' – 'Then, you will not follow better counsel! but here you may trust in me: I will watch for you, and warn you of any alteration in the town.' I asked, 'And what of the Emir?' – 'You may also trust Zâmil; but even Zâmil cannot at all times refrain the unruly multitude.'

The Nasrâny is Driven from Aneyza

One day when I returned to my lodging, I found that my watch had been stolen! I left it lying with my medicines. This was a cruel loss, for my fortune was very low; and by selling the watch I might have had a few reals: suspicion fell upon an infamous neighbour. The town is uncivil in comparison with the desert! I was but one day in the dokân, and all my vaccinations pens were purloined: they were of ivory and had cost ten reals; – more than I gained (in twice ten months) by the practice of medicine, in Arabia. I thought again upon the Kenneyny's proffer, which I had passed over at that time; and mused that he had not renewed it! There are many shrewd haps in Arabia; and even the daily piastre spent for bread divided me from the coast; and what would become of my life, if by any evil accident I were parted from the worthy persons who were now my friends?

– Handicraftsmen here in a Middle Nejd town (of the sanies'

caste), are armourers, tinkers, coppersmiths, goldsmiths; and the workers in wood are turners of bowls, wooden locksmiths, makers of camel saddle-frames, well-wheel-rights, and (very unhandsome) carpenters [for they are nearly without tools]; the stone-workers are hewers, well-steyners and sinkers, besides marble-wrights, makers of coffee mortars and the like; and house-builders and pargeters. We may go on to reckon those that work with the needle, seamsters and seamstresses, embroiderers, sandal makers. The sewing men and women are, so far as I have known them, of the libertine blood. The gold and silver smiths of Aneyza are excellent artificers in filigrane or thread-work: and certain of them established at Mecca are said to excel all in the sacred town. El-Kenneyny promised that I should see something of this fine Arabian industry; but the waves of their fanatical world soon cast me from him.

The salesmen are clothiers in the sûk, sellers of small wares [in which are raw drugs and camel medicines, sugar-loaves, spices, Syrian soap from Medina, coffee of the Mecca Caravans], and sellers of victual. In the outlying quarters are small general shops – some of them held by women, where are sold onions, eggs, iron nails, salt, (German) matches, girdle-bread [and certain of these poor wives will sell thee a little milk, if they have any]. On Fridays, you shall see veiled women sitting in the mejlis to sell chickens, and milk-skins and girbies that they have tanned and prepared. Ingenuous vocations are husbandry, and camel and horse dealing. All the welfaring families are land owners. – The substantial foreign merchants were fifteen persons.

Hazardry, banqueting, and many running sores and hideous sinks of our great towns are unknown to them. The Arabs, not less frugal than Spartans, are happy in the Epicurean moderation of their religion. Aneyza is a welfaring civil town more than other in Nomadic Arabia: in her B.Temîm citizens is a spirit of industry, with a good plain understanding – howbeit somewhat soured by the rheum of the Waháby religion.

Seeing that few any more chided the children that cried after me in the street, I thought it an evil sign; but the Kenneyny had not warned me, and Zâmil was my friend: the days were toward the end of May. One of these forenoons, when I returned to my house, I saw filth cast before the threshold; and some knavish children had flung stones as I passed by the lonely street. Whilst I sat within, the little knaves came to batter the door; there was a Babel of cries; the boldest climbed by the side walls to the house terrace; and hurled down stones and clay bricks by the stair head. In this uproar I heard a skritching of fanatical women, 'Yá Nasrâny! thou shalt be dead! – they are in the way that will do it!' I sat on an hour whilst the hurly-burly lasted: my door held, and for all their hooting the knaves had no courage to come down where they must meet the kafir. At this hour the respectable citizens were reposing at home, or drinking coffee in their friends' houses; and it was a desolate quarter where I lodged. At length the siege was raised; for some persons went by who returned from the coffee companies, and finding this ado about Khalîl's door, they drove away the truants, – with those extreme curses which are always ready in the mouths of Arabs. ...

... I thought I had slumbered an hour, when the negro voice of Aly awakened me! crying at the gate, 'Khalîl! – Khalîl! the Emir bids thee open.' I went to undo for him, and looked out. It was dark night; but I perceived, by the shuffling feet and murmur of voices, that there were many persons. *Aly*: 'The Emir calls thee; he sits yonder (in the street)!' I went, and sat down beside him: could Zâmil, I mused, be come at these hours! then hearing his voice, which resembled Zâmil's, I knew it was another. 'Whither, said the voice, would'st thou go, – to Zifty?' – 'I am going shortly in the company of Abdullah el-Bessàm's son to Jidda.' 'No, no! and Jidda (he said, brutally laughing) is very far off: but where wilt thou go this night?' – 'Aly, what sheykh is this?' – 'It is Aly the Emir.' Then a light was brought: I saw his face which, with a Waháby brutishness, resembled Zâmil's; and with him were some of his ruffian ministers. – 'Emir Aly, Ullah lead thy parents into paradise! Thou knowest that I am sick; and I have certain debts for medicines here in the town; and to-day I have

tasted nothing. If I have deserved well of some of you, let me
rest here until the morning; and then send me away in peace.'
– 'Nay, thy camel is ready at the corner of the street; and this
is thy cameleer: up! have out thy things, and that quickly. Ho!
some of you go in with Khalîl, to hasten him.' – 'And whither
will ye send me, so suddenly? and I have no money!' – 'Ha-
ha! what is that to us, I say come off': as I regarded him
fixedly, the villain struck me with his fist in the face. – If the
angry instinct betray me, the rest (I thought) would fall with
their weapons upon the Nasrâny: – Aly had pulled his sword
from the sheath to the half. 'This, I said to him, you may put
up again; what need of violence?'

Rasheyd, Zâmil's officer, whose house joined to mine from
the backward – though by the doors it was a street about, had
heard a rumour; and he came round to visit me. Glad I was to
see him enter, with the sword, which he wore for Zâmil. I inquired of him, if Aly's commandment were good? for I could
not think that my friends among the chief citizens were con-
senting to it; and that the philosophical Zâmil would send by
night to put me out of the town! When I told Rasheyd that
the Waháby Aly had struck me; he said to me apart, 'Do not
provoke him, only make haste, and doubtless this word is
from Zâmil: for Aly would not be come of himself to compel
thee.' Emir Aly called from without, 'Tell Khalîl to hasten! is
he not ready?' Then he came in himself; and Rasheyd helped
me to lift the things into the bags, for I was feeble. 'Whither,
he said to the Emir Aly, art thou sending Khalîl?' 'To Khubbera.' – 'El-Helâlîeh were better, or er-Russ; for these lie in the
path of caravans.' – 'He goes to Khubbera.' 'Since, I said,
you drive me away, you will pay the cameleer; for I have little
money.' Emir Aly: 'Pay the man his hire and make haste; give
him three reals, Khalîl.' – Rasheyd: 'Half a real is the hire to
Khubbera: make it less, Emir Aly.' – 'Then be it two reals, I
shall pay the other myself.' – 'But tell me, are there none the
better for my medicines in your town?' – 'We wish for no
medicines.' – 'Have I not done well and honestly in Aneyza?
answer me, upon your conscience.' Emir Aly: 'Well, thou
hast.' – 'Then what dealing is this?' But he cried, 'Art thou

ready? now mount!' In the meanwhile, his ruffian ministers had stolen my sandals (left without the chamber door); and the honest negro Aly cried out for me, accusing them of the theft, 'O ye, give Khalîl his sandals again!' I spoke to the brutal Emir; who answered, 'There are no sandals': and over this new mishap of the Nasrâny [it is no small suffering to go barefoot on the desert sòil glowing in the sun] he laughed apace. 'Now, art thou ready? he cries, mount then, mount! but first pay the man his hire.' – After this, I had not five reals left; my watch was stolen: and I was in the midst of Arabia.

Rasheyd departed: the things were brought out and laid upon the couching camel; and I mounted. The Emir Aly with his crew followed me as far as the Mejlis. 'Tell me (I said to him) to whom shall I go at Khubbera?' – 'To the Emir, and remember his name is Abdullah el-Aly.' – 'Well, give me a letter for him.' – 'I will give thee none.' I heard Aly talking in a low voice with the cameleer behind me; – words (of an adversary), which doubtless boded me no good, or he had spoken openly: when I called to him again, he was gone home. The negro Aly, my old host, was yet with me; he would see me friendly to the town's end. – But where, I mused, were now my friends? The negro said, that Zâmil gave the word for my departure at these hours, to avoid any further tumult in the town; also the night passage were safer, in the desert. Perhaps the day's hubbub had been magnified to Zâmil; – they themselves are always ready!

Aly told me that a letter from the Muttowwa of Boreyda had been lately brought to Zâmil and the sheykhs of Aneyza; *exhorting them, in the name of the common faith, to send away the Nasrâny!* – 'Is this driver to trust? and are they good people at Khubbera?' Aly answered with ayes, and added, 'Write back to me; and it is not far: you will be there about dawn, and in all this, believe me Khalîl, I am sorry for thy sake.' He promised to go himself early to Kenneyny, with a request from me, to send 'those few reals on account of medicines': but he went not (as I afterward learned); for the negro had been bred among Arabs, whose promises are but words in the air, and forged to serve themselves at the moment. – 'Let this cameleer swear to keep faith with me.' *Aly*: 'Ay, come here thou Hásan! and swear thus and thus.' Hásan swore all that he would; and at the town walls the negro departed. There we passed forth to the dark Nefûd; and a cool night air met us breathing from the open sand wilderness, which a little revived me to ride: we were now in the beginning of the stagnant summer heat of the lower Rummah country.

The Nasrâny after being Conveyed to Khôbra is Recalled by Zâmil to Aneyza and Lodged in a Plantation

When I had been more than three weeks in this desolation, I wrote on a leaf of paper, *katálny et-taab wa ej-jû'a*, 'I am slain with weariness and hunger'; and sent these words to Kenneyny. – I hoped ere long to remove, with Zâmil's allowance, to some of the friends' grounds; were it Bessàm's jeneyny, on the north-east part of the town [there is the *black stone*, mentioned by some of their ancient poets, and 'whereof, they say, Aneyza itself is named']; or the palms of the good father Yahŷa, so kind to my guiltless cause. My message was delivered: and at sunrise on the morrow came Abdullah's serving lad, who brought girdle-bread and butter, with a skin of butter-milk; and his master's word bidding me be of good comfort; and they (the friends) would ere long be able to provide for my departure.

Wars of Kahtân

The sheukh of Meteyr were now in Aneyza, to consult finally with Zâmil and the sheykhs for the common warfare. The Kahtân thought themselves secure, in the khála, that no townsfolk would ride against them in this burning season; and as for el-Meteyr, they set little by them as adversaries. – Zâmil sent word to those who had thelûls in the town, to be ready to mount with him on the morrow. He had 'written' for this expedition 'six hundred' thelûls. The ghrazzu of the confederate Beduw was '300 thelûls, and 200 (led) horses.'

The day after el-Meteyr set forward at mid-afternoon. But
Zâmil did not ride in one company with his nomad friends:
the Beduins, say the townspeople, are altogether deceitful – as
we have seen in the defeat of Saûd the Waháby. And I heard
that some felony of the Aarab had been suffered two years
before by Aneyza! It is only Ibn Rashîd, riding among the rajajîl and villagers, who may foray in assurance with his subject
Beduw.

Zâmil rode out the next day, with 'more than a thousand' of
the town: and they say, 'When Zâmil mounts, Aneyza is confident.' He left Aly to govern at home: and the shops in the
sûk were shut; there would be no more buying or selling, till
the expedition came home again. The morning market is not
held, nor is any butcher's meat killed in these days. Although
so many were in the field with Zâmil, yet 'the streets, said
Sâlih, seemed full of people, so that you should not miss
them!' I inquired, 'And what if anyone opens his dokân – ?'
Answer: 'The Emir Aly would send to shut it: but if he per-
sisted, such an one would be called before the emir, and
beaten': only small general shops need not be closed, which
are held by any old broken men or widows. ...

... The townsmen rode in three troops, with the ensigns of
the three great wards of Aneyza; but the town banners are
five or six, when there is warfare at home.

Early in the afternoon I heard this parley in the garden, between Fáhd and a poor Meteyry, – who having no thelûl
could not follow with his tribesmen. Fáhd: 'By this they are
well in the way! and please Ullah they will bring back the
heads of them.' – 'Please Ullah! the Lord is bountiful! and kill
the children from two years old and upward; and the hareem
shall lament!' I said to them, 'Hold your mouths, kafirs! and
worse than kafirs.' The Beduwy: 'But the Kahtân killed our
children – they killed even women!' The Meteyr were come
in to encamp nigh the town walls; and two small menzils of
theirs were now our neighbours. These southern Aarab were
such as other Beduw. I heard in their mouths the same nomad
Arabic; yet I could discern that they were of foreign dîras.

I saw their girbies suspended in cane-stick trivets. Some of them came to me for medicines: they seemed not to be hospitable; they saw me tolerated by Zâmil, and were not fanatical. ...

... Tidings of this foray came to Boreyda, and messengers rode out to warn the Kahtân. Zâmil made no secret of the town warfare, which was not slackness in such a politic man, but his long-suffering prudence. 'He would give the enemies time, said Sâlih, to sue for peace': – how unlike the hawks of er-Riâth and Jebel Shammar!

– The Kahtân were lately at el-ʿAyûn; and the ghrazzu help thither. But in the way Zâmil heard that their menzils were upon *ed-Dellamîeh*, a water between the mountain Sàk and er-Russ. The town rode all that day and much of the night also. By the next afternoon they were nigh er-Russ; and alighted to rest, and pitched their (canvas) tents and (carpet) awnings. Now they heard that the enemy was upon the wells *Dókhany*, a march to the southward. As they rode on the morrow they met bye and bye with the Meteyr; and they all alighted together at noon. – The scouts of Meteyr brought them word, that they had seen the booths of the Aarab, upon *Dókhany*! and so many they could be none other than the Kahtân; who might be taken at unawares! – The young literates of Aneyza boasted one to another at the coffee fires, 'We shall fight then to-morrow upon the old field of *Jebel Kezâz*, by *Dókhany*; where Tubbʿa (lord the king, signeur) of el-Yémen fought against the *Wâilyîn* (sons of Wâil, that is the Annezy), – *Koleyb, sheykh Rabîʿa*; and with them B. Temîm and Keys' [Kahtân against Ishmael: – that was little before the héjra]. The berg Kezâz is 'an hour' from the bed of the Wady Rummah.

Zâmil and the town set forward on the morrow, when the stars were yet shining: the Meteyr had mounted a while before them, and Dókhany was at little distance. In this quarrel it was the Beduins which should fall upon their capital foemen; and Zâmil would be at hand to support them. The town fetched a compass to envelope Kahtân from the southward.

Meteyr came upon their enemies as the day lightened: the Kahtân ran from the beyts, with their arms, sheykhs leapt upon their mares; and the people encouraged themselves with shouting. Then seeing they were beset by Meteyr they contemned them, and cried, *jàb-hum Ullah*, 'A godsend' – but this was a day of reckoning upon both parts to the dreary death. The Meteyr had 'two hundred' mares under them; but they were of the less esteemed northern brood. The *Kahatîn* in the beginning were sixty horse-riders. Then thirty more horsemen joined them from another great menzil of theirs pitched at little distance. The Kahtân were now more than the ghrazzu of Meteyr, who finally gave ground.

– Then first the Kahtân looked about them; and were ware of the town bands coming on! The Kahatîn, of whom not many were fallen, shouted one to another, in suspense of heart, 'Eigh! is it Ibn Rashîd? – but no! for Ibn Rashîd rides with one bàrak: but these ride like townsfolk. – Ullah, they are *hâthr*!' – Now as the town approached some knew them, and cried, 'These be the Kusmân! – they are the *Zuâmil* (Zamils, or the people of Zâmil).' When they saw it was so, they hasted to save their milch-camels.

– Zâmil, yet distant, seeing Beduin horsemen driving off the camels, exclaimed, 'Are not these the *Moslemîn* [those of our part]?' 'Nay! answered him a sheykh of Meteyr (who came riding with the town to be a shower of the way in the khála), they are billah el-Kahtân!' The town cavaliers were too few to gallop out against them. And now the Kahtân giving themselves to save the great cattle forsook their menzil: where they left booths, household stuff, and wives and children in the power of their foemen.

The horsemen of Meteyr pursued the flying Kahtân; who turned once more and repulsed them: then the Aneyza cavaliers sallied to sustain their friends. The rest of the Meteyr, who alighted, ran in to spoil the enemies' tents. – And he and he, whose house-wives were lately pierced by the spears of Kahtân, or whose babes those fiend-like men slew, did now the like by their foemen; they thrust through as many hareem, and slit the throats of their little ones before the mothers' faces, crying to them, 'Oh, wherefore did your men so with our little ones that other day!' Some frantic women ran on the spoilers with tent-staves; and the Meteyries, with weapons in their hands, and in the tempest of their blood, spared them not at all. – Thus there perished five or six wives, and as many children of Kahtân.

In their most tribulation a woman hid her husband's silver, 600 reals [that was very much for any Beduwy]! in a girby; and stript off her blue smock – all they wear besides the haggu on their hunger-starved bodies: and hanging the water-skin on her shoulder, she set her little son to ride upon the other. Then she ran from her tent with a lamentable cry, *weylêy, weylêy!* woe is me! and fled naked through the tumult of the enemies. The Meteyr, who saw it, supposed that one of the people had spoiled the woman, and thought shame to follow her; yet some called to her, to fling down that she bore on her shoulder: but she, playing the mad woman, cried out, 'She was undone! – was it not enough to strip a sheykh's daughter? and would they have even this water, which she carried for the life of her child!' Others shouted, to let the woman pass: and she fled fast, and went by them all; – and saved her good-man's fortune, with this cost of his wife's modesty.

There fell thirty men of Kahtân – the most were slain in the flight; and of Meteyr ten. – These returned to bury their dead: but the human charity is here unknown to heap a little earth over the dead foemen!

A woman messenger came in from the flying Kahtân, to Zâmil. The town now alighted at the wells (where they would rear up the awnings and drink coffee): she sought safe conduct for some of their sheykhs, to come and speak with him; which Zâmil granted. – Then the men returned and kissing him as suppliants, they entreated him, 'since their flocks, and the tents and stuff, were now (as he might see) in the hands of Meteyr, to suffer them to come to the water, that they might drink and not perish.' They had sweated for their lives, and that summer's day was one of greatest heat; and having no girbies, they must suffer, in flying through the desert, an extremity of thirst. But who might trust to words of Beduin enemies! and therefore they bound themselves with a solemn oath, – *Aleyk âhad Ullah wa amàn Ullah, in mâ akhûnak! el-khàyin yakhûnhu Ullah* – 'The covenant of the Lord be with thee, and His peace! I will not surely betray thee! who betrayeth, the Lord shall him betray.'

Such was the defeat of the intruded Kahtân, lately formidable even to Ibn Rashîd. [Ibn Saûd had set upon them last summer here at Dókhany! but the Kahtân repulsed the decayed Wahâby!] – This good success was ascribed to the fortune of Zâmil: the townsmen had made no use of their weapons. The Meteyr sent messengers from the field to Ibn Rashîd, with a gift of two mares out of the booty of Kahtân. – Even Boreyda would be glad, that the malignant strange tribesmen were cast out of the country. – Many Kahtân perished in their flight through the khála: even lighter wounds, in that extremity of weariness and thirst, became mortal. They fled southward three days, lest their old foes, hearing of their calamity, should fall upon them: we heard, that some Ateyba had met with them, and taken 'two hundred' of the saved milch camels. Certain of them who came in to el-Ethellah said, that they were destroyed and had lost 'an hundred men': – so dearly they bought the time past [now two full years] of their playing the wolf in Nejd!

When I asked what would become of the Kahtân? the Shuggery answered, 'The Beduw are hounds, – that die not; and these are sheyatîn. They will find twenty shifts; and after a year or two be in good plight again.' – 'What can they do now?' – 'They will milk the nâgas for food, and sell some camels in the villages, to buy themselves dates and cooking vessels. And they will not be long-time lodged on the ground, without shelter from the sun: for the hareem will shear the cattle that remain to them, and spin day and night; and in few weeks set up their new woven booths! besides the other Kahtân in the south will help them.' – We heard after this, that the defeated Kahtân had made peace with the Ateybân; and reconciled themselves with Ibn Saûd! But how might they thus assure themselves? had the Kahtân promised to be confederate with them against Ibn Rashîd?

– Hayzàn was fallen! their young Absalom; 'a young man of a thievish false nature,' said his Beduin foes: it was he who threatened me last year, in a guest-chamber at Hâyil: Hayzàn was slain for that Meteyry sheykh, who lately fell by his hand in the north. A sheykhly kinsman of the dead sought him in the battle: they ran together; and Hayzàn was borne through the body with a deadly wide wound. The young man was very robust for a Beduwy, and his strong hand had not swerved; but his lance-thrust was fended by a shirt of mail which his foeman wore privily under his cotton tunic. That Meteyry was a manly rider upon a good horse, and after Hayzàn, he bore down other five sheykhs. – When the fortune of the day was determined by the coming of 'the Zuâmil', he with his brother and his son, yet a stripling [principal sheykh's sons soon become horsemen, and ride with their elders to the field], and a few of his Aarab, made prize of eighty milch camels! In that day he had been struck by lances and shot in the breast, eleven times; but the dints pierced not his 'Davidian' shirt of antique chain work. They say, that the stroke of a gun-shot leaves upon the body fenced by such harness, only a grievous bruise.

A brother of Hayzàn, Terkey, was fallen; and their sheykhly sister. She was stripped, and thrust through with a spear! – because Kahtân had stripped and slain a Meteyry sheykh's daughter. The old Kahtân sheykh – father of these evil-starred brethren, hardly escaped upon a thelûl. Hayzân, mortally wounded, was stayed up in the saddle, in the flight, till evening; and when they came to the next *golbân* (south of Dókhany) the young sheykh gave up the ghost: and his companions cast his warm body into one of those well-pits...

The Kâfily for Mecca

Now in Aneyza the jammamîl made ready their gear; for the samn kâfily was soon to set out for Mecca. The *zemmel*, bearing camels, were fetched in from the nomads; and we saw

them daily roaming at pasture in the Nefûd about us. A
caravan departed in these days with dates and corn for
Medina.

Zâmil and Kenneyny rode out one day to the Wady together, where Zâmil has a possession; and they proposed to
return by Rasheyd's plantation, to visit Khalîl. But in the hot
noon they napped under the palms: Abdullah woke quaking
with ague! and they rode the next way home.

One evening there came a company of young patricians
from Aneyza; to see some sheep of theirs, which the Beduin
herds had brought in, with a disease in the fleece. The gallants
stripped off gay kerchiefs and mantles; and standing in the
well-troughs, they themselves washed their beasts. When it
was night, they lay down on the Nefûd sand to sleep, before
the shepherds' tents. Some of them were of the fanatical
Bessàms; and with these came a younger son of the good
Abdullah. The lad saluted me affectuously from his father;
who sent me word, 'that the kâfily would set out for Mecca
shortly; and I should ride with Abd-er-Rahmàn (his elder
son)'; I had languished now six weeks in Rasheyd's plantation.

I had passed many days of those few years whose sum is our
human life, in Arabia; and was now at the midst of the Peninsula. A month! – and I might be come again to European
shipping. From hence to the coast may be counted 450 desert
miles, a voyage of at least twenty great marches in the uneasy
camel-saddle, in the midsummer flame of the sun; which is a
suffering even to the homeborn Arabs. Also my bodily languor
was such now, that I might not long sit upright; besides I
foresaw a final danger, since I must needs leave the Mecca
kâfily at a last station before the (forbidden) city. There was
come upon me besides a great disquietude: for one day twelve
months before, as I entered a booth (in Wady Thirba), in the
noon heat, when the Nomads slumber, I had been bitten by
their greyhound, in the knee. I washed the wound; which in a
few days was healed, but a red button remained; which now
(justly at the year's end) broke, and became an ulcer; then
many like ulcers rose upon the lower limbs (and one on the

wrist of the left hand). – Ah! what horror, to die like a rabid hound in a hostile land.

The friends Kenneyny and Bessàm purchased a thelûl, in the Friday market, for my riding down to Jidda, where the beast, they thought, might fetch as much as they gave; and if no, one of their kinsmen, who was to come up from Jidda in the returning kâfily would ride home upon her. – I received then a letter from the good Bessàm: 'All (he wrote) is ready; but because of the uncivil mind [Waháby malice] of the people he would not now be able to send me in his son's company! I must excuse it. But they had provided that I should ride in the company of Sleymàn el-Kenneyny, to whom I might look for that which was needful [water, cooking, and the noon shelter] by the way.' – He ended in requesting me to send back a little quinine: and above his seal was written – 'God's blessing be with all the faithful Moslemîn.'

I sent to Zâmil asking that it might be permitted me to come one day to town, to purchase somewhat for the journey, and bid my friends farewell: but my small request could not be vouchsafed, – so much of the Waháby misery is in the good people of Aneyza.

Departure of the Butter Caravan for Mecca. The Journey to the Ayn Ez-Zemya. The Nomad Sherîf, Sâlem

On the morrow, when the sun was setting, there came a messenger for me, from Abdullah el-Kenneyny; with the thelûl upon which I should ride to Jidda. We mounted; and Rasheyd's labourers who had left their day's toil, and the poor slave woman, approached to take my hand; and they blessed me as we rode forth. We held over to the Kenneyny's plantation: where I heard I should pass the morrow. The way was not two miles; but we arrived, after the short twilight, in the dark: there my rafîk forsook me; and I lay down in that lonely palm ground to sleep, by the well side.

At the sun-rising I saw Abdullah el-Kenneyny! who arrived riding upon an ass, before the great heat. A moment later came

Abdullah el-Bessàm, on foot: 'Ah! Khalîl, said he, taking my hand, we are abashed, for the things thou hast suffered, and that it should have been here! but thou knowest we were overborne by this foolish people.' Kenneyny asked for more of that remedy which was good for his mother's eyes; and I distributed to them my medicines. Now came Hàmed es-Sâfy; and these friends sat on with me till the sun was half an hour high, when they rose to return to breakfast, saying they would see me later. In the afternoon came es-Sâfy again; who would perfect his writing of English words. – None of my other friends and acquaintance came to visit the excommunicated Nasrâny.

The good Kenneyny arrived again riding upon an ass, in the cooling of the afternoon, with his son Mohammed. He was feeble to-day, as one who is spent in body and spirit; and I saw him almost trembling, whilst he sat to talk with me: and the child playing and babbling about us, Abdullah bade him be still, for he could not bear it. I entreated him to forget whatsoever inquietude my coming to Aneyza had caused him: he made no answer.

It was now evening; and Sleymàn arrived, upon a thelûl, with his little son. He was riding-by to the caravan menzil and would speak the last words with his kinsman, who lent him money for this traffic. Abdullah called to him, to set down the child; and take up Khalîl and his bags. – I mounted with Sleymàn; and we rode through a breach of the town wall, which bounded Kenneyny's tillage. Abdullah walked thus far with us; and here we drew bridle to take leave of him: I gave hearty thanks, with the Semitic blessings; and bade this gentle and benificent son of Temîm a long farewell. He stood sad and silent: the infirm man's mortal spirit was cut off (Cruel stars!) from that Future, wherefore he had travailed – and which we should see! ....

We went on riding an hour or two in that hollow roadway worn in the Nefûd, by which I had once journeyed in the night-time in the way to Khubbera. It was dark when we came to the caravan menzil; where Sleymàn hailed his drivers, that had arrived before us, with the loads. They brought us to our place in the camp; which, for every fellowship, is where they have alighted and couched their camels. Here was a coffee fire, and I saw Sleymàn's goat-skins of samn (which were twenty-four or one ton nearly) laid by in order: four of them, each of fifteen sah (of el-Kasîm), are a camel's burden, worth thirty reals, for which they looked to receive sixty in Mecca. – Many persons from Aneyza were passing this last night in the camp with their outfaring friends and brethren. This assembling place of the Mecca kâfily is by the outlying palms *'Auhellàn*;. where are said to be certain *ancient caves hewn in the sand-rock!* I only then heard of it, and time was not left me to search out the truth in the matter.

– But now first I learned, that no one in the caravan was going to Jidda! they were all for Mecca. Abdullah el-Kenneyny had charged Sleymàn; and the good Bessàm had charged his son (*Abd-er-Rahmàn*) for me, that at the station next before Mecca [whether in Wady Laymûn, or the Seyl] they should seek an *'adamy*, to convey me (without entering the *hadûd* or sacred limit) to Jidda. – The good Kenneyny, who had never ridden on pilgrimage, could not know the way; and his perspicuous mind did not foresee my final peril, in that passage.

In our butter kâfily were 170 camels, – bearing nearly 30 tons of samn – and seventy men, of whom forty rode on thelûls, – the rest were drivers. We were sorted in small companies; every master with his friends and hired servants. In each fellowship is carried a tent or awning, for a shelter over their heads at the noon stations, and to shadow the samn, – that is molten in the goat-skins (*jerm* pl. *jerûm*) in the hot hours: the *jerûm* must be thickly smeared within with date syrup. Each skinful, the best part of an hundredweight, is suspended by a loop (made fast at the two ends) from the saddle-tree. Sometimes a jerm bursts in the caravan journeys, and the precious humour is poured out like water upon the dust of the waste: somewhiles the bearing-camels thrust by acacia trees, and jerms are pricked and ripped by the thorny boughs. It was well that there rode a botcher in the kâfily; who in the evening station amended the daily accidents to butter-skins and girbies.

– All this samn, worth more than £2,000 in Mecca, had been taken up, since the spring, in their traffic with the Beduw: the Aneyza merchants store it for the time in marble troughs.

There is an emir, named by Zâmil, over such a great town caravan: he is one of the princely kin; and receives for every camel a real. – El-Kenneyny had obtained a letter from Zâmil, commending me to the emir; and charging him to provide for my safety, when I should leave the kâfily 'at the Ayn.' – We sat on chatting about the coffee fire, till we were weary; and then lay down to sleep there, on the Nefûd sand.

Rising with the dawn, there was yet time to drink coffee. The emir and some young Aneyza tradesmen in Mecca, that would return with the kâfily, had remained all night in the town: they would overtake us riding upon their fleet 'omanías. [The thelûls of the Gulf province 'Omân or 'Amân' are of great force and stature; but less patient of famine and thirst than some lesser kinds. A good 'omanîa, worth 50 to 70 reals at Aneyza, may hardly be bought in the pilgrim season at Mecca – where they are much esteemed – for 150 reals.] When the sun was up the caravaners loaded, and set forward. We soon after fell into the Wady er-Rummah; in which we journeyed till two hours before noon: and alighted on a shaeb, *es-Shibbebîeh*, to rest out the midday heat (*yugŷilûn*). In that place are some winter granges of Aneyza, of ruinous clay building, with high-walled yards. They are inhabited by well-drivers' families, from the autumn seed time till the early harvest. Here we drew brackish water, and filled our girbies. The day's sultry heat was great; and I found under the awnings 105 F. Principal persons have canvas tents made Beduin-wise, others have awnings of Bagdad carpets. I saw but one or two round tents – bargains from the coast, and a few ragged tilts of hair-cloth [that I heard were of the Kahtân booty!] in poorer fellowships. – Sleymàn el-Kenneyny's six loads of samn were partly Abdullah's: he was a jemmâl, and the beasts were his own.

It might be three o'clock ere they removed, – and the hot sun was going down from the meridian: the signal is made with a great shout of the Emir's servant, ES-SHÎ-ÎL! In the next instant all awnings are struck, the camels are led-in and couched, the caravaners carry out the heavy butter-skins; and it is a running labour, with heaving above their strength, to load on their beasts, before the kâfily is moving: for the thelûl riders are presently setting forth; and who is unready will be left in the hindward. The emir's servant stands like a shepherd before the kâfily – spreading his arms to withhold the foremost! till the rest shall be come up; or, running round, he cries out on the disobedient. Now they march; and – for the fear of the desert – the companies journey nigh together. Our path southward was in the Wady Rummah, which is a wide plain of firmer sand in the Nefûd. The Abàn mountains are in sight to the westward, covered with haze. [The Abànát may be seen, lifted up in the morning twilight, from the dunes about Aneyza.] At sun-setting we alighted by other outlying granges – that are of er-Russ, *el-Hajnowwy*, without the Wady: we were there nearly abreast of Khubbera.

Their tents are not pitched at night; but in each company the awning is now a sitting carpet under the stars; and it will be later for the master to lie on. One in every fellowship who is cook goes out to gather sticks for fuel; another leads away the beasts to browse, for the short half-hour which rests till it is dark night. With Sleymàn went three drivers: the first of them, a poor townsman of Aneyza, played the cook in our company; another was a Beduwy. – After an hour, the supper dish (of seethed wheaten stuff) is set before us. Having eaten, we sip coffee: they sit somewhile to chat and smoke tobacco; and then wrapt in our cloaks we lie down on the sand, to sleep out the short hours which remain till toward sunrising.

An hour before the dawn we heard shouted, 'THE REMOVE!' The people rise in haste; the smouldering watch-fires are blown to a flame, and more sticks are cast on to give us light: there is a harsh hubbub of men labouring; and the ruckling and braying of a multitude of camels. Yet a minute or two, and all is up: riders are mounted, and they which remain afoot look busily about them on the dim earth, that nothing be left.

- They drive forth; and a new day's march begins; to last through the long heat till evening. After three hours journeying, in the desert plain, we passed before er-Russ; – whose villagers, two generations ago, spared not to fell their palm stems for a breastwork, and manfully resisted all the assaults of Ibrahîm Pasha's army. The Emir sent a thelûl rider to the place for tidings: who returned with word, that the samn caravaners of er-Russ were gone down with the Boreyda kâfily, which had passed-by them two days before. Er-Russ (which they say is greater than Khubbera) appears as three oases lying north and south, not far asunder. In the first, er-Ruéytha, is the town; in the second, er-Rafya, a village and high watch-tower showing above the palms; the third and least is called Shinàny. Er-Russ us the last settlement southward and gate of el-Kasîm proper. – We are here at the border of the Nefûd; and bye and bye the plain is harsh gravel under our feet: we reenter that granitic and basaltic middle region of Arabia, *which lasts from the mountains of Shammar to Mecca*. The corn grounds of er-Russ are in the Wâdy er-Rummah; their palms are above.

I saw the Abànát – now half a day distant westward, to be a low rebel coast, such as Ajja, trending south. There are two mountains one behind other; and the bed of the Wady (there of no great width) lies betwixt them. The northern is named *el-Eswad*, and oftener *el-Esmar*, the brown and swart coloured; and the southerly, which is higher, *el-Ahmar*, the red mountain: this is perhaps granite; and that basaltic.

We came at noon to *Umm Tÿeh*, other outlying granges of er-Russ, and inhabited; where some of us, riding-in to water, found a plot of growing tobacco! The men of Aneyza returned laughing, to tell of this adventure in the caravan menzil: for it was high noon, and the kâfily halted yonder. – From this *mogÿil* we rose early; and journeyed forth through a plain wilderness full of basaltic grey-red granite bergs [such as we have seen in the Harb and Shammar dîras westward]. Finally when the sun was descending, with ruddy yellow light behind the Abàn mountains, we halted to encamp. ...

... The caravaners, after three days, were all beside their short Semitic patience; they cry out upon their beasts with the passionate voices of men in despair. The drivers beat forward the lingering cattle, and go on goading them with the heel of their spears, execrating, lamenting and yelling with words of evil augury, *Yâ mâl et-teyr – hut!* eigh! thou carrion for crows, *Yâ mâl eth-thubbah,* eigh! butcher's meat: if any stay an instant, to crop a stalk, they cry, *Yâ mâl ej-jú´a,* O thou hunger's own! *Yelaan Ullah abu hâ'l ras,* or *hâ'l kalb* or *hâ'l hulk,* May the Lord confound the father of thy head, of thy heart, of thy long halse. – Drivers of camels must have their eyes continually upon the loaded beasts: for a camel coming to any sandy place is likely to fall on his knees to wallow there, and ease his itching skin; – and then all must go to wreck! They discern not their food by sight alone, but in smelling; also a camel will halt at any white stone or bleached *jella,* as if it were some blanched bone, – which if they may find at anytime they take it up in their mouth, and champ somewhile with a melancholy air; and that is 'for the saltiness,' say the Arabs. The caravaners in the march are each day of more waspish humour and fewer words; there is naught said now but with great *by-gods*: and the drivers, whose mouths are bitter with thirst, will hardly answer each other with other than crabbed and vaunting speech; as 'I am the son of my father! I the brother of my little sister!' 'Am I the slave of thy father (that I should serve or obey thee)?' And an angry soul will cry out on his neighbour, *Ullah la yubârak fîk, la yujîb 'lak el-kheyr,* 'The Lord bless thee not, and send thee no good.'

The heat in our mid-day halt was 102° F. under the awnings, and rising early we made haste to come to the watering; where we arrived two hours before the sunsetting. This is *'Afîf,* an ancient well of ten fathoms to the water, and steyned with dry building of the wild basalt blocks. – Sleymàn, and the other master caravaners, had ridden out before the approaching kâfily, with their tackle; each one contending to arrive before other at the well's mouth, and occupy places for the watering. When we rode-in they stood there already by their gear; which is a thick stake pight in the ground, and made fast with stones:

the head is a fork, and in that they mount their draw-reel, *mahâl*, – as the nomads use at any deep golbân, where they could not else draw water. The cord is drawn by two men running out backward; a third standing at the well-brink receives the full bucket, as it comes up; and runs to empty it into the camel trough, – leather or carpet piece spread upon a hollow, which they have scraped with stick or stone and their hands in the hard gravel soil. When so many camels must be watered at a single *jelîb*, there is a great ado of men drawing with all their might and chanting in cadence, like the Beduw. I went to drink at the camel troughs, but they bade me beware; 'I might chance to slip in the mire, and fall over the well brink,' which, without kerb, [as in all desert golbân] is even with the soil. The well-drawers' task is not therefore without peril; and they are weary. At their last coming down, an unhappy man missed his footing, – and fell in! He was hastily taken up – for Arabs in the sight of such mischiefs are of a sudden and generous humanity! and many are wont from their youth to go down in all manner of wells: – His back was broken: and when the caravan departed, the sick man's friends laid him upon a camel; but he died in the march. – To the first at the well succeeded other drawers; and they were not all sped in three hours. This ancient well-mouth is mounded round with earth once cast up in the digging: thus the waterers, who run backward, draw easily; and the sinking sludge returns not to infect the well.

By that well side, I saw the first token of human life in this vast wilderness, – the fresh ashes of a hunters' fire! whereby lay the greatest pair of gazelle horns that I have seen at any time. The men doubtless were Solubba; and some in the kâfily had seen their asses' footprints to-day. It is a marvel even to the Arabs, how these human solitaries can live by their shooting, in the khála. The Solubby may bear besides his long matchlock only a little water; but their custom is to drink a fill of water or mereesy two hours before dawn: and then setting out, they are not athirst till noon. I now learned to do the like; and that early draught sustained me until we halted at midday, though in the meanwhile my companions had drunk thrice. –

They would hardly reach me the bowl, when they poured out for themselves to drink; and then it was with grudges and cursing; if Sleymàn were out of hearing, they would even deny the Nasrâny altogether. Sleymàn, who was not good, said, 'We shall suffer by the way, I cannot amend it, and these are Arabs: Abdullah would find no better, were he here with his beard, (himself). See you this boy, Khalîl? he is one from the streets of Aneyza: that other (a Beduwy lad, of Annezy in the North) has slain, they say, his own father; and he (the cook) yonder! is a poor follower from the town: wellah, if I chided them, they would forsake me at the next halt!' – It were breath lost to seek to drink water in another fellowship: one day I rode by a townsman who alighted to drink; and ere he put up the bowl I asked him to pour out a little for me also. His wife had been a patient of mine, and haply he thought I might remember his debt for medicines; for hastily tying up again the neck of his girby, he affected not to know me. When I called him by name! – he could no longer refuse; but undoing the mouth of the skin, he poured me out a little of the desert water, saying, 'Such is the road and the toil, that no man remembers other; but the word is *imshy hâl-ak!* help thyself forward.' – A niggard of his girby is called *Bîa'a el-má*, Water-seller, by his angry neighbours. My thelûl was of little stature, wooden and weak: in walking she could not keep pace with the rest; and I had much ado to drive her forward. The beast, said Sleymàn, was hide-bound; he would make scotches in her side, when they were come down to Mecca.

Betwixt us and the lava country is the hard blackish crusted mire of yesterday; a flat without kerb or stone, without footprint, and white with *subbakha*: tongues of this salty land stretch back eastward beyond our path. A little before noon we first saw footprints of nomad cattle, from the Harra-ward; – whereunder is a good watering, in face of us. In the mid-day halt our thirst was great: the people had nothing to drink, save of that sour and black water from Shurrma; and we could not come to the wells, till nightfall, or early on the morrow. I found the heat of the air under the awnings 107° F.; and the

simûm was blowing. In the caravan fellowships they eat dates
in the mogŷil, and what little burghrol or temmn may be left
over from their suppers. Masters and drivers sit at meat together; but to-day none could eat for thirst. I went to the
awnings of Ibrahîm and Bessàm – each of them carried as
many as ten girbies – to seek a fenjeyn of coffee or of water.
The young men granted these sips of water and no more; for
such are Arabians on the journey: I saw they had yet many
full waterskins!

That nooning was short, because of the people's thirst, –
and the water yet distant. As we rode forth I turned and saw
my companions drinking covertly! besides they had drunk
their fills in my absence, after protesting to me that there was
not any; and I had thirsted all day. I thought, might I drink
this once, I could suffer till the morning. I called to the fellows
to pour me out a little; 'we were rafîks, and this was the will
of Abdullah el-Kenneyny': but they denied me with horrible
cursing; and Sleymàn made merchant's ears. I alighted, for
'need hath no peer,' and returned to take it whether they
would or no. The Beduwy, wagging his club and beginning
to dance, would maintain their unworthy purpose: but Sleymàn (who feared strife) bade them then pour out for Khalîl. –
It was sweet water from 'Afîf, which they had kept back and
hidden this second day from the Nasrâny: they had yet to
drink of it twice in the afternoon march. – Sleymàn was under
the middle age, of little stature, of a sickly nature, with some
sparkles of cheerful malice, and disposed to fanaticism. I had
been banished from Aneyza, and among these townsmen were
many of the Waháby sort; but the most saluted me in the long
marches with a friendly word, 'How fares Khalîl, art thou
over weary? well! we shall be soon at our journey's end.'
Once only I had heard an injurious word; that was in the
evening rest at 'Afîf, when crossing in the dark towards
Ibrahîm and Múthkir I lighted on some strange fellowship,
and stumbled at the butter skins. 'Whither O kafir,' cried their
hostile voices; but others called to them 'to hold their mouths!
and pass by, mind them not Khalîl.' ...

... Before us is a solitary black jebel, *Biss*, which is perhaps of basalt. – And now we see again the main Harra; that we are approaching, to water at Sh'aara. Múthkir tells me, 'the great Harrat el-Kisshub is of a round figure [some say, It is one to two days to go over]; and that the Kisshub is not solitary, but a member of the train of Harras between Mecca and Medina: the Kisshub and the Ahràr el-Medina are not widely separated.' There met us a slender Beduin lad coming up after the cattle; and beautiful was the face of that young waterer, in his Mecca tunic of blue! – but to Northern eyes it is the woman's colour: the black locks hanged down dishevelled upon his man-maidenly shoulders. 'Hoy, weled! (cries our rude Annezy driver, who as a Beduwy hated all Beduw not his tribesfolk). – I say fellows, is this one a male or a female?' The poor weled's heart swelled with a vehement disdain; his ingenuous eyes looked fiercely upon us, and almost he burst out to weep. – Sh'aara, where we now arrived, is a bay in the Harra that is here called *A'ashiry*. The end of the lava, thirty feet in height, I found to overlie granite rock, – which is whitish, slacked, and crumbling, with the suffered heat: the head of lava has stayed at the edge of the granite reef. Sh'aara is a sh'aeb or seyl-strand which they reckon to the *Wady Adzíz* and *Wady el-'Agíg*. Here are many narrow-mouthed wells of the ancients, and dry-steyned with lava stones; but some are choked. We heard from the Aarab that the Boreyda caravan watered here last noon: since yesterday the desert paths are one. I found the altitude, 4,900 feet.

. .. We have passed from Nejd; and here is another nature of Arabia! We rode a mile in the narrow *Seyl* plain, by thickets of rushy grass, of man's height! with much growth of peppermint; and on little leas, – for this herbage is browsed by the caravan camels which pass by daily between Mecca and Tâyif. Now the kâfily halted, and we alighted: digging here with their hands they find at a span deep the pure rain water. From hence I heard to be but a march to Tâyif: and some prudent and honest persons in the kâfily persuaded me to go thither, saying, 'It was likely we should find some Mecca cameleers

ascending to et-Tâyif, and they would commit me to them, –
so I might arrive at et-Tâyif this night; and they heard the
Sherîf (of Mecca) was now at et-Tâyif: and when I should be
come hither, if I asked it of the Sherîf, he would send me
down safely to Jidda.'

– What pleasure to visit Tâyif! the Eden of Mecca, with
sweet and cool air, and running water; where are gardens of
roses, and vineyards and orchards. But these excellencies are
magnified in the common speech, for I heard some of the
Kusmàn saying, 'They tell wonders of et-Tâyif! – well, we
have been there; and one will find it to be less than the report.'
– The maladies of Arabia had increased in me by the way; the
lower limbs were already full of the ulcers, that are called *hub*
or *bîzr* or *bethra et-támr*, 'the date button', on the Persian Gulf
coast [because they rise commonly near the time of date
harvest]. The boil, which is like the Aleppo button, is known
in many parts of the Arabic world, – in Barbary, in Egypt
('Nile sores'); and in India ('Delhi boil'): it is everywhere ascribed to the drinking of unwholesome water. The flat sores
may be washed with carbolic acid, and anointed with fish oil;
but the evil will run its course, there is no remedy: the time
with me was nearly five months. – Sores springing of themselves are common among the Beduw. For such it seemed
better to descend immediately to Jidda; also I rolled in my
heart, that which I had read of (old) Mecca Sherîfs: besides,
were it well for me to go to et-Tâyif, why had not el-Bessàm –
who had praised to me the goodness of the late Sherîf – given
me such counsel at Aneyza? Now there sat a new Sherîf: he is
also Emir of Mecca; and I could not know that he would be
just to a Nasrâny. ...

This is a worn camping-ground of many generations of
pilgrims and caravaners; and in summer the noon station of
passengers between the Holy City and et-Tâyif. Foul rákhams
were hawking up and down; and I thought I saw mortar clods
in this desert place, and some old substruction of brick building! – My Aneyza friends tell me, that this is the old station
Kurn e-menâzil; which they interpret of the interlacing stays

of the ancient booths, standing many together in little space. I went barefoot upon the pleasant sward in the mid-day sun, – which at this height is temperate; for what sweetness it is, after years passed in droughty countries, to tread again upon the green sod! Only the Nasrâny remained clad among them; yet none of the Kusmàn barked upon me: they were themselves about to arrive at Mecca; and I might seem to them a friend, in comparison with the malignant Beduin people of this country [*el-Hathèyl*].

I found Bessàm's son, girded only in the ihràm, sitting under his awning. 'Khalîl, quoth he, yonder – by good fortune! are some cameleers from et-Tâyif: I have spoken with one of them; and the man – who is known – is willing to convey thee to Jidda.' – 'And who do I see with them?' – 'They are *Jàwwa*. [Java pilgrims so much despised by the Arabians: for the Malay faces seem to them hardly human! I have heard Amm Mohammed say at Kheybar, 'Though I were to spend my lifetime in the *Béled ej-Jàwwa*, I could not –! wellah I could not wive with any of their hareem.' Those religious strangers had been at Tâyif, to visit the Sherîf; and the time was at hand of their going-up, in the 'little pilgrimage,' to Medina.] Khalîl, the adventure is from Ullah: wellah I am in doubt if we may find anyone at *el-'Ayn*, to accompany thee to the coast. And I must leave the kâfily ere the next halt; for we (the young companions with Ibrahîm) will ride this night to Mecca; and not to-morrow in the sun, because we are bare-headed. Shall we send for Sleymàn, and call the cameleer? – but, Khalîl, agree with him quickly; for we are about to depart, and will leave thee here.'

– That cameleer was a young man of wretched aspect! one of the multitude of pack-beast carriers of the Arabic countries, whose sordid lives are consumed with daily misery of slender fare and broken nights on the road. In his wooden head seemed to harbour no better than the wit of a camel, so barrenly he spoke. *Abd-er-Rahmàn*: 'And from the 'Ayn carry this passenger to Jidda, by the Wâdy Fâtima.' – 'I will carry him by Mecca, it is the nigher way.' *Abd-er-Rahmàn, and Sleymàn*: 'Nay, nay! but by the Wâdy, – Abd-er-Rahmàn added; This one goes not to Mecca,' – words which he spoke with a fanatical strangeness, that betrayed my life; and thereto Sleymàn rolled his head! So that the dull cameleer began to imagine there must be somewhat amiss! – he gaped on him who should be his charge, and wondered to see me so white a man! I cut short the words of such tepid friends: I would ride from the 'Ayn in one course to Jidda, whereas the drudge asked many days. The camels of this country are feeble, and of not much greater stature than horses. Such camels move the Nejd men's derision: they say, the Mecca cameleers' march is *mîthil, en nimml*, 'at the ants' pace.'

That jemmâl departed malcontent, and often regarding me, whom he saw to be unlike any of the kinds of pilgrims. [As he went he asked in our kâfily, what man I were; and some answered him, of their natural malice and treachery, *A Nasrâny!* When he heard that, the fellow said '*Wullah-Bullah*, he would not have conveyed me, – no, not for an hundred reals'!] 'Khalîl, there was a good occasion, but thou hast let it pass!' quoth Abd-er-Rahmàn. – 'And is it to such a pitiful fellow you would commend my life, one that could not shield me from an insult, – is this the man of your confidence? one whom I find to be unknown to all here: I might as well ride alone to Jidda.' *Sleymàn*: 'Khalîl, wheresoever you ride in these parts, they will know by your saddle-frame that you are come from the east [Middle Nejd]' – And likewise the camel-furnitures of these lowland Mecca caravaners seemed to us to be of a strange ill fashion.

Whilst we were speaking Ibrahîm's servant shouted to remove! The now half-naked and bare-headed caravaner loaded hastily: riders mounted; and the Nejd kâfily set forward. – We were descending to Mecca! and some of the rude drivers *yulubbûn* [the devout cry of the pilgrims at Arafát]; that is, looking to heaven they say aloud *Lubbeyk! Lubbeyk!* 'to do Thy will, to do Thy will (O Lord)!' This was not a cheerful song in my ears: my life was also in doubt for those worse than unwary words of the son of Bessàm. Such tidings spread apace and kindle the cruel flame of fanaticism; yet I hoped, as we had set out before them, that we should arrive at the 'Ayn

ere that unlucky Mecca jemmâl. I asked our Annezy driver,
why he craked so? And he – 'Auh! how fares Khalîl? to-
morrow we shall be in Mekky! and thus we cry, because our
voyage is almost ended, – Lubbeyk-lubbeyk!'

From the Seyl we descend continually in a stony valley-bed
betwixt black plutonic mountains, and half a mile wide: it is a
vast seyl-bottom of grit and rolling stones, with a few acacia
trees. This landscape brought the Scandinavian *fjelde*, earlier
well-known to me, to my remembrance. The carcase of the
planet is alike, everywhere: it is but the outward clothing that
is diverse, – the gift of the sun and rain. They know none other
name for this iron valley than *Wady es-Seyl*. In all yonder horrid
mountains are *Aarab Hathèyl* [gentile pl. *el-Hetheylân*], – an
ancient name; and it is said of them in the country, 'they are a
lineage by themselves, and not of kindred with the neighbour
tribes.' When Mecca and Tâyif cameleers meet with strangers
coming down from Nejd, they will commonly warn them with
such passing words, '*Ware the Hathèyl! they are robbers.*' – The
valley way was trodden down by camels' feet! The Boreyda
caravan had passed before us with 200 camels, – but here
I saw the footprints of a thousand. I knew not that this is
the Mecca highway to Tâyif, where there go-by many trains
of camels daily. When the sun was setting we alighted – our
last menzil – among the great stones of the torrent-valley. The
height was now only 3,700 feet.

– It had been provided by the good Bessàm, in case none
other could be found at the station before Mecca, that his own
man (who served his son Abd-er-Rahmàn by the way) should
ride down with me to Jidda. Abd-er-Rahmàn now called this
servant; but the fellow, who had said 'Ay-ay' daily in our long
voyage now answered with *lilla*, 'nay-nay – thus the Arabs do
commonly fail you at the time! – He would ride, quoth he,
with the rest to Mecca.' Abd-er-Rahmàn was much displeased
and troubled; his man's answer confounded us. 'Why then
didst thou promise to ride with Khalîl? go now, I entreat thee,
said he; and Khalîl's payment is ready: thou canst not say nay.'
Likewise Ibrahîm the Emir persuaded the man; – but he had

no authority to compel him. The fellow answered shortly, 'I am free, and I go not to Jidda!' and so he left us. Then Ibrahîm sent for another in the kâfily, a poor man of good understanding: and when he came he bade him ride with Khalîl to Jidda; but he beginning to excuse himself, they said, 'Nothing hastens thee, for a day or two, to be at Mecca; only set a price, – and no nay!' He asked five reals; and with this slender assurance they dismissed him: 'Let me, I said, bind the man, by paying him earnest-money.' Ibrahîm answered, 'There is no need to-night; – in the morning!' I knew then in my heart that this was a brittle covenant; and had learned to put no trust in the evening promises of Arabs. – 'Yâ Múthkir! let one of your Beduins ride with me to Jidda.' – 'Well, Khalîl, if that might help thee; but they know not the way.' Ibrahîm, Abd-er-Rahmàn and the young companions were to mount presently, after supper, and ride to Mecca, – and then they would abandon me in this sinister passage. I understood later, that they had deferred riding till the morning light: – which came all too soon! And then we set forward.

It needed not that I should await that Promiser of overnight; who had no thoughts of fulfilling Ibrahîm and Abd-er-Rahmàn's words, – and they knew this. Though to-day was the seventeenth of our long marches from Aneyza; yet, in the sameness of the landscape, it seemed to me, until yesterday, when we passed es-Sh'aara, as if we had stood still. – The caravan would be at Mecca by mid-day: I must leave them now in an hour, and nothing was provided.

We passed by a few Beduins who were moving upward: light-bodied, black-skinned and hungry looking wretches: their poor stuff was loaded upon the little camels of this country. I saw the desolate valley-sides hoary with standing hay – these mountains lie under the autumn (moonsoon) rains – and among the steep rocks were mountain sheep of the nomads; all white fleeces, and of other kind than the great sheep in Nejd. Now in the midst of the wady we passed through a grove of a tree-like strange canker weed (el-'esha), full of green puff-leaves! the leafy bubbles, big as grape-shot, hang in noisome-looking clusters, and enclose a roll of seed.

This herb is of no service, they say, to man or cattle; but the country people gather the sap, and sell it, for a medicine, to the Persian pilgrims; and the Beduins make charcoal of the light stems for their gunpowder. There met us a train of passengers, ascending to Tâyif, who had set out this night from Mecca. The hareem were seated in litters, like bedsteads with an awning, charged as a houdah upon camel-back: they seemed much better to ride-in than the side cradles of Syria.

I was now to pass a circuit in whose pretended divine law is no refuge for the alien; whose people shut up the ways of the common earth; and where any felon of theirs in comparison with a Nasrâny is one of the people of Ullah. I had looked to my pistol in the night; and taken store of loose shot about me; since I had no thought of assenting to a fond religion. If my hard adventure were to break through barbarous opposition, there lay thirty leagues before me, to pass upon this wooden thelûl, to the coast; by unknown paths, in valleys inhabited by *ashrâf* [sherîfs], the seed of Mohammed. – I would follow down the seyl-strands, which must needs lead out upon the seabord. But I had no food nor water; and there was no strength left in me. – Ibrahîm who trotted by, gazed wistfully under my kerchief; and wondered (like a heartless Arab) to see me ride with tranquillity. He inquired, 'How I did? and quoth he, seest thou yonder bent of the Wady? when we arrive there, we shall be in sight of '*Ayn ez-Zeyma*.' – 'And wilt thou then provide for me, as may befall?' – 'Ay, Khalîl'; and he rode further: I saw not Abd-er-Rahmàn! he was in the van with the companions.

The thelûl of one who was riding a little before me fell on a stone, and put a limb out of joint, – an accident which is without remedy! Then the next riders made lots hastily for the meat; and dismounting, they ran-in to cut the fallen beast's throat: and began with their knives to hack the not fully dead carcase. In this haste and straitness, they carved the flesh in the skin; and every weary man hied with what gore-dropping gobbet his hand had gotten, to hang it at his saddle bow; and that should be their supper-meat at Mecca! they re-mounted immediately, and hastened forward. Between the fall of the thelûl, and an end of their butchery, the caravan camels had not marched above two hundred paces! – Now I saw the clay banks of 'Ayn ez-Zayma! green with thùra; – and where, I thought, in few minutes, my body might be likewise made a bloody spectacle. We rode over a banked channel in which a spring is led from one to the other valley-side. Besides the fields of corn, here are but few orchards; and a dozen stems of sickly palms; the rest were dead for fault of watering; the people of the hamlet are Hathèyl. I read the altitude, under my cloak, 2,780 feet. ...

... In the (southern) valley-side stands a great clay kella, now ruinous; which was a fort of the old Wahábies, to keep this gate of Nejd: and here I saw a first coffee-station *Kahwa* (vulg. *Gahwa*) of the Mecca country. This hospice is but a shelter of rude clay walling and posts, with a loose thatch of palm branches cast up. – Therein sat Ibrahîm and the thelûl riders of our kâfily; when I arrived tardily, with the loaded camels. Sleymàn el-Kenneyny coming forth led up my riding-beast by the bridle to this open inn. The Kusmàn called *Khalîl!* and I alighted; but Abd-er-Rahmàn met me with a careful face. – I heard a savage voice within say, '*He shall be a Moslem*': and saw it was some man of the country, – who drew out his bright *khânjar!* 'Nay! answered the Kusmàn, nay! not so.' I went in, and sat down by Ibrahîm: and Abd-er-Rahmàn whispered to me, 'It is a godsend, that we have found one here who is from our house at Jidda! for this young man, *Abd-el-Azîz*, is a nephew of my father. He was going up, with a load of carpets, to et-Tâyif; but I have engaged him to return with thee to Jidda: only give him a present, – three reals. Khalîl, it has been difficult! – for some in the Kahwa would make trouble: they heard last night of the coming of a Nas-rány; but by good adventure a principal slave of the Sherîf is here, who has made all well for you. Come with me and thank him: and we (of the kâfily) must depart immediately.' – I found a venerable negro sitting on the ground: who rose to take me by the hand: his name was *Ma'abûb*. Ibrahîm, Sley-man, and the rest of the Kusmàn now went out to mount

their thelûls; when I looked again they had ridden away. The
son of Bessàm remained with me, who cried, 'Mount! and
Abd-el-Azîz mount behind Khalîl!' – 'Let me first fill the
girby.' 'There is water lower in the valley, only mount.'
'Mount, man!' I said; and as he was up I struck-on the thelûl:
but there was no spirit in the jaded beast, when a short trot
had saved me.

I heard a voice of ill augury behind us, 'Dismount, dismount! – Let me alone I say, and I will kill the kafir.' I looked
round, and saw him of the knife very nigh upon us; who with
the blade in his hand, now laid hold on the bridle. – 'Ho! Jew,
come down! ho! Nasrâny (yells this fiend); I say down!' I was
for moving on; and but my dromedary was weak I had then
overthrown him, and outgone that danger. Other persons
were coming, – 'Nôkh, nôkh! cries Abd-er-Rahmàn, make her
kneel and alight! Khalîl!' This I did without show of reluct-
ance. He of the knife approached me, with teeth set fast, 'to
slay, he hissed, the Yahûdy-Nasrâny'; but the servitor of the
sherîf, who hastened to us, entreated him to hold his hand. – I
whispered then to the son of Bessàm, 'Go call back some of
the kâfily with their guns; and let see if the guest of Aneyza
may not pass. Can these arrest me in a public way, without the
hadûd?' (borders of the sacred township). But he whispered,
'Only say, Khalîl, thou art a Moslem, it is but a word, to ap-
pease them; and to-morrow thou wilt be at Jidda: thou thyself seest – ! and wellah I am in dread that some of these will
kill thee.' – 'If it please God I will pass, whether they will or
no.' 'Eigh Khalîl! said he in that demiss voice of the Arabs,
when the tide is turning against them, what can I do? I must
ride after the kâfily; look! I am left behind.' – He mounted without more; and forsook his father's friend among
murderers.

A throng of loitering Mecca cameleers, that (after their night
march) were here resting-out the hot hours, had come from the
Kahwa, with some idle persons of the hamlet, to see this
novelty. They gathered in a row before me, about thirty together, clad in tunics of blue cotton. I saw the butchery sword-
knife, with metal scabbard, of the country, jambîeh, shining in

all their greasy leathern girdles. Those Mecca faces were black as the hues of the damned, in the day of doom: the men stood silent, and holding their swarthy hands to their weapons.

The servitor of the Sherîf (who was infirm and old), went back out of the sun, to sit down. And after this short respite the mad wretch came with his knife again and his cry, 'that he would slay the Yahûdy-Nasrâny'; and I remained standing silently. The villain was a sherîf; for thus I had heard Maabûb name him: these persons of the seed of Mohammed 'are not to be spoken against,' and have a privilege, in the public opinion, above the common lot of mankind. The Mecca cameleers seemed not to encourage him; but much less were they on my part. [The sherîf was a nomad: his fellows in this violence were one or two thievish Hathèylies of the hamlet; and a camel driver, his rafîk, who was a Beduwy. His purpose and theirs was, having murdered the kafir – a deed also of 're-ligious' merit! to possess the thelûl, and my things.]

When he came thus with his knife, and saw me stand still, with a hand in my bosom, he stayed with wonder and dis-couragement. Commonly among three Arabians is one media-tor; their spirits are soon spent, and indifferent bystanders inclined to lenity and good counsel: I waited therefore that some would open his mouth on my behalf! – but there was no man. I looked in the scelerat's eyes; and totter-headed, as are so many poor nomads, he might not abide it; but, heaving up his khánjar, he fetched a great breath (he was infirm, as are not few in that barren life, at the middle age) and made feints with the weapon at my chest; so with a sigh he brought down his arm and drew it to him again. Then he lifted the knife and measured his stroke: he was an undergrown man; and watch-ing his eyes I hoped to parry the stab on my left arm, – though I stood but faintly on my feet, I might strike him away with the other hand; and when wounded justly defend myself with my pistol, and break through them. Maabûb had risen, and came lamely again in haste; and drew away the robber sherîf: and holding him by the hand, 'What is this, he said, sherîf Sâlem? you promised me to do nothing by violence! Re-member Jidda bombarded! – and that was for the blood of

some of this stranger's people; take heed what thou doest.
They are the Engleys, who for one that is slain of them send
great battleships; and beat down a city. And thinkest thou our
lord the Sherîf would spare thee, a bringer of these troubles
upon him? – Do thou nothing against the life of this person,
who is guilty of no crime, neither was he found within the
precincts of Mecca. – No! sherîf Sâlem, for *Hasseyn* (the Sherîf
Emir of Mecca) our master's sake. Is the stranger a Nasrâny?
he never denied it: be there not Nasâra at Jidda?'

Maabûb made him promise peace. Nevertheless the wolvish
nomad sherîf was not so, with a word, to be disappointed of
his prey: for when the old negro went back to his shelter, he
approached anew with the knife; and swore by Ullah that now
would he murder the Nasrâny. Maabûb seeing that, cried to
him, to remember his right mind! and the bystanders made as
though they would hinder him. Sâlem being no longer coun-
tenanced by them, and his spirits beginning to faint – so God
gives to the shrewd cow a short horn – suffered himself to be
persuaded. But leaping to the thelûl, which was all he levelled
at, 'At least, cries he, this is *nâhab*, rapine!' He flung down my
coverlet from the saddle, and began to lift the great bags.
Then one of his companions snatched my headband and kerchief; but others blamed him. A light-footed Hathèyly ran to
his house with the coverlet; others (from the backward)
plucked at my mantle; the Mecca cameleers stood still in this
hurly-burly. I took in all patience; and having no more need,
here under the tropic, I let go my cloak also. Maabûb came
limping again towards us. He took my saddle-bags to himself;
and dragging them apart, made me now sit by him. Sâlem re-
penting – when he saw the booty gone from him – that he had
not killed the stranger, drew his knife anew; and made toward me, with hard-set (but halting) resolution appearing in
his squalid visage, and crying out, that he would put to death
the Yahûdy-Nasrâny: but now the bystanders withheld him.
Maabûb: 'I tell thee, Sherîf Sâlem, that if thou have any cause
against this stranger, it must be laid before our lord the Sherîf;
thou may'st do nothing violently.' – 'Oh! but this is one who
would have stolen through our lord's country.' – 'Thou canst

accuse him; he must in any wise go before our lord Hasseyn. I commit him to thee Sâlem, *teslîm*, in trust: bring him safely to Hasseyn, at et-Tâyif.' The rest about us assenting to Maabûb's reasons, Sâlem yielded, – saying, 'I hope it may please the Sherif to hang this Nasrâny, or cut off his head; and that he will bestow upon me the thelûl.' – Notwithstanding the fatigue and danger of returning on my steps, it seemed to make some amends that I should visit et-Tâyif. ...

Journey to Tâyif. The Nasrâny Assailed. Arrival at Tâyif. Audience of the Sherîf, Emir of Mecca

... Late in the day he [Sâlem] came to me with Maabûb and Abd-el-Azîz; who had rested in another part of the kahwa! – surely if there had been right worth in them (there was none in Abd-el-Azîz), they had not left me alone in this case. Maabûb told me, I should depart at evening with the caravan men; and so he left me again. Then Sâlem, with a mock zeal, would have an inventory taken of my goods – and see the spoil! he called some of the unlettered cameleers to be witnesses. I drew out all that was in my bags, and cast it before them: but '*El-f'lûs, el-f'lûs!* cries Sâlem with ferocious insistance, thy money! thy money! that there may be afterward no question – show it all to me, Nasrâny!' – 'Well, reach me that medicine box; and here, I said, are my few reals wrapped in a cloth!'

The camel-men gathered sticks; and made watch fires: they took flour and water, and kneaded dough, and baked '*abûd* under the ashes; for it was toward evening. At length I saw this daylight almost spent: then the men rose, and lifted the loads upon their beasts. These town caravaners' camels march in a train, all tied, as in Syria. – My bags also were laid upon the Bessàm's thelûl: and Sâlem made me mount with his companion, *Fheyd*, the Beduin, or half-Beduin master of these camels. – 'Mount in the shidàd! Khalîl Nasrâny.' [But thus the radîf might stab me from the backward, in the night!] I said, I would sit back-rider; and was too weary to maintain myself in the saddle. My words prevailed! for all Arabs tender the infirmity of human life, – even in their enemies. Yet Sâlem

293

was a perilous coxcomb; for if anyone reviled the Nasrâny in his hearing, he made me cats' eyes and felt for his knife again.

In this wise we departed; and the Nasrâny would be hanged, as they supposed, by just judgement of the Sherîf, at et-Tâyif: all night we should pace upward to the height of the Seyl. Fheyd was in the saddle; and the villain, in his superstition, was adread of the *Nasrâny*! Though malignant, and yet more greedy, there remained a human kindness in him; for understanding that I was thirsty he dismounted, and went to his camels to fetch me water. Though I heard he was of the Nomads, and his manners were such, yet he spoke nearly that bastard Arabic of the great government towns, Damascus, Bagdad, Mecca. But unreasonable was his impatience, because I a weary man could not strike forward the jaded thelûl to his liking, – he thought that the Nasrâny lingered to escape from them!

A little before us marched some Mecca passengers to et-Tâyif, with camel-litters. That convoy was a man's household: the goodman, swarthy as the people of India and under the middle age, was a wealthy merchant in Mecca. He went beside his hareem on foot, in his white tunic only and turban; to stretch his tawny limbs – which were very well made – and breathe himself in the mountain air. [The heat in Mecca was such, that a young Turkish army surgeon, whom I saw at et-Tâyif, told me he had marked there, in these days, 46° C.] Our train of nine camels drew slowly by them: but when the smooth Mecca merchant heard that the stranger riding with the camel-men was a Nasrâny, he cried, 'Akhs! a Nasrâny in these parts!' and with the horrid inurbanity of their (jealous) religion, he added, 'Ullah curse his father!' and stared on me with a face worthy of the koran!

The caravan men rode on their pack-beasts eating their poor suppers, of the bread they had made. Sâlem, who lay stretched nomad-wise on a camel, reached me a piece, as I went by him; which beginning to eat I bade him remember, 'that from henceforth there was bread and salt between us, – and see, I said, that thou art not false, Sâlem.' – 'Nay, wellah,

I am not *khayin*, no Khalîl.' The sickly wretch suffered old
visceral pains, which may have been a cause of his splenetic
humour. – He bye and bye blamed my nodding; and bade me
sit fast. 'Awake, Khalîl! and look up! Close not thine eyes all
this night! – I tell thee thou mayest not slumber a moment;
these are perilous passages and full of thieves, – the Hathèyl!
that steal on sleepers: awake! thou must not sleep.' The camels
now marched more slowly; for the drivers lay slumbering
upon their loads: thus we passed upward through the weary
night. Fheyd left riding with me at midnight, when he went to
stretch himself on the back of one of his train of nine camels;
and a driver lad succeeded him. Thus these unhappy men
slumber two nights in three: and yawn out the daylight hours,
– which are too hot for their loaded beasts – at the 'Ayn
station or at the Seyl.

The camels march on of themselves, at the ants' pace. –
'Khalîl! quoth the driver lad, who now sat in my saddle, beware of thieves!' Towards morning, we both nodded and
slumbered, and the thelûl wandering from the path carried us
under a thorny acacia: – happy I was, in these often adventures
of night-travelling in Arabia, never to have hurt an eye! My
tunic was rent! – I waked; and looking round saw one on foot
come nigh behind us. – 'What is that?' quoth the strange man,
leaping up he snatched at the worsted girdle which I wore in
riding! I shook my fellow-rider awake, and struck-on the
thelûl; and asked the raw lad, 'If that man were one of the
cameleers?' – 'Didst thou not see him among them? but this
is a thief and would have thy money.' The jaded thelûl trotted
a few paces and stayed. The man was presently nigh behind me
again: his purpose might be to pull me down; but were he an
Hathèyly or what else, I could not tell. If I struck him, and the
fellow was a cameleer, would they not say, 'that the Nasrâny
had beaten a Moslem?' He would not go back; and the lad
in the saddle was heavy with sleep. I found no better rede than
to show him my pistol – but I took this for an extreme ill fortune: so he went his way. – I heard we should rest at the rising
of the morning star: the planet was an hour high, and the day
dawning when we reached the Seyl ground; where I alighted

with Sâlem, under the spreading boughs of a great old acacia tree.

There are many such menzil trees and shadows of rocks, in that open station, where is no Kahwa: we lay down to slumber, and bye and bye the sun rose. The sun comes up with heat in this latitude; and the sleeper must shift his place, as the shadows wear round. 'Khalîl (quoth the tormentor) what is this much slumbering? – but the thing thou hast at thy breast, what is it? show it all to me.' – 'I have showed you all in my saddle-bags; it is infamous to search a man's person.' – 'Aha! said a hoarse voice behind me, he has a pistol; and he would have shot at me last night.' – It was a great mishap, that this wretch should be one of the cameleers; and the persons about me were of such hardened malice in their wayworn lives, that I could not waken in them any honourable human sense. *Sâlem*: 'Show me, without more, all that thou hast with thee there (in thy bosom)!' – There came about us more than a dozen cameleers.

The mad sherîf had the knife again in his hand! and his old gall rising, 'Show me all that thou hast, cries he, and leave nothing; or now will I kill thee.' – Where was Maabûb? whom I had not seen since yester-evening: in him was the faintness and ineptitude of Arab friends. – 'Remember the bread and salt which we have eaten together, Sâlem!' – 'Show it all to me, or now by Ullah I will slay thee with this knife.' More bystanders gathered from the shadowing places: some of them cried out, 'Let us hack him in morsels, the cursed one! what hinders? – fellows, let us hack him in morsels!' – 'Have patience a moment, and send these away.' Sâlem, lifting his knife, cried, 'Except thou show me all at the instant, I will slay thee!' But rising and a little retiring from them I said, 'Let none think to take away my pistol!' – which I drew from my bosom.

What should I do now? the world was before me; I thought, Shall I fire, if the miscreants come upon me; and no shot amiss? I might in the first horror reload, – my thelûl was at hand: and if I could break away from more than a score of persons, what then? – repass the Rî'a, and seek Sh'aara again? where 'Atey-

bân often come-in to water; which failing I might ride at adventure: and though I met with no man in the wilderness, in
two or three days, it were easier to end thus than to be presently rent in pieces. I stood between my jaded thelûl, that
could not have saved her rider, and the sordid crew of camel-
men advancing, to close me in: they had no fire-arms. - Fheyd
approached, and I gave back pace for pace: he opened his arms
to embrace me! - there was but a moment, I must slay him, or
render the weapon, my only defence; and my life would be at
the discretion of these wretches. - I bade him come forward
boldly. There was not time to shake out the shot, the pistol
was yet suspended from my neck, by a strong lace: I offered
the butt to his hands. - Fheyd seized the weapon! they were
now in assurance of their lives and the booty: he snatched the
cord and burst it. Then came his companion Sâlem; and they
spoiled me of all that I had; and first my aneroid came into
their brutish hands; then my purse, that the black-hearted
Siruân had long worn in his Turkish bosom at Kheybar. -
Sâlem feeling no reals therein gave it over to his confederate
Fheyd; to whom fell also my pocket thermometer: which
when they found to be but a toy of wood and glass, he res-
stored it to me again, protesting with nefarious solemnity,
that other than this he had nothing of mine! Then these robbers sat down to divide the prey in their hands. The lookers-on
showed a cruel countenance still; and reviling and threatening
me, seemed to await Sâlem's rising, to begin 'hewing in pieces
the Nasrâny.'

Sâlem and his confederate Fheyd were the most dangerous
Arabs that I have met with; for the natural humanity of the
Arabians was corrupted in them, by the strong contagion of
the government towns. - I saw how impudently the robber
sherîf attributed all the best of the stealth to himself! Sâlem
turned over the pistol-machine in his hand: such Turks' tools
he had seen before at Mecca. But as he numbered the ends of
the bullets in the chambers, the miscreant was dismayed; and
thanked his God, which had delivered him from these six
deaths! He considered the perilous instrument, and gazed on
me; and seemed to balance in his heart, whether he should not

prove its shooting against the Nasrâny. 'Akhs – akhs! cried some hard hostile voices, look how he carried this pistol to kill the Moslemîn! Come now and we will hew him piece-meal: – how those accursed Nasrânies are full of wicked wiles! – O thou! how many Moslems hast thou killed with that pistol?' 'My friends, I have not fired it in the land of the Arabs. – Sâlem, remember Ayn ez-Zeyma! thou camest with a knife to kill me, but did I turn it against thee? Render therefore thanks to Ullah! and remember the bread and the salt, Sâlem.'

– He bade his drudge Fheyd, shoot off the pistol; and I dreaded he might make me his mark. Fheyd fired the first shots in the air: the chambers had been loaded nearly two years; but one after another they were shot off, – and that was with a wonderful resonance! in this silent place of rocks. Sâlem said, rising, 'Leave one of them!' This last shot be reserved for me; and I felt it miserable to die here by their barbarous hands without defence. 'Fheyd, he said again, is all sure? – and one remains?'

Sâlem glared upon me, and perhaps had indignation, that I did not say, *dakhîlak*: the tranquillity of the kafir troubled him. When he was weary, he went to sit down and called me, 'Sit, quoth he, beside me.' – 'You hear the savage words of these persons; remember, Sâlem, you must answer for me to the Sherîf.' – 'The Sherîf will hang thee, Nasrâny! Ullah curse the Yahûd and Nasâra.' Some of the camel-men said, 'Thou wast safe in thine own country, thou mightest have continued there; but since thou art come into the land of the Moslemîn, God has delivered thee into our hands to die: – so perish all the Nasâra! and be burned in hell with your father, Sheytàn.' 'Look! I said to them, good fellows – for the most fault is your ignorance, ye think I shall be hanged to-morrow: but what if the Sherîf esteem me more than you all, who revile me to-day! If you deal cruelly with me, you will be called to an account. Believe my words! Hasseyn will receive me as one of the ullema; but with you men of the people, his subjects, he will deal without regard.' 'Thou shalt be hanged, they cried again, O thou cursed one!' and after this they dispersed to their several halting places.

– Soon afterward there came over to us the Mecca burgess; who had now alighted under some trees at little distance. From this smooth personage, a flower of merchants in the holy city – though I appealed to his better mind, that he should speak to Sâlem, I could not draw a human word; and he abstained from evil. He gazed his fill; and forsook me to go again to his hareem. I watched him depart, and the robber sherîf was upbraiding me, that I had 'hidden' the things and my pistol! – in this I received a shock! and became numbed to the world: I sat in a swoon and felt that my body rocked and shivered; and thought now, they had mortally wounded me, with a knife, or shot! for I could not hear, I saw light thick and confusedly. But coming slowly to myself so soon as I might see ground I saw there no blood: I felt a numbness and deadness at the nape of the neck. Afterward I knew that Fheyd had inhumanly struck me there with his driving-stick, – and again, with all his force.

I looked up and found them sitting by me. I said faintly, 'Why have you done this?' *Fheyd*: 'Because thou didst withhold the pistol.' 'Is the pistol mine or thine? I might have shot thee dead! but I remembered the mercy of Ullah.' A caravaner sat by us eating, – one that ceased not to rail against me: he was the man who assailed me in the night, and had brought so much mischief upon me. I suddenly caught his hand with the bread; and putting some in my mouth, I said to him, 'Enough man! there is bread and salt between us.' The wretch allowed it, and said not another word. I have never found any but Sâlem a truce-breaker of the bread and salt, – but he was of the spirituality.

– There came one riding to us on an ass! it was Abd-el-Azîz! He and Maabûb had heard the shots, as they sat resting at some distance yonder! For they, who were journeying together to et-Tâyif, had arrived here in the night-time; and I was not aware of it. Maabûb now sent this young man (unworthy of the name of Bessàm) to know what the shots meant, and what were become of the Nasrâny, – whether he yet lived? Abd-el-Azîz seeing the pistol in Sâlem's hands and his prisoner alive, asked, 'Wherefore had he taken away the man's pistol?' I said to him, 'You see how these ignorant men threaten me: speak some word to them for thine uncle Abdullah's sake.' But he, with sour fanatical looks; 'Am I a Frenjy?' – and mounting again, he rode out of sight.

After these haps; Sâlem having now the spoil in his hands, and fearing to lose it again at et-Tâyif, had a mind to send me down to Jidda, on the Bessàm's thelûl. – 'Ha! Khalîl, we are become brothers; Khalîl, are we not now good friends? there is nothing more betwixt us. What sayest thou? wilt thou then that we send thee to Jidda, and I myself ride with thee on the thelûl?' – But I answered, 'I go to visit the Sherîf, at Tâyif; and you to accuse me there, and clear yourselves before him; at Jidda you would be put in prison.' Some bystanders cried, 'Let him go to et-Tâyif.'

– A messenger returned from Maabûb, bidding Sâlem, Khalîl and Fheyd come to him. As we went I looked back, and saw Fheyd busy to rifle my camel-bags! – after that he followed us. The young Bessàm was sitting under the shadow of some rocks with Maabûb. – 'Are you men? quoth Maabûb, are you men? who have dealt so with this stranger!' I told him how they robbed me, and what I had suffered at their hands: I was yet (and long afterward) stunned by the blows on the neck. *Maabûb*: 'Sherîf Sâlem, thou art to bring this stranger to our lord Hasseyn at et-Tâyif, and do him no wrong by the way. How canst thou rob and wound one who is committed to thy trust, like the worst Beduin thieves? but I think verily that none of the Beduw would do the like.' *Sâlem*: 'Is not this a Nasrâny? he might kill us all by the way: we did but take his pistol, because we were afraid.' *Maabûb*: 'Have you taken his silver from him and his other things, because ye were afraid? – I know thee, Sâlem! but thou wilt have to give account to our lord the Sherîf' – so he dismissed us; and we returned to our place.

It came into my mind, bye and bye, to go again to Maabûb: the sand was as burning coals under my bare feet, so that after every few steps I must fall on my knees to taste a moment's relief. – Maabûb was Umbrella-bearer of the Sherîf; and an old faithful servitor of his brother, the late Sherîf. 'Wherefore, I asked, had he so strangely forsaken me hitherto? Or how could he commit me to that murderous Sâlem! whom he himself called *a mad sherîf*; did he look to see me alive at Tâyif! – I am now without defence, at the next turn he may stab me; do thou therefore ride with me on the thelûl!' – 'Khalîl, because of an infirmity [sarcocele] I cannot mount in a saddle.' When I said, I would requite his pains, the worthy negro answered, 'That be far from me! for it is my duty, which I owe to our lord, the Sherîf; but if thou have a remedy for my disease, I pray thee, remember me at et-Tâyif.' – The young Bessàm had fever, with a daily crisis. It came on him at noon; and then he who lately would not speak a word to shelter the Frenjy's life, with a puling voice (as they are craven and unmanly), besought me to succour him. I answered, 'At et-Tâyif!' Had he aided me at the first, for his good uncle's sake, I had not now been too faint to seek for remedies. I promised, if he would ride with me to-night, to give him a medicine to cut the fever to-morrow: but Arabs put no trust in distant promises.

It drew to the mid-afternoon, when I heard we should remove: and then the foolish young Bessàm bade me rise and help to load the carpets on his camel. I did not deny him; but had not much strength; and Maabûb, blaming the rashness of the young man, would have me sit still in the shadow. – Maabûb rode seated on the load of carpets; and when the camel arose under him, the heavy old negro was nigh falling. Once more I asked him, not to forsake me; and to remember how many were the dark hours before us on the road.

I returned hastily to our menzil tree. The caravaners had departed; and the robber sherîf, who remained with the thelûl, was chafing at my delay: he mounted in the saddle, and I mounted again back-rider. – Sâlem had a new companion, who rode along with us, one Ibrahîm of Medina, lately landed at Jidda; and who would soon ride homeward in the 'little pilgrimage.' Ibrahîm hearing what countryman I was began to say, 'That an Engleysy came in the vessel with him to Jidda; – who was wellah a good and perfect Moslem! yesterday he entered Mecca, and performed his devotion: – and this

Engleysy that I tell you of, sherîf Sâlem, is now sojourning at Mecca, to visit the holy places.' – Ibrahîm was one who lying under our awning tree, where he had arrived late, had many times disdained me, crying out despitefully, 'Dog! dog! thou dog!' But as we rode he began to smile upon the Nasrâny betwixt friendly and fiendly: at last quoth he, 'Thou wast at Hâyil; and dost thou not remember me? – I have spoken with thee there; and thou art Khalîl.' – How strange are these meetings again in the immensity of empty Arabia! but there is much resort to Hâyil: and I had passed a long month there. The light-bodied Arabian will journey, upon his thelûl, at foot-pace, hundreds of leagues for no great purpose: and little more troubles him than the remembrance that he is absent from his household and children. 'Thou hast known me then a long time in these countries; now say on before these strangers, if thou canst allege aught against me.' – 'Well none, but thy misreligion.'

Ibrahîm rode upon a dromedary; his back-rider was an envenomed cameleer; who at every pause of their words shook his stick at me: and when he walked he would sometimes leap two paces, as it were to run upon the kafir. There was a danger in Sâlem's seeing another do me wrong, – that in such he would not be out-done, and I might see his knife again: so I said to Ibrahîm (and stroked my beard), 'By thy beard, man! and for our old acquaintance at Hâyil –!' Ibrahîm acknowledged the token; and began to show the Nasrâny a more friendly countenance. 'Ibrahîm, did you hear that the Engleys are a bad people?' 'Nay, *kullesh tâyib*, good every whit.' – 'Are they the Sultan's friends, or foes?' – 'His friends: the Engleys help him in the wars.' *Sâlem*: 'Well Khalîl, let this pass; but tell me, what is the religion of the Nasâra? I thought surely it was some horrible thing!' – 'Fear God and love thy neighbour, this is the Christian religion, – the way of Aysa bin-Miriam, from the Spirit of Ullah.' – 'Who is Aysa? – hast thou heard this name, Ibrahîm?' – 'Ullah curse Aysa and the father of Aysa, cries Ibrahîm's radîf. Akhs! what have we to do with thy religion, Nasrâny?' Ibrahîm answered him very soberly, 'But thou with this word makest thyself a kafir, blaspheming a prophet of the prophets of Ullah!' The cameleer answered, half-aghast, 'The Lord by my refuge! – I knew not that Aysa was a prophet of the Lord!' 'What think'st thou, Sâlem?' – 'Wellah Khalîl, I cannot tell: but how sayest thou, *Spirit of Ullah*! – is this your kafir talk?' – 'You may read it in the koran, – say, Ibrahîm?' – 'Ay, indeed, Khalîl.'

There were many passengers in the way; some of whom bestowed on me an execration as we rode-by them, and Sâlem lent his doting ears to all their idle speech: his mind wavered at every new word. – 'Do not listen to them, Sâlem, it is they who are the Nasâra!' He answered, like a Nomad, 'Ay billah, they are Beduw and kafirs; – but such is their ignorance in these parts!' Ibrahîm's radîf could not wholly forget his malevolence; and Sâlem's brains were beginning again to unsettle: for when I said, 'But of all this ye shall be better instructed to-morrow': he cried out, 'Thou liest like a false Nasrâny, the Sherîf will cut off thy head to-morrow, or hang thee: – and, Ibrahîm, I hope that our lord will recompense me with the thelûl.'

We came to a seyl bed of granite-grit, with some growth of pleasant herbs and peppermints; and where holes may be digged to the sweet water with the hands. Here the afternoon wayfarers to Tâyif alight, to drink and wash themselves to prayerward. [This site is said to be '*Okâtz*, the yearly parliament and vaunting place of the tribes of Arabia before Islâm: the altitude is between 5,000 and 6,000 feet.] As we halted Abd-el-Azîz and Maabûb journeyed by us; and I went to ask the young Bessàm if he would ride with me to-night, – and I would reward him? He excused himself, because of the fever: but that did not hinder his riding upon an ass. – Sâlem was very busy-headed to know what I had spoken with them; and we remounted.

Now we ascended through strait places of rocks; and came upon a paved way, which lasts for some miles, with steps and passages opened by blasting! – this path had been lately made by Turkish engineers at the Government cost. After that we journeyed in a pleasant steppe which continues to et-Tâyif.

We had outmarched the slow caravan, and were now alone
in the wilderness: Ibrahîm accompanies us, – I had a doubtful
mind of him. They said they would ride forward: my wooden
dromedary was cruelly beat and made to run; and that was to
me an anguish. – Sâlem had responded to some who asked the
cause of our haste, as we outwent them on the path, 'that he
would be rid of the Nasrâny': he murmured savage words; so
that I began to doubt whether these who rode with me were
not accorded to murder the Nasrâny, when beyond sight. The
spoilers had not left me so much as a penknife: at the Seyl I
had secretly bound a stone in my kerchief, for a weapon.

At length the sun set: it is presently twilight; and Ibrahîm
inquired of Sâlem, wherefore he rode thus, without ever
slacking. *Sâlem*: 'But let us outride them and sleep an hour at
the mid-way, till the camels come by us. – Khalîl, awake thou
and sleep not! (for I nodded on his back;) Auh! hold thine
eyes open! this is a perilous way for thee': but I slumbered on,
and was often in danger of falling. Bye and bye looking up, I
saw that he gazed back upon me! So he said more softly,
'Sleepest thou, Khalîl Nasrâny? – what is this! when I told
thee *no*; thou art not afraid!' – 'Is not Ullah in every place?' –
'Ay, wellah Khalîl.' Such pious words are honeycombs to the
Arabs, and their rude hearts are surprised with religion. –
'Dreadest thou not to die!' – 'I have not so lived, Moslem,
that I must fear to die.' The wretch regarded me! and I beheld
again his hardly human visage: the cheeks were scotched with
three gashes upon a side! It is a custom in these parts, as in
negro Africa; where by such marks men's tribes may be
distinguished.

Pleasant is the summer evening air of this high wilderness.
We passed by a watering-place amongst trees, and would have
halted: but Ibrahîm answered not to our call! – he had out-
ridden us in the gloom. Sâlem, notwithstanding the fair words
which lately passed between them, now named him 'impudent
fellow' and cursed him. 'And who is the man, Sâlem? I
thought surely he had been a friend of thine.' – 'What makes
him my friend? – Sheytàn! I know of him only that he is from
Medina.' – Bye and bye we came up with him in the darkness;

and Ibrahîm said, 'They had but ridden forward to pray. And here, quoth he, is a good place; let us alight and sup.' They had bread, and I had dates: we sat down to eat together. Only the radîf held aloof, fearing it might be unlawful to eat with a kafir: but when, at their bidding, he had partaken with us, even this man's malice abated. – I asked Ibrahîm, Did he know the Nejûmy family at Medina? 'Well, he said, I know them, – they are but smiths.'

We mounted and rode forward, through the open plain; and saw many glimpsing camp-fires of nomads. Sâlem was for turning aside to some of them; where, said he, we might drink a little milk. It had been dangerous for the kafir, and I was glad when we passed them by; although I desired to see the country Aarab. – We came at length to the manôkh or midway halting-place of passengers; in the dim night I could see some high clay building, and a thicket of trees. Not far off are other outlying granges and hamlets of et-Tâyif. We heard asses braying, and hounds barking in nomad menzils about us. We alighted and lay down here on the sand in our mantles; and slumbered two hours: and then the trains of caravan camels, slowly marching in the path, which is beaten hollow, came by us again: the cameleers lay asleep upon their loads. We remounted, and passing before them in the darkness we soon after lost the road: Ibrahîm said now, they would ride on to et-Tâyif, without sleeping; and we saw him no more.

In the grey of the morning I could see that we were come to orchard walls; and in the growing light enclosures of vines, and fig trees; but only few and unthriving stems of palms [which will not prosper at Tâyif, where both the soil and the water are sweet]. And now we fell into a road – a road in Arabia! I had not seen a road and green hedges since Damascus. We passed by a house or two built by the way-side; and no more such as the clay beyts of Arabia, but painted and glazed houses of Turkey. We were nigh et-Tâyif; and went before the villa of the late Sherîf, where he had in his life-time a pleasure-ground, with flowers! [The Sherîfs are commonly Stambûl bred men.] – The garden was already gone to decay.

Sâlem turned the thelûl into a field, upon our right hand; and we alighted and sat down to await the day. He left me to go and look about us; and I heard a bugle-call, – Tâyif is a garrisoned place. When Sâlem returned he found me slumbering; and asked if I were not afraid? We remounted and had ado to drive the dromedary over a lukewarm brook, running strongly. So we came to a hamlet of ashrâf, which stands a little before et-Tâyif; and drew bridle a moment ere the sunrising, at the beyt of a cousin of Sâlem.

He called to them within, by name! – none answered. The goodman was on a journey; and his wives could not come forth to us. But they, hearing Sâlem's voice, sent a boy, who bore in our things to the house; and we followed him. This poor home in the Mecca country was a small court of high clay walling; with a chamber or two, built under the walls There we found two (sherîf) women; and they were workers of such worsted coverlets in yarns and colours as we have seen at Teyma. And it was a nomad household; for the hareem told me they lived in tents, some months of the year, and drank milk of the small cattle and camels. Nomad-like was also the bareness of the beyt, and their misery: for the goodman had left them naught save a little meal; of which they presently baked a cake of hardly four ounces, for the guests' breakfast. Their voices sounded hollow with hunger, and were broken with sighing; but the poor noble-women spoke to us with a constant womanly mildness: and I wondered at these courtly manners, which I had not seen hitherto in Arabia. They are the poor children of Mohammed. The Sultàn of Islam might reverently kiss the hand of the least sherîf; as his wont is to kiss the hand of the elder of the family of the Sherîfs of Mecca (who are his pensioners – and in a manner his captives), at Stambûl.

It had been agreed between us, that no word should be said of my alien religion. Sâlem spoke of me as a stranger he had met with in the way. It was new to me, in these jealous countries, to be entertained by two lone hareem. This pair of pensive women (an elder and younger) were sister-wives of one, whom we should esteem an indigent person. There was

no coffee in that poor place; but at Sâlem's request they sent
out to borrow of their neighbours: the boy returned with six
or seven beans; and of these they boiled for us, in an earthen
vessel (as coffee is made here), a thin mixture, – which we
could not drink! When the sun was fairly risen, Sâlem said he
would now go to the Sherîf's audience; and he left me. – I
asked the elder hostess of the Sherîf. She responded, 'Hasseyn
is a good man, who has lived at Stambûl from his youth; and
the best learned of all the learned men here: yet he is not fully
such as Abdullah (his brother), our last Sherîf, who died this
year, – the Lord have him in His mercy! And he is not white
as Abdullah; for his mother was a (Galla) bond-woman.' – It
seemed that the colour displeased them, for they repeated,
'His mother was a bond-woman! – but Hasseyn is a good man
and just; he has a good heart.'

Long hours passed in this company of sighing (hunger-
stricken) women; who having no household cares were busy,
whilst I slumbered, with their worsted work. – It was toward
high noon, when Sâlem entered. 'Good tidings! 'nuncle
Khalîl, quoth he: our lord the Sherîf sends thee to lodge in
the house of a Tourk. Up! let us be going; and we have little
further to ride.' He bore out the bags himself, and laid them
on my fainting thelûl; and we departed. From the next rising-
ground I saw et-Tâyif! the aspect is gloomy, for all their building is of slate-coloured stone. At the entering of the town
stands the white palace of the Sherîf, of two stories; and in
face of it a new and loftier building with latticed balconies,
and the roof full of chimneys, which is the palace of Abdillah
Pasha, Hasseyn's brother. In the midst of the town appears a
great and high building, like a prison; that is the soldiers'
quarters.

– The town now before my eyes! after nigh two years'
wandering in the deserts, was a wonderful vision. Beside our
way I saw men blasting the (granite) rock for building-stone.–
The site of Tâyif is in the border of the plutonic steppe, over
which I had lately journeyed, a hundred leagues from el-
Kasîm. I beheld also a black and cragged landscape, with low
mountains, beyond the town. We fell again into the road from

the Seyl, and passed that lukewarm brook; which flows from yonder monsoon mountains, and is one of the abounding springs which water this ancient oasis. The water-bearers – that wonted sight of Eastern towns! went up staggering from the stream, under their huge burdens of full goat-skins; – there are some of their mighty shoulders that can wield a camel load! Here a Turkish soldier met us, with rude smiles; and said, he came to lead me to the house where I should lodge. The man, a Syrian from the (Turkish) country about Antioch, was the military servant of an officer of the Sherîf: that officer at the Sherîf's bidding would receive me into his house.

The gate, where we entered, is called *Bab es-Seyl*; and within is the open place before the Sherîf's modest palace. The streets are rudely built, the better houses are daubed with plaster: and the aspect of the town, which is fully inhabited only in the summer months, is ruinous. The ways are unpaved: and we see here the street dogs of Turkish countries. A servant from the Sherîf waited for me in the street, and led forward to a wicket gate: he bade me dismount, – and here, heaven be praised! he dismissed Sâlem. 'I will bring thee presently, quoth the smiling servitor, a knife and a fork; also the Sherîf bids me ask, wouldst thou drink a little tea and sugar?' – these were gentle thoughts of the homely humanity of the Prince of Mecca!

Then the fainting thelûl, which had carried me more than 450 miles without refreshment, was led away to the Sherîf's stables; and my bags were borne up the house stairs. The host, *Colonel Mohammed,* awaited me on the landing; and brought me into his chamber. The tunic was rent on my back, my mantle was old and torn; the hair was grown down under my kerchief to the shoulders, and the beard fallen and unkempt; I had bloodshot eyes, half blinded, and the scorched skin was cracked to the quick upon my face. A barber was sent for, and the bath made ready: and after a cup of tea, it cost the good colonel some pains to reduce me to the likeness of the civil multitude. Whilst the barber was doing, the stalwart Turkish official annointed my face with cooling ointments; and his hands were gentle as a woman's, – but I saw no breakfast in that hospice! After this he clad me, my weariness and faintness being such, like a block, in white cotton military attire; and set on my head a fez cap.

Toward evening, after a Turkish meal with my host, there entered a kawàs of the Sherîf; who brought a change of clothing for me. – And when they had clad me as an Arab sheykh; Colonel Mohammed led me through the twilight street, to the Sherîf's audience: the ways were at this hour empty.

Some *Bîsha* guards stand on the palace stairs; and they made the reverence as we passed to the Sherîf's officer; other men-at-arms stand at the stair's head. There is a waiting chamber; and my host left me, whilst he went forward to the Sherîf. But soon returning he brought me into the hall of audience; where the Sherîf Emir of Mecca sits daily at certain hours – in the time of his summer residence at et-Tâyif – much like a great Arabian sheykh among the *musheyikh*. Here the elders, and chief citizens, and strangers, and his kinsmen, are daily assembled with the Sherîf: for this is the mejlis, and coffee-parliament of an Arabian Prince; who is easy of access and of popular manners, as was Mohammed himself.

The great chamber was now void of guests: only the Sherîf sat there with his younger brother, Abdillah Pasha, a white man and strongly grown like a Turk, with the gentle Arabian manners. Hasseyn Pasha [the Sherîf bears this Ottoman title!] is a man of pleasant face, with a sober alacrity of the eyes and humane demeanour; and he speaks with a mild and cheerful voice: his age might be forty-five years. He seemed, as he sat, a manly tall personage of a brown colour; and large of breast and limb. The Sherîf was clad in the citizen-wise of the Ottoman towns, in a long blue *jubba* of pale woollen cloth. He sat upright on his diwan, like an European, with a comely sober countenance; and smoked tobacco in a pipe like the 'old Turks'. The simple earthen bowl was set in a saucer before him: his white jasmine stem was almost a spear's length. – He looked up pleasantly, and received me with a gracious gravity. A chair was set for me in face of the Sherîf; then Colonel Mohammed withdrew, and a servitor brought me a cup of coffee.

The Sherîf inquired with a quiet voice, 'Did I drink coffee?'
I said, 'We deem this which grows in Arabia to be the best of
all; and we believe that the coffee plant was brought into
Arabia from beyond the (Red) Sea.' – 'Ay, I think that it was
from Abyssinia: are they not very great coffee-drinkers where
you have been, in Nejd?' Then the Sherîf asked me of the
aggression at 'Ayn ez-Zeyma; and of the new aggression at
the Seyl. 'It were enough, he said, to make any man afraid.
[Alas! Hasseyn himself fell shortly, by the knife of an assassin,
– it was the second year after, at Jidda: and with the same
affectuous cheerfulness and equanimity with which he had
lived, he breathed forth his innocent spirit; in the arms of a
countryman of ours, Dr Gregory Wortabet, then resident
Ottoman Officer of Health for the Red Sea.] – But now you
have arrived, he added kindly; and the jeopardy (of your long
voyage) is past. Take your rest at Tâyif, and when you are refreshed I will send you down to the English Consul at Jidda.'
He asked, 'Had I never thought of visiting et-Tâyif? – it had
been better, he added, if I were come hither at first from the
Seyl; and he would have sent me to Jidda.' The good Sherîf
said further, 'Neither is this the only time that Europeans
have been here; for – I think it was last year – there came one
with the consul of Hollanda, to visit an inscription near the
Seyl; – I will give charge that it may be shown to you, as you
return.' I answered, 'I knew of one (Burckhardt) who came
hither in the time of the Egyptian warfare.' – The Sherîf
looked upon me with a friendly astonishment! [from whence,
he wondered, had I this knowledge of their home affairs?] –
The then subtle Sherîf of Mecca, who was beguiled and dispatched by the old Albanian fox Mohammed Aly, might be
grand uncle of this worthy Prince.

'And how, he asked, had I been able to live with the Beduw,
and to tolerate their diet? – And found you the Beduw to be
such as is reported of them [in the town romances] or, fall
they short of the popular opinion [of their magnanimity]? –
Did you help at the watering? and draw up the buckets hand
over hand – thus?' And with the Arabian hilarity the good
Sherîf laid by his demesurate pipe-stem; and he made himself

the gesture of the nomad waterers! (which he had seen in an expedition). There is not I think a natural Arabian Prince – but it were some sour Waháby – who might not have done the like; they are all pleasant men.– 'I had not strength to lift with them.' He responded, with a look of human kindness, 'Ay, you have suffered much!'

He inquired then of my journey; and I answered of Medáin Sâlih, Teyma, Hâyil: he was much surprised to hear that I had passed a month – so long had been the tolerance of a tyrant! – in Ibn Rashîd's town. He asked of Mohammed ibn Rashîd, 'Did I take him for a good man?' – plainly the Sherîf, notwithstanding the yearly presents which he receives from thence, thought not this of him: and when I answered a little beside his expectation, 'He is a worthy man,' Hasseyn was not satisfied. Then we spoke of Aneyza; and the Sherîf inquired of Zâmil, 'Is he a good man?' Finally he asked, 'if the garments [his princely gift] in which I sat clad before him, pleased me?' and if my host showed me (which he seemed to distrust) a reasonable hospitality? Above an hour had passed; then Colonel Mohammed, who had been waiting without, came forward; and I rose to take my leave. The Sherîf spoke to my host, for me; and especially that I should walk freely in et-Tâyif, and without the walls; and visit all that I would,– Colonel Mohammed kissed the venerable hand of the Sherîf, and we departed. ...

Colonel Mohammed entered, – and then Sâlem: whom the Sherîf had commanded to restore all that he and his confederate robbed from me. The miserable thief brought the pistol (now broken!), the aneroid, and four reals, which he confessed to have stolen himself from my bags. He said now, 'Forgive me, Khalîl! and, ah! remember the *zád* (food) and the *melh* (salt) which is between us.' 'And why didst thou not remember them at Seyl, when thou tookest the knife, a second time, to kill me?' *Colonel Mohammed*: 'Khalîl says justly; why then didst thou not remember the bread and salt?' – 'I am guilty, but I hope the Sherîf may overlook it; and be not thou against me, Khalîl!' I asked for the purse and the other small things. But Sâlem denying that they had anything more! Colonel Mohammed drove him out, and bade him fetch them instantly. – 'The cursed one! quoth my host, as he went forth: the Sherîf has determined after your departure to put him in irons, as well as the other man who struck you. He will punish them with severity. – but not now, because their kindred might molest you as you go down to Jidda. And the Sherîf has written an injunction, which will be sent round to all the tribes and villages within his dominion, '*That in future, if there should arrive any stranger among them, they are to send him safely to the Sherîf*: for who knows if some European may not be found another time passing through the Sherîf's country; and he might be mishandled by the ignorant people. Also the Sherîf would have no after-questions with their governments.'

(*From Tâyif, Doughty with a guard of three men journeyed to Jidda, where ended his wanderings in Arabia Deserta.*)

GLOSSARY

Abd: slave; in Arabia a black, bond or free.

Abd-el-Azîz: a Bessàm, of Aneyza.

Abd el-Hâdy: a householder of Kheybar.

Abd el-Kâder: the Algerian Sherîf Prince and Imam, resident at Damascus.

Abd er-Rahmàn: son of Abdullah el-Bessàm of Aneyza.

Abdillah Pasha: brother of Sherîf Hasseyn.

Abdullah el-Bèssàm: a Jidda merchant of Aneyza and a constant friend.

Abdullah el-Kenneyny: a friend at Aneyza.

Abdullah es-Siruân: Kurdish captain at Kheybar.

Abdullah Ibn Saûd: Waháby prince.

Abdullah weled Mahanna: brother of the Emir of Boreyda.

Abeyd Ibn Rashîd: brother of Abdullah.

Abu: father.

Abûd: hasty-bread, baked under the embers.

Adamy: child of Adam; a man.

Adan: sand dune.

Adu: an enemy.

Aga: captain.

el-Agab: small black eagle.

Ageyl: government dromedary riders of Nejd.

Ahl Gibly: the southern Aarab.

Ajàj: sand-driving wind.

Ajamy: Persian.

Ajjr: impotent, infertile.

Akaba: a steep slope.

Akkâm: a camel driver in the Haj.

Aleykom es-salaam: response to the greeting of peace.

Allayda: a kindred of Wélad Aly.

Aly aklu: 'according to his understanding.'

Aly el-Ajid: aforetime stud servant at Hâyil.

Am'dan: stakes of Bed. booths or large tents.

Amm Mohammed: Mohammed en-Nejûmy.

Anâz: great crater hill on the Harrat el-Aueyrid.

Aneyza: metropolis of Nejd, chief town of el-Kasîm.

Annez y: the great Ishmaelitish nomad tribe.

Ard Suwwan: Arabia Patraea, flint ground.

Arûth: 'I depart.'

Ashîra: tribe.

Ashrâf: pl. of *Sherîf,* the seed of Mohammed.

Askar: soldier.

el-Assr: time of the third prayer, the sun being at half afternoon height.

Auâjy: sheykhs' clan of Bishr in Nejd.

Ayb: 'shame!'

Ajîb: a shame.

Ayn er-Reyih: a spring at Kheybar.

Ayn ez-Zeyma: station before Mecca in the way to et-Tâyif.

Aysa-bin-Miriam: Jesus son of Mary.

Azab: said of camels pasturing apart from the menzils.

Azîz: a beloved.

el-Bâdia: the great waste wilderness.

Baggl (Mereesy): dry milk shards.

Bakhorra: camel driving-stick with bent handle.

Bàrak: banner.

Battâl: bad, idle.

Bédan: wild goat.

Bedr ibn Rashîd: younger brother of Bunder, and murderer of his uncle Metaab.

Beduwy: Beduins, inhabitants of the *bâdia* or great waste lands.

Béled: country, the land, the soil.

Béled mât: a died-out place.

Beny Sôkhr: Beduin tribe of Moab and Ammon.

Beny Temîm: liberal-minded tribe inhabiting Gofar.

Berber: descendant of people of Barbary.

Berkoa: woman's veil or face cloth.

Bernûs: white mantle of the Moors of Barbary.

Bessàm: a wealthy family of many households at Aneyza.

Bethr-ak: used at Hâyil for *b'ithnak,* 'by thy leave.'

Beyt el-mâl: treasure house at Hâyil.

Beyt-es-shaar: Nomadic tent of hair.

el-Bil: the camels of a tribe.

Billah: By Ullah, the common B. oath.

Billî: ancient Teháma tribe, of the Red Sea border.

Bint: daughter, girl; also young married woman until she has borne a child.

Bîr: a well.

Bîr-el-Ghrannem: well of the flocks, below Medáin Sâlih.

Birket: a cistern.

Bîsàn: Galla word for water.

Bîsha, Bîshy: negro armed band serving the Sherîf Emir of Mecca.

Bishr: a great sub-tribe of Annezy in the W. Nejd.

Bismillah: 'In the name of God.'

Boábat Ullah: a gate of Damascus facing the Holy Cities.

Boghrâz: strait between cliffs.

Boreyda: a great clay-built town in the Nefûd of el-Kasîm.

Borj Selmàn: desert ground in Fejîr dîra or boundaries.

Bottîn: a blunt hilly height.

Bukkra: young cow-camel with first calf.

Bunder ibn Rashîd: eldest son of Telâl.

el-Bunn: coffee powder.

Búrghrol, borghrol: a boiled wheaten dish of Syria and the Nejd.

Burr: high desert-land.

Chai: tea.

Dakhîlak: 'having entered thy roof I need thy protection.'

Dalîl: guide.

Dàr: Teyma word for house.

Dellàl: Coffee pots.

Dellâls: criers, running brokers.

Derâhim: money (from the Greek *Drachmi*).

Deh: imitative word.

Derwish: poor man, *fakîr.*

Dîra: circuit of the Nomads, and of the oasis settlements.

Dîrat er-Rasûl: The Apostles' country (of Mohammed).

Dinya el-jedîda: America, the New World.

Dokân: a shop.

Dokhân: (lit. smoke), tobacco leaf.

Dowla: the Turkish government.

Dubbush: small cattle, sheep, goats.

Ekîms: sleeping carpets.

El-hamd-illah: ' The Lord be praised.'

el-Elûm: the liberal sciences.

Emir: he in whom is the *umr* or word of command.

Entha: female; said commonly of a woman of a poorer condition.

Erkâl: ' mount!'

Ethel: long tamarisk timber, grown in the oases for building.

Eyâda ibn Ajjuèyn: an Heteymy Sheykh.

Eyyâl: a family fellowship.

Eyyâl es-sheukh: children of the princely house.

Fáhd: the distracted elder son of Abeyd ibn Rashîd.

Fáhd: the brindled and spotted wild cat.

Fáras: mare.

Fàsidîn: corrupt, depraved.

Fatya: basket for coffee pots.

Fehját: a poor small Heteym kindred.

Fejîr: the Fukara.

el-Fejr: the dawn.

Fendy: a kindred, natural division of a tribe.

Fenjeyn: small coffee cups.

Ferîj: nomad hamlet.

Fèysal: a child of Hamûd ibn Rashîd.

Ferth: the cud.

el-Figgera: the brow of the Harra about Kheybar.

el-Fukara, or *el-Fejîr:* Annezy Aarab of el-Hejr.

Fulûs: (fish scales): silver or gold coins.

Galla: blacks, from Abyssinia and beyond.

Galliûn: tobacco pipe.

Gatta: sand-grouse.

Ghrannem: small cattle.

Ghrazel: the gazelle.

Ghrazzu: a foray, raid.

Ghroceyb: sheykh rafîk to Kheybar.

Ghrósh: perforce, by effort.

Girby: water-skin of goat or sheep, without seam.

Golbân: wells (sing. jellib, or kellib).

Gôm: enemies.

el-Gúsh: the Beduins' household gear and baggage.

Gussha: pasture bushes, never burned in the fires.

Gutîa: coffee-cup box.

Habalîs, pl. of *Hablus* (a word heard only in the Teyma and Hejr country): murderers, thieves, rovers.

Habâra, a kind of bustard.

Hábashy: Abyssinian.

Hadàj: camel pack-saddle.

Haddàj: the well pit of Teyma.

Haderûn: '(we are) ready!'

el-Hadûd: the bounds of Mecca, the forbidden country.

Haggu: plaited leathern loin ribbon worn by both sexes.

Haj, or *Hajjy:* pilgrim, to the Holy places.

Haj (es-Shem): the great Syrian convoy of pilgrims to Mecca.

Hajr el-kra: red granite.

Hakîm: healer, doctor (of medicine), wise man.

Halàl: lawful.

Halîb: milk.

Halla: Harra hill of black powder and slag.

Hammàm: bath.

Hammam (Syrian): the purse (human).

Hameydy: a kind of tobacco.

Hamûd ibn Rashîd: deputy ruler in Hâyil.

Hánash: large white poisonous snake.

Harameyn: the holy cities, forbidden to unbelievers.

Haràmy: thief.

Harb: a great Nejd tribe.

Hareem: pl. of *horma,* woman.

Harra(t): lava field, vulcanic country.

el-Hása: the stone (malady).

Hâthr: townsfolk.

Haurân: vulcanic country in Syria beyond Jordan.

Hauta: orchard.

Hayâtakl: 'By thy life!'

Hâyil: village capital of Jebel Shammar.

Házam: gunner's belt.

Házm: vulcanic hills bearing vegetation.

Hejâz: the part lying between Nejd or highland Arabia and the hot lowland border or Teháma. Used also of the peoples.

Héjra: a summer tent.

Helw: sweet.

Helwàn: mountain east of Teyma.

el-Heteym: a great nomad nation, not accounted Beduw by the Arabs.

Hillî, hellowatt, hilliân: the Harra hills together.

Himyaric: of the old language of el-Yémen.

Hisma: a high country of sand stones, extending from Petra to Tebûk.

Horma: woman (pl. *hareem*).

Hosseny: fox.

Howeytât: Beduin nation.

Hubts: companies of marketing nomads.

W. el-Humth: great valley of the Hejâz, unknown to Europeans until 1876, when the author first traced it from el-Héjr.

Hurr: dromedary stallion.

Hurra, hurrî: heavy hard black basalt.

Hût: fish.

Huthb: hilly mountain coast.

Ibn: son of.

Ibn Rashîd: Prince of West Nejd.

Ibn Shalan: chief of the Annezy tribe el-Ruwalla, in the north.

Ibn Saud Abdullah: Waháby prince.

Ibràm: the loin cloth of pilgrims that enter Mecca.

Imbârak: captain of the guard at Hâyil.

Inshallah!: 'if the Lord will!'

el-Irâk: Mesopotamia.

Isa ibn Miriam: Jesus son of Mary.

Ithin: one of the prayers.

Jabbàr: high-handed, tyrannical.

Jdhash: ass.

Jáhil: ignorant, muddle-headed.

Jambieh: sword-knife of Mecca.

Jâra: housewife.

Jau: valley-like passage between the Harras; also watering place in low ground.

Jauf: a great oasis in the S. of Syrian desert. Taken by Abeyd Ibn Rashîd.

Jebel: mountain.

el-Jebel: Jebel Shammar, the dîra of Ibn Rashîd; said also of the people.

Jebel Tar: Gibraltar.

Jebel Tor: Sinai.

Jedûm: hatchet.

Jehâd: religious war.

Jehennem: hell.

Jelámy: small brown desert lizard.

Jelîb: well.

Jella: camel dung, used for fuel.

Jemmamîl: camel masters.

Jeneyny: palm orchard pleasure grounds.

Jerboa: spring rat.

Jerm, pl. *jerûm:* goat skins to hold butter.

Jet: a kind of vetch.

Jeyber: Emir's officer at Boreyda.

Jezzîn: abstaining from water.

Jidda: Red Sea port.

Jîdda: Beduin caldron.

Jiddar, pl. *Jiddrân:* camel path in the Harra.

Jiss: gypsum or pipe-clay.

Jubba: long coat worn in Turkish towns,

Jurdy: government provisions relief sent down to meet the returning Haj.

Jurraba: mangy riding camel.

Kaaba: sacred pre-Islamic idol stone at Mecca.

Kaak: Damascus biscuits.

Kabíla: a tribe.

Kâdy: justice, man of the religious law.

Kâfily: caravan.

Kafir: a heathen.

Kahl: antimony, used to paint the eyes.

Kahtân: southern Aarab, reputed to exceed all others in fanatical wildness and cruel malice.

Kahwa: coffee tent or house.

Kâhwajy: coffee-server.

Kanakína: quinine.

Kâramak Ullah!: 'The Lord requite thee!'

el-Kasím: a province of Middle Nejd.

Kâsim ibn Barâk: great sheykh of the midland Heteym.

Kasr: clay-built chamber, house, or castle.

Kawàs: javelin man.

Kef: hand, or palm.

Kella: tower defending a cistern; redoubt.

Kellâjy: a kella keeper.

Kerakôl: 'sentinel!'

Khâla: desert waste; the land that is empty.

Khâlas: 'He is ended!'

Khalíl: Sheykh; title of honour.

el-Khamâla: a kindred of the Fukhara tribe.

Khânjar: crooked girdle knife.

Khára: vile.

Khayin: treacherous.

Kheybar: large oasis in the Prophet's country.

eh-Kheyr Ullah!: 'The Lord's bounty!'; a present from God.

Khíbel: mentally unsound.

Kh'lúy: solitary wayfarer.

el-Khreyma: an oasis N.E. of Hâyil.

el-Khuèyra: a sick camel.

Khusshm: a headland.

Kuffâr: Kafir, heathen.

Kumbâz: man's gown of the towns.

Kúmr: girdle.

Kúnfuth: the hedgehog.

Kurdy Aga: Abdullah es-Siruân, Kurdish captain at Kheybar.

Lâba: lava.

Léban: sour milk, butter-milk.

Lilla: la-la; no-no.

Loghrat: dialect.

Lullilu: joyful cry of women.

Maabûb: negro umbrella-bearer to the Sherîf Emir of Mecca.

Maan: 9th station of the Haj.

Maasub: head cord.

Mâ aleyk!: 'No evil shall befall thee!'

Mâ el-enab: grape juice.

Mâ es-Sáma: well of sweet water at Hâyil.

Máhal: extreme barrenness of desert soil; waterless.

Mahâl: nomad's pulley-wheel over deep wells.

Mahál-el-Mejlis: principal monument of the past at Medáin Sâlih.

Mâjid: elder son of Hamûd ibn Rashîd.

Mákbara: burying ground.

Makhzans: guest-chambers.

Márhabba!: 'welcome!'

Marra: woman.

Matàra, or *zemzemîyeh:* the leathern bucket-bottle, hung from the saddle.

Mecca: chief holy city, 245 miles S. of Medina.

Medáin Sâlih: cities of Sâlih the prophet.

Medina: the prophet's (holy) city.

Mehsan: the bountiful blind Allayda sheykh.

Mejîdy: Turkish silver dollar.

Mejlis: the daily council of elders.

Mejlis: the open market-place in every oasis-town of Kasîm.

Mejnûn: a fool; possessed by the jân (spirits).

Melh: salt.

Menzil: camping ground of nomads and caravans.

Mereesy: dried butter-milk.

Mèrguba: round, infolding nomad mirror.

Merkez: a principal rest station of the pilgrimage.

Méshab: open place in town.

Meshghrûll: 'we are too busy!'

Mesîhiyûn: Arabic Christians of the border lands.

Mesjid: mosque; 'place of kneeling down to worship.'

Meskîn: mean, paltry.

Metaab ibn Rashîd: Prince, after Telâl.

Min?: Who?

Mîry: tribute.

Mishaab, also *Mehján* and *Bakorra:* camel driving-stick with double hook.

Moahîb: a kindred of the Sb'Annezy.

Moallakât: collection of pre-Islamite poetry.

Moghreby: a Moor.

Mogŷil: the noon resting of passengers in a march.

Mohâfuz: guardian.

Mohammed en-Nejûmy: a friend at Kheybar.

Mohammed ibn Rashîd: Emir of Hâyil.

Moslemîn: 'the-submitted-to-the-divine-governance-of-the-world.'

Mothif: guest-hall.

Motlog Allayda: sheykh of the Welad Aly.

el-Mowla: The Lord God.

Mûbrak: camel's night lair.

Mudd yédak!: 'Reach forth thine hand!'

Mudowwy: Hakîm, doctor (of medicine).

Muéthin: he who utters the cry to the formal prayers.

Mufarrij: Steward of the Prince's hall at Hâyil.

Muhafûth: title of Ibn Rashîd.

Múkàad: sitting place of the men in an Arab house or booth.

Mukowwem: camel master in the Haj.

Munâkh: a couching place of camels.

Mûsa: Moses.

Musky: poisoned in his drink.

Múthkir: an Ateyba sheykh, guide in the Aneyza butter caravan.

Muttowwa: religious elder.

Muzayyin: circumcision feast.

Muzeyrîb: assembling place of the Haj, 40 miles south of Damascus.

Nabateans: powerful widespread war-like Arabian people flourishing 700 B.C.–A.D. 105, destroyed by Trajan. The centre of the cult of their god Dusares was Petra. Aramaic their inscriptions.

Nâga: cow-camel.

Nâhab: spoil, plunder.

Nasrâny: Nazarene, Christian.

Nêby: The Prophet.

Neffera: shy.

Nefûds: deep sand deserts.

Nejd: inner highland of N. Arabia.

Nejûmy, The: Mohammed en-Nejûmy, a friend at Kheybar.

Nimmr: brindled leopard.

Nô'kh!: 'make (the camel) kneel!'

Omanîas: fleet riding-camels from the Gulf Province Omân or Amân.

Piastre: half a groat, at Damascus.

Pilaw: dish of boiled rice and mutton.

Rabeyby: Arabian one-stringed viol.

Rabîa: young desert herbs after autumn or winter showers.

Radîf (pl., *râduffa*): dromedary-back rider.

Rafîk: way-fellow.

Râfuthy: a heretic.

Rahîl: about to remove.

Râhla: camp removal.

Rajajîl: the prince's armed band, at Hâyil.

Râjil: a man.

er-Râkham: small white carrion eagle.

Ramta: camping-place.

Ramathân: month of fasting.

Real: a crown, a dollar.

Rîa: passage in a gap in the mountains.

er-Riâth: Waháby metropolis in East Nejd.

er-Rîhh: ague, rheumatism.

Rikâb: dromedary.

Rimth: saline bush; the dry twigs are used for the desert fires.

Rizelleyn: a pair of villains.

Rubba: fellowship.

Rûhh!: 'Go, then!'

Wady er-Rummah (el-Wady): a great dry valley and torrent bed, 'whereunto flow seventy considerable wadies.'

Ruwàlla: a great sub-tribe of Annezy in the north.

Sabûny: soap.

es-Sâfy-Hàmed: a young Aneyza citizen.

Sàhilat et Khammashîeh: a plain near Hâyil.

Sahs: measures; at Teyma they are two pints, at Medina and Kheybar nearly five.

Salaam aleyk!: 'Peace be with thee!'

Samn: clarified (liquid) butter.

Samrà: desert bergs of hard stone.

Sâny: smith.

Sbâite (es-Sh'aa): a sub-tribe of Annezy.

Sbeydy: small wild tuber.

Sebîl: wayside fountain.

Sehamma: a branch of the Billî tribe.

Semîly: sheepskin milk-bag.

Seyadîn: Beduin petty tradesmen.

Seyl: torrent, and dry bed of.

Shaeb: side of a deep, dry torrent bed, where might be shade.

Shahûd: martyrs (those dying in the Haj).

Sham: Damascus, Syria.

Shammar : a great Beduin tribe extending from Irak to Teyma and Hâyil.

Sîdr: apple-thorn tree.

Simm: poison.

Simûm: hot wind.

Sirrúk: a thievish night-bird.

Sîr Amîn: an Emir of the Haj.

Strûr: a Galla Ageyly at Kheybar.

Sherarát: a tribe between Ma'an and Jauf.

Sherîf: of the seed of Mohammed.

Sherîf Hasseyn: Emir of Mecca.

Sheykh (pl. Sheukh): elder noble, leader, chieftain by blood (Fem. *Sheykha*).

Sheytàn: Satan.

Shidàd: camel riding-saddle.

es-Shî-îll: 'lift the loads!'

Shimbel: Annezy district in Syria.

Shôbek: village of Mount Seir.

es-Shor: the counsels (of the nomads).

es-Shoth: a deep cleft in sandstone rock.

Shuggery, The: A Shuggera labourer of Rasheyd's orchards.

Sleymàn: uncle of Hamûd ibn Rashîd, personage of Hâyil.

Sleymàn el-Kenneyny: a poor kinsman of the good Abdullah el-k.

Sleyb: the Solubba.

es-Sokhûr (Beny Sókhr): a sub-tribe of Annezy.

Solubby: nomad tinker and hunter, despised by Beduin. Also *Sleyb*.

Suânies: draw-wheel frames of the wells of irrigation.

Subbakha (Kheybar *summakha*) salt crust on the soil.

Suffa: ground rock.

Suffa: an upper-house-chamber at Kheybar.

Sûk: street, bazaar.

Surbût: coffee-pestle.

Surra: payment to Beduins for right of way.

Sweydiâ: small pied rock bird.

Tâga: long casements.

Tábal: ague, rheumatic pains.

Tájir: tradesman.

Takht: carpeted settle.

Takht-er-Rûm: camel litter, of great personages.

Tarbûsh: fez.

et-Tâyif: an ancient town in the highlands above Mecca; summer residence of the Emirs of Mecca.

Tannûr: girdle-pans of iron plate.

Tchôl Bagdad: steppes of Bagdad.

Telûl ibn Rashîd: the second Prince of Jebel Shammar.

Temim, Beny: A widespread tribe, in whom is the spirit of industry and a good plain understanding.

Temmn: river rice from Mesopotamia.

Teslîm: in trust.

Teyma: an ancient oasis. The Tema of O.T.

Tháhab el-asfr: gold.

Thalûk: wild desert bush, chewed by the nomads.

Thamûd: ancient tribe of South Arabia, which came north after a defeat.

Thelûl: dromedary or riding camel.

Thôb: a desert lizard.

Thùbba: hyena.

Thubîha: beast for slaughter.

Thulla: mountain.

Thunma: small wild tubers.

Thùra: a kind of millet.

Tiryâk: treacle, as antidote.

Tittun: tobacco.

Tôma: cupidity, gain.

Towîl: peak, landmark.

et-Towîlan: a sandstone needle 60 feet high near Teyma.

Túrfah: dry tamarisk wood.

et-Tursh: the driven flocks and great cattle of the nomads.

Ullah: Allah, God.

Ullema: doctors (of religion) learned men.

Wába: the plague.

Wabar, wabbar: a rodent animal in the desert mountains.

Wady (pl. *wadiàn*): low valley-ground.

Wady Mûsa: Moses' valley, or Petra.

Wahábis: a puritanical sect of militant reformers, centred in Nejd.

Wàly: governor of the Weliát or Turkish Province of Syria.

Wâsit: a ruined suburb of Hâyil.

Weled: young man.

Wélad Aly: a great sub-tribe of Annezy; the southern half-tribe are treacherous and fanatical.

Wéled Mahanna: Emir of Boreyda.

Wellah: lit. 'By God!' but it has come to signify *verily, indeed.*

Wittr: pad under pack-saddle.

Wothŷhi: wild cow or antelope, *Oryx Beatrix*, probably the Reem or Unicorn of Scripture.

Yahûdy: Jews.

Ya sámy: 'O my namesake!'

Ybba: said for *Abu,* father, in Medina.
el-Yémen: Arabia Felix.
Ymgebâs: desert owl.

Zabtîyah: police soldiery.
Zád: food.
Zahlán: sorrowful.
Zamîl: Emir of Aneyza.
Zikma: cold in the head.
Zillamy: one of the people.
Zmèyem: nose-ring.
Zôra: the natural stay under the chest of the camel.

MORE ABOUT PENGUINS
AND PELICANS

For further information about books available from Penguins
please write to Dept EP, Penguin Books Ltd, Harmondsworth, Middlesex UB7 ODA.

In the U.S.A.: For a complete list of books available from
Penguins in the United States write to Dept CS, Penguin
Books, 625 Madison Avenue, New York, New York 10022.

In Canada: For a complete list of books available from
Penguins in Canada write to Penguin Books Canada Ltd,
2801 John Street, Markham, Ontario L3R 1B4.

In Australia: For a complete list of books available from
Penguins in Australia write to the Marketing Department,
Penguin Books Australia Ltd, P.O. Box 257, Ringwood,
Victoria 3134.

In New Zealand: For a complete list of books available from
Penguins in New Zealand write to the Marketing Department, Penguin Books (N.Z.) Ltd, P.O. Box 4019, Auckland
10.